REFORMATION AND REACTION
IN TUDOR CAMBRIDGE

REFORMATION AND REACTION IN TUDOR CAMBRIDGE

BY

H. C. PORTER
M.A., Ph.D.

Lecturer in History, University of Cambridge

ARCHON BOOKS
1972

Library of Congress Cataloging in Publication Data

Porter, Harry Culverwell.
   Reformation and reaction in Tudor Cambridge.

   Reprint of the 1958 ed., with a new preface. Includes
bibliographies.
   1. Cambridge. University—History. 2. Reformation—
England. I. Title.
[LF116.P6 1972]   378.425'72   77-179573
ISBN 0-208-01228-1

L u t h
L F
1 1 6
P G
1 9 7 2

First published 1958 by Cambridge University Press.
Reprinted 1972 with permission and with a new preface as an
Archon Book by The Shoe String Press, Inc., Hamden,
Connecticut

Printed in the United States of America

1972 PREFACE

PATRICK COLLINSON has pointed out (*Letters of Thomas Wood, Puritan, 1566–77*, 1960) that I was wrong in my identification of Thomas Wood on p. 116. I thought him to be a 1561 Trinity College sizar. In fact, Wood, Beaumont and Gilbey were all veterans of the Geneva congregation—and all Leicestershire men. Wood apparently studied at Cambridge about 1530. Collinson (pp. 24–25) prints the text of Wood's letter to Gilbey, 4 October 1565.

On p. 169 Whitgift is described as a Yorkshireman; in fact he was born at Grimsby, Lincolnshire. On p. 103 the date of the Act of Supremacy is given as January 1559; in fact the bill was first read in February, and was signed in April. Richard Rogers the Marian exile and Richard Rogers the Elizabethan puritan diarist are not separated in the Index (p. 458). With regard to the question of the threat of praemunire proceedings against the prelates (p. 374); this had been discussed from 1589; the story that Elizabeth used the threat in 1595 occurs in Richard Montague's *Appello Caesarem* (1625).

This book was published in the autumn of 1958. Of books and articles published since then, the following seem especially relevant: the place of publication being London if not otherwise noted.

BAINTON, R. *Erasmus of Christendom*, New York, 1969.
BENNETT, H. S. *English Books and Readers 1558–1603*. Cambridge, 1965. *English Books and Readers 1603–1640*. Cambridge, 1970.
BLENCH, J. W. *Preaching in England in the late 15th and 16th Centuries*. Oxford, 1964.
BREWARD, I. (ed.). *William Perkins*. Abingdon, 1970.
BUCER, M. *De Regno Christi*, tr. by W. Pauck and P. Larkin, in 'The Library of Christian Classics', Vol. XIX, *Melanchthon and Bucer*, ed. by W. Pauck. London and Philadelphia, 1969.
CALVIN, J. *Concerning the eternal Predestination of God* (1552), tr. by J. K. S. Reid. 1961.

v

CHAMBERS, D. D. C. 'A Catalogue of the Library of Andrewes', *Transactions of the Cambridge Bibliographical Society*, Vol. V, Pt. II. 1970.

CHARLTON, K. *Education in Renaissance England*. 1965.

City of Cambridge, 2 parts, Royal Commission on Historical Monuments in England. 1959.

COBBAN, A. B. *The King's Hall within the University of Cambridge in the later Middle Ages*. Cambridge, 1969.

COLLINSON, P. *The Elizabethan Puritan Movement*. 1967.

COSTELLO, W. T. *The Scholastic Curriculum at early 17th Century Cambridge*. Cambridge, Mass., 1958.

CRAGG, G. R. (ed.). *The Cambridge Platonists*. New York, 1968.

CRESSY, D. 'The Social Composition of Caius College, Cambridge, 1580–1640', *Past and Present*, Number 47. May 1970.

CROSS, C. (ed.). *The Royal Supremacy in the Elizabethan Church*. 1969.

CURTIS, M. H. *Oxford and Cambridge in Transition 1558–1642: an essay on changing relations between the English Universities and English Society*. Oxford, 1959.

DEWAR, M. *Sir Thomas Smith*. 1964.

DICKENS, A. G. *The English Reformation*. 1964.

DICKENS, A. G. and CARR, D. (eds.). *The Reformation in England to the Accession of Elizabeth I*. 1967.

ELTON, G. R. (ed.). *The Reformation* (New Cambridge Modern History, Vol. II). Cambridge, 1958.

GEORGE, C. H. 'Puritanism as History and Historiography', *Past and Present*, Number 41. December 1968.

GEORGE, C. H. and K. *The Protestant Mind of the English Reformation*. Princeton, 1961.

GREEN, V. H. H. *Religion at Oxford and Cambridge*. 1964.

HARRISON, W. *The Description of England (1587)*, ed. G. Edelen. Cornell, 1968.

HAUGAARD, W. P. *Elizabeth and the English Reformation*. Cambridge, 1968.

HILL, C. *Society and Puritanism in Pre-Revolutionary England*. 1964. 'A Note on the Universities', *Appendix to Intellectual Origins of the English Revolution*. Oxford, 1965.

HOOPES, R. *Right Reason in the English Renaissance*. Cambridge, Mass., 1962.

KEARNEY, H. *Scholars and Gentlemen: Universities and Society in Pre-Industrial Britain 1500–1700*. 1970.

JONES, R. F. *Ancients and Moderns: a study of the rise of the scientific movement in 17th century England*, second edition. St Louis, 1961.

KNOX, S. J. *Walter Travers: Paragon of Elizabethan Puritanism*. 1962.

Lamont, W. M. 'Puritanism as History and Historiography', *Past and Present*, Number 44. August, 1969.

LEHMBERG, S. E. *Sir Walter Mildmay and Tudor Government.* Austin, Texas, 1964.

LITTLE, D. *Religion, Order and Law: a study in pre-revolutionary England.* New York, 1969.

LOADES, D. M. *The Oxford Martyrs.* 1970.

MacCAFFERY, W. *The Shaping of the Elizabethan Regime.* 1969.

McCONICA, J. K. *English Humanists and Reformation Politics under Henry VIII and Edward VI.* Oxford, 1965.

MCGRATH, P. *Papists and Puritans under Elizabeth I.* 1967.

MORGAN, E. S. *Visible Saints: the History of a Puritan Idea.* New York, 1963. (ed.) *Puritan Political Ideas.* New York, 1965. *The Puritan Family,* revised edition. New York, 1966.

PARKER, T. H. L. *English Reformers* (Library of Christian Classics Vol. XXVI). London and Philadelphia, 1966.

PARKER, W. I. *Milton: a biography.* Oxford, 1968.

PATRIDES, C. A. (ed.). *The Cambridge Platonists.* 1969.

RIDLEY, J. *Thomas Cranmer.* Oxford, 1962.

RYAN, L. V. *Roger Ascham.* Stanford and London, 1963.

SALTMARSH, J. *King's College and its Chapel.* Norwich, 1969.

SEAVER, P. S. *The Puritan Lectureships: the Politics of Religious Dissent 1560–1662.* Stanford, 1970.

SIBERCH, J. The subject of Monograph No. 6 of the Cambridge Bibliographical Society. Cambridge, 1970.

SIMON, J. 'The Social Origins of Cambridge Students 1603–1640', *Past and Present,* Number 26. November 1963. *Education and Society in Tudor England.* Cambridge, 1966.

STONE, L. 'The Educational Revolution in England 1560–1640', *Past and Present,* Number 28. July 1964. *The Crisis of the Aristocracy.* Oxford, 1965. (ed.) *Social Change and Revolution in England 1540–1640.* 1965.

SURTZ, E. *The Work and Days of John Fisher.* Cambridge, Mass., 1967.

WALZER, M. *The Revolution of the Saints: a study in the origins of radical politics.* 1966.

WERNHAM, R. B. (ed.). *The Counter-Reformation and Price Revolution 1559–1610* (New Cambridge Modern History, Vol. III). Cambridge, 1968.

WRIGHT, L. B. and LAMAR, V. A (eds.). *Life and Letters in Tudor and Stuart England.* Cornell, 1962.

Perhaps I might be permitted to note that since 1958 I have dealt more extensively with Erasmus, in collaboration with Professor D. F. S. Thomson of Toronto, in *Erasmus and Cambridge* (Toronto, 1963, 1970); Thomson translated Erasmus' Cambridge letters, and I supplied the introduction and notes. I also included Cambridge material (Barnes, Bucer, Perkins, Emmanuel College) in my anthology *Puritanism in Tudor England* (1971).

H. C. PORTER

FACULTY OF HISTORY
WEST ROAD
CAMBRIDGE
March 1971

PREFACE

In its original form, this book was awarded the Archbishop Cranmer Prize for 1952, and its publication has been made possible by a grant from the Cranmer Prize Fund. This prize is for an essay 'which shall relate to the intention and result of the changes in doctrine, organization and ritual within the Church of England between 1500 and 1700'. My work, concerning aspects of religious life and thought in the University of Cambridge between 1500 and 1650, may be thought of as fitting between two previous Cranmer Prize essays, both published by the Cambridge University Press: E. G. Rupp, *Studies in the Making of the English Protestant Tradition: mainly in the reign of Henry VIII* (1947); and G. R. Cragg, *From Puritanism to the Age of Reason: a Study of Changes in Religious Thought within the Church of England, 1660–1700* (1950).

My greatest thanks are due to Professor Norman Sykes, who has supervised and guided my work—whether essay, thesis or book—with great kindness and concern.

I should also like to thank those who have discussed various sections with me: Professor Rupp of Manchester; Dr Owen Chadwick, Master of Selwyn College; Dr John Roach of Corpus Christi College; and Mr Edward Miller of St John's College. I have also been helped at Cambridge by the Rev. R. C. Walls of Corpus, at Princeton by Professor W. F. Craven, and at Toronto by Professor E. R. Fairweather, Professor D. F. S. Thomson and Mr E. E. Rose. And the friendly interest and advice over the years of Professor Bruce Dickins of Corpus have been greatly appreciated.

With the manuscripts I have been expertly helped by Miss H. E. Peek, Deputy Keeper of the University Archives; Miss J. Iselis, Assistant Librarian of Hatfield House; Mr Adams of Trinity,

Mr White of St John's and Mr Bury of Corpus; and by the staffs of the Manuscript Room of the British Museum, the Search Room of the Public Record Office, and the Anderson Room of the Cambridge University Library. The staff of the University Press, both in England and New York City, has been helpful in many more ways than an author could have the right to expect. I wish in particular to thank my friend Mr R. A. Becher of the Cambridge office.

In all quotations, the spelling, capitalization and punctuation have been modernized. The datings throughout are new style: that is, although a date from 1 January to 24 March was written as (say) 15 February 1551, and could pedantically be printed by the historian as 15 February 1551/2, I have preferred to put 15 February 1552.

H. C. PORTER

TRINITY COLLEGE, TORONTO
February 1958

A NOTE ON THE ENDPAPERS

The illustrations on the endpapers are reproduced by permission of the University Library, Cambridge. They show, respectively, George Braun's Cambridge plan of 1575, and part of the central sheet of John Hammond's plan of 1592. The Braun plan first appeared in the second book of a folio collection of maps entitled *Civitates Orbis Terrarum* (Cologne, 1575); it measured $17\frac{5}{8}$ in. wide and $13\frac{1}{4}$ in. high, and was probably copied from Richard Lyne's plan of 1574, the earliest known plan of Cambridge. Of Hammond's important plan, only one complete copy is known to be in existence; it is kept in the Bodleian, and measures $46\frac{3}{4}$ in. long by $34\frac{1}{2}$ in. high. All but the central portion is in poor condition.

CONTENTS

CONTENTS

INTRODUCTION

'Certain forms of existence are so abnormal that they
are bound to produce certain characteristic faults.'
MARCEL PROUST

Ideas, wrote Burke, 'entering into common life, like rays of light
which pierce into a dense medium, are, by the laws of nature,
refracted from their straight line'.[1] The ideas discussed in this
essay are those of the Protestant Reformers, the Calvinist Puritans,
and the moderating Anglicans. The common life, the dense
medium, is that provided by the University of Cambridge. The
ideas are the important thing—of the relation between man and
God, nature and grace. But ideas can be historically appreciated
only in so far as they achieve a local habitation and a name; here,
that is, as they were developed by the teachers and students, the
masters and pastors, of a particular collegiate university at a
particular time, whether in the dramatic conflict or the trivial
round.

The story is that of the Reformation in England, told from a
certain angle. The universities are traditionally the nurseries of
the Church, and the contribution of Cambridge to the ecclesiastical
history of England in the sixteenth and early seventeenth centuries
has never passed unrecognized. But it could be argued that much
of the history of the Church of England cannot be written by
anyone not intimately acquainted with the life and the habits of
the older universities: the history, for instance, of the Reformation, the Evangelical Revival, or the Oxford Movement.
Certainly the vicissitudes of the story can best be appreciated (and
most fully enjoyed) by those who have experience of the senior
and the junior combination room, and can savour their peculiar
blend of the sublime and the ridiculous. (The charges against

[1] *Reflections on the Revolution in France.*

Degory Nichols, a Puritan Master of Magdalene in the reign of Elizabeth, included the regrettable facts that he had sworn to root out all Welshmen in the college; that he was in the habit of leaving his cows to graze in the court, to the peril of the hall and the chapel; and that he had taken to wife a vociferous scold, whose voice penetrated to the farthest corners of the college, 'to the disturbance of the students, so that it were to be wished she had another dwelling house'.[1]) At one moment, the historian of the sixteenth-century university breathes the intellectual air which St Augustine breathed; the next moment he is in the world of Sir Charles Snow's *The Masters*, with its dons 'victims of some-thing like war hysteria'.[2] Mr John Saltmarsh has compared Tudor Cambridge, with its bees and butterflies and cornfields, to Hardy's Casterbridge.[3] It was no less like Hardy's Hintock: 'where reasoning proceeds on narrow premises, and results in inferences wildly imaginative; yet where, from time to time, dramas of a grandeur and unity truly Sophoclean are enacted in the real, by virtue of the concentrated passions and closely-knit inter-dependence of the lives therein'.[4]

For the religious disputes of Tudor Cambridge were greatly concerned with the passions and prejudices of academic persons. Erasmus was guilty of unpardonable (if picturesque) exaggeration when he described the Cambridge dons he knew as 'Cyprian bulls and dung-eaters'.[5] Bucer was slightly more serious when he wrote of them as 'profligate epicureans'.[6] But both men had been shocked by expecting to discover in Cambridge groups of rational beings associated on the basis of a common affection and respect, and finding instead

[1] J. B. Mullinger, *The University of Cambridge*, II, 287.
[2] C. P. Snow, *The Masters*, 181.
[3] 'Tudor Cambridge', *Journal of the Institutional Management Association*, August 1952, 121.
[4] *The Woodlanders*, chapter I.
[5] Letter of November, 1511. P. S. Allen (ed.). *Erasmi Epistolae*, I, 492. Translated by F. M. Nichols, *The Epistles of Erasmus*, II, 49.
[6] *Original Letters relative to the English Reformation* (Parker Society), II, 546.

The slaves unrespited of low pursuits
Living amid the same perpetual flow
Of trivial objects.

Again, what can be learned of the donnish character from Winstanley's four volumes on the later history of the university is
directly relevant to the Tudor theme; though it might be a little
optimistic to take as a general rule his deduction from the tangled
tale of Robinson's vote that 'stupidity is far more common than
deliberate wickedness'.[1]

Anglicanism, it has been said, is a religion for dons. Was
Puritanism any the less so?

However that may be, the religious movements in Cambridge
from Erasmus to Whichcote both influenced and were influenced
by the structure and balance of power within the academic
community; they were canalized in (or vitiated by) considerations
of college feeling and scholarly animosity, as well as by constitutional questions of visitorial interference, local jurisdiction and
university rights and privileges. That is the nature of the refraction:
and that is the interest of the story.

[1] D. A. Winstanley, *Later Victorian Cambridge*, 19.

PART I

HUMANISTS, REFORMERS AND EXILES

CHAPTER I

THE CAMBRIDGE OF JOHN FISHER

CARDINAL JOHN FISHER, emaciated and 'a very image of death',[1] was beheaded on Tower Hill in June 1535, the first of five Tudor Chancellors of the University of Cambridge to meet death on the scaffold.[2] For over forty years he had been a man of high authority in Cambridge: perhaps at no other time has the university owed so much, for so long, to one man. Indeed, of all the formative periods in the development of Cambridge—the bursts of acceleration, as it were, or the changes of gear—those years have claim to be considered the most important; they were, without doubt, the most dramatic and the least dull; they were also—and this especially fits them for the historian's pen—the most ironic. The Cambridge of Fisher was the seed-time of a strange harvest: the corn would have been alien to him. Fate, as Tudor poets were fond of pointing out, has a way of altering design. For instance, the two colleges which Fisher founded, with the Lady Margaret, as homes of orthodox religion and true learning, were to be notorious strongholds of factious Calvinist Puritanism. 'He looked that it should bring forth grapes, and it brought forth wild grapes.'

Fisher had first made the long journey to Cambridge from his home in Yorkshire when he was fourteen.[3] That was in 1483, the year of Edward IV's death. The college chosen for the boy was Michaelhouse, founded in 1324 by Edward II's Chancellor of the Exchequer, and situated where today stand the south-west corner of Trinity Great Court and the Bishop's Hostel. This choice was

---

[1] Philip Hughes (ed.), *St John Fisher: the Earliest English Life*, 184.
[2] The other four were Thomas Cromwell (executed 1540), Somerset (executed 1552), Northumberland (executed 1553), and Essex (executed 1601).
[3] Fisher was born in 1469; A. H. Lloyd, *The Early History of Christ's College*, 391.

3

probably dictated by the fact that John there came under the tutoring eye of another Yorkshireman, William Melton, then in his middle twenties—Melton was later to be Master of the college, Chancellor of York, and a preacher of some renown. For nearly eight years Fisher studied the arts course under Melton, the seven liberal arts and the three philosophies.[1] To achieve the status of bachelor he worked at the *trivium*—Latin grammar (Priscian), rhetoric (Boethius, Cicero and Aristotle), and logic (Aristotle again, with the *Parva Logicalia*, a portion of the *Summulae Logicales* written in the late thirteenth century by Petrus Hispanus, a native of Lisbon who taught in Paris, and who became Pope John XXI). In his second year—1485, the time of Bosworth Field—he became sophister, able to take part in (and not merely to attend) certain disputations in the Schools. In his third and fourth years he came to grips with natural, moral and metaphysical philosophy, as expounded (yet again) in the works of Aristotle, with the commentaries of Duns Scotus or Alexander Hales as guide. From 'questionist', involving a nominal examination by the praelector, Fisher commenced bachelor in the Lent of 1488, four and half years after entering the university, when he was nineteen. This involved standing in the Schools with his fellow determinists on the afternoon of each week-day for a month, arguing his 'questions' with those who cared to test him. A successful 'determination' meant admission as bachelor of arts. There were now a further three years of study until the inception as master of arts: a hard core of the *quadrivium* (arithmetic, geometry, music and astronomy), much more Aristotle, some disputing and a little lecturing. Then, after the grant of an approving testimonial by twelve masters of arts and of a licence to incept, he took part in the solemn public disputations of the Commencement in the July of 1491, and, being successful, was himself admitted master. So

---

[1] The course of studies in medieval Cambridge is described in J. B. Mullinger, *The University of Cambridge*, I, 342–58; S. M. Leathes, Introduction to *Grace Book* A, xxi–xxvii; and S. E. Morison, *The Founding of Harvard College*, 26–35.

from 1491 Fisher assumed for a few years the mantle of the regent, or teaching, master: lecturing, disputing, attending congregations of the regents—the 'upper house' of the Senate. In 1491 he was also elected Fellow of his college, and ordained priest—after obtaining a dispensation from Pope Innocent VIII, for he was only twenty-two, below the canonical age.[1] Eventually, by lecturing on the Bible and on the standard text-book of sound theological teaching (the *Libri Sententiarum* drawn up in the middle of the twelfth century by Peter Lombard), after preaching to the university, and passing through the detailed series of oppositions, responsions and replications, Fisher became qualified to receive, in 1501, the degree of doctor of divinity. By that time he had been for ten years a busy administrator: proctor in the year 1494/5, and Master of Michaelhouse (in succession to Melton) in 1497.[2] As proctor, concerned with the raising of funds for the rebuilding of Great St Mary's, he had met the Lady Margaret Beaufort, mother of the King, at Greenwich in 1495.[3] In 1501 she appointed Dr Fisher her chaplain-confessor. In the following year he was named, in the deed of foundation, the first Lady Margaret Professor of Divinity in the University of Cambridge. He was obviously, from all points of view, the appropriate choice.

So Fisher's Cambridge career—extending now over twenty years—had been brilliantly successful. The stars were dancing for him, this tall, direct and grave young doctor, slender and sad, but with a ruddy countenance and a witty turn of phrase which nicely balanced the more highly serious of his virtues. In 1504, in swift succession, he was appointed Bishop of Rochester and Chancellor of the university. He was to hold both offices until his death thirty-one years later. (For three of these years—from 1505 to 1508—he was also President of Queens'.) Like Matthew

[1] A. H. Lloyd, *op. cit.* 391.
[2] There is no direct evidence that either Melton or Fisher was Master; A. E. Stamp, *Michaelhouse*, 50.
[3] Mary Bateson, Introduction to *Grace Book* B, *Part I*, xv. For Margaret Beaufort, see Mrs Sorley's *Kings' Daughters*.

Parker, Fisher may be regarded, so far as his Cambridge career is concerned, as a born don who drifted naturally into administration. Certainly he had the qualities which were considered necessary for a successful university administrator and reformer—caution, prudence, soundness.[1] As Chancellor he 'looked very straitly to the orders and rules of the university',[2] and the value of his work as patron and benefactor can scarcely be over-estimated:

calling every man to his duty, as well in the schools for profit of their learning, as in their churches and colleges for due keeping and observing the service of God, endeavouring himself by all the means he could to reduce the university to their ancient rules and statutes, which began even then to grow out of frame.[3]

As Bishop, 'his palace for continence seemed a very monastery, and for learning an university'.[4] As Chancellor, Master, President and Professor, 'many times, for the encouragement of the younger sort, himself would be present at their disputations and readings and in disputing among them would bestow sometimes many hours together'.[5] The 'very mirror', then, and 'lantern of light'.[6] And though in 1506, when the King came to Cambridge, with the Lady Margaret and Prince Henry, and perhaps Erasmus too, the Chancellor could oratorically declare that in his young days 'there had stolen over well nigh all of us a weariness of learning and study, so that not a few did take counsel in their own minds how they might effect their departure',[7] of the three reasons he gave for this, one was conspicuously no longer applicable. The strife with the town continued, and the plague; but no one could say that in 1506 'there were few or no helpers and patrons of letters'. Weariness—if weariness there had been—had given way to a new spirit of assurance and achievement. The chancellorship

[1] H. O. Evennett, 'John Fisher and Cambridge', *Clergy Review*, IX, 378.
[2] Hughes (ed.), *St John Fisher*, 40. [3] *Ibid.* 40–1.
[4] *Ibid.* 38. [5] *Ibid.* 41.
[6] *Ibid.* 192.
[7] Oration translated and quoted in Mullinger, *op. cit.* 427.

of Fisher marked the spring of Renaissance Cambridge, no less surely than it witnessed the Indian summer of the medieval university.

For the Cambridge of Fisher was, in sharp degree, a combination of the medieval and the new; and much of the religious history of Tudor England is reflected or implied in the uses to which the new men were putting the ancient institutions—the hostels, for example, or the religious houses.

There were, in the early sixteenth century, about twenty hostels. During the whole period from the thirteenth century to the sixteenth there had been, all told, over one hundred and thirty.[1] The students and teachers of medieval Cambridge and Oxford did not necessarily house themselves in a college. In fact only a minority did so.[2] The thirteen colleges which existed in 1500 have been described as 'essentially charitable and moral institutions for poorer men who could not afford to live in lodgings or the hostels'.[3] Thomas Lever made a statement to the same effect when he spoke of the hostels serving those 'having rich friends or being beneficed men'.[4] The collegiate ideal (which received its earliest English expression in the rule of Merton) was confined at first to Fellows and scholars, and though during the fifteenth century there began to be provision for pensioners within the colleges, or some of them, not every young man would relish the prospect of a strict communal discipline. But just as the fifteenth century was a great period of Cambridge growth— until by the early 1500's the numbers were almost as great as those at Oxford—the Cambridge of Fisher marked the most important stage in the rise of the colleges to power and importance. The statutes of God's House drawn up in 1496 provided, for the first time, college lectures and college teaching, as distinct from the

[1] See H. P. Stokes, *The Mediaeval Hostels of Cambridge* (Camb. Antiq. Soc. Pubn., XLIX).

[2] E. F. Jacob, 'English university clerks in the later Middle Ages', *Essays in the Conciliar Epoch*, 215.

[3] Evennett, *loc. cit.*   [4] Thomas Lever, *Sermons*, 121.

university lectures of the masters of arts such as those Fisher had given in the early 'nineties.

Thus, although several hostels were marked on Richard Lyne's map of Cambridge in 1574, there was not a single reference to the use of hostels for teaching and residence in the University Grace Book containing records for the years 1542–89.[1] Trinity Hostel, east of Holy Trinity Church, was, according to Thomas Fuller, 'the longest liver, surviving all the rest':[2] but there do not appear to have been students there after 1540.

Some of the hostels had been 'absolute corporations, entire within themselves'.[3] Others were attached to the colleges. Borden Hostel, near the modern site of Deighton Bell's shop, was jointly owned by Peterhouse and Clare; it was sold in 1536 to a wealthy alderman, who made an inn of it.[4] St Mary's Hostel, where the Senate House now stands, was once the Hall of the Guild of St Mary (attached to the Church of St Mary the Great). This guild combined with that of Corpus Christi (attached to St Bene't's), and the amalgamated guild founded, by 1352, the College of Corpus Christi and the Blessed Virgin Mary, to which college the old hall now belonged. Matthew Parker spent some of his student days there in the 1520's. Later, Parker bought it from his college, to use as a private house, and his son, Sir John Parker, died there in poverty in 1619.[5] Physwick Hostel, with its twenty or thirty students, was an annexe of Gonville Hall; in 1533 a newly elected Fellow called John Caius was appointed Principal. Physwick Hostel, with Michaelhouse and King's Hall, went to the making of Trinity in 1546. The Hostel of St Nicholas, south of the Barnwell Gate, was distinguished for its brawls. Indeed, inter-hostel feuds were as striking a contemporary nuisance as 'town and gown' riots. In 1507, for instance, the men of this hostel carried on a boisterous battle with the students of Christ's

[1] J. Venn, Introduction to *Grace Book* Δ, vi.
[2] Thomas Fuller, *History of the University of Cambridge*, 62.
[3] *Ibid.* 66.   [4] Stokes, *Mediaeval Hostels*, 25.
[5] Stokes, *Corpus Christi College*, 50.

for two nights running![1] When most of its latter-day inmates had long since heard the chimes at midnight for the last time, the hostel became the home of the puritan Laurence Chaderton, Fellow of Christ's and first Master of the godly house of Emmanuel.

The religious houses are more significant for the story. There may indeed have been an intimate connection between the monastic orders and the start of Cambridge studies, though the group of monks from the Lincolnshire house of Crowland who arrived in Cambridge early in the twelfth century[2] must regretfully be relegated, as theoretical founders of the university, to the crowded limbo of picturesque persons for whom the same honour has been claimed, in company, that is, with such worthies as the Spanish Prince Cantaber, King Arthur, and the Saxon King Sigebert. Be that as it may, to speak of the medieval university is to speak of monks and canons and friars; the disappearance of the religious habit from the streets and courts of Cambridge in the late 1530's must be numbered among the real breaks in academic history. Monastic houses had the obligation to send some of their number to study at the university, to take a degree in theology or canon law.[3] The obligation was often ignored, in the fourteenth century as in the early sixteenth.[4] After all, a leave of absence of at least seven years from the monastery, for a religious in early manhood, with the prospect of ample opportunity for all sorts and conditions of dissipation, would not necessarily be warmly encouraged by every abbot. Many monks, however, were sent. These 'university monks' may have gone to their own houses of study. The Benedictines had three such houses at Oxford, but none at Cambridge until 1428. In that

---

[1] Mary Bateson, Introduction to *Grace Book* B, xvii.

[2] H. Rashdall, *The Universities of Europe in the Middle Ages*, III, 276.

[3] For monks at the university, David Knowles, *Religious Orders in England*, II, chapter 2, 'Monks and canons at the university, 1300–1450'; and J. Venn, *Early Collegiate Life*, chapter 6, 'Monks in Cambridge'.

[4] Some sixteenth-century complaints are quoted in Philip Hughes, *The Reformation in England*, I, 60–1.

year 'the hostel called monks' place' was founded, a small community, drawn mainly from Crowland. From the 1480's the house was referred to as Buckingham College—a name assumed to derive from Henry, second Duke of Buckingham.[1] The first record of the name Buckingham College is dated 1483. Thus at Cambridge, and even at Oxford, the monks often lived in the ordinary colleges or hostels. The house of Augustinian canons at Butley in Suffolk had an *honesta camera* reserved for their men at Gonville Hall, Cambridge; and of the sixteen pensioners resident in that college in 1513, three were Austin canons from Westacre, in Norfolk, and there were monks also from Norwich and Lewes.[2] Conversation in the Gonville Hall of the 1520's was lively enough, when the young monks found as their collegiate seniors such Lutheran reformers as Edward Crome, Nicholas Shaxton and Sygar Nicholson. And by 1523 the prior of the house of Augustinian canons at Barnwell was himself in sympathy with the reformers: he was Thomas Rawlyn.

Thus many others besides Hugh Latimer of Clare may have remembered with affection, in later days, a 'merry monk' of their college.[3] And the minor revolution of their disappearance seems perhaps the more shocking when it is remembered that the royal injunctions of 1535 had once more attempted to enforce the obligation of houses to send monks to the university.

The site and buildings of Buckingham College were granted by the King to Lord Chancellor Audley, and so Magdalene was founded. Such transformations were not a new thing. Over forty years before, in 1496, the Cambridge house of Benedictine nuns had been refounded as Jesus College by Bishop Alcock of Ely (like Fisher, a Beverley man), who had found at his last visitation only two rather fallen sisters. And at four o'clock on

---

[1] D. M. B. Ellis and L. F. Salzman, 'Religious Houses', *Victoria History of the County of Cambridge*, II, 312.
[2] Venn, *Early Collegiate Life*, 77; 68–9.
[3] Latimer, *Sermons*, I, 153.

the afternoon of 12 March 1511 the half dozen or so remaining Austin canons of the Hospital of St John (founded at the very beginning of the thirteenth century) left Cambridge by water and were rowed to Ely. The previous week an order had been placed at Greenwich for 800,000 bricks; 'to engraft a college upon the old stock, that might bring forth better fruit'[1]—the college, that is, of St John's, the founding of which had been first discussed by Fisher and the Lady Margaret in 1505.[2] The foundation charter was issued in April 1511. The burden of the suppression of the old hospital and the organization of the new college was borne by Fisher, for the Lady Margaret died before the final licences had been drawn up; and it is typical of Fisher that he also bore, out of his own pocket, a considerable proportion of the expense.

The history of the friaries provides examples no less striking of the conversion of old institutions to the new uses of the university. The conversion seems easy, almost without incident. The surrender of the Cambridge houses in 1538 does not appear to have occasioned great protest; but that may be because we are ill fitted to catch the echoes of the searchings of conscience, the bitter regrets, and the shock. There can be no doubt that by the sixteenth century, as Dr Moorman has written, the Franciscan house 'had lost a good deal of its former glory',[3] and it may be assumed that the Cambridge Dominicans, Carmelites and Augustinian friars had shared in the apparently general failure of nerve. The Franciscan deed of surrender had twenty-four signatures,[4] the Dominican sixteen.[5] These men found themselves compelled profoundly to consider that the perfection of Christian living did not consist in ceremonies, the wearing of habit, and other such papistical tricks, which tended to hypocrisy and fained

[1] T. Baker, *History of St John's College*, I, 61.
[2] E. A. Benians, *John Fisher*, 20.
[3] J. R. H. Moorman, *The Grey Friars in Cambridge*, 131.
[4] *Ibid.* 129. September, 1538.
[5] W. Gumbley, *The Cambridge Dominicans*, 38.

dissimulation.[1] It was a sorry end, after three hundred years in Cambridge of doing good works, praying, learning and teaching. But there was a personal continuity of sorts. Gregory Dodds, the last prior of the Dominican house, was to end his days as Elizabethan Dean of Exeter; and John Scory, who also signed the deed of surrender, and was the last Dominican to receive a degree in the university,[2] died, as Bishop of Hereford, in 1585—the year after the foundation of Emmanuel College on the site of the old Dominican house.

The Franciscans, three clerks and some lay brothers, had arrived in Cambridge in 1225, barely a generation after students had first begun to settle in the town.[3] Thirteen years later, in 1238, the Dominicans were building on their large site south of the Barnwell Gate, flanking what on Lyne's map was still called Preachers' Street. In 1249 the Carmelites came to Chesterton, moving two years later to a three-acre site at Newnham,[4] and later still to property in Milne Street just north of where Queens' College was to be built. At one time there were fifty friars in the Carmelite convent; but at the time of the suppression the house had been abandoned by all but two. The Augustinian friars arrived in 1291, and obtained the spacious and attractive site bounded by the present-day Bene't Street, Corn Exchange Street, Pembroke Street and Free School Lane.[5] The surrender of the Austin friars was to be signed by the prior and three friars. The Franciscans, after forty years of sharing an old synagogue with the town jailbirds, of worshipping in a chapel of 'the simplest model, a day's work of a single carpenter',[6] moved in 1266 to the site upon which today stands Sidney Sussex College. There they constructed the setting for a life of academic yet industrious piety: a kitchen,

[1] The text of the deed of surrender is in Moorman, *op. cit.* 132.
[2] Gumbley, *op. cit.* 38.   [3] Moorman, *op. cit.* 6.
[4] David Knowles and R. Neville Hadcock, *Medieval Religious Houses: England and Wales*, 196.
[5] D. H. S. Cranage and H. P. Stokes, 'The Augustinian Friary in Cambridge', *Trans. Camb. Antiq. Soc.* XXII, 56.
[6] Knowles, *Religious Orders*, I, 141.

garner, brew house and mill house, a chapel, cloister, refectory, school house and library (from which Erasmus was to borrow a manuscript text of the Greek New Testament).[1] In the 1320's the friars laid on abundant fresh water to their house by buying a strip of ground two feet wide stretching to a spring on the Madingley Road, and laying down a pipe below the strip.[2] Eccleston wrote that the Grey friars in Oxford laughed unceasingly, that the only thing to sadden them was the necessity of parting.[3] The Cambridge brethren, too, brought to the infant university that 'delicacy and intuition of sympathy' which was the legacy from the mind of their founder, 'exquisitely sensitive and keenly receptive of all beauty'.[4] They had few great names to put against the Franciscan school of Oxford: no Grosseteste, Roger Bacon, or William of Occam, although Duns Scotus was probably at Cambridge for a few years at the very end of the thirteenth century. But their school of theology did prosper, and Dr Moorman ascribes in great part the growth of a faculty of theology in Cambridge to 'the presence of the Franciscan school, which was attracting good teachers and was proving a popular and important element in the life of the university'.[5]

The relations between the Orders and the university were not always happy. But the buildings of both the Augustinians and the Franciscans were often used by the university for ordinary academic purposes. Between 1478 and 1519, when the Church of St Mary the Great was almost completely demolished and rebuilt, the church of the Grey friars was sometimes used for the disputations and ceremonies of the Commencement. Fuller styled their church 'the St Mary's, before St Mary's, the commencement, acts and exercises being kept therein'.[6] Even after 1519 the practice continued: by a University Grace of 1523[7] the friars

[1] Moorman, op. cit. 58.
[2] W. W. R. Ball, The King's Scholars and King's Hall, 38–9.
[3] Knowles, Religious Orders, I, 140.   [4] Ibid. 122.
[5] Moorman, op. cit. 30.   [6] Fuller, History of Cambridge, 66.
[7] R. Willis and J. W. Clark, Architectural History of the University of Cambridge, II, 724.

were paid ten shillings for use of their church, and storage of the wooden tiers for seating. A last Commencement was held there in 1540: but this was an appendix to the story, for the friars were gone, and the church was soon to be demolished.

The property of the friars was not allowed to decay. Cambridge men could never have countenanced the slow, natural dissolution of good buildings—nor was this an age which would have found particularly moving the romantic but melancholy fate of the statue of Ozymandias. The Carmelite site was sold to Queens', and is today part of the college garden.[1] The Augustinian property passed into private hands: the succession of owners included John Hatcher, Regius Professor of Physic, and, in 1614, Stephen Perse; finally, in 1636, the estate was bought by Thomas Buck, esquire bedell and sometime University Printer. The old refectory, immediately opposite the east wall of the court of Corpus Christi, was used in the 1630's as a printing house for the University Press. Buck's nephew, to whom the property passed, died in 1746; and William Cole described the demolition of the refectory and the sale of the last effects, all that remained of the 'old monastery'.[2] The Dominican site had also passed into private hands. It was bought by Sir Walter Mildmay in 1583, to found a college for the puritan order of preachers, and the church of the Black friars became the hall of Emmanuel.[3] As if in compensation, the refectory of the Grey friars was transformed into the chapel of Sidney Sussex[4] in 1596, when the executors of Frances, Countess of Sussex, had bought the site after six years of negotiation. The buildings were in ruins, for in 1546 the stonework had been 'defaced and taken towards the building of the King's Majesty's new college'[5]—nearly three thousand loads of stone

[1] J. H. Gray, *The Queens' College*, 15.
[2] D. H. S. Cranage and H. P. Stokes, 'The Augustinian Friary', *Trans. Camb. Antiq. Soc.* XXII, 53–75. See also S. C. Roberts, *History of the Cambridge University Press: 1521–1921*, 50.
[3] Willis and Clark, *op. cit.* II, 694.
[4] *Ibid.* 730.   [5] *Ibid.* 725.

were carried to Trinity in one year alone.[1] Today, all that remains of the Franciscan buildings is an old wall in the garden of Sidney Sussex. But the water pipe from Madingley—which the friars had shared with King's Hall from 1445—survived; and on Christmas Eve 1546 the King granted to Trinity College the conduit head at Madingley, all springs contributing thereto, and all conduits, leaden pipes and underground water courses extending therefrom to the site of the college.[2] And so, at Trinity, 'even now, in these days of ample supply, the Franciscan water is still used for the college Fountain, whose splash at midnight has been grateful to the ears of so many generations of·dwellers in the Great Court'.[3]

The charter of foundation of Trinity College was dated 17 December 1546.[4] To this college, with its sixty Fellows and scholars, founded for 'the amplification and establishment of the Christian religion, the extirpation of heresy and false opinion',[5] Henry VIII granted the estates of twenty-six dissolved religious houses.[6] This was abundant recompense for the scare of the early 1540's, when it had seemed possible that the colleges might follow the way of the monasteries. Indeed an Act of 1544[7] had given the King power to dissolve any college at either university, and appropriate its possessions. This Act was in fact used for the dissolution of Michaelhouse and King's Hall, and of Physwick Hostel, and so for the foundation of Trinity; a college given its name, said Fuller, 'not only because dedicated to God, One in three persons, but also because made by King Henry the Eighth, one of three colleges'.[8]

King's Hall was a wealthy college, founded by Edward II in 1317; its entrance gate, begun in 1518, was to be Trinity Great Gate; its last warden the first Master of Trinity. At the other end of the collegiate scale was the poor God's House, dating back to

---

[1] *Ibid.* 562.
[2] Trinity College, Cambridge, Senior Bursar's Muniments, Box 34.
[3] G. M. Trevelyan, *Trinity College*, 14.   [4] W. W. R. Ball, *op. cit.* 63.
[5] Cooper, *Annals*, I, 144.   [6] *Ibid.* 446–51.
[7] 37 Hen. VIII, cap. iv.   [8] Fuller, *History of Cambridge*, 83.

1439, but refounded by Henry VI. John Sycling, the proctor of the college at the end of the fifteenth century, was a good friend of Fisher and the Lady Margaret,[1] and in 1505, under their patronage, the old house began to blossom into Christ's College, as hall, kitchen and chambers took shape beneath the scaffolding and the cranes and the ropes. In October 1506 Sycling became the first Master of Christ's; and the last four Fellows of God's House became senior Fellows of the new foundation,[2] which was to have twelve Fellows and nearly fifty scholars. Fisher was appointed Visitor for life. The buildings were largely completed by 1511.[3] In that year rebuilding and building began on the site of the old Hospital of St John, until by 1513 the chapel, hall and master's lodge were almost finished.[4] Many times Fisher was sorry that he ever took the business upon him, such had been the difficulties and the obstructions, but these regrets were laid aside in the summer of 1516, when he went to Cambridge formally to open the new college. He drew up statutes for St John's, as he had done for Christ's; more, he founded four fellowships, a number of scholarships and lectureships, and made generous gifts of vestments and plate to the chapel; he intended also to bequeath to the college his beloved library—but this was seized at Rochester after his arrest, and dispersed.

In the first twenty years of the century, then, extensive building was in progress at Christ's and St John's; and also at Great St Mary's and King's. The roof of the nave of Great St Mary's was completed in 1508, thirty years after the first stone of the building had been laid;[5] a gift of timber from the King and the Lady Margaret had spurred on the building appeal, an appeal to which bishops and heads of religious houses subscribed, as well as kings. The porch and vestry were finished, and the windows

[1] Evennett, loc. cit. 382.
[2] H. Rackham, Christ's College in Former Days, 7.
[3] Willis and Clark, op. cit. II, 200.
[4] Ibid. 242. The chapel was that of the hospital, restored.
[5] E. Venables, Annals of Great St Mary's, 62.

glazed, in 1514, and the church was first used in 1519.[1] In 1508 also, work was resumed on the chapel of King's, after an interval of a quarter of a century. The master mason there was John Wastell.[2] The account books of the college tell of 140 workmen—masons, carpenters, sawyers, plumbers, labourers—under whose hands the vaulting, the buttresses and the towers took shape, until by 1515 the stonework was complete. The other fine artist at work in King's was Barnard Flower, under whose supervision four of the windows were in place by 1517. The glazing was resumed in 1526—perhaps spurred on by Fisher—and nearly all the glass was finished by 1531. Mr Kenneth Harrison has written of the importance of this work in King's, which gave to the diffusion of Renaissance work in English painted glass 'the greatest, and perhaps the earliest, impetus'.[3] It is significant and appropriate that it was under the chancellorship of Fisher that a Gothic building was decorated in the Renaissance style.

In 1536 the old chapel of King's collapsed one evening after vespers, and the new chapel was used for the first time. The year before, Fisher had been executed: he was the only Henrician Bishop to die for the papal supremacy, though not the only one to refuse to repudiate it. In that year were also martyred William Exmew of Christ's, vicar and steward of the London Charterhouse, Richard Reynolds, Fellow of Corpus Christi and monk of Sion, and Thomas More, who had been high steward of the university from 1525 to 1529. Dr Thomas Greenwood, Fellow of St John's and Carthusian, was to die in prison in June 1537. Stories were brought back to Cambridge of the heroic end of the

[1] S. Sanders, *Historical and Architectural Notes on Great St Mary's*, 19–20.

[2] A sketch, probably by Wastell, of the north side and east end of the chapel, in perspective, showing the detail of the projected completion, and introducing figures in academic dress, is in the Cotton manuscripts (British Museum). It was discussed and reproduced as 'the earliest-known English technical drawing showing a complete building of large size' by John Harvey in his article on 'Early Tudor draughtsmen' in *The Connoisseur Coronation Year Book* (1953, ed. L. G. G. Ramsey), 98–100. Harvey dates the drawing as 1512. Wastell also worked at Saffron Walden; W. J. Fancett, *The Story of Saffron Walden Parish Church*, 20.

[3] K. Harrison, *The Windows of King's College Chapel*, 72.

Chancellor. An unknown Cambridge man, recollecting years later what he had 'heard say credibly' in 1535 when he was 'but a young scholar of St John's college', could remember many of the details of that day.[1] How Fisher was awakened at five in the morning, and told that his execution was to be between nine and ten; how he dressed himself especially carefully, saying to his servant, 'What, man! Do you not know that this is our marriage day? I must be gay this day for honour of the marriage'; how he went to the scaffold reciting and meditating upon a verse from St John's Gospel, 'this is life eternal, that they might know thee the only true God, and Jesus Christ, whom thou hast sent'. 'And coming up the stairs of the scaffold, the sun being in the south east did shine marvellous bright upon his face, that he could not well see. And therewithal he said: *Accedite ad eum et illuminamini; et facies vestrae non confundentur.* And so what he said upon the scaffold I cannot tell.' The 'headless carcass' of the Chancellor was left naked on the scaffold for the rest of that hot June day, 'saving that one for pity and humanity cast a little straw upon it'.[2] And his tomb stood unfinished in the chapel of St John's.

On balance, the Cambridge of Fisher was one of the pleasanter spots of early Tudor England. True, the climate was not good. Erasmus, Ascham and Bucer all complained of the damp and the cold; and William Harrison was to write in 1577 that although the town 'standeth very well', it was 'somewhat near unto the fens, whereby the wholesomeness of the air is not a little corrupted'.[3] Also, the streets—and the King's Ditch, which served the town as a sanitary moat—stank to high heaven. Elizabethan sanitary regulations[4] were to mention the mire and the dung in the busy thoroughfares, the pigs and the cattle and the geese

---

[1] This account, used, with other sources, in the life of Fisher issued under the name of Richard Hall, was separately printed (from British Museum Arundell MS. 152) by F. van Ortroy, in *Analecta Bollandiana*, x (1891), 164–7.   [2] Hughes (ed.), *St John Fisher*, 187.
[3] *A Description of England* (ed. L. Withington, 1876), p. 249.
[4] Such as those of 1575; Cooper, *Annals*, II, 332.

wandering through the narrow lanes and sometimes through the colleges, the carcasses mouldering in the Ditch and the alleys— all the sights and smells of a medieval market and trading town. Then there were the slaughter-houses, behind the Augustinian friary, in the lane which took its name from them, a lane running with blood and littered with entrails. How many Cambridge men would have echoed the humanitarian appeal of John Foxe: 'I can scarce pass the shambles where beasts are slaughtered, but that my mind secretly recoils with a feeling of pain'?[1] With the summer came the plague. Lectures were broken off, students evacuated, almost yearly through the sixteenth century, until the climax of this horror was reached in the appalling 'great plague' of 1630. The emergency plague-houses were an especially unsavoury addition to the clusters of gimcrack tenements which sprang up in Tudor Cambridge. There were the dunghills too, improvised or authorized. The metaphors of the Puritan preachers were nothing if not homely, and to speak to a Cambridge congregation, as did William Perkins of Christ's, of the sinner who 'is nothing else but a filthy dunghill of all abomination and uncleanness, the stink whereof hath infected heaven and earth',[2] was to strike a chord which does not reverberate quite so effectively for a modern reader.

Yet, on the other hand, there were the open spaces, the orchards, the vineyards, the gardens, within the town and within the colleges. Cambridge can still be called, even in the 1950's, a 'garden city',[3] and the sixteenth-century university town has been compared to the Dorchester which Hardy knew. Beyond the town were the wharves and the trading vessels and the swans on the river, the open fields, the pleasant walks, the corn and the woods. And the atmosphere of the Cambridge spring, early spring, was surely delightful, with the new brick courts of

---

[1] Letter of Foxe to the Queen (1575) quoted by Gordon Rupp in *Six Makers of English Religion, 1500–1700*, 62.
[2] Perkins, *Works*, I (1616), 378.   [3] Ernest Barker, *Age and Youth* (1953), 5.

Queens' and St John's to give a unique and domestic flavour to the scene. The charm and variety were there: the charm, later, of Hammond's map (1592) and the prints of David Loggan (1688). In a turbulent age there was opportunity here for quiet lives.

In 1500 Queens' laid out an especially extensive garden, on the west bank of the river.[1] This may have delighted even the crotchety Erasmus, and compensated in some measure for the bad beer. If, as tradition has it, he lodged in the tower at Queens', the view must have atoned for the stairs: over to the Trumpington woods, and the open country beyond Newnham. Perhaps, as Thomas Fuller, also of Queens', was to imagine, the Dutchman really was 'allured with the situation of this college so near the river (as Rotterdam his native place to the sea)'.[2] It was, at the least, a charitable thought.

[1] Willis and Clark, *op. cit.* III, 579.   [2] Fuller, *History of Cambridge*, 166.

CHAPTER II

ERASMUS IN CAMBRIDGE

I

THERE occurred in 1469 two births which were to condition the course of Cambridge history. The one was obscure enough, that of a boy, baptized John, to a Beverley mercer called Robert Fisher. The other was both obscure and dubious—the son of a serving maid and a cleric, secretly born in Rotterdam.[1] The servant girl, mother of Erasmus, died in 1483 (the year in which John Fisher went up to Michaelhouse) and the father followed her within twelve months. The not unhappy schooldays at Gouda and Deventer were over; and in the period when Fisher was working through the arts course at Cambridge, the resentful Dutch boy was first fretting in an inferior school at s'Hertogen-bosch, and then adjusting himself to the regular monastic life at the house of Steyn, near Gouda: a house of the Brethren of the Common Life, under the Augustinian rule. For a year or two Erasmus was happy enough here, in his own way. But then the boredom set in, and the bitterness; what relief for that spirit, fearing above all things to be 'cabin'd, cribb'd, confin'd', when he was sent, a university monk, to study theology in Paris (at a time when Fisher was studying the duties of a proctor at the University of Cambridge). In some ways Paris was a disappointment, a betrayal of the Erasmian vision. For one thing, the Collège de Montaigu was notoriously squalid. Erasmus's own later attacks on it were to be echoed and equalled by such otherwise diverse French stylists as Calvin and Rabelais. But there were consolations: his pupils, for instance, among whom two lively English boys, lodging in his own hostel with a testy Scots guardian, came to

[1] A. Hyma, *The Youth of Erasmus*, 51.

Erasmus to be taught Latin grammar. One of these boys was Robert Fisher, cousin of John. There were friends too, such as another Englishman, whom Erasmus met in 1497, a Fellow of Queens' named Richard Whitford, who had come to Paris as chaplain to Lord Mountjoy. The little Dutch monk, though he could be difficult and moody, was popular with the English 'set'. He was kind and affectionate—too affectionate for the silly suspicious Scot, who removed Thomas Grey, the other English lad, from his care. And he was an original, making for himself a nice little reputation with his Latin verses.[1] He was perhaps a little shocked, but surely envious, at the stories Whitford told him of the comparatively pleasant collegiate life of Cambridge, of such architectural splendours as the court of Queens', bright in warm red brick, of such rising hopes as Robert's cousin, elected Master of Michaelhouse in 1497.

Fourteen years later, on a rainy day in August 1511, Erasmus rode bad-tempered into Cambridge, handed over his lame horse to be stabled, and crossed that very court of Queens' to the room provisionally reserved for him. This was almost certainly not his first stay in Queens'; in the spring of 1506, when Fisher was President of the College, and Henry VII and the Lady Margaret visited the university, Erasmus was probably one of the company of distinguished guests who lodged there.[2] But that had been a flying visit. Now Erasmus came to Cambridge with a definite purpose, to lecture in Greek. The appointment was Fisher's work, needless to say. 'I look to you', the Chancellor was to tell Erasmus, 'as necessary to the university, and will not suffer you to want, so long as there is anything to spare out of my own poor means.'[3] So for the first few weeks, into the autumn, the Dutch-

---

[1] See *The Poems of Erasmus,* ed. C. Reedijk (Leiden, 1956).

[2] P. S. Allen (ed.), *Erasmi Epistolae*, I, 591. An application for a D.D. degree is in the University Grace Book for this year, but Erasmus in fact took his degree in Italy in September 1506 (*ibid.*; cf. *ibid.* 432).

[3] November 1511. Allen (ed.), *Erasmi Epistolae*, I, 485. Translated by F. M. Nichols, *The Epistles of Erasmus*, II, 75. P. S. Allen's edition of the *Opus Epistolarum* of Erasmus was

man worked over his lectures on the basic elements of Greek grammar. The attendance at these lectures was to prove disappointing. But by the Michaelmas Term, in October, there was talk of his lecturing on divinity, and he began to collect his thoughts and his notes about Jerome, always his favourite of the Fathers: 'Deum immortalem', he had written in 1500,

shall the names of Scotus, Albertus, and writers still less polished be shouted in all the schools, and that singular champion, exponent and light of our religion (*ille unicus religionis nostrae pugil illustrator ac lumen*) who deserves to be the one person celebrated,—shall he be the only one of whom nothing is said?[1]

It is probable that he was appointed to the chair of divinity founded ten years before by the Lady Margaret, the chair first held by Fisher, which entailed the duty of lecturing for one hour on each week-day during term.

Of the letters which Erasmus wrote from Cambridge, only thirty have survived.[2] The first was written to Colet on 24 August 1511, the last to Warham in January 1514. Erasmus, then, was connected with the university for less than three years. Moreover, there are regular series of letters for only two periods, each of about five months, until December 1511, and again from July 1513. He seems to have spent a great part of 1512 in London, perhaps confined to a sick bed—he was so ill in that year that rumours of his death were spread about Europe.[3] It is uncertain, again, where he lived. In August and September of 1511 he was lodged in Queens', certainly.[4] But afterwards? Perhaps in Queens', more probably with Garrett Godfrey, the Dutch

published at Oxford in eleven volumes, 1906–47. F. M. Nichols's three volumes of translations appeared from 1901 to 1918. I have used Nichols's translations largely, with alterations where appropriate.

[1] Allen (ed.), *Erasmi Epistolae*, I, 332. Nichols (ed.), *Epistles*, I, 289.

[2] They are printed among numbers 225 to 285 in the first volume of Allen (ed.), *Erasmi Epistolae*.

[3] Allen (ed.), *Erasmi Epistolae*, I, 526.

[4] Three letters of August and September are dated from there. The 'Erasmian' tradition at Queens' was first expressed in print by Thomas Fuller, who went up in 1622.

stationer, and later churchwarden of Great St Mary's. Erasmus was always an impatient guest. Dr Rupp has felicitously called him the original Flying Dutchman. Cambridge cannot boast the privilege of knowing him for long.

II

The little Dutchman, 'a clever man, and a very merry one too' (as, in his wry way, he thought of himself),[1] though teaching in the damp obscurity of East Anglia, had a reputation as scholar, publicist and wit which extended throughout Europe. A university has a habit of moulding visiting celebrities in its own image; and one wonders how many of Erasmus's Cambridge colleagues appreciated his originality, or how many, for that matter, had ever heard of him. He was now well into his forties, and before leaving London for Cambridge in 1511 he had taken a two months' trip to Paris to supervise the printing of *The Praise of Folly*, which appeared in June—and was to run through five editions in the next year and a half. But perhaps the Cambridge dons would best know their guest by way of his *Adages*, a dictionary of Latin and Greek quotations, a sort of reader's digest of the wisdom of the ancients, the augmented edition of which, in 1508, had made his name. They might perhaps have come across his recent editions of Cicero; or his translation into Latin verse of the *Hecuba* and *Iphigenia* of Euripides, published in 1506, and presented to Archbishop Warham. They might also have known that this Austin canon in the garb of a secular cleric[2] was more than a mere classical scholar. *Enchiridion militis christiani*, 'the handsome weapon of a Christian knight', written while Erasmus was staying in the Franciscan house at St Omer, had

---

[1] Erasmus, 'The Profane Banquet', *Colloquies*, 69.

[2] Erasmus obtained a dispensation from wearing the habit of his order in 1507. While at Cambridge, he spent a great deal of money endeavouring to receive formal confirmation of this dispensation: Allen (ed.), *Erasmi Epistolae*, I, 466.

been published in 1503.[1] This was the first Erasmian exposition of the *philosophia Christi*, the first of his great tilts at the windmills of the Christian Pharisees. It sprang, like everything Erasmus wrote, from a vision of Christian simplicity, purity and harmony, in a balanced world of order and justice, owing allegiance to the undefiled Christ—a Christ known from the pure and original sources. The mind of the creator of the *Enchiridion* and *The Praise of Folly* was cool, sardonic, disciplined; and also fully comic. The way to the realization of the vision is blocked—by the grotesques, those who lack charity. God is spirit, and they who worship him must worship him in spirit and truth. But where is truth? Not in monastic rules, nor in the casuistries of the divines. 'I see the modern theologians too freely and with a certain captious subtlety drinking in the letter, rather than plucking out the mysteries and giving their attention (as if Paul had not spoken the truth) to the fact that our law is spiritual.'[2] The clowns do not realize this: those who have perverted the ways of Christian love, arguing dryly or living shamefully, dancing to the measure piped not by God but by Folly. But judgement will come upon the insincere, the insipid, upon those who forget that Christ demands above all obedience to the law of charity. At that judgement the Christ will interrupt the self-justifying recitals of formal works, dry bones stripped of faith and love, and he will ask: 'Who are they, this new tribe of Jews? I do not recognize them as my own.'[3] It is high time, then, that we awoke; and we can awake, God's kingdom is at hand, we may have the key. That key must be accepted, the crooked must be made straight, or we perish in a sea of pride and inordinacy and

[1] *A booke called in latyn Enchiridion militis christiani and in englysshe the manuell of the christen knyght replenyssed with most holsome preceptes made by the famous clerke Erasmus of Roterdame to the which is added a newe and mervaylous profytable preface.* (London, 1533; translation usually attributed to Tyndale.) Note also *A short Recapitulation or abrigment of Erasmus Enchiridion brefely comprehending the summe and contentes thereof...Drawne out by M. Coverdale* (Antwerp, 1545). There is a new translation of the *Enchiridion*, by Dr F. L. Battles, in *Advocates of Reform* (ed. by Matthew Spinka, Library of Christian Classics, 1953).
[2] *Enchiridion* (tr. Battles), *op. cit.* 305.
[3] Erasmus, *The Praise of Folly*, section LIV.

25

folly. That was the Erasmian message. The villains of his morality play were as twisted and worthy of laughter as the absurdly distorted gargoyles of medieval masons. And most of the villains were academic. Erasmus's greatest comic scorn was always reserved for the *theologi*: 'genus hominum mire superciliosum atque irritabile'.[1] They made mock of the word of God, toying with theology—the study praised by Erasmus in 1501 as

> that excellent Queen, whom the inspired Psalmist describes, according to the interpretation of Jerome, as standing on the King's right hand, not mean and ragged as she is now seen in the schools of Sophists (*non sordidatam, non pannosam, qualis nunc visitur in ludis sophistarum*) but in vesture of gold, wrought about with divers colours, to whose rescue from degradation my nightly studies are devoted.[2]

He had written to Colet of that 'sordid and supercilious crowd of divines, who think nothing of any learning but their own' (*de sordido hoc ac supercilioso vulgo theologorum, qui prae se omnes omnium litteras pro nihilo ducunt*).[3] That, of course, was a description of the theologians of Oxford; and Whitford may have given his Cambridge friends advance notice of Erasmus's jibes at the superannuated sophists of the Sorbonne. But suppose the same touch were to be applied to Cambridge! What an unpleasant thought! The Erasmian attack sprang from indignation and was clothed in wit. The indignation might be ignored, but the wit was more dangerous. The academic mind is constitutionally suspicious of any wit which does not cater for its own rather inbred humour. And the cool smile of Erasmus, the sharp eyes, his whole habit of standing, as it were, on the periphery of things, on the outside looking in—what was Cambridge to make of it?

And how could Cambridge provide Erasmus with liberal spirits?—this friend of Colet, of the gentle More, the learned Grocin, the acute and delicate Linacre, of all that circle of

---

[1] Erasmus, *The Praise of Folly*, section LIII.
[2] Nichols (ed.), *Epistles*, I, 296. Allen (ed.), *Erasmi Epistolae*, I, 344.
[3] Nichols (ed.), *Epistles*, I, 220–1. Allen (ed.), *Erasmi Epistolae*, I, 247.

attractive scholars who owed their loyalty to Oxford, not quite yet the home of lost causes. In the three months which he had spent at Oxford in 1499—the three very last months of the fifteenth century—Erasmus, fresh from Paris and thirty-three years old, had discovered his vocation: to use the humanities of Greek and Latin for the advancing of Scripture study and the knowledge of Christ. He heard Colet's lectures on Paul: and he had found a kindred spirit.

In offering to do battle, my dear Colet, with this indomitable race of men for the restoration of genuine theology to its pristine brightness and dignity (*in pristinum nitorem ac dignitatem*) you have undertaken a pious work as regards theology itself, and a most wholesome one in the interest of all studies, and especially of this flourishing university of Oxford.[1]

Colet, certainly, went to the heart, making a bare text into a living gospel. He lectured on the Vulgate, knowing no Greek. But Greek, Erasmus now came to see, was the key at once to good letters and to Christian living. He wrote in 1501:

Latin erudition, however ample, is crippled and imperfect without Greek. We have in Latin at best some small streams and turbid pools, while they have the clearest springs and rivers flowing with gold (*fontes purissimi et flumina aurum volventia*). I see it is the merest madness to touch with the little finger that principal part of theology, which treats of the divine mysteries, without being furnished with the apparatus of Greek.[2]

So, after the oasis of Oxford, Erasmus elected to return to France and the Low Countries, to hardship and poverty, to teach himself Greek. By the end of 1502 he could write the language tolerably well;[3] when he visited England again in 1505 he had mastered it completely, at the age of nearly forty. Colet, now dean of St Paul's, lent him Greek manuscripts from the cathedral library,

[1] Nichols (ed.), *Epistles*, I, 221. Allen (ed.), *Erasmi Epistolae*, I, 247.
[2] Nichols (ed.), *Epistles*, I, 313. Allen (ed.), *Erasmi Epistolae*, I, 352.
[3] Nichols (ed.), *Epistles*, I, 353. Allen (ed.), *Erasmi Epistolae*, I, 381.

and he began to work on the New Testament. Then, in 1506, after the visit to Cambridge, Erasmus realized one of the dreams of his youth, to visit Italy. Here, albeit a northerner, he was welcomed, in the very home of the Renaissance: fêted in Bologna, Florence, Venice, Padua and the Rome of Julius II. For three years he travelled, making a bee-line, always, for the libraries. In the Florence of Leonardo, Michaelangelo and Raphael he collated texts of Lucian; in the Venice of Bellini, Giorgione and Titian he added Greek proverbs to the *Adages*. The furrow might seem narrow. But he had set his hand to the plough and only death could release the hold.

So this well-travelled and mature scholar faced his scanty audience in a chilly lecture hall of the Cambridge Schools in the autumn of 1511; and placed on the desk the elementary Greek grammar of the Byzantine Manuel Chrysoloras.

III

This then was Erasmus of Rotterdam: a slight man, rather reserved and inclined to be irritable, with a smile, half understanding, half supercilious, hovering at the corners of his thin, wide mouth, a mouth appropiately balanced in the fine bone structure of his face by the over-long, sharp nose; a man hesitating, in his high-pitched voice, over the few words in his English vocabulary; slightly over-playing his part as the prematurely aged scholar; suffering from the stone, a prey to vicious insomnia, and nervously fastidious about dirt. ('The dainty hands', wrote Dr T. M. Lindsay, 'and the general primness of his appearance, suggest a descent from a long line of maiden aunts.'[1]) Huizinga has pin-pointed as the core of Erasmus's character his need for purity: but that 'passionate desire for cleanliness and brightness, of the home and of the body',[2] would find little fulfilment in the

[1] T. M. Lindsay, *History of the Reformation*, I, 177. A. C. Benson madethe same remark about A. E. Housman.
[2] J. Huizinga, *Erasmus of Rotterdam*, 117.

Fenland market town in which he now found himself. One may imagine him taking roundabout ways to avoid the slaughter-houses or the fish stalls or the dung heaps. He certainly preferred riding to walking. When Roger Ascham went up to St John's in 1530 men still talked of the scholar 'which when he had been sore at his book, for lack of better exercise would take his horse and ride about the Market Hill'.[1] There was, after all, quite a lot for any visitor to see in Cambridge, and admire too. The building operations at Christ's, St John's, Great St Mary's and King's, for instance, were worth inspecting, and Erasmus must often have drawn up his horse for a glance at them. He unfortunately arrived six months too late to see the last remaining Austin canons of the Hospital of St John rowed away to Ely.

Yet, as everyone knows, Erasmus was not particularly happy at Cambridge. He was never a very happy or contented person, except for rare periods of calm in Oxford or London. He could not find in Cambridge what he had glimpsed at Oxford—the ideal of the Paradise Garden. 'The whole Renaissance', wrote Huizinga, 'cherished that wish of reposeful, blithe, yet serious intercourse of good and wise friends in the cool shade of a house under trees, where serenity and harmony would dwell.'[2] Erasmus realized that wish, on paper, in his dialogue, *The Religious Banquet*. At Oxford he may have felt it fulfilled in fact. Certainly, at Oxford, they had respected his 'sense of decorum, his great need of kindly courtesy, his pleasure in gentle obliging treatment, in cultured and easy manners'.[3] He needed to be surrounded by sympathetic affection. Perhaps he found amusing those diversions which a Fellow of St John's, ten years later, was to indicate as the most typical of Cambridge university activities: 'those tiresome visits of formality,...the backbiting and discussion of others, the canvassing for offices and pursuit of votes by all means fair or foul'.[4] But it was amusement in a wilderness. There was

---

[1] R. Ascham, *Toxophilus*, 46. [2] Huizinga, *op. cit.* 104.
[3] *Ibid.* 105. [4] Nicholas Darynton. Quoted in P. S. Allen, *Erasmus*, 161.

no Colet at Cambridge. And the old serenity, with much else, had gone for ever.

So we picture Erasmus as a sort of academic Mrs Gummidge. He complained of the Cambridge dons. He objected to the Cambridgeshire beer and had casks of Greek wine sent up from London.[1] (This was not the whim of a connoisseur but the revulsion of an invalid. For the sake of his health Erasmus preferred to risk the plague in Cambridge rather than drink the Fenland brew of his friends the Gonnells, out at Landbeach.) The wine casks took too long to arrive, or else they were tampered with—occasions for sizzling displays of Erasmian invective against the carriers or 'the common sort of people at Cambridge'.[2] He complained, as always, of poverty: 'money slips away here, where everything is done at my own cost'.[3] (This in spite of the stipend from a rectory in Kent, which he never visited, and a permanent grant from Lord Mountjoy, who also augmented his stipend as Greek lecturer.) During his first Cambridge winter he dwelt on the prospect of a room free from draughts, with a well-burning fire: 'de cubiculo tantum optem nidum aliquem probe defensum a ventis, et foco luculento'.[4] If only, he wrote, he could have 'some warm hive, where I can stow myself for the winter'![5] Occasionally he gave way to a perhaps ironically factitious feeling of revolt:

We have been living...for some months a snail's life. We shrink and hide ourselves indoors, and are as busy as bees in study. There is a great solitude here, most people away for fear of plague; though when all are here it is still a solitude. The expense is beyond bearing, the profit not a farthing...I am determined to take flight, I know not whither. If nothing else, at any rate I should die elsewhere.[6]

[1] Nichols (ed.), *Epistles*, II, 20. Allen (ed.), *Erasmi Epistolae*, I, 466. 25 August 1511: 'I do not like the beer of this place at all, and the wines are not satisfactory.'
[2] Nichols (ed.), *Epistles*, II, 39. Allen (ed.), *Erasmi Epistolae*, I, 482.
[3] November 1511. Nichols (ed.), *Epistles*, II, 33. Allen (ed.), *Erasmi Epistolae*, I, 484.
[4] December 1511. Nichols (ed.), *Epistles*, II, 52. Allen (ed.), *Erasmi Epistolae*, I, 495.
[5] November 1511. Nichols (ed.), *Epistles*, II, 43. Allen (ed.), *Erasmi Epistolae*, I, 483: 'alvearium aliquod tepidum in quod me condam hac bruma'.
[6] Nichols (ed.), *Epistles*, II, 103. Allen (ed.), *Erasmi Epistolae*, I, 542.

This letter was written in November 1513. Three months later Erasmus was in fact gone away, to London, and thence to Basle, his baggage stuffed with notes and memoranda and works in progress, all to be worked over at breakneck speed—the work of six years, Erasmus said, in six months—many to be published during 1516, the greatest year of his life.

In 1516 Erasmus was hailed by scholars all over Europe as finest among their number. Some of these scholars were his Cambridge friends. The Erasmian genius for friendship was as apparent by the Cam as it was by the Thames or the Seine or the Rhine or the Tiber. To a handful of Cambridge men he appeared as Huizinga has pictured him: 'the bearer of a new liberty of the mind, a new clearness, purity and simplicity of knowledge, a new harmony of healthy and right living'.[1] His influence, inevitably, was most effective on his young pupils. In his relations with them he fell into neither effusion nor spite—two easy snares for his shy, feminine spirit. Stephen Gardiner had been a pupil of Erasmus's host in Paris in 1511; to the end of his days he remembered the guest's finicky way with a salad. Another young friend now in Paris was Richard Croke of Eton and King's, just turned twenty-one in 1511. Seven years later Croke was Greek lecturer in his old university, after teaching Greek at Cologne, Louvain, Leipzig and Dresden; in 1522 he became the first public orator. Other Cambridge friends were Henry Bullock, a young Fellow of Queens', also avid for Greek, and Robert Aldrich, another young man of Eton and King's, who helped Erasmus in his work on Seneca, and also accompanied him on the famous pilgrimage to Walsingham in 1512: he was to be Bishop of Carlisle and Provost of Eton. John Bryan, a Kingsman of eighteen when Erasmus came to Cambridge, was another pupil in whom his master's voice was later to be heard, when he lectured upon Aristotle in the schools 'disregarding altogether the subtleties of the realists and nominalists'.[2] There was also Thomas Lupset, a favourite of

[1] Huizinga, *Erasmus*, 100.   [2] C. H. and T. Cooper, *Athenae Cantabrigienses*, I, 87.

Colet's at St Paul's, and now, although at Pembroke, Erasmus's daily companion and assistant. Erasmus wrote of him to More in July 1513: 'Lupset esteems himself born anew by our aid, and simply saved from perdition. The masters make every exertion to drag the young man back to their treadmill; for on the very first day he had thrown away their sophistical books and bought Greek.'[1]

Bullock was the most favoured disciple, the Cambridge man Erasmus most loved. He died in 1526; and Erasmus wrote regularly to him till the end. In these letters, from Basle, or Freiburg, or Louvain, he often asked to be remembered to his Cambridge friends. We can draw up a kind of 'Residence List' of them: Richard Foxe, Bishop of Winchester and Master of Pembroke, founder of Corpus Christi College, Oxford, and prime mover in the commissioning of Barnard Flower as glazier for King's Chapel in 1515; Thomas Green, Master of St Catharine's from 1507 to 1529; the Franciscan Richard Brinkley; and Fellows of Queens' such as Humphrey Walkden, John Vaughan, and Dr John Fawne, Vice-President of the College and Erasmus's successor as Lady Margaret Professor. Dr Richard Sampson of Trinity Hall met Erasmus abroad in 1518: 'one with whom', wrote the primate of literary Europe, 'formerly at Cambridge and more lately at Tournai, I have had the sweetest possible companionship (*consuetudo*)'.[2] Sampson was to become Dean of St Paul's. Another friend was John Laer, of Siegburg near Bonn, generally known as John Siberch. Bookseller, bookbinder and printer, Siberch came to Cambridge to set up his press at the beginning of 1521, obtaining a loan from university funds to do so. His bond was guaranteed by four resident members, including Henry Bullock; and the 'principal driving spirit behind the venture'[3] was Richard Croke, whose elementary Greek primer

---

[1] Nichols (ed.), *Epistles*, II, 76–7. Allen (ed.), *Erasmi Epistolae*, I, 528.
[2] Nichols (ed.), *Epistles*, III, 348. Allen (ed.), *Erasmi Epistolae*, III, 261.
[3] E. P. Goldschmidt, *The First Cambridge Press in its European Setting*, 38.

had been reprinted in Cologne, commissioned and financed by Siberch, in 1520.[1] Siberch remained in Cambridge for only a year or two. The first product of his press was the oration which Bullock had made before Wolsey when the Cardinal had visited Cambridge in the autumn of 1520; and the first use of Greek type in England was in an edition of Lucian printed in Cambridge in 1521 (with a Latin translation by Bullock).[2] Siberch greatly annoyed Erasmus by printing at Cambridge, probably from Bullock's copy, but entirely without Erasmus's permission, a *Libellus de conscribendis epistolis* which had been dashed off for Robert Fisher in Paris in the 1490's, worked over a little in Cambridge in 1511, but still, according to the author, 'worthless rubbish'.[3] Erasmus calmed down, however, and he was soon writing of the German printer in the old way.

John Watson was a Fellow of Peterhouse from 1501 to 1517. Erasmus wrote him a charming little note in 1517: 'to whatever part of the world I go, I carry my friends with me in my mind, and my Watson among the first, and remembering our delightful friendship (*familiaritas*) and those nights that passed in amusing talk of which one never tired'.[4] Perhaps Cambridge—cold damp unsympathetic Cambridge—had pleased him more than might appear. 'I had rather pass the summer than the winter here',[5] he wrote: an understandable point of view, it must be confessed. But, he went on, 'I do not dislike this place, where I see there is something to be earned, if one can play the part of man of all work': 'hic locus non omnino mihi displicet'.[6] It is not a gushing vote of confidence in the university; but it serves to correct, a little, the popular impression—created, it must be noted, by Erasmus himself, with his delight in grumbling, sometimes about

---

[1] R. Croke, *Introductiones ad Rudimenta Graeca*. First printed in Leipzig some years before (1514–17); Goldschmidt, *op. cit.* 1.
[2] Goldschmidt reproduced a page of this; *op. cit.* 85.
[3] *Ibid.* 5–9.
[4] Nichols (ed.), *Epistles*, II, 453. Allen (ed.), *Erasmi Epistolae*, II, 429.
[5] Nichols (ed.), *Epistles*, II, 38. Allen (ed.), *Erasmi Epistolae*, I, 480.
[6] *Ibid.*

the things he most liked. Writing to Croke in 1518 to congratulate him on his Greek lectureship, Erasmus said that he still took an especial interest in the welfare of Cambridge University, 'on account of the hospitality I have enjoyed there'.[1]

IV

At Cambridge, as elsewhere, Erasmus had talked freely and written comparatively cautiously; written and dictated, however, in those two and a half years, with almost unbelievable industry and energy. Rushing off a satirical essay or dialogue; revising his *De Copia*, first printed in 1512 and five times reissued during the next three years; preparing for translation a treatise by Plutarch— the first of the series was printed in 1512; working over a manuscript of Seneca from Peterhouse or King's, ready for publication by 1513; selecting moral and religious precepts from the *Disticha Catonis*; editing some of Aesop's fables for an edition which appeared in 1513; planning the *Institutio Principis Christiani*, the 'Education of a Christian Prince', to be published in 1516 and dedicated to the imperial Prince Charles; enlarging still further the *Adages*; editing a Greek grammar, in conjunction with his lectures; or smiling over his last rapier thrust at the academic old guard—before he had been a month in Cambridge he wrote to Colet of 'pitched battles on your behalf with these Thomists and Scotists'.[2] The battles begun in Paris and Oxford were to be continued in Cambridge.

These battles were not only planned but also fought in the study (though the results in the history of Europe were to go beyond the compass of the quiet lives of scholars, living in their libraries and dying in their beds). The battle cry was 'Back to the Sources': 'fontes purissimi et flumina aurum volventia'. Victory could spring

[1] Nichols (ed.), *Epistles*, III, 355. Allen (ed.), *Erasmi Epistolae*, III, 293.
[2] September 1511. Nichols (ed.), *Epistles*, II, 22. Allen (ed.), *Erasmi Epistolae*, I, 467: 'dimicatio pro te cum his Thomistis et Scotistis'.

only from that decisive retreat. As it was for William Turner in the natural sciences, so it was for Erasmus in theology; and he became, in the opinion of Melanchthon, 'the first to call back theology to her fountain head'.[1] So, in Cambridge, he worked upon his Jerome and his New Testament. In September 1513, two years after his arrival in the university, he wrote: 'The work of correcting and commenting upon Jerome interests my mind so warmly that I feel as if I were inspired by some god. I have already emended almost the whole by collating many ancient copies.'[2] The technique of collation was also forwarding the Greek text of the New Testament. Erasmus borrowed one manuscript, dating from the late fifteenth century, from the library of the Cambridge Franciscans. This manuscript was later to pass into the possession of William Charke of Peterhouse, disciple of another Lady Margaret Professor, Thomas Cartwright.[3] (Another Greek text of the Gospels, probably of the twelfth century, was in the Franciscan library, borrowed from the Oxford house in the sixteenth century by Richard Brinkley, who carefully neglected to return it, and later (in 1567) given to the library of Caius by Thomas Hatcher, son of the Regius Professor of Physic.[4])

The edition of Jerome was published at Basle in 1516, in nine volumes, dedicated to the Archbishop of Canterbury. A matter of weeks before, the *Novum Instrumentum* had appeared, the first Greek text of the New Testament ever printed, face to face with a new Latin translation, with an introduction and notes. This edition was dedicated to Pope Leo X, though Erasmus had at first intended to dedicate it to Fisher. Erasmus was now nearly fifty. This was his golden year. 'To this destiny I was born,' he wrote to Bullock, with amused mock rhetoric, when the revised

[1] Quoted in F. Seebohm, *The Oxford Reformers* (third edition), 477.
[2] Nichols (ed.), *Epistles*, II, 87. Allen (ed.), *Erasmi Epistolae*, I, 531.
[3] J. Rendel Harris, *The Origin of the Leicester Codex of the New Testament* (1887), 19, 33–45.
[4] M. R. James, *Catalogue of the Manuscripts at Gonville and Caius*, II, 469–70.

edition of the New Testament appeared in 1518, 'and it is not for me to fight against Providence.'[1]

Fisher received his copy of the New Testament in June, as he was on the point of leaving Rochester for Cambridge for the consecration of the chapel of St John's.[2] The book, Colet wrote to Erasmus in June, was 'bought with avidity, and read everywhere here'.[3] Warham heartily approved of it.[4] In August, Bullock wrote from Queens' to the 'glory of our age': 'People here are hard at work upon Greek and earnestly hope for your arrival. The same set are much delighted with the publication of the New Testament. Great heavens, how elegant it is, how clear-cut, how pleasing to every person of sound taste, and how much required.'[5] Erasmus received Bullock's letter at Rochester, where he was staying with Fisher. He was, he replied, glad to hear that the restored New Testament was approved by those of sound taste. However, there had been opposition, even in Cambridge: 'one of the most theological of your colleges, composed of pure Areopagites, has passed a serious resolution, that no one shall either by horse, or boat, or cart or porter bring that volume within the precincts of the college'.[6] But on the whole the humanists could be pleased. (Colet, like Fisher, had been inspired by the publication to take up Greek.[7]) 'About thirty years ago', continued Erasmus—at the time, that is, when Fisher went up to Michaelhouse—

nothing was taught at Cambridge but Alexander, the *Parva Logicalia*, as they are called, those old 'dictates' of Aristotle, and questions from Scotus (*vetera illa Aristotelis dictata Scoticasque questiones*). In process of time literature (*bonae literae*) was introduced; the study of mathe-

---

[1] Nichols (ed.), *Epistles*, III, 296. Allen (ed.), *Erasmi Epistolae*, III, 220.
[2] Nichols (ed.), *Epistles*, II, 292. Allen (ed.), *Erasmi Epistolae*, II, 268.
[3] Nichols (ed.), *Epistles*, II, 286. Allen (ed.), *Erasmi Epistolae*, II, 257.
[4] Nichols (ed.), *Epistles*, II, 289. Allen (ed.), *Erasmi Epistolae*, II, 262.
[5] 'dii boni quam eleganti, argutae ac omnibus sani gustus suavi et pernecessariae'; Allen (ed.), *Erasmi Epistolae*, II, 313. Nichols (ed.), *Epistles*, II, 318.
[6] Nichols (ed.), *Epistles*, II, 324. Allen (ed.), *Erasmi Epistolae*, II, 321.
[7] Nichols (ed.), *Epistles*, II, 396. Allen (ed.), *Erasmi Epistolae*, II, 351.

matics was added, and a new or at least a renovated Aristotle. Then came some acquaintance with Greek, and with many authors whose very names were unknown to the best scholars of a former time. Now, I ask, what has been the result to the university? It has become so flourishing that it may vie with the first schools of the age, and possesses men, compared with whom those old teachers appear mere shadows of theologians (*viros ad quos veteres illi collati umbrae theologorum videantur, non theologi*).[1]

In a letter of December 1517 Erasmus repeated this point: 'Cantabrigia mutata'—'Cambridge is a changed place, and this school detests those chill subtleties, which make more for disputation than for piety.'[2] And in 1518, when Croke returned to the university as lecturer in Greek, he could in all conscience claim that at Greek Cambridge was better than Oxford.

V

The Erasmian edition of the New Testament did not, however, have interest merely for students of Greek. 'By your correction of the New Testament', wrote John Watson in the summer of 1516, 'accompanied by your notes you have thrown a marvellous light on Christ, and deserved well of all his zealous followers.'[3] Erasmus's introduction to his edition was translated into English in 1529,[4] with the title 'An Exhortation to the diligent study of Scripture'.

For this purpose we need but little the painted arguments and coloured conclusions of the rhetoricians, for nothing so surely can garnish and perform that that we desire as the truth itself, which when it is most plain and simple is of most vehement efficacy in persuading.[5]

A mockery has been made of 'this immortal fountain of Christ's pure philosophy',[6] a mockery continuing because 'men's

---

[1] Nichols (ed.), *Epistles*, II, 331. Allen (ed.), *Erasmi Epistolae*, II, 328.
[2] Nichols (ed.), *Epistles*, III, 158. Allen (ed.), *Erasmi Epistolae*, III, 177.
[3] Nichols (ed.), *Epistles*, II, 335. Allen (ed.), *Erasmi Epistolae*, II, 315.
[4] Probably by William Roy, assistant to Tyndale.
[5] Erasmus, *An Exhortation to the diligent Studye of Scripture*, 3.   [6] *Ibid.*

doctrines and traditions (besides the promising of false felicity) do confound many men's wits and make them clear to despair because they are so dark, crafty and contentious'.[1] But why be so blind? The relief is at hand, for those with 'simple and plain hearts', with 'a godly and ready mind chiefly endowed with plain and pure faith'.[2] The relief once applied, 'We should see verily within a few years a true and godly kind of Christian spring up in every place, which would not only in ceremonies, dispositions, and titles profess the name of Christ, but in their very heart and true conversation of living'.[3] There is in Erasmus always this thread of hope, of the imminent end of darkness and folly. He wrote in 1517 of the approaching peace and unanimity of European politics: 'at the present moment I could almost wish to be young again, for no other reason but this, that I anticipate the near approach of a golden age. I am led to a confident hope, that not only morality and Christian piety, but also a genuine and purer literature may come to renewed life or greater splendour.'[4] There was this one pre-eminent obstacle to the Christian golden age: that 'call we them Christian, yea and divines, which have never read the Scriptures of God'.[5] But if all men did? And all women too—and Scots, Irishmen, Turks, and Saracens? If we could ensure that 'the ploughman would sing a text of the scripture at his plough. And that the weaver at his loom, with this would drive away the tediousness of time. I would the wayfaring man with this pastime would expel the weariness of his journey.'[6] Then there would be an end of ignorance and barbarousness: and a hope for 'a restoring or repairing of our nature which in his first creation was good'.[7]

So in August 1516 Erasmus congratulated Bullock on 'having adopted the practice of public preaching', 'especially as you teach

[1] Erasmus, *Exhortation*, 7.
[2] *Ibid.*   [3] *Ibid.* 13.
[4] Nichols (ed.), *Epistles*, II, 506. Allen (ed.), *Erasmi Epistolae*, II, 488.
[5] Erasmus, *Exhortation*, 14.   [6] *Ibid.* 9.
[7] *Ibid.* 15.

Christ in simplicity, without any displaying of the subtleties of men'.[1] And in the Michaelmas term of 1516, when he began to lecture in Cambridge on the Gospel of St Matthew, Bullock used the notes of Erasmus as his guide.[2]

The New Testament, Erasmus had been pleased to note, was approved at Cambridge by the best people. As for the not so good—'Are your friends displeased that in future the Gospels and Apostolic Epistles will be read by more persons and with more attention?...And would they prefer that our whole life should be consumed in the useless subtleties of "Questions"?'[3] Is it not well, in fact, to recall such divines to the *fontes*: to the original sources?[4] That indeed was the point. If the discipline of humanist studies was built upon exact textual criticism, enlivened by imagination, the trend of theological studies was also towards exact criticism, informed by grace. The New Testament in the printed Greek and Latin was to all scholars, as to Bullock, elegant, clear-cut, pleasing. (But what of the English translation by Tyndale, prepared during 1524 and 1525 from the text of Erasmus, and reaching England in the spring of 1526, just under ten years after the *Novum Instrumentum*?) Many began like Bullock, but went on to the very heart of a new spiritual experience—the revelation of grace in and through the reading of the printed Scripture. Thomas Bilney of Trinity Hall 'heard speak of Jesus, even then when the New Testament was first set forth by Erasmus: which ...I understood to be eloquently done by him, being allured rather by the Latin than by the word of God'. He read St Paul: 'It is a true saying and worthy of all men to be received, that Christ Jesus came into the world to save sinners.'

This one sentence, through God's instruction and inward working, which I did not then perceive, did so exhilarate my heart, being before

---

[1] Nichols (ed.), *Epistles*, II, 332. Allen (ed.), *Erasmi Epistolae*, II, 329: 'cum Christum pure doceas'.
[2] Bullock to Erasmus, May 1517. Nichols (ed.), *Epistles*, II, 553. Allen (ed.), *Erasmi Epistolae*, II, 555.
[3] Nichols (ed.), *Epistles*, II, 332. Allen (ed.), *Erasmi Epistolae*, II, 328.   [4] *Ibid.*

wounded with the guilt of my sins, and being almost in despair, that immediately I felt a marvellous comfort and quietness, insomuch that my bruised bones leaped for joy.[5]

From the experience of grace the next step was inevitable: that is, the preaching of it—and the consequences.

[1] Bilney to Tunstall; quoted by Foxe, *Acts and Monuments*, IV, 635.

CHAPTER III

THE CAMBRIDGE REFORMERS

I

By the type of Midas touch described by Thomas Bilney, secular scholarship was transformed into prophecy, and the Reformation in Cambridge at first appeared as an aspect of the New Learning. For the history of England, as well as for that of the university, it was the most important aspect. 'The university', writes Dr Rupp, 'bore its own coherent part in the making of the English Reformation by providing a series of theological and ecclesiastical leaders such that its contribution...might have become known to historians as "the Cambridge Movement".'[1] The university of Fisher and Erasmus was that of Cranmer also; he commenced bachelor, from Jesus College, in 1512, having gone up about 1503. It was also that of Hugh Latimer, who was a Fellow of Clare by 1510.

It is to two Corpus men that the historian may look for the beginning of the story. The details of the life of Thomas Dusgate are notoriously mysterious, but it has been claimed that he was born in Cambridge in 1480 and that he was a Fellow of Corpus before 1500.[2] It is certainly true that in the 1520's he gave up his fellowship and secretly took a wife—he had discussed the matter of clerical marriage, after all, with Luther himself; it is also true that out of affection for his old college he assumed the name of Thomas Benet; and it is recorded that in December 1531 he was arrested for heresy at Exeter, in which city he was burnt on the tenth day of the following January.[3] Corpus can therefore claim

[1] E. G. Rupp, *Studies in the Making of The English Protestant Tradition*, 15.
[2] G. E. Tapley Soper, 'Thomas Benet and Master Dusgate', *Trans. Devonshire Assoc. for Advancement of Science, Literature and Art*, LXIII (1931), 369–80.
[3] Act Books of Exeter Chamber, 55, fol. 89. *Historical·Manuscripts Commission, Records of Exeter*, 361.

the second of the twenty-five Protestant martyrs of Cambridge, Thomas Bilney being the first. The other Corpus reformer was William Warner, who commenced B.A. from that college in 1498,[1] when Cranmer was a young schoolboy. Matthew Parker was to dub Warner the Cambridge Colet: one of the first in the university to ignore Scotus and Aquinas and the rest of 'the tribe of prying and worthless pseudo-theologians', and concentrate upon the Holy Scriptures.[2] A greater than Warner in the exposition of the pure word of God was George Stafford, who became a Fellow of Pembroke in 1513, the year in which Erasmus left the university. Many a future reformer was to remember hours spent in the Schools at the feet of Stafford in the 1520's, when the message of the apostolic preaching became urgently alive. Thomas Becon, recalling his undergraduate days, told of Stafford's lectures on Paul: 'he seemed of a dead man to make him alive again and...to set him forth in his native colours'.[3] His lectures on the Gospels were no less inspiring: 'likewise did he learnedly set forth in his lectures the native sense and true understanding of the four evangelists, vively restoring unto us...the mind of those holy writers, which so many years before had lain hid unknown and obscured through the darkness and mists of the Pharisees and Papists'.[4] Stafford died of the plague in 1529, a young man still. Nicholas Shaxton was another reformer educated in Cambridge in the first decade of the century; he became Fellow of Gonville Hall in 1507. As Bishop of Salisbury in the thirties, Shaxton was a firm hammer of abuses. In less happy days, faced with death, he discarded his character of Valiant-for-Truth and recanted. He was to be among the judges of John Hullier of King's, burnt to death on Jesus Green in 1556.

Between 1510 and 1520, many other future reformers commenced bachelor: Thomas Forman (1512) and Simon Heynes

[1] Cooper, *Athenae Cantabrigienses*, I, 116. Warner became Doctor of Divinity in 1513.
[2] Parker's tribute is in Robert Masters' *History of the College of Corpus Christi and the Blessed Virgin Mary* (ed. J. Lamb), 316.
[3] Thomas Becon, 'The Jewel of Joy', in *Catechism, etc.*, 426.   [4] *Ibid.*

(1516), both of Queens', each to be President of the College; George Joye of Peterhouse (1513), Fellow of the college from 1517 to 1528;[1] John Thixtell of Pembroke (1515); Thomas Arthur of Gonville Hall (1513) and John Lambert of Queens'— both, like Bilney, Forman, Shaxton, Thixtell, Barnes and Becon, being Norfolk men; John Skipp (1515), later Master of Gonville Hall; Edward Fox (1517), later Provost of King's. William Tyndale probably deserted Oxford for Cambridge in 1519.[2] Some men of this generation were to bridge events and survive until the reign of Elizabeth. Edward Crome, Fellow of Gonville Hall in 1507 and later Master, was also a London rector under Henry VIII, and constantly in trouble for his attacks on abuses. He was in prison during the reign of Mary. But Cranmer paid him a graceful tribute: 'when he was but President of a College in Cambridge his house was better ordered than all the houses in Cambridge besides';[3] and he lived until 1562. John Bale, the unpleasant ex-Carmelite of Norwich, 'foul-mouthed' and 'bilious', was probably a friend of Cranmer at Cambridge.[4] He became Bishop of Ossory in 1552, went into exile under Mary, and died in 1562 as a canon of Canterbury.

These men were among the lesser players in the Cambridge movement. But in their decade, when Latimer was at Clare, Robert Barnes was a young student at the Augustinian priory; and Bilney, born in 1495, was up at Trinity Hall before 1510. In 1519 Bilney was ordained, and Cranmer, after the death of his wife and his re-election to a fellowship at Jesus, set himself seriously to study the Scriptures. In 1519 also, Beza was born; the year before, Zwingli had begun to preach in the minster at Zürich; and, in 1517, the year in which Erasmus wrote of an imminent golden age in Europe, Martin Luther, Augustinian friar, had nailed his Theses to the door of the Church at Wittenberg.

[1] For Joye, see J. F. Mozley, *Coverdale and his Bibles*, Appendix G.
[2] J. F. Mozley, *William Tyndale*, 19.
[3] C. H. and T. Cooper, *Athenae Cant.* I, 216.
[4] *Ibid.* 226.

II

The 1520's saw the effective beginnings of the Reformation in Cambridge. Thomas Bilney is usually reckoned the first of the few, who became the many: Foxe called him 'the first framer of that university in the knowledge of Christ'.[1] Latimer's tribute to Bilney, in a sermon preached in 1552, is a justly famous account of emotion recollected in comparative tranquillity. In the early 1520's Latimer was the bearer of the university Cross, and an unduly officious keeper of the Schools, warning the young men against the methods of biblical study employed by such popular lecturers as Bullock and Stafford. Then his views were changed.

Here I have occasion to tell you a story which happened at Cambridge. Master Bilney, or rather Saint Bilney, that suffered death for God's word sake; the same Bilney was the instrument whereby God called me to knowledge; for I may thank him, next to God, for that knowledge that I have in the word of God. For I was as obstinate a papist as any was in England, insomuch that when I should be made Bachelor of Divinity, my whole oration went against Philip Melanchthon and against his opinions. Bilney heard me at the time, and perceived that I was zealous without knowledge: and he came to see me afterward in my study, and desired me, for God's sake, to hear his confession. I did so; and, to say the truth, by his confession I learned more than before in many years. So from that time forward I began to smell the word of God, and forsook the school-doctors and such fooleries.[2]

That was in 1524. Latimer was about thirty-four, Bilney four years his junior. (The previous year, the Zürich City Council had accepted the theses of Zwingli, who was then forty: the year after, Luther, aged forty-two, quarrelled irrevocably with Erasmus.) 'He came to see me afterward in my study': at the end of the century John Cotton was in like manner to seek out Richard Sibbes, and later John Preston was in his turn to consult Cotton. For Bilney and Latimer it was the beginning of a mutually

[1] Foxe, *Acts and Monuments*, IV, 651.   [2] Latimer, *Sermons*, I, 334–5.

44

beneficial friendship, nurtured on long, talkative tramps through the Cambridgeshire fields and lanes, or on 'Heretics' Hill', a friendship which, made firm by frequent reception of the Sacrament, became the central core of the evangelical group of Cambridge dons in the 1520's. The first-fruits of the Cambridge Holy Club were in the sphere of practical divinity. 'Now after I had been acquainted with him', continued Latimer, 'I went with him to visit the prisoners in the Tower at Cambridge; for he was ever visiting prisoners and sick folk. So we went together, and exhorted them as well as we were able to do; moving them to patience, and to acknowledge their faults.'[1] William Perkins was to do the same thing half a century later; and so was Richard Greenham.

This group was probably the nucleus of the study and discussion circle which met in the inn called the White Horse, between King's and St Catharine's. Luther was excommunicated and his books condemned to be burnt in December 1520. Shortly afterwards there was a bonfire before the new west door of Great St Mary's, and some cakes and ale too: two shillings was granted in the proctors' accounts to the deputy Vice-Chancellor 'for drink and other expenses about the burning of the works of Martin Luther'.[2] In May there was another ceremonial burning, in London at Paul's Cross, preceded by a sermon from Fisher. But the forbidden works still circulated; and the Society of Christian Brethren—'a kind of "forbidden book of the month" club'[3]—found Cambridge a demanding market. Among those to be accused of circulating Lutheran writings was Sygar Nicholson of Gonville Hall. The meetings of the White Horse circle were probably not fixed or formal. In procedure, they perhaps resembled nothing so much as the gatherings in Elizabethan Cambridge of pious scholars of all shades of opinion to read and interpret the Bible—Lancelot Andrewes meeting William

[1] *Ibid.* 335.   [2] Cooper, *Annals,* I, 304.
[3] E. G. Rupp, *The Righteousness of God,* 37.

Whitaker in that co-operation of equal though contrary minds which is possible, though not inevitable, in *Academe*.[1] Stephen Gardiner went to the White Horse on occasion. There was virtue, after all, in knowing what the Germans were up to. There was also the spice of being aware that Authority might intervene: on one such raid the wily Dr Forman of Queens' 'concealed and kept Luther's books when sought for to be burnt'.[2] The members whose names are known were mostly young men, though they were joined, surely, by the occasional elderly don, hoping to be thought broad-minded by his juniors. (The reforming zeal could not be doubted of a man such as John Edmunds, Master of Peterhouse, of whom it was rumoured that he kept a wife privately.[3]) The most important of the group was Robert Barnes, prior of the Augustinian friars. It was he who, of all the Cambridge reformers, 'came closest in sympathy and opinions to Luther'[4]—they were, for one thing, members of the same Order. In the mid 1520's Robert Barnes lectured and preached in the priory behind Corpus. His pupils included Miles Coverdale, now in his thirties, who by 1528 had thrown off his friar's habit and was preaching in Essex against image worship, confession and the mass.[5] It is possible that Coverdale had been in Cambridge until 1527, when he began 'to taste of holy scriptures';[6] from 1529 he worked with Tyndale in Germany. Tyndale was in Cambridge in the 1520's too: one of his disciples was John Frith, who commenced bachelor from King's in 1526.[7] Christopher Coleman was another Augustinian friar whose name has come down to us as a Lutheran reformer; he appeared to history again in 1568, an

[1] It is perhaps permissible here (it is certainly suggestive) to draw a parallel with that 'study group of some sort' formed in Washington, D.C., in the mid 1930's 'of men who were interested in knowing something about Russia and Russian policy and the general communist theory of life, and so on'; testimony of Whittaker Chambers to Adolf Berle, Jr, September 1939, quoted by Alger Hiss, *In the Court of Public Opinion* (New York, 1957), 157. Cf. Chambers' later (1952) account: *Witness*, 26–34.
[2] Fuller, *History of Cambridge*, 202.   [3] J. Strype, *Life of Parker*, I, 13.
[4] Rupp, *The Righteousness of God*, 39.   [5] Mozley, *Coverdale*, 3.
[6] Coverdale to Cromwell, 1527; quoted in Mozley, *Tyndale*, 4.
[7] *Ibid.* 20.

active member of the London puritan congregation at Plumbers'
Hall.[1] John Rogers, a B.A. of Pembroke in 1526 at the age of
sixteen, was to be chaplain to the English colony at Antwerp, and
another friend and collaborator of Coverdale and Tyndale. He
ended in 1555, in the fire, refusing to recant even at the affecting
sight of his wife and eleven children assembled by the pyre.
Richard Taverner was a Norfolk man at Corpus Christi, who
went to Oxford, but returned to take his B.A. from Gonville Hall
—a more sympathetically advanced college than his original
choice—in 1529. In 1530 he translated into English a letter of
Erasmus in praise of matrimony; and he continued his Erasmian
labours with an English version of the *Adages* (1539).[2] Taverner
ended his days, an amiable eccentric, as the Elizabethan high
sheriff of Oxfordshire, distributing fruit and scripture texts to
street urchins, and preaching in the university church in sword
and gold chain. Another Corpus man who would, at the least,
have been well aware of the new breezes blowing through the
university—the more so because he was a Norwich boy—was
Matthew Parker. Parker went up to Corpus, just turned sixteen,
in September 1520: in the following March he was elected to a
bible clerkship.[3] He became a Fellow of his College in 1527.

Many of these men, the youngest especially, were to treasure
the memory of their meetings in the 1520's to recall themselves,

[1] C. Burrage, *The Early English Dissenters*, II, 12.

[2] *Proverbs or adagies with newe addicions gathered out of the Chiliades of Erasmus by Richard
Taverner* (1539). Taverner probably also had a hand in the translation published in 1542
of Erasmus's *Apophthegmes, that is to saie, prompte, quicke, wittie and sentencious saiynges of
certain Emperours, Kynges, Capitaines, Philosophiers and Oratours, aswel Grekes, as Romaines.*

[3] Parker's name first appears in the Corpus Christi College accounts in March 1520/1.
(Volume of accounts 1479–1574, in the college bursary.) Parker's so-called autobio-
graphy (printed in the Parker Society edition of his letters, and by Strype in an appendix
to his *Life of Parker*), and also a marginal note in Parker's hand in Corpus Christi College
MS. cvi, 15, give 8 September as the date of his going to Corpus; this must therefore have
been September 1520. Both the 'autobiography', and a biographical entry in Grace
Book B, added in the 1560's (*Grace Book B, Part Two*, 86) give March as the date of
Parker's election to a bible clerkship; it can be assumed that his name first appeared in the
accounts for that reason. Thus Strype's date of 1520 for Parker's going up to Corpus is
confirmed, as against Parker's own memory (the 'autobiography' has 1522) and as
against Robert Masters, H. P. Stokes and W. M. Kennedy, who compromised with 1521.

47

in later years, from the trivial and the mean. 'So oft as I was in their company', wrote Thomas Becon of St John's, 'methought I was clean delivered from Egypt and quietly placed in the new glorious Jerusalem.'[1] It is a sweet thing to be in the company of godly learned men: or so Becon assures us.[2] But by 1529 the godly were stricken. Stafford was dead, Barnes a prisoner, and Bilney, newly released from prison, a broken man. 'When Master Stafford read, and Master Latimer preached, then was Cambridge blessed.'[3] And now the leadership passed naturally to Latimer. To 1529 belong his memorable Sermons on the Card, preached in St Edward's Church, from the pulpit which is still in use there. One of those who sat at his feet was Becon:

I was sometime a poor scholar of Cambridge, very desirous to have the knowledge of good letters; and in the time of my being there this godly man preached many learned and Christian sermons both in the Latin and English tongue, at which I for most part was present; and although at that time I was but a child of sixteen years, yet I noted his doctrine so well as I could, partly reposing it in my memory, partly commending it to letters, as most faithful treasures unto memory.[4]

There we have the essence of a university education; and the consequences in the sixteenth century were unusually far-reaching.

The time for mere talk, even in 1530, had passed. Mercade brings a black shadow to the circle of young wits, the humane revellers disperse, with only suffering and trial to come. In 1525 Barnes had been examined before the Vice-Chancellor, in the Common Schools and then in Clare Hall. Both meetings were interrupted by student demonstrations and Barnes was taken to London to be tried before Wolsey, who imprisoned him.[5] Another fifteen years of life were left him. But he was never

[1] Becon, Catechism, etc., 426.
[2] Ibid.
[3] Ibid. 425. Becon quoted this as 'a common saying which remaineth unto this day'.
[4] Ibid. 424.
[5] The story is told in Barnes's Supplication; quoted in Cooper, Annals, I, 13–23, and in Rupp, The English Protestant Tradition, 31–8.

again to pluck the flower safety from the nettle danger, and he came in the end to the fire. Joye and Bilney were summoned before Wolsey, in their turn, in 1527; and promised to conform.[1] Latimer too had his interview with the cardinal, after a brush in Great St Mary's with the pompous Bishop of Ely, Nicholas West. But Wolsey gave Latimer a courteous hearing and confirmed his licence to preach.[2]

In 1531 (six months before Zwingli was killed at Kappel) the Cambridge movement received its baptism of blood. The sorrowful Bilney, to whom the comfort of friends was now as naught, for he had compromised with untruth, left Trinity Hall one evening to go 'up to Jerusalem'.[3] He preached at Norwich, was arrested, condemned as a relapsed heretic, and burnt in the Lollards' Pit. The burning drew a large crowd. Among them were William Warner and Matthew Parker.

III

A year earlier, in the spring of 1530, the university had pronounced that marriages with a brother's widow were so contrary to the law of God that not even a papal dispensation could make them valid.[4] Time might after all be on the side of those who attacked the authority of Rome. In March 1533 Cranmer was consecrated Archbishop of Canterbury; the Statute of Appeals and the Act of Supremacy in 1534 stated the official case and the national myth for royal headship of the Church; and from 1536 all men proceeding to degrees were to renounce the authority, power, and jurisdiction of the Bishop of Rome, and accept the King as the Supreme Head in earth of the Church of England.[5] In that year Calvin published the first version of the *Institutes*,

[1] Cooper, *Annals*, I, 325.
[2] J. B. Mullinger, *The University of Cambridge*, I, 584.
[3] Foxe, *Acts and Monuments*, IV, 642.
[4] Mullinger, *op. cit.* 617–21.
[5] 28 Hen. VIII, c. 10; quoted in Cooper, *Annals*, I, 382.

and Erasmus died at Basle—in a world to which he was almost a stranger, though he had helped to call it into being: a family ghost, without a corridor to haunt. (The hopes of 1516 rang strangely in the English translation of 1529: 'if schoolmasters would instruct their children rather with this simple science than with the witty traditions of Aristotle and Averroes, then should the Christian be more at quietness, and not be disturbed with such perpetual storms of dissension and war.'[1]) Erasmus lived to know that two of his English friends, More and Fisher, had ended their days under the axe. Fisher was succeeded as Chancellor of Cambridge by Thomas Cromwell: his successors—and the history of England is reflected in the succession—were Stephen Gardiner (1539–47), Somerset (1547–52), Northumberland (1552–3), Gardiner again (1553–6), and Cardinal Pole (1556–8).

Yet in 1535 some of the ideals of Erasmus, and many of the hopes of the reformers, were recognized in Cambridge, in the new royal injunctions which Mullinger took as 'the line that in university history divides the mediaeval from the modern age'.[2] Degrees and lectures in canon law were abolished; all divinity lectures were to be 'according to the true sense' of the Scriptures, and not after the manner of the scholastic commentators; all students were to be encouraged to read the Scriptures privately, and Melanchthon as well as Aristotle was listed as a prescribed author; in every college, every day, there should be one lecture on Latin, and one on Greek.[3] The pattern of studies in arts and theology was still not wholly different from that which Fisher had known as a student. But the differences, whether of addition or omission, were, to say the least, significant.

Some collegiate studies of the Elizabethan undergraduate were detailed in a time-table prepared by the Master of Corpus, Robert Norgate, in the 1570's.[4] Each day of the week began with morning

[1] Erasmus, *Exhortation to the diligent Studye of Scripture*, 12.
[2] Mullinger, *The University of Cambridge*, I, 631.   [3] *Ibid.* 630.
[4] From photographs in the Corpus Christi College library of an original MS. in the possession of the Norfolk Record Society.

prayer, between five and six. Then there was a lecture in the hall on Aristotle's natural philosophy, lasting one hour. At noon there were read 'two Greek lectures, one of construction, as Homer or Demosthenes or Hesiod or Isocrates; the other of the grammar'. At three there was a lecture on rhetoric, with Cicero as text-book. This was daily routine. On Wednesdays and Fridays the morning chapel concluded with a commonplace, in which 'one of the Fellows in his order handleth some place of the Scripture, whereupon he taketh occasion to entreat of some common place of doctrine, the which he proveth by the Scripture and Doctors'. Such a programme might not have displeased Erasmus. But it would arouse the scorn of John Milton. It was the eventual success of the attack on Aristotle which was finally to end the medieval curriculum in Cambridge: an attack which owed much to the new logic and rhetoric of Peter Ramus, violently discussed in Elizabethan Cambridge,[1] but most of all to the scientific methods and philosophical novelties of the seventeenth century.

Erasmus would certainly have rejoiced at the foundation, in 1540, of the Regius professorship of Greek, to which John Cheke was appointed. This was one of five Regius professorships founded in that year: the four others being in Civil Law (given to Thomas Smith), Physic, Hebrew (to be held in 1549 by Paul Fagius), and Divinity. At the suggestion of Cranmer the divinity chair was offered, in 1549, to Martin Bucer.

Bucer (who was born in Alsace in 1491) was the most distinguished foreigner to hold office in the university since Erasmus; and his appointment set the seal upon the success of the Cambridge reformers. His works had been well known in England for

---

[1] The works of Pierre de la Ramée (1515–72) were influential in Cambridge from the late 1560's, when Laurence Chaderton, Fellow of Christ's, lectured on his *Ars Logica*; Gabriel Harvey became the most enthusiastic supporter of the Ramist methods for reform of the liberal arts, and William Temple and William Gouge of King's, and perhaps William Perkins of Christ's, were also the Frenchman's disciples. The most recent study of Ramus, containing much concerning the intellectual and religious history of Cambridge, is by Professor W. S. Howell of Princeton: *Logic and Rhetoric in England, 1500–1700*, chapter 4.

twenty years—the Latin commentary on the Psalms was translated in 1530.[1] Also, since 1538, he had been in correspondence with Cranmer, to whom he had dedicated his commentary on Romans. By 1548 he was the doyen of the Continental Reformation, with over twenty years at Strasbourg to incite respect, and with a gentleness of person which earned the affection of those English theologians who wrote to him or knew him. Cranmer first invited him to England in October 1548,[2] and he arrived at Lambeth six months later, with his wife and family.[3] For Bucer the offer of the Cambridge chair was a reassurance that, although Strasbourg had fallen before the armies of the Emperor, his work as pastor and teacher had not yet been accounted useless. A more recent victim of tyranny, Pastor Franz Hildebrandt, has described the consolations and serenity of the Cambridge of the 1940's, after the agonies of Europe.[4] Four hundred years have not altered the picture. For Bucer too the university held prospects of a pleasant exile.

It was to be a short exile; for Bucer died in March 1551. It began ominously with the death of Paul Fagius, who expired in Bucer's arms on 13 November 1549, after having suffered—so Bucer was to write to Strasbourg—

most severely from a quartan fever since the 28th of August. For he was burned up with dark bile, which rendered him delirious, so that he drank things that were injurious to him; and at first he was in a room without a fire, where he was severely affected by the cold; at last inflammation came on, and ulceration of the throat, which, together with the fever, put an end to his life.[5]

[1] C. Hopf, *Martin Bucer and the English Reformation*, 5.
[2] *Original Letters relative to the English Reformation* (ed. H. Robinson, Parker Society, 1846–7), I, 19.   [3] *Ibid.* II, 535.
[4] F. Hildebrandt, *Melanchthon: Alien or Ally?*, ix: 'the traveller who has left the Third Reich behind and walks for the first time through King's or Clare towards the University Library cannot help feeling both drunk at the taste of freedom and overwhelmed by the unbroken unity of mediaeval tradition and modern life'.
[5] *Original Letters relative to the English Reformation*, II, 549. A possible successor to Fagius in the Hebrew chair was Wolfgang Musculus of Augsburg, now at Berne: but Musculus rejected the offer (*ibid.* 680) and the chair was given to Tremellius.

Bucer was a sick man too; nearly sixty, with little English, and now no close friend in Cambridge. But he determined to sing the Lord's song in a strange land. The seeds of true doctrine (Cranmer had assured him)[1] were beginning to be sown in England, and he too would become a labourer in this foreign vineyard. He began his Cambridge lectures in January 1550.[2] But the Cambridge weather brought to a head the illness which had dogged him for six months; and during the March and April of 1550 he was seriously ill. He complained in May of excessive weakness in his legs, arms, and hands.

In my left hand one, and in my right hand two fingers, still refuse their office; so that I am not yet able to write. The Lord gave me some respite about Christmas, so that from that time until the middle of March I was enabled tolerably to perform my office; but since that time my most painful disorders returned, from which the Lord began to relieve me a little more than a month ago, so that I have since then returned to my duty. My disorder consisted of incredibly cold and slow humours in all my muscles and joints; colic pains, gravel; severe pains at first in all my limbs, succeeded afterwards by the greatest weakness and prostration of strength; together with a constant obstruction of the bowels.[3]

Even in June—he wrote to Calvin—his arms, legs and hands were still weak and his bowels obstinate.[4] But he could perform his academic duty: and, in Cambridge, 'I am permitted to set forth the kingdom of Christ with the most entire freedom, in my lectures, disputations and Latin sermons'.[5] He had found good friends. Edward VI gave him £20 with which to buy a stove.[6] The Duchess of Suffolk, whose two sons were among his Cambridge pupils, helped to nurse him in his illness and gave him a cow and a calf (rumoured by the papists to be two devils, inspiring his lectures).[7] In spite of these kindnesses, and his

[1] *Ibid.* I, 20. [2] Hopf, *Bucer*, 17.
[3] *Original Letters relative to the English Reformation*, II, 544.
[4] *Ibid.* 548. [5] *Ibid.* 543. (Letter of May 1550.)
[6] Hopf, *Bucer*, 16.
[7] Charles Smyth, *Cranmer and the Reformation under Edward VI*, 169.

stipend, he was a poor man. His last letter was a sad scribble to Matthew Parker, Master of Corpus, begging for a loan;[1] and his widow was to find herself compelled to write to Cranmer asking for assistance.[2] Cambridge was in other respects not completely the promised land. The colleges are excellent—he wrote to Calvin —well endowed and with good statutes; the young men on the whole well educated and well kept. And so there should have gone from the university 'swarms of faithful ministers'.[3] But this was not so:

such connivance has so long existed, and is especially so prevalent at this time, that by far the greater part of the Fellows are either most bitter papists, or profligate epicureans, who, as far as they are able, draw over the young men to their way of thinking, and imbue them with an abhorrence of sound christian doctrine and discipline.[4]

On some young men, however, Bucer made a great impression. During a visit to Oxford to see Peter Martyr he preached a sermon which Laurence Humphrey remembered in detail twenty years later.[5] At Cambridge, the comments have been preserved of Thomas Horton, Fellow of Pembroke and future Marian exile.

Dr Bucer cries incessantly, now in daily lectures, now in frequent sermons, that we should practise penitence, discard the depraved customs of hypocritical religion, correct the abuses of fasts, be more frequent in hearing and having sermons, and constrain ourselves by some sort of discipline. Many things of this kind he impresses on us even *ad nauseam*.[6]

To most of his Cambridge hearers Bucer seemed, as he was to John Bradford, 'God's prophet and true preacher'.[7]

His voice was heard in the university for only fifteen months. He died on the first day of March 1551, after rebuking those

---

[1] J. Strype, *Memorials of Cranmer*, II, 301.
[2] *Original Letters relative to the English Reformation*, I, 363.
[3] *Ibid.* II, 546.   [4] *Ibid.*
[5] Hopf, *Bucer*, 21.   [6] Smyth, *Cranmer*, 163.
[7] J. Bradford, *Sermons, etc.*, 445.

doctors who attributed his failing strength to the change of the moon, and flinging down the fine final challenge: 'It is He, it is He, who ruleth and ordereth all things.'[1]

Dead, he took his place in the great tradition of Cambridge funerals. (One is reminded of the burial of William Whitaker in St John's in 1596 or of Charles Simeon in King's in 1836.) In 1551 a crowd of three thousand townsmen and gownsmen is said to have followed the coffin to Great St Mary's. A Latin sermon was preached by the Master of Corpus on a text from the Wisdom of Solomon ('He pleased God and was beloved of Him: so that living among sinners he was translated'); and Parker availed himself of the obvious opportunity to call the university to repentance: 'Prospice tibi Cantabrigia, cui Deus misit prophetas suos.'[2] The next day there were four hundred communicants at St Mary's, when the preacher was the Master of Trinity, John Redman.

The wheel of fortune then spun strangely. On a drizzly Monday morning at the beginning of January 1557, a visitation of the university was formally opened by a high mass in King's and a sermon in Great St Mary's 'against heresies and heretics, as Bilney, Latimer, Cranmer, Ridley &c'.[3] One of the first acts of the Visitors, headed by Cuthbert Scot, Master of Christ's and Bishop of Chester, was to place Great St Mary's under interdict, because Bucer was interred there, and also St Michael's, where Fagius was buried.[4] On Tuesday 12 January, in the early afternoon, the heads met in the Schools and decided that 'for as much as Bucer had been an arch-heretic teaching by his life time many detestable heresies and errors suit should be made unto the Visitors by the university that he might be taken up and ordered according

---

[1] Martin Bucer, *Scripta Anglicana*, 875. Account of Bucer's death by Nicholas Carr, Fellow of Pembroke and Regius Professor of Greek.
[2] *Ibid.* 895.
[3] Account of the Marian Visitation by John Mere, Esquire Bedell, printed by John Lamb, *Original Documents from the Library of Corpus Christi College Cambridge*, 200.
[4] E. Venables, *Annals of Great St Mary's*, 78.

to the law and likewise P. Fagius'. At seven o'clock the next morning (a windy Wednesday) the Vice-Chancellor went to the Visitors, at Trinity College, to obtain the sentence of condemnation and exhumation; at nine, in the presence of a full congregation of the Senate, graces announcing the sentence were read. On the Friday the condemnation was read again in congregation, and sealed with the common seal of the university.[1] Soon after 8 a.m. on Tuesday the 26th the Visitors came to Great St Mary's, where 'the Vice-Chancellor with the university and the Mayor with the town' were already gathered, and walked in procession to the 'little scaffolding made for them within the choir'. The Vice-Chancellor then came forward and read the citation for the condemnation. Scot pronounced the formal sentence of condemnation and exhumation, after which the Vice-Chancellor preached until eleven o'clock on the text, 'Behold how good and joyful a thing it is, brethren, to dwell together in unity'.[2] During his sermon some of the undergraduates pasted over the west doors of the church with scribbled verses making mock of the name of Bucer.[3] (It is only fair to add that a number of verses in favour of Bucer were later discovered in St John's.[4]) Then, twelve days later, on a fine Saturday morning, the bodies of Bucer and Fagius were 'taken up out of their graves and about nine of the clock burnt in the market place and a cart load of books with them'; and Dr Thomas Watson, Bishop of Lincoln and sometime Master of St John's, preached in Great St Mary's for almost two hours 'setting forth Bucer's wickedness and heretical doctrine'. At seven the next morning the Master of Christ's hallowed 'a great tub full of water' and proceeded once round the outside of Great St Mary's and thrice within, hallowing the church; after which he preached at Mass.[5] The next day, Monday, there was a general procession of the university and town to Great St Mary's: the

[1] Lamb, *op. cit.* 201–3.
[2] Foxe, *Acts and Monuments*, VIII, 280.   [3] Lamb, *op. cit.* 210.
[4] *Ibid.* 215.   [5] *Ibid.* 217.

university cross-bearer led the line of undergraduates, bachelors, masters and doctors; followed by the Visitors and heads of houses, each with a blazing torch; then, under a canopy carried by four doctors, came the Master of Christ's in the finest cope his college could provide, bearing the Sacrament in a monstrance borrowed from Gonville Hall; and, bringing up the rear, the mayor and aldermen, also with torches, and lastly the bailiffs and burgesses. The procession left Trinity at seven in the morning, and walked past St John's and down Bridge Street, past the Round Church and the old Franciscan House, to Petty Cury, then round the Market Hill, past the slaughter-houses and St Bene't's, and down High Street to the university church, singing 'Salva festa dies' all the way. (The solemnity was marred slightly by the fact that the day was muddy and many a gown was liberally bespattered; and substantially by an awkward few minutes when the canopy caught fire.) Mass was sung in Great St Mary's by the Vice-Chancellor, who afterwards dined with the Visitors in Trinity.[1] The Vice-Chancellor was the Master of Peterhouse, Andrew Perne.

Three years later, in July 1560, the university restored Bucer and Fagius to honour. There was a sermon by James Pilkington, Master of St John's; and an oration by the new public orator, George Acworth, who, comparing Cambridge with London and Oxford, nicely commented that 'whereas in every singular place was executed a singular kind of cruelty, insomuch, that there was no kind of cruelness that could be devised, but it was put in use in one place or other, this was proper or peculiar to Cambridge, to exercise the cruelty upon the dead, which in other places was extended but to the quick'.[2]

The Vice-Chancellor at the time was again Andrew Perne, Master of Peterhouse. This fact, as Canon Charles Smyth has observed,[3] is at least gratifying to human frailty.

[1] *Ibid.* 218.   [2] Foxe, *Acts and Monuments*, VIII, 289.
[3] Smyth, *Cranmer*, 177.

IV

What did the Cambridge reformers wish to reform? How far did they come to fit into the European tradition of Protestant faith and works? In the early 1520's, humanists avid for Greek and piously orthodox spirits disturbed by the weaknesses of the Church might find themselves in some matters at one with more destructive and far ranging minds, nurtured by the new theology. Fisher was as much a 'reformer' as Barnes in his Christian consciousness that empty works and temporal excesses were an affront to the majesty of God. But Robert Barnes, in his famous sermon preached in St Edward's in 1525[1] against prelatical pomp and pride and the abuses of the ecclesiastical courts, went beyond anything Fisher could tolerate, both in matter and manner. At the same time Bilney was preaching in the diocese of Norwich against images, prayers to the saints, pilgrimages and vows, and against the feigned miracles at Walsingham and Canterbury.[2] Thomas Becon praised Latimer as attacking 'temple-works, good intents, blind zeal, superstitious devotion, etc.; as the painting of tabernacles, gilding of images, setting up of candles, running on pilgrimage, and such like other idle inventions of men, whereby the glory of God was obscured'.[3] The university which had given hospitality to Erasmus might have taken that in its stride. But the violence of Latimer's attacks on 'unpreaching prelates',[4] and his emphasis on the contrast between episcopal magnificence and the simplicity of Christ—a theme he dramatically exploited when the Bishop of Ely unexpectedly stormed into Great St Mary's during one of his sermons[5]—was something rather new. He was, said the sympathetic Edward Fox, 'more vehement than becometh the very evangelist of Christ'.[6] The voice of indignation, springing from a full heart and an outraged conscience, from a deep sense

[1] Cooper, *Annals*, I, 312.
[2] Foxe, *Acts and Monuments*, IV, 627.
[3] Becon, *Catechism, etc.* 425.
[4] Latimer, *Sermons*, I, 154.
[5] J. Strype, *Ecclesiastical Memorials*, III, 369.
[6] Lamb (ed.), *Documents from Corpus Christi College Library*, 17.

of shock, began to assume a strident tone far removed from the sharp but controlled periods of Erasmus. 'Whereby the glory of God was obscured': but does the Universe find its harmony only in the contrast between the absolute impotence of man and the unconditional sovereignty of God? The Protestant reformers came to believe so. That is the basis of the Protestant world picture. Bilney and Latimer and Barnes in 1525, like Luther in 1515, were appalled beyond measure by those who seemed to deny the gravity of the web of human perversity, and the blinding power of grace. 'In no condition', preached Latimer in 1529, 'we shall either know ourselves or God, unless we do utterly confess ourselves to be mere vileness and corruption.'[1] The attacks on abuses, springing from this un-qualified assertion, were therefore not minor; nor were they merely negative. They were as significant in the sphere of theology as was, in the sphere of political theory, the seemingly petty attack of the House of Commons on pluralities in the late 1520's. 'The great thing to be attended to is that God's glory be main-tained entire and unimpaired.'[2]

Roger Ascham commenced bachelor from St John's, at the age of eighteen, in 1534. In that year—when the matter of the papal supremacy was under discussion in the university—Ascham 'chanced among my companions to speak against the Pope'. He was at that time a candidate for a fellowship, and his indiscretion came to the ears of the Master, Nicholas Metcalf, who summoned the young man before himself and the senior Fellows. There, 'after grievous rebuke and some punishment, open warning was given to all the Fellows, none to be so hardy as to give me his voice at that election'. That was the public example; but, in private, the Master told Ascham that he could be quite certain of being elected.[3] The unpredictable currents and treacherous breezes of the early 1530's made it difficult for even the most perceptive

---

[1] Latimer, *op. cit.* 8.   [2] Calvin, *Institutes*, 3/13/12.
[3] R. Ascham, *The Schoolmaster*, 161.

Machiavellian correctly to set his sails. But it was the issue of the papacy which was, until 1534, the vital thing. In the early 'twenties the 'reformers' had been a fairly comprehensive group; but implicitly their ranks were already divided. There had been at first no clear line of common action, no very precise idea of the issues which were to become the chief debating points of the Reformation: issues of the papal primacy, of justification, of the eucharist. The Protestant reformers had not called the tune, for they were learning it as they went along. But the major chords were already in their minds. Cranmer had prayed for the overthrow of the Pope's authority from 1525,[1] and though he swore an oath of spiritual allegiance to the Pope at his consecration in 1533, he had previously made a declaration on oath before witnesses that this oath would be no more than a matter of form.[2] Others besides Pole might have felt this to be close to perjury. And when, a bare year after the cautious nuances of Ascham's election, Chancellor Fisher gave up his life for the papal primacy, that issue was as clear as the noon-day sun which almost blinded him on the scaffold.

Ten years before his death Fisher had preached in St Paul's, as Robert Barnes bore the penitent's faggot. And the Chancellor attacked not the specific errors enumerated in the articles which had been drawn up against the Augustinian prior, but Lutheranism in general. The Reformation in Cambridge did indeed begin 'with love of letters, among a company devoted to the New Learning'.[3] But, as 1530 came closer, the advanced spirits in the university became less and less capable of being described in such phrases as 'the Erasmian group at Cambridge'.[4] They parted company with Erasmus where Erasmus parted company with Luther. The articles upon which Bilney was examined in 1527 were concerned not only with his attacks upon abuses, and upon

[1] Philip Hughes, *The Reformation in England*, i, 241.   [2] *Ibid.* 243.
[3] E. G. Rupp, *The English Protestant Tradition*, 196.
[4] M. M. Knappen, *Tudor Puritanism*, 27.

the authority of the Pope, but also with such problems as whether the Church may err, whether natural and moral philosophy may help towards the understanding of the Scriptures, whether the will is overridden by necessity in salvation or damnation, and whether good works and charity must go with faith towards justification.[1] A decree of the Vice-Chancellor[2] after the trial of Nicholas Shaxton in 1531 imposed an oath upon those proceeding to degrees in divinity to renounce errors 'in all those articles wherein there hath been controversy': the errors, that is, 'of Wyclif, Luther, or any other condemned of heresy'. The list of errors was long. It concerned matters such as Communion in both kinds, fasting, clerical celibacy, and the authority of the Church, besides such points as the importance of pilgrimages and images. It also included more central matters: of 'faith and works', 'sin in a good work', and 'grace and free will'. The next Vice-Chancellor was Simon Heynes and the oath was dropped. But in that year (when Bilney was burnt at Norwich) Robert Barnes published at Wittenberg his summary of the Christian faith in nineteen articles. The articles appeared in German, under the name 'Antonius Anglus'. A Latin version was published in the same volume as Barnes's *Vitae Romanorum Pontificum*,[3] which came out in Basle in 1535, with a preface by Luther himself. The articles dealt with the prime points of controversy: the commands of God are impossible of achievement by our strength; the will, by itself, cannot but sin; even good works have the nature of sin; the Lord's Supper should be communicated in both kinds, bread and wine; priests should be permitted to marry; private confession is not necessary to salvation; church councils can err. Cambridge controversies, in the late 1520's, had covered the same ground. But the escape to Wittenberg and the friendship with Luther had given Barnes the courage to place at the head of his

[1] Foxe, *Acts and Monuments*, IV, 624–5.
[2] Strype, *Ecclesiastical Memorials*, V, 573.
[3] R. Barnes, *Vitae Romanorum Pontificum*, 298–9.

confession of faith the watchword of the Reformation: justification is by faith alone.

In the twenty years which passed between the burning of Bilney and the arrival of Bucer that watchword was extensively debated in England, until, in Cranmer's *Homily of Salvation*, probably written in 1546, it received its classic statement in the vernacular. Justification not by contrition, faith and charity, not for our own works or deservings: but 'sola fide'.

Because all men be sinners and offenders against God, and breakers of His law and commandments, therefore can no man by his own acts, works, and deeds, seem they never so good, be justified and made righteous before God; but every man of necessity is constrained to seek for another righteousness or justification, to be received at God's own hands, that is to say, the remission, pardon, and forgiveness of his sins and trespasses in such things as he hath offended. And this justification or righteousness, which we so receive by God's mercy and Christ's merits, embraced by faith, is taken, accepted, and allowed of God for our perfect and full justification.[1]

However, even when Bucer came to Cambridge the battle for that doctrine was not unreservedly won. Stephen Gardiner was Master of Trinity Hall; and he had argued with Bucer at Ratisbon in 1541, where the central issue of debate was justification.[2] For Gardiner, such discussions seemed a recreation for unworldly dons. Indeed they were: but some dons were more right than others, and Bucer's conviction, at Cambridge as at Ratisbon, that salvation is granted through faith alone, and that faith is given by grace alone, and that to be accounted righteous is not·the same thing as to be inherently righteous, was crucial to the Reformation. In his Cambridge disputations in 1550 Bucer did not have it all his own way. Most significantly, he debated with Andrew Perne and John Young about the sinfulness of works before justification.[3] (The manuscript copies of Bucer's arguments were carefully

---

[1] *The Book of Homilies* (S.P.C.K. ed. 1938), 20.
[2] Hopf, *Bucer*, 183.   [3] *Ibid.* 18.

preserved in the reign of Mary by Matthew Parker: however, when they were brought from their hiding places in 1559, some had been 'gnawed by the rats and entirely spoiled'.[1]) Young (who was called, not 'Jungus', but 'Fungus' by his enemies)[2] was to have Bucer's chair under Mary.

But Bucer had the better of the argument. He was the master, in the royal chair. The Cambridge reformers had won through.

V

Bucer, in April 1549, had been refreshed to find that in the land of exile 'all the services in the churches are read and sung in the vernacular tongue, that the doctrine of justification is purely and soundly taught, and the Eucharist administered according to Christ's ordinance'.[3] The communion office of the new Book of Common Prayer seemed to him especially 'pure', 'scrupulously faithful to the word of God'.[4] This judgement was hardly surprising, since that office was in some part based on the so-called 'Consultation of Hermann of Cologne',[5] drawn up five years previously by Melanchthon and Bucer himself. There were things in the Book, certainly, which Bucer did not like. While at Cambridge in 1550 he prepared a detailed 'Censura' of the 1549 Liturgy.[6] He did not recommend the priest's wearing a 'white albe plain with a vestment or cope', as laid down in the ornaments rubric of the communion office; he objected to the making of the sign of the cross in the consecration prayer; he disliked anointing in baptism, prayers for the dead, and the blessing of water for the font; he criticized the directive that 'kneeling, crossing, holding up of hands, knocking on the breast and other gestures:

[1] Grindal to Conrad Hubert of Strasbourg, May 1559. *Zürich Letters*, Second Series, 18.
[2] *Ibid.*
[3] *Original Letters of the English Reformation*, II, 536.
[4] Smyth, *Cranmer*, 238.
[5] E. C. Ratcliff, *The Book of Common Prayer* (1949), 13.
[6] Hopf, *Bucer*, 65–79.

they may be used or left as every man's devotion serveth without blame'.[1] Some of Bucer's suggestions were incorporated in the Prayer Book of 1552, which he did not live to see. But the important point is that the great man, fresh from the very battle-fields of the European Reformation, had not sold the pass to the extremists; and the extremists were furious.

The moderation of Bucer was quickly made clear to the English reformers. In 1550 there flared up in Cambridge, as in London, a controversy about vestments, such as was to divide the university again a decade later, 'like an ancestral ghost prophesying disaster'.[2] William Bill, the Master of St John's, asked for Bucer's judgement in the matter:[3] and so, a month later, did Cranmer.[4] It seemed to men such as Bill that the Strasbourg reformer might reasonably be expected to oppose the vestments, root and branch. But Bucer's reply anticipated the reasoning of Whitgift and the classic Anglican arguments of Richard Hooker. Vestments, briefly, are things indifferent, neither prescribed nor proscribed in the Word of God: if their use is ordered by the magistrate, as a condition of liturgy and order, they may and must in all conscience be worn.[5] Whitgift, in the 1570's, was to quote this judgement against Cartwright. Indeed, in more ways than one the Cambridge of 1550 was the overture to the Elizabethan controversies: for in that year, when Thomas Cartwright was elected scholar of St John's under William Bill, John Whitgift, aged eighteen, matriculated from Pembroke.

More important (though equally moderate) was Bucer's theology of the Eucharist. Important, because by 1550, the doctrine of Justification being 'soundly taught' and therefore *hors de combat*, the issue of the Real Presence had come to be the focal point of controversy: just as, in the early 1530's, the issue had been the primacy of the Pope. John Bradford of Pembroke,

---

[1] *Ibid.* 66.
[2] Smyth, *Cranmer*, 17.
[3] Hopf, *Bucer*, 135.
[4] *Ibid.* 132.
[5] *Ibid.* 133–6.

64

pupil and friend of Bucer, in his farewell to Cambridge before martyrdom in 1555,[1] gave two reasons why he had elected to die. First, 'I will not grant the antichrist of Rome to be Christ's vicar-general and supreme head of his Church'; secondly, 'I will not grant such corporal, real and carnal presence of Christ's body and blood in the sacrament, as doth transubstantiate the substance of bread and wine'.

Bradford was a successor of John Frith of King's and John Lambert of Queens', both burnt to death in the 1530's for their denials of the doctrine of transubstantiation, after Fisher had argued with the former[2] and the King himself with the latter. But Frith and Lambert were of the school of Robert Barnes, the orthodox Lutheran, who repeated, in his 1531 articles of belief, the firm assertion of Melanchthon in the Augsburg Confession of 1530, that the body and blood of Christ are 'truly present' in the elements of bread and wine. 'Hoc est Corpus Meum.' By 1555 the English reformers were less conservative. But in the 1530's Bucer, with Calvin, had carefully emphasized that the bread and wine are not mere 'naked and bare signs', and that in the Eucharist 'under the symbols of bread and wine', 'the very body and the very blood of Christ is received'.[3] As Regius professor, Bucer held fast to these truths in his Cambridge lectures and sermons of 1550: to audiences which included Matthew Parker, Master of Corpus, Edmund Grindal, Fellow of Pembroke, and John Whitgift, in his first year at Pembroke. In a letter to Calvin written from Cambridge in May 1550[4] Bucer emphasized that although 'no one supposes a local presence of Christ in the supper' it is nonsense to say that 'nothing else but the bread and wine is there distributed'; the body of Christ, though it cannot be locally circumscribed, is verily present—to those who feed upon him by faith. Indeed Bucer had advised Peter Martyr to revise the preface to his

[1] Bradford, *Sermons, etc.* 441–2.   [2] Philip Hughes (ed.), *St John Fisher*, 113.
[3] Calvin, *Theological Treatises* (ed. Reid), 169.
[4] *Original Letters relative to the English Reformation*, II, 544–5. I have slightly revised the awkward translation in one or two places.

treatise on the Eucharist, and insert more passages 'whereby to express more fully his belief in the presence of Christ'. This section of Bucer's letter is worth quoting in full. Through it there runs the thread of insistence on 'Discipline' which coloured all Bucer's thought and argument, and was to be so well remembered by his Cambridge hearers. Among the nobility of England, he wrote, there are those

who would reduce the whole of the sacred ministry into a narrow compass, and who are altogether unconcerned about the restoration of church discipline. While they seek to provide against our bringing down Christ the Lord from heaven and confining him in the bread, and offering him to the communicants to be fed upon without faith, a thing that none of our party ever thought of; they themselves, without any warrant of holy scripture, go so far as to confine him to a certain limited place in heaven; and talk so vapidly about his exhibition and presence in the supper (nay, some of them cannot even endure these words), that they appear to believe that nothing else but the bread and wine is there distributed. No one has as yet found fault with me for my simple view of the subject; nor have I ever heard of any one who has been able to confute it from any solid passage of scripture, nor indeed has anyone yet ventured to make the attempt. Their principal argument is, that the mysteries of Christ can be well and intelligibly explained: (which would be true, if they would add, 'to faith but not to reason'). They now assume, that it cannot with reason be supposed of Christ, that he is in heaven without being circumscribed by physical space; and since he is thus in heaven, as they take for granted, they insist, not only upon what no one will allow them, but also without any solid reason, that it cannot be understood that the same body of Christ is in heaven and in the Supper: and when we reply, that no one supposes a local presence of Christ in the Supper, they again say that the body of Christ cannot be understood to be present anywhere without being locally circumscribed. The sum therefore of their argument is this. Reason does not comprehend what you teach respecting the exhibition and presence of Christ in the Supper: therefore these teachings are not true, and the scriptures which seem to prove them must be otherwise interpreted. Let us pray for these persons.

It was perhaps unfortunate that Cranmer's careful phrases in the Forty-two Articles, drawn up in 1552, could be interpreted as confirming the arguments of the 'persons' Bucer had been so careful to refute. When Cranmer wrote that 'a faithful man ought not either to believe, or openly to confess the real and bodily presence (as they term it) of Christ's flesh and blood in the sacrament of the Lord's Supper', the extremists could unreservedly claim that he 'oppugned and took away the Real Presence in the Eucharist'.[1] The extremists were unsubtle. Parker, significantly, omitted this phrase of Cranmer's when he revised the articles in 1562; and, even more significantly, he substituted a passage which neatly summed up the official Cambridge theology of 1550: 'The Body of Christ is given, taken and eaten in the Supper, only after an heavenly and spiritual manner. And the mean whereby the Body of Christ is received and eaten in the Supper is Faith.' That was a hit—a palpable hit—at the Real Absence.

VI

The debates about the 'Holy Communion, commonly called the Mass' were not only theological but also liturgical. They affected, that is, not only the pulpit and the rostrum, but also the college chapel.

On 4 September 1548 Protector Somerset, the new Chancellor, wrote to the Vice-Chancellor that there should be a uniformity of worship 'such as is presently used in the King's Majesty's Chapel, and none other'; this was to be observed 'until further order be taken'.[2] The next six months were very disturbed. In November there was a disputation about the mass in the chapel of St John's, in which Thomas Lever took part.[3] Ascham wished to repeat this disputation in the Schools, but this was forbidden by

[1] Sampson and Humphrey to Bullinger, 1566, Zürich Letters, First Series, 165.
[2] A. Peel (ed.), The Second Part of a Register, I, 45.
[3] Strype, Cranmer, II, 45.

5-2

the Vice-Chancellor, though Ascham wrote letters of protest to Parker and William Cecil. Previously, there had been a great commotion when someone cut the pyx string in St John's. Then, in June 1549, on and after the feast of Pentecost, the new Book of Common Prayer was commanded to be used. The second Book followed in April 1552. These three intervening years saw a systematic upheaval in the Cambridge chapels. The splendid furnishings, the images, the plate and the vestments were prudently stored away; and how splendid these were may be indicated by reading the list of the gifts of the Lady Margaret to Christ's[1] (nearly £400 worth of ornaments, nearly £600 of vestments), or the kindred bequests of Fisher to St John's. In Christ's, at the very beginning of 1548, workmen spent two days 'helping down with images and mending the pavement under Christ's image': three years later a carpenter and two assistants took down the high altar and two tabernacles; and a communion table was provided for six shillings.[2] The University Visitors of 1549 pulled down six altars in Jesus Chapel, which once had 'glittered with splendid furniture';[3] also the high altar and at least two side altars at Queens'—earlier, the walls of Queens' Chapel had been white-washed, and a communion table introduced.[4] The junior bursar of Trinity, only three years after the foundation, raised £140 by the sale of missals, silver basins, plate, copes and other vestments,[5] formerly belonging to King's Hall and Michaelhouse, some of them once used by Fisher himself. The Provost and Fellows of King's were compelled to remove their high altar, which had been in position for only five years. At Great St Mary's, even in the 1540's, there had been sales of vestments and property, 'by the consent of most part of the parishioners'.[6] In 1550 the high altar was removed, along with five side altars, the images were taken

[1] J. Peile, *Christ's College*, 34.
[2] R. Willis and J. W. Clark, *Architectural History of the University of Cambridge*, II, 206–7.
[3] *Ibid.* 141.   [4] *Ibid.* 38–9.
[5] *Ibid.* 561.
[6] E. Venables, *Annals of Great St Mary's*, 74–5.

down, the frescoes painted over with whitewash, and Scripture texts pasted on the walls.[1] Also, the Crucifix and the figures of St John and the Blessed Virgin, dedicated in 1523, were taken from the rood loft, although the rood loft and screen (1520–3) remained, to be repaired and painted in the next reign, and the figures replaced.[2] The churchwardens of Great St Mary's, who had bought four copies of the English translation of the litany in 1545,[3] now bought, in 1550, two copies of the Prayer Book, two copies of the communion office, and the Book of Homilies. They also bought a copy of the new English translation (supervised by Nicholas Udall) of Erasmus's paraphrases of the Gospels and Epistles,[4] which at the beginning of the reign of Edward (as at the beginning of the reign of Elizabeth) were ordered to be placed in every church in the land. Three years later they paid for psalters, with the settings of John Merbecke, and four copies of the 1552 Prayer Book.[5] The dirges in Great St Mary's—of which nearly a score had been sung each year— had ceased in 1547: the endowments were to be used for the provision of sermons.

Thus much of the colour had gone, most of the 'scenic apparatus of divine worship'.[6] Some of it was to be restored under Mary. But the most picturesque event in the religious life of medieval Cambridge had been abandoned as early as 1535: that is, the Corpus Christi Day procession. Fuller has reconstructed the proceedings:[7] the sermon by the Vice-Chancellor in Great St Mary's; the procession to St Bene't's, headed by the aldermen and elders of the amalgamated Guild of Corpus Christi and the Blessed Virgin, and by the Master of Corpus 'in a silk cope under a canopy, carrying the host in the pyx'; followed by the Vice-

[1] Ibid. 76. J. E. Foster (ed.), *Churchwardens' Accounts of St Mary the Great: 1504–1635* (Camb. Antiq. Soc. Pubn.), 118–19, 123.
[2] Venables, *op. cit.* 78.
[3] Foster (ed.), *Churchwardens' Accounts*, 107.
[4] Ibid. 120.   [5] Ibid. 127.
[6] The phrase was Jewel's. *Zürich Letters*, First Series, 23.
[7] Fuller, *History of Cambridge*, 99–100.

Chancellor, 'the university men in their seniorities', and the mayor and burgesses of the town.

Thus from Bene't Church, they advanced to the great bridge,[1] through all the parts of the town, and so returned with a good appetite to the place where they began. Then in Corpus Christi College was a dinner provided them, where good stomachs meeting with good cheer and welcome, no wonder if mirth followed of course.

Even the Fellows of Corpus (Matthew Parker among them), normally and traditionally given to prayer and fasting, must have regretted the passing of the dinner, and the mirth.

VII

But the time for mirth had passed. In 1547, when the young John Knox was slaving in the galleys, the shock troops of Henry II of France exterminated the Huguenot congregation at Meaux; and after the battle of Mühlberg, the victorious armies of the Christian Emperor entered Strasbourg, Constance, and Augsburg, as, in Italy, the delegates at the Council of Trent were debating the decrees on justification. Luther had died at Eisleben (Saxony) on 18 February 1546. Eleven days before, George Wishart of Corpus Christi College, who had taught the elements of New Testament Greek in the grammar school at Montrose when Stafford was lecturing on St Paul in the Cambridge Schools, was burnt at St Andrews. The lights of charity were going out all over Europe: the Church of Christ, though it spoke of patience and love, both endured and employed the most cruel persecution; pious men were forced to argue more harshly about what they most revered; and in the process the iron entered their souls.

Even in Cambridge the arteries of the Reform Movement were hardening. Roger Ascham, writing in 1547,[2] described how the

---

[1] That is, the present Magdalene Bridge.   [2] Strype, *Cranmer*, II, 73.

doctrine of election was forcing its ominous way into lecture halls and pulpits. Men did not forget John Randall of Christ's, found hanged in his room, his Bible open at a passage concerning pre-destination.[1] Yet in spite of the hardening, there was much new blood; and some of it was to be spilt. The twenty-five men from the university who died as martyrs between 1531 and 1558[2] perished as much for the Protestant movement in Cambridge as they did for the Reformation in England. The two, indeed, tended to be the same thing.

However erratically 'the prices of martyrs' ashes rise and fall in Smithfield Market'[3] (and today, when historians of the Reformation tend to be considered virtuous only in so far as they are 'neither Protestant nor Catholic and free from the instinctive prejudices of both creeds', quotations have seldom been lower), it is difficult not to be moved and edified by an end such as that of John Bradford. A Manchester man, Bradford had been con-verted in 1547, at the age of thirty-seven—converted to the extent of confessing that his master, John Harington, as army pay-master, had swindled the government out of some hundreds of pounds. He went up to St Catharine's in the summer of 1548, and was given the degree of M.A. in October 1549. Within a year of his arrival, Ridley, Master of Pembroke, made him a Fellow of that college. He was an intimate friend of Latimer, the comforter of Bucer in his painful last illness, and the tutor of John Whitgift. He was imprisoned in the Tower in 1553, and read the works of Bucer for consolation in his cell, in the intervals of discussing Eucharistic theology with Latimer and predestination with Ridley. In the spring of 1555 he wrote his farewell to Cambridge: 'O Perne, repent; O Thomson,[4] repent; O ye doctors, bachelors and masters, repent; O mayor, aldermen, and town-dwellers repent, repent, repent, that you may escape the near vengeance

[1] J. Peile, *Biographical Register of Christ's College*, I, 19. Foxe suggested that Randall was hanged by his tutor; 'pour encourager les autres', no doubt.
[2] Rupp, *English Protestant Tradition*, ch. 9.   [3] Fuller, *Holy State*, 275.
[4] John Thomson, Fellow of St John's and Canon of Gloucester (1552–9).

of the Lord.'[1] And he was burnt at Smithfield on Monday 1 July 1555, after consoling the young man who was his fellow martyr: 'Be of good comfort brother: for we shall have a merry supper with the Lord this night.'

The death of Ridley followed in that winter. The youngest of the Edwardian bishops, he was burnt with Latimer (then aged seventy) on 16 October, at Oxford; and he atoned for his comparative lack of years by the singular suffering of his death. His farewell to Cambridge is justly famous. He dwelt affectionately upon the university, 'my loving mother and tender nurse': 'where I have dwelt longer, found more faithful and hearty friends, received more benefits (the benefits of my natural parents only excepted), than ever I did in mine own native country'.[2] Then, as in private duty bound, he praised his own college of Pembroke. William Turner was to remember that the behaviour of the Master was 'very obliging and very pious, without hypocrisy or monkish austerity; for very often he would shoot the bow or play at tennis with me'.[3] And, at the end, Ridley's thoughts turned back to the college orchard: where '(the walls, butts, and trees, if they could speak, would bear me witness) I learned without book almost all Paul's Epistles'.[4]

The martyrdom of John Hullier, of Eton and King's, is less familiar. But for the history of Cambridge it is the most directly relevant of all, because he was burned to death, the Maundy Thursday of 1556, on Jesus Green.[5] 'I am bidden to a Maundy, whither I trust to go, and there to be shortly. God hath laid the foundation, as I by his aid shall end it.' But his end was not short, for it was a blustery Cambridge day, the fire was badly set, and the flames blew to his back. His friends caused the sergeants to turn it and 'fire it to that place where the wind might blow it to his face'. One of them gave him bags of gunpowder to hang

---

[1] Bradford, *Sermons, etc.* 446.
[2] Foxe, *Acts and Monuments*, VII, 557.
[3] Strype, *Ecclesiastical Memorials*, III, 386.
[4] Foxe, *loc. cit.*
[5] *Ibid.* VIII, 379.

round his neck, but this errand of mercy failed too, for the powder did not catch fire until after Hullier was dead. Splendidly, in the sickening horrors of his last hour, he found consolation in the Book of Common Prayer: 'there was a company of books which were cast into the fire; and by chance a communion book fell between his hands, who received it joyfully, opened it, and read so long till the force of the flame and smoke caused him that he could see no more'.

One suffering for the truth, wrote Hugh Latimer, turneth more than a thousand sermons.[1] Many of the Cambridge reformers who succeeded Hullier and his generation, a new and rather different race of Protestants, were to have less respect than he for Cranmer's liturgy. Yet the suffering was not unacknowledged. Providence, in its inscrutable fashion, sent the future historian of the English martyrs to Oxford.[2] But Cambridge, undeniably, has the more cause to rejoice in and mourn their deaths.

[1] Quoted in the programme for the service in St Edward's Church, Cambridge, 16 October 1955, the four hundredth anniversary of the martyrdom of Ridley and Latimer, when a memorial tablet to Bilney, Barnes and Latimer, designed by David Kindersley, was unveiled by the Master of Magdalene, after a sermon by Dr Owen Chadwick.

[2] John Foxe went up to Oxford in 1534, at the age of sixteen or seventeen (J. F. Mozley, *John Foxe and his Book*, 12, 17).

CHAPTER IV

THE CAMBRIDGE EXILES

I

DURING the reign of Mary the English Reformation came of age. The fires of Smithfield provided insular Protestantism with its most potent popular 'myth': and the experience of those who migrated to Europe summed up (and developed) the existing achievements of English worship and theology, and also laid down the lines of future retrenchment and reform. Indeed, it has been usual to approach the ecclesiastical history of the first years of the reign of Elizabeth by way of the returning exiles. Such a route may be helpful, though not necessarily edifying: 'few things', remarked Philip Guedalla, 'are more depressing than the exaggerated deference of English revolutionaries to foreign models'. But, for the history of Cambridge, the exiles find their importance not in any future influence within the university, but in the fact that their story serves as an appendix to, and a commentary upon, certain aspects of Cambridge life and thought in the reigns of Henry VIII and Edward VI.

II

On Thursday, 6 July 1553, Edward VI died at Greenwich. The news was brought to Princess Mary Tudor at Hoddesdon (ten miles east of Hatfield); and immediately she set out, disguised, for her manor of Kenninghall (in Norfolk, near Thetford), spending the night *en route* and hearing mass the next morning at the manor house of Sawston, seven miles south of Cambridge. The Duke of Northumberland contrived to keep pretty secret the news of the King's death until Saturday the 8th. On Sunday the 9th Bishop Ridley, Master of Pembroke, preached in London against Mary; and the next day Lady Jane Dudley was proclaimed Queen—the Lady Jane Grey, grand-daughter of the sister of Henry VIII, had been married six weeks before to Northumberland's son, Lord Guilford Dudley. During the following week, Mary's supporters rallied and armed themselves in the eastern counties, as Northumberland collected in London a troop of horse and foot, some 4000 strong—a troop which on Sunday the 16th clattered its way through the streets of Cambridge. Northumberland, Chancellor of the University, had arrived in the town the previous afternoon, and dined, so it was said, with Edwin Sandys, Master of St Catharine's and Vice-Chancellor, Thomas Lever, Master of St John's, William Bill, Master of Trinity, and Matthew Parker, Master of Corpus. Another of his strong supporters was Sir John Cheke, Provost of King's, former tutor of the late King. The Chancellor could then be fairly confident of support in the university; a support which was crystallized on the Sunday in a sermon preached to the university by the Vice-Chancellor, on a text from the first chapter of Joshua: 'According as we hearkened unto Moses in all things, so will we hearken unto thee.' But in fact the position was precarious. Northumberland might march out from Cambridge on the Monday, as if into the land of his possession; he was back again by Tuesday, his forces decimated by desertion. Within the university, there were riots in the Schools and the Regent House, and on Wednesday the 19th, as Thomas Lever and his brother Ralph, booted and spurred, were about to carry to the London printers the text of Sandys's sermon, the news reached Cambridge that Lady Jane and her husband had been imprisoned and Mary acclaimed as Queen. The next morning—Thursday the 20th, two weeks after the death of Edward—Northumberland tearfully swallowed his pride and cut his losses, by publicly proclaiming Mary as Queen on Market Hill. But that last card was as ineffective as the rest. The Chancellor was arrested in Cambridge that evening, and the Vice-Chancellor

75

on the following day. As he left the university for the Tower on a borrowed horse (his own stable having been robbed) Sandys was jeered in the streets. He began his captivity in the Tower on Tuesday the 25th; on the Friday he was joined by John Cheke.

Cheke was released, and given a licence to travel, in September. Sandys was not so favoured, for he remained in the Tower for six months in all, before being transferred in January 1554 to the Marshalsea, from which he was not released for another two months. On 6 May, after lying low for two days in a marshlands farmhouse, he set sail for Antwerp, in company with Richard Cox (who had escaped from house arrest) and Thomas Sampson (who had been in hiding). In the late summer of 1554 Sandys arrived in Strasbourg. Cheke had passed through the city in April, two months after the arrival of a party of Englishmen headed by Thomas Lever.

Lever had left Cambridge in September 1553, with his brothers John and Ralph. In fact over twenty Fellows of St John's were obliged to leave the college about that time. More than half of them lived on in England, with the consolation that they had seen better days. But nine decided that they who would valiant be, must follow the Master. The senior of these nine Fellows of St John's to go abroad was James Pilkington, who had been a Fellow, aged twenty, when young Lever had come up from Bolton at the age of seventeen in 1539. Pilkington too was a Bolton man; and it is worth noting that the original statutes of the college, drawn up by the Yorkshireman John Fisher, had made great provision for northerners: 'forasmuch as of the two regions, the north and the south, into which England is divided,, he noted the north to be more barren of learning and so ruder in manners than the south'.[1] Lever—a man, said Thomas Baker, 'that had the spirit of Hugh Latimer'[2]—was elected Master in 1550, when he was twenty-nine. And the eight other Johnian dons who went

[1] Philip Hughes (ed.), *St John Fisher*, 52.
[2] T. Baker, *History of St John's College*, I, 130.

abroad in 1553 did so under the sway of this forceful Lancashire reformer. They were Roger Kelke, three years younger than Lever, elected Fellow in 1545; Leonard Pilkington, brother of James, also elected in 1545; William Ireland, a former Benedictine (1547); Thomas Lakin (1548); Thomas Wilson (1548), the Elizabethan Dean of Worcester (not to be confused with his more famous namesake of King's, who was also an exile); Ralph Lever, younger brother of Thomas (1549); Percival Wiborne, elected Fellow in 1552 at the age of eighteen; and young Robert Swift, elected three months before the death of Edward, having matriculated in 1549: he was, in due season, to marry Thomas Lever's daughter. John Lever, another brother, eight years younger than the Master, was also of the company: he proceeded master of arts in 1553, but did not stay to be elected Fellow. In Thomas Lever's party must also be included the Johnian William Birch, one of the two Fellows of Corpus who resigned in 1553; and two Trinity Fellows, Henry Cockcroft and John Pedder.

In addition to Cockcroft and Pedder, six Fellows of Trinity left England at the beginning of the new reign. John Banks and James Haddon (originally of Michaelhouse and King's respectively), who were in Strasbourg by July 1554; Matthew Carew, who went to Padua in the summer of 1554 with his elder brother Roger, who had also been a Fellow; Thomas Donnell, a Christ's man by origin, who appeared in Frankfurt with his colleague John Jefferay; and the Johnian John Orphinstrange, who also went to Padua.

At the tail of the roll there were Nicholas Carvell, Fellow of King's, who was in Zürich by October 1554; Thomas Wilson of King's, who went to Frankfurt with the Provost; Robert Beaumont, bursar of Peterhouse, who was in Zürich at the same time as Carvell; Thomas Jeffreys of Clare, resident in Strasbourg by December 1554; and James Taylor of St Catharine's, who may have joined Sandys, his former Master. Other dons stayed in Cambridge for the moment but went abroad later in the reign:

George Acworth of Peterhouse, for example, and William Masters and William Temple of King's. But, so far as the records tell, there were at least twenty-three Cambridge dons resident at the beginning of the reign of Mary who left the university for the Continent as soon as they could conveniently manage to do so.

III

But that is not the whole story. Miss C. H. Garrett, in a definitive study published in 1938,[1] gave a list of 472 Marian exiles. Of these men, seventy-six were or had been members of Cambridge colleges: fifteen colleges—every one, that is, except Magdalene— had nurtured future exiles. There were also two old members of the Cambridge religious houses—the ex-Franciscan Bartholomew Traheron and the ex-Dominican John Scory, Edwardian Bishop of Rochester and Chichester. Ten men, in addition, are known to have been educated at Cambridge, but have left no trace of their college: including Edmund Cranmer, brother of the Archbishop, who commenced bachelor of arts in 1514, two years after Thomas. So the list of Cambridge exiles can with propriety contain about ninety names,[2] a fifth, that is, of the total number listed by Miss Garrett.

The names span the generations. John Bale was born in 1495; Percival Wiborne lived until 1606, a canon of Westminster for over forty-five years; and Matthew Carew died in 1618. Three of the exiles—Bale, Cox, and Cranmer—had gone up to Cambridge in the decade 1510-20, the decade which began with the lectures of Erasmus and ended with the burning of the works of Luther. At the other end of the scale, ten of the Cambridge men were undergraduates or young bachelors when they went abroad. Edward Frencham matriculated from St Catharine's in 1552; abroad, he was smiled at as a hypochondriac; but the boy's fussing must have had its cause, for he died in 1559. Edmund Chapman

[1] C. H. Garrett, *The Marian Exiles.*   [2] See the Appendix to this chapter.

of Gonville Hall, who spent some time in Aarau, had matriculated in 1554 at the age of sixteen. John Pelham, who went up to Queens' in 1549, went to Padua and Geneva with his tutor, William Morley. At Frankfurt the names were registered of Walter Austen and Thomas Watts of Christ's, John Hilles and Thomas Walker of Jesus, Thomas Acworth of Trinity and Christopher Southhouse of Trinity Hall—all of them hovering on the near or far side of twenty. John Watson, who matriculated from Corpus in 1550, was probably also of their number.

Between those extreme generations, seven future exiles, including Cheke and William Turner of Pembroke, had gone up between 1520 and 1530, the years of the 'little Germany' in the White Horse; fifteen, including Robert Horne, had been undergraduates in the 1530's; and over thirty—more than a third of the total number—had gone up in the 1540's.

The figures and the bare names, dry bones of the story, give some indication of the growth of the reform movement in Cambridge, rising to the great names of the 1540's. A closer examination would show the peculiar importance of college loyalties and tradition: a tradition expressed and perhaps formed by the personality of a strong Master—a Shorton or a Ridley at Pembroke, a Forman or a Heynes at Queens', a Lever at St John's. Only some of the men, of course, had stayed in Cambridge. Many had been itinerant preachers or troublesome priests: Anthony Gilbey of Christ's, John Bale, Thomas Becon of St John's. Other priests had married in the reign of Edward, and therefore forfeited their ministry in December 1553. Some had been schoolmasters: Laurence Nowell, a B.A. of Christ's in 1541 (though an Oxford man by origin) was headmaster of Sutton Coldfield School in the early 1550's; in later years he was to be the intellectual father of William Lambarde and 'the chief reviver of the Anglo-Saxon language and learning'.[1] Thomas Cole of King's, who was to complete William Whittingham's narrative

[1] A. L. Rowse, *The England of Elizabeth*, 35.

of 'The Troubles begun at Frankfurt', was headmaster of Maidstone School. Another Kingsman, a very distinguished one, was Richard Cox. Cox had migrated to Oxford in the 1520's, to the Cardinal's College; in the early 1530's he was headmaster of Eton and in the early 1540's tutor to Prince Edward; from 1541 to 1553 he was Archdeacon of Ely; in 1547 he was appointed dean of his old Oxford college, now called Christ Church, and Chancellor of the University; in the reign of Edward he was also Canon of Windsor and Dean of Westminster, and Cranmer's most trusted adviser in liturgical matters. Richard Jugge, a Kingsman again, was a printer; Francis Russell of King's Hall a member of Parliament and a lord lieutenant; the gentle Christopher Hales of St John's a patron and man of letters.

Of the seventy-six collegiate exiles, forty-four were Fellows or sometime Fellows. Many of these had of course risen to high national authority under Edward VI. John Ponet had been Bishop first of Rochester then of Winchester. The peevish Robert Horne had been Dean of Durham. Thomas Sampson, William Turner and James Haddon were also deans, of Chichester, Wells and Exeter respectively. Edmund Grindal and Richard Alvey were canons of Westminster. Edmund Allen of Corpus, one of the translators (under Udall) of the *Paraphrases* of Erasmus, was also chaplain to Princess Elizabeth. They were, these forty-four dons, a remarkable collection, of various and striking talents. A slight sketch of four of them will illustrate the fact: William Turner, George Acworth, John Aylmer and John Ponet.

The handsome, witty and outspoken William Turner went up to Pembroke in 1526, two years after Ridley became Fellow. He loved the orchard, as the future Master also loved it; but Turner paced its paths not to peruse the Epistles of Paul but to study the plants, for he was to go down to history as 'the true pioneer of natural science in England'.[1] Yet his fight against error and

[1] C. E. Raven, *English Naturalists from Neckham to Ray*, 127. Dr Raven devoted four chapters of this book to a study of Turner.

superstition in the sciences (akin to that of Erasmus in the humanities and the Scriptures) led him to join the struggle for the pure and simple Gospel. He learned Greek from Ridley and sat at the feet of Latimer, to whom, in 1551, he was to dedicate his *Preservative against the Poison of Pelagius.* Leaving Cambridge in 1537, Turner became an itinerant preacher, was imprisoned for a time, and went abroad in 1540. This first exile, of six years' duration, showed the double thread of his life and work: the scientific interwoven with the prophetic. From Cologne, Bonn and Basle he went south to Italy, where he proceeded to the degree of doctor of medicine. Then back north again, to Switzerland, Strasbourg, the Low Countries. He met Bucer and wrote *The Huntyng and Fynding Out of the Romishe Fox* (1543). He also met Gesner, the great naturalist of Zürich, and made volumes of botanical notes. He wrote a treatise on birds in 1544 and dedicated it to Prince Edward.[1] In 1547 he returned to England, to serve Protector Somerset in the unusual but satisfactory combination of physician and chaplain. In 1551 he was appointed Dean of Wells. Another seventeen years of life remained to the inquisitive Turner of Pembroke; but now, in his early forties, he was an outstandingly many-sided and original figure, in an age of versatile dons.

George Acworth of Peterhouse remained in Cambridge until 1555, when he signed the Marian articles; condemning heretics such as Bucer, affirming the seven Sacraments, and agreeing that justification was by faith in company with repentance and hope and charity, and not by faith alone. Then Acworth went abroad, to Louvain, Paris and Padua, ostensibly to study law, though it may have been true, as he explained later to Parker, that he turned to the study of law 'lest I might appear to be approving those dogmas of religion to which I have never assented'.[2]

[1] William Turner, *Avium praecipuarum, quarum apud Plinium et Aristotelem mentio est, brevis et succincta historia.* There is a modern edition, edited in 1903 by A. H. Evans (Cambridge University Press).
[2] L. G. H. Horton-Smith, *George Acworth* (1953), 16.

John Aylmer took his M.A. degree from Queens'. An Henrician prebendary of Wells, and an Edwardine archdeacon of Stow, Aylmer was also tutor to Lady Jane Grey, who was to pay a prim but touching tribute to the effects of his teaching: 'all their sport in the park is but a shadow to that I find in Plato'.[1]

John Ponet was also a Queens' man, bursar and dean of the college. Ponet was a curious combination of the Renaissance man and the Reformation bishop, with a touch thrown in of the White Knight. As proficient in mathematics and astronomy as in Greek, Italian and German, he presented to Henry VIII an elaborate scientific dial tabulating, amongst much else, details of the ebb and flow of the tides. A pity that in him the milk of human kindness had been somewhat soured by an unfortunate youthful love match with the sometime spouse of a Nottingham butcher. Ponet was never to see Queens' again after he went to Strasbourg, nor England either, for he died of the plague in 1557, meditating to the last upon the Christian duty of active disobedience to the ungodly ruler, awaiting the purgative murder of Mary by such virtuous plotters as the Cambridge exile-diplomats William Pickering, sometime pupil of Cheke, and Thomas Dannett of St John's, cousin of William Cecil.

There were exiled Fellows from nine Cambridge colleges. Their names will be found in the appendix to this chapter. But it is worth pointing out here that in addition to the nine Fellows who followed Thomas Lever into exile, five sometime dons of St John's also went abroad: Cheke, Sandys, William Jackson, Richard Alvey and Robert Horne (who once taught Hebrew in the college and who was to teach it to the English colony in Frankfurt). The second great foundation of Fisher and the Lady Margaret, a house not yet half a century old, therefore sent more dons than any other college as exiles into Protestant Europe. At times, in fact, the story of the Cambridge exiles seems little more than a footnote to the history of St John's.

[1] R. Ascham, *The Schoolmaster*, 33.

IV

Once abroad, the paths of the exiles diverged. Even Thomas Lever's party soon split up: there were no organized Cambridge 'companies' among the migrants, except in so far as university men in far-flung outposts might naturally tend to see life as a series of reunions. Not every exile, after all, went abroad strictly for conscience' sake; many were like John Ponet's friend Sir Peter Carew, who left England 'to travel countries and to see strange fashions'.[1] Others went abroad primarily to continue their education in a sympathetic atmosphere. Switzerland was a favourite finishing school for young men in a hurry: the Cambridge men who entered themselves at the University of Basle included Francis Walsingham and two young dons, John Banks of Trinity and William Temple of King's. William Amondesham reversed the process. He had migrated to Switzerland with his family, and matriculated from Basle in 1556; he was to matriculate from Cambridge, a fellow commoner of Pembroke, in 1564.

Other men went to Italy—the Italy (if they knew about such things) of Titian, Tintoretto and Veronese. Acworth, Nowell, Walsingham and Thomas Wilson of King's were to settle down in Padua, where there was quite a large Cambridge colony. Wilson proceeded there to the degree of doctor of law, and was to be imprisoned for heresy in the midst of some incomprehensible negotiations with the Pope. Francis Russell, second Earl of Bedford, a King's Hall man, left his English prison by arrangement in 1555 and went to Padua, Venice, Rome and Naples; then back north to Zürich, where he spent the winter of 1556/7, for religion was to him—we have Gualter as witness[2]—dearer than all else. The doyen of the English exiles in Italy was the peripatetic Provost of King's. At Padua Cheke studied law and Italian and lectured on Greek—perhaps winning converts to his new system of

---

[1] J. Vowell, *Life of Sir Peter Carew*, 16; quoted in Garrett, *Marian Exiles*, 104.
[2] *Zürich Letters*, Second Series, 9.

pronunciation, which had split academic opinion in Cambridge in the 1530's; Stephen Gardiner, suspicious of this attempt to base authority not on usage but on reason, had asked a pertinent question: 'What does not the itch of seeking out Truth compel men to do?'[1] But in the spring of 1555, after only nine months in Padua, Cheke fell dangerously ill. He went north, to spend the winter in Strasbourg: he wrote to Calvin from there in October. He travelled north again, almost to the North Sea, to visit Emden, the seat of the ministry of information of the organized propaganda campaigns carried out by the exiles, a sort of pamphlet warfare against occupied England. Cambridge men such as the printer Richard Jugge, John Bale, Robert Hutton of Pembroke (a pupil of William Turner), John Scory, and perhaps William Turner himself, are known to have been at Emden. Robert Cole and Thomas Horton, both Fellows of King's, were both messengers between the exiles and their sympathizers in England, purveyors of prohibited literature and underground gossip, conscientious and successful go-betweens in a highly dangerous game. Cheke came to be suspected by the English government— no one knows how justly—of being a master mind of the Emden organization. In May 1556 he was kidnapped near Brussels, and imprisoned in London on a charge of sedition. He died in prison in 1557, at the age of forty-three. One of his kidnappers may have been William Paget, who had lectured on Melanchthon in the Trinity Hall of the 1520's.

The fatal connection between the love of letters and the zeal for reform was ending, for some, in high tragedy. Life, as it were, had broken in.

But most of the exiles found their haven not in Italy, nor by the North Sea, but in the established centres of the Reformation in Germany and Switzerland. Many of them, by 1558, were well-travelled men. The generous but restless Thomas Sampson, who had crossed to the Low Countries with Sandys, thereafter left a

[1] Strype, *Ecclesiastical Memorials*, I, 576

bewildering trail of short visits. Ralph Lever, again, left no permanent trace. Thomas Lever was not quite so much a wandering scholar. He spent 1554 in Switzerland, sometimes in Zürich (with James Pilkington and Robert Horne), sometimes in Geneva; in January 1555 he was called to Frankfurt, at the height of the troubles, and quarrelled with John Knox—two of whose sons, in spite of this, were later to be Fellows of St John's;[1] in the summer of 1555 he returned to Geneva, and then went far north, up the Rhine to Wesel; finally, from September 1556, he settled down for eighteen months, thirty miles south-east of Basle, as pastor of the little English congregation at Aarau, where he lived in the house of his brother John. William Turner also wandered triumphantly, in the 1550's as in the 1530's, collecting plants up and down the Rhine from Bonn to Basle, setting up experimental gardens at Cologne, writing his *New Booke of Spirituall Physik* and *The Huntyng of the Romyshe Wolfe* (both published by the press at Emden), and practising as a physician. Turner, at times, seems made of quicksilver.

Frankfurt-am-Main, strategically central between the Low Countries and Switzerland, was the most popular resort. The really influential Cambridge men there were Richard Cox and Robert Horne. By the winter of 1554 it had become clear that John Knox, pastor of the English congregation, by refusing to use the Prayer Book of 1552 because it was too conservative, was endangering the somewhat shaky unity of the exiled English front. Grindal, under orders from Ponet, hurried north from Strasbourg in November; and Thomas Lever—the subtle underminer, com-plained Knox, of the whole congregation—took up pastoral duties there in January. Knox appealed for a ruling to Calvin, who, surprisingly, counselled moderation. Cox, the champion of

---

[1] Nathaniel Knox (born in 1557) matriculated from St John's with Eleazor (born in 1558), in 1572, shortly after the death of their father. Nathaniel was elected Fellow in 1577 and died in 1580; Eleazor was elected in 1580 and died in 1591. T. R. Glover contributed a note on the two Knoxes to *Collegium Divi Johannis Evangelistae, 1511–1911*; their autographs are there reproduced (plate XI).

conformity, arrived in March, and called in the city authorities of Frankfurt. Less than a fortnight later, at the end of March 1555, Knox was driven out of Frankfurt, with the dubious consolation, for a mile or two, of a triumphal procession of his admirers. The Coxians, having defeated the Knoxians, called in Horne to assist in a revised version of the 1552 rite—the so-called 'liturgy of Frankfurt'. Horne became pastor of the English congregation in 1556. He continued the tradition of troubles by quarrelling about finance and the powers of the pastor in relation to those of the congregation and resigned early in 1557, having conducted himself throughout, says Miss Garrett, 'with a lack of dignity bordering on the ludicrous'.[1]

From Frankfurt, Knox had gone to Geneva: 'the most perfect school of Christ', he believed, 'that ever was in the earth since the days of the Apostles'.[2] He arrived just as Calvin, after twenty years of struggle, had finally tamed the city by obtaining a majority on the councils. The English church was founded in November of that year (1555); and Anthony Gilbey, with Christopher Goodman, was elected to preach and administer the Sacraments.[3] Thomas Lever and William Amondesham had arrived in Geneva in the summer, shortly after Knox. During 1556 they were followed by James Pilkington, Robert Beaumont, John Scory, and Thomas Sampson. Wiborne arrived in 1557, and Coverdale in 1558; the latter was made an elder of the English church in November of that year, and left Geneva in the following August.[4] During the three years between its foundation and the death of Mary that English church had about 180 members.[5]

Calvin had saved Geneva by his exertions. It was the hope of his disciples to save Europe by his example. But could England be saved? Could Calvin be an example to Cambridge?

[1] Garrett, *Marian Exiles*, 189.
[2] Knox, *Works*, IV, 240.
[3] Charles Martin, *Les Protestants anglais réfugiés à Genève: 1555–60*, 39.
[4] Mozley, *Coverdale*, 21–7.
[5] Martin, *op. cit.* 45. The figure he gave is 186.

V

'O Zürich! Zürich!', wrote Jewel to Peter Martyr in 1559, 'how much oftener do I think of thee than ever I thought of England when I was at Zürich.'[1] Even allowing for stylistic exaggeration (Jewel was an Oxford man) there is no denying the perverse nostalgia of it; and to some—perhaps most—of the returned exiles, such nostalgia was to be a spur to action, a hankering after the pattern of the best reformed churches. Everyone had known that this would be so. 'I warn you,' preached Bishop White of Winchester at the funeral of Queen Mary in December 1558, 'the wolves be coming out of Geneva, and other places of Germany, and hath sent their books before.'[2] Thomas Sampson refused to accept a bishopric, though his conscience allowed him to be dean of Christ Church; four years later, with the President of Magdalen, he was called before Parker to answer for their stirring-up of the university of Oxford against the surplice and the cap. Sampson was not the only Cambridge exile to make his mark on Oxford: Robert Horne as Visitor, with George Acworth as his commissary, had a sharp way with 'the scenic apparatus of divine worship'. William Turner was restored to his deanery of Wells in 1559 but suspended from it in 1564 for vestiarian irregularities. Perhaps this gave him time to bring himself up to date in English botany, to work on a collation of the Hebrew, Greek, Latin and English texts of the Bible, and to publish a book on baths and a treatise on wines. Turner died in 1568, and his widow married Richard Cox. His funeral sermon was preached by Thomas Lever, who, refusing to wear the surplice, had lost his prebend at Durham, and who would undoubtedly have run into trouble as archdeacon of Coventry for his encouragement of the 'prophesyings', had it not been for his timely death in 1577. The names of Cambridge exiles were to crop up also amongst the recalcitrant inferior clergy, those

[1] J. Jewel, *Works*, IV, 1210. Also in *Zürich Letters*, First Series, 23.
[2] Strype, *Ecclesiastical Memorials*, VI, 542.

to whom the verdict of Sir George Paule on Thomas Cartwright may justly be applied: 'he was so far carried away with an affection of that new devised discipline, as that he thought all churches and congregations for government ecclesiastical, were to be measured and squared by the practice of Geneva'.[1] Such men as Antony Gilbey of Christ's, the puritan pope of Ashby-de-la-Zouch; Robert Edmunds, also of Christ's, a member of the London *classis* in 1572; Thomas Walker, a Jesus sizar of 1549, deprived of his living in 1571; Edmund Lawrence of Michaelhouse, to be deprived by the Bishop of Norwich; and those who, in the momentous Convocation of 1562, were to lose by only one vote their motion for a discipline and the alteration of rites and ceremonies—Thomas Becon, Percival Wiborne, and the rest. Wiborne was still a troublemaker in 1586, when he was suspended for a sermon preached at Rochester—and he had another twenty years to live.

Not all the Marian exiles were to be troublesome on their return. Some, after all, became Bishops: the quarrelsome and obstinate Sandys, whose 'Germanic' qualities, complained of by Parker, had naturally been accentuated by his German sojourn, was appointed Bishop of Worcester, and then Archbishop of York; Grindal was to go to London, Cox to Ely, Horne to Winchester, James Pilkington to Durham; Aylmer, after fourteen years as archdeacon of London, was consecrated Bishop of the diocese in 1577; Scory, once Bishop of Rochester and Chichester, was to be Bishop of Hereford from 1559 until he died in 1585—the sole survivor of all the Edwardian Bishops and survivor of all but one of the original Elizabethan.

The grievance of the Puritans against these men was clear enough: 'What talk they of their being beyond the seas in Queen Mary's days because of the persecution, when they in Queen Elizabeth's days, are come home to raise a persecution.'[2]

[1] G. Paule, *Life of Whitgift* (second edition, 1699), 11.
[2] 'Second Admonition to Parliament', W. H. Frere and C. E. Douglas, *Puritan Manifestos* (reprinted 1954), 112.

And in fact the legacy of the exile to many of those who returned was a divided mind and an uneasy conscience. James Pilkington and his colleagues had firmly declared, in January 1559: 'we trust that both true religion shall be restored; and that we shall not be burdened with unprofitable ceremonies'.[1] Party programmes have more than once proved an embarrassment to returning exiles; and the Church of England after 1559 (like the State of Germany after Hitler's war) was to be administered by one who had watched and waited under the tyrant, not by those who had fled from the Cities of the Plain. Pilkington had also declared: 'We purpose to submit ourselves to such orders as shall be established by Authority, being not of themselves wicked.'[2] The operative phrase was the last. But what was to happen when one became Master of St John's and Bishop of Durham? In his years of authority Pilkington gently reminded the froward: 'We are under authority and can innovate nothing without the Queen; nor can we alter the laws; the only thing left to our choice is, whether we will bear these things, or break the peace of the Church.'[3] The career of Pilkington clearly illustrates the trials of a divided allegiance. So does that of Robert Beaumont, Master of Trinity, and twice Vice-Chancellor before his death in 1567, in whom there was an especially dramatic tension between the memory of the best reformed churches, and the obligation, as a local magistrate of the supreme Governor, to keep 'the mean between the two extremes, of too much stiffness in refusing, and of too much easiness in admitting any variation'.

In fact, only a dozen of the Cambridge exiles returned to the university. Percival Wiborne took up his fellowship at St John's; Thomas Wilson went back for a time to King's; Anthony Mayhew may have been reinstated in his fellowship at Pembroke,

[1] William Whittingham, A Brief Discourse of the Troubles begun at Frankfurt, 226.
[2] Ibid.
[3] D. Neal, History of the Puritans, I, 159.

but he died in October 1559; Thomas Jeffreys of Clare became a Fellow of St John's in 1560, but stayed there for only a year or two; Ralph Lever also returned to St John's, but went to Durham in 1561, as chaplain to Bishop Pilkington. George Acworth, through the influence of Parker, was appointed public orator in August 1559, a post in which he was succeeded in 1563 by William Masters of King's. Acworth, in spite of his unfortunate private habits, was a great friend of Parker: with John Bale and Laurence Nowell he was the Archbishop's assistant in building up the collection of manuscripts later bequeathed to Corpus—an arsenal to refute the charges, whether popish or presbyterian, that the Church of England as by law established was a new-fangled institution.[1] Five of the returned exiles were to be Masters: Edmund Grindal of Pembroke, Roger Kelke of Magdalene, Leonard Pilkington of St John's; and the Geneva men, Robert Beaumont and James Pilkington. Beaumont was the first Elizabethan Lady Margaret Professor, and he was also (*O tempora, o mores!*) to minister at Little St Mary's.

The exiled faction may have become, in England, the Puritan party. Be that as it may, the influence of the returned exiles on the history of the Elizabethan Church was obviously crucial. Its importance has never gone unnoticed, nor has the part which Cambridge men were to play in that national story. But it would be incorrect to assume that the exiles who returned to Cambridge were to bear any direct responsibility for the growth of Puritanism in the university. There was, certainly, Edmund Chapman of Gonville Hall, who was elected Fellow of Trinity in 1560; in 1570 he was among the supporters of Thomas Cartwright; in the early 1580's he was to be one of the organizers of the Dedham *classis*, in close touch with the sympathizers at Cambridge. And it may be that the troubles in Elizabethan St John's would have been less

---

[1] C. E. Wright, 'The dispersal of the monastic libraries', *Trans. Cambridge Bibliographical Society*, 1951. Sir Edwin Hoskyns (ed. Charles Smyth), *Cambridge Sermons*, 204–17.

violent had it not been for the policy of the Pilkingtons from 1559 to 1564. But such swallows do not make a summer, not even a Puritan one.

No: the story of the Cambridge exiles is not the most fruitful approach to the study of the origins of Puritanism in Elizabethan Cambridge. It is an epilogue to the history of the university under Henry VIII and Edward VI.

APPENDIX

Names of Fellows of colleges are printed in italic; those of heads of houses are printed in capitals. *D.N.B.* means that there is a biography in the *Dictionary of National Biography*.

THE CAMBRIDGE MARIAN EXILES

CHRIST'S

Richard Alvey. *See under* St John's.

Walter Austen. Matric. 1551. B.A. 1553. (Frankfurt.)

Henry Cockcroft. Matric. 1544. *Fellow of Trinity*, 1547–54. Ordained, 1551. (Zürich, Frankfurt.) Died 1567.

Thomas Donnell. Matric. 1540. *Fellow of Trinity*, 1546–53. (Frankfurt.) Elizabethan Essex rector. Died 1572.

Robert Edmunds. Matric. 1544. Elizabethan Essex rector.

Anthony Gilbey (1510–85). B.A. 1532. (Frankfurt, Geneva, Basle.) Vicar of Ashby-de-la-Zouch, 1564–83. (*D.N.B.*)

Thomas Jeffreys. Matric. 1547. *Fellow of Clare*, 1552. (Strasbourg.) Ordained, 1559; returned to Clare, 1559. *Fellow of St John's*, 1560. B.D. 1561. Wiltshire rector, 1564.

Laurence Nowell. From Oxford. Scholar 1538; B.A. 1541. Master at Sutton Coldfield School, 1546. Rector in Staffs, 1553–6; 1560–76. (France and Italy.) Eliz. archdeacon of Derby, Dean of Lichfield, preb. of York. Brother of Alexander. (*D.N.B.*)

Richard Rogers (1533–97). B.A. of Oxford. M.A. from Christ's. (Frankfurt.) B.D. from Christ's, 1562. Bishop suffragan of Dover, 1568–97. Dean of Canterbury 1584–97. (*D.N.B.*)

Thomas Watts. Matric. 1549. B.A. 1553. (Frankfurt.) Ordained, 1560. Archdeacon of Middlesex and chaplain to Grindal. Preb. of St Paul's and canon of Westminster from 1560. Died, 1577.

CLARE

Thomas Jeffreys. See under Christ's.

CORPUS

Edmund Allen. B.A. 1535. Ordained, 1536. Fellow, 1536. Chaplain to Princess Elizabeth (1549). One of the translators (1540's) of Erasmus's Paraphrases. Nominated Bishop of Rochester (1559), but died before consecration. (*D.N.B.*)

William Birch. Fellow, 1548–53. Matric. from St John's, 1544. Friend of Thomas Lever. Ordained, 1552. (Frankfurt.) Preb. of Durham, 1562–7; deprived. Died, 1575.

John Watson. Matric. 1550.

GONVILLE HALL

Edmund Chapman (1538–1602). Matric. 1554. (Aarau.) B.A. from Trinity, 1559. *Fellow of Trinity,* 1560. B.D. 1569. D.D. 1578. Canon of Norwich, 1569–76 (deprived). Preacher at Dedham, 1577. Dedham *classis.*

JESUS

John Bale (1495–1563). Educated first at the Carmelite house Norwich, then at Jesus. In Germany and Switzerland, 1540–7. Bishop of Ossory, 1552. (Emden, Wesel, Frankfurt, Basle.) Elizabethan canon of Canterbury. (*D.N.B.*)

John Hilles. Matric. 1549. (Frankfurt.) Ordained, 1561.

Thomas Walker. Matric. 1549. (Frankfurt.) Elizabethan parson at Ipswich.

KING'S

Nicholas Carvell (1528–66). Matric. 1545. Fellow, 1548–57. (Zürich, Frankfurt.) (*D.N.B.*)

JOHN CHEKE (1514–57.) Provost, 1548–53. Born in Cambridge. B.A. from St John's, 1530. *Fellow of St John's,* 1530. Regius Professor of Greek, 1540. Tutor to Prince Edward, 1544. Knighted, 1551. (Strasbourg, Basle, Padua, Emden.) (*D.N.B.*)

Robert Cole (1524–77). Matric. 1544. Fellow till 1551. Elizabethan rector in London.

Thomas Cole. M.A. 1550. Headmaster of Maidstone School, 1552. (Frankfurt, Strasbourg.) Elizabethan archdeacon of Essex. D.D. 1564. (*D.N.B.*)

Richard Cox (1500–81). Adm. 1519. B.A. 1524. Canon of Cardinal College, Oxford, 1525. Cambridge M.A. 1535. D.D. 1537. Headmaster of Eton, 1530–4. Archdeacon of Ely, 1541–53. Dean of Christ Church and Chancellor of Oxford, 1547. Canon of Windsor, 1547. Dean of Westminster, 1548. (Duisburg, Strasbourg, Frankfurt, Zürich, Worms.) Elizabethan bishop of Ely. (*D.N.B.*)

James Haddon. Adm. 1539. *Fellow of Trinity*, 1546–50. Dean of Exeter, 1553–4. (Strasbourg, Frankfurt.) Died of plague in 1556. (*D.N.B.*)

Thomas Horton (1520–64). Adm. 1537. Fellow, 1540–2. *Fellow of Pembroke*, 1548. Ordained deacon, 1550. (Frankfurt.) Ordained priest, 1560. Elizabethan preb. of Durham.

Richard Jugge (1514–77). Adm. 1531. (Emden.) Elizabethan Master and Warden of Stationers' Company; Queen's Printer. (*D.N.B.*)

William Masters (1532–90). Adm. 1549. B.A. 1554. M.A. 1557. Fellow, 1552–69. (Frankfurt.) Proctor and Public Orator in the 1560's. Vicar general of Norwich diocese.

William Temple. Adm. 1545. Fellow, 1548–57. (Basle.)

Francis Walsingham (1530–90). Fellow commoner, 1548–50. Gray's Inn, 1552. (Basle, Padua, and other universities.) Elizabethan Secretary of State. (*D.N.B.*)

Thomas Wilson (1525–81). Adm. 1541. Fellow, 1545–71. (Padua, Rome, Ferrara.) Elizabethan Secretary of State, Dean of Durham. Author, *The Art of Rhetoric*. (*D.N.B.*)

KING'S HALL

Francis Russell (1527–85). Second Earl of Bedford, 1555. Edwardian M.P. and Lord Lieutenant. (Padua, Venice, Rome, Naples, Ferrara, Zürich.) (*D.N.B.*)

MICHAELHOUSE

John Banks. Matric. 1544. *Fellow of Trinity*, 1551–4. (Strasbourg, Basle.)

John Jefferay. Matric. 1546. *Fellow of Trinity*, 1551–4. (Frankfurt, Strasbourg.) Sussex rector, 1566–1618.

Edmund Lawrence. Matric. 1544. (Basle.) Suspended, in Suffolk, 1579.

PEMBROKE

(William Amondesham.) (In Geneva and Basle, 1555–7. Fellow commoner, 1564.)

Anthony Denny. Fellow commoner, 1551. Son of Sir Anthony D., Henrician Privy Councillor. (Padua and Basle.) Middle Temple, 1557.

Edmund Grindal (1519–83). B.A. 1538. Fellow, 1538–53. Edwardian proctor. Edwardian precentor of St Paul's, chaplain to Ridley and Edward VI, and (1552) canon of Westminster. (Strasbourg, Frankfurt, Wasselheim, Speyer.) (*D.N.B.*)

Thomas Horton. See under King's.

Robert Hutton. Sizar of William Turner. Ordained, 1553. (Emden.) Died, 1568.

Anthony Mayhew. Matric. from Queens', 1544. Fellow of Pembroke, 1547. (Frankfurt, Basle). Died, 1559.

Thomas Sampson (1517–89). Fellow, 1548. Dean of Chichester, 1553. (Strasbourg, Zürich, Frankfurt, Geneva.) Elizabethan dean of Christ Church; deprived, 1565. (*D.N.B.*)

William Turner. B.A. and Fellow, 1530. Ordained, 1530. Edwardian and Elizabethan Dean of Wells. Physician and naturalist, etc. (Bonn, Strasbourg, Speyer, Worms, Frankfurt, Basle, Emden, etc.) Died, 1568. (*D.N.B.*)

PETERHOUSE

George Acworth. Matric. 1548. Fellow, 1552–62. (Louvain, Paris, Padua.) LL.D. 1561. Public orator, 1559. Chancellor and vicar general of Winchester diocese. Died, 1582. (*D.N.B.*)

Robert Beaumont. Bible clerk, 1542. From Westminster School. B.A. 1544. M.A. 1550. Fellow, 1550. Bursar, 1550–2. (Zürich, Geneva.) Lady Margaret Professor, minister at Little St Mary's, 1559. Archdeacon of Huntingdon, 1560. Master of Trinity, 1561. D.D. and canon of Ely, 1564. Twice Vice-Chancellor. Died, 1567. (*D.N.B.*)

Nicholas Horneby. B.A. 1529. Fellow, 1531–43. (Frankfurt.)

John Pedder (1520–71). B.A. 1539. Fellow, 1540–50; bursar, 1546–50. *Fellow of Trinity,* 1550–3. (Strasbourg, Frankfurt.) Elizabethan Dean of Worcester. (*D.N.B.*)

QUEENS'

John Aylmer (1521–94). B.A. 1541. M.A. 1545. Henrician preb. of Wells. Tutor to Lady Jane Grey. Edwardian archdeacon of Stow. (Strasbourg, Zürich, Basle.) Archdeacon of Lincoln, 1562–77. Bishop of London, 1577–94. (*D.N.B.*)

Anthony Mayhew. *See under* Pembroke.

William Morley. Matric. 1545. Fellow, 1548–50. (Padua, Geneva.)

John Pelham. Matric. 1549. (Padua, Geneva.) Knighted, 1573.

John Ponet (1514–56). B.A. 1533. Fellow, 1533. B.D. 1547. Edwardian Bishop of Rochester and Winchester. (Strasbourg.) Died of the plague. (*D.N.B.*)

ST CATHARINE'S

Edward Frencham. Matric. 1552. (Zürich.) Died, 1559.

EDWIN SANDYS (1519–88). Master, 1549–53. B.A. from St John's, 1539. D.D. 1549. Vice-Chancellor, 1552–3. (Augsburg, Strasbourg, Zürich, Frankfurt.) Bishop of Worcester (1559); London (1570). Archbishop of York, 1577–88. (*D.N.B.*)

James Taylor. Matric. 1544. Fellow, c. 1550. M.A. 1553.

ST JOHN'S

Richard Alvey. Scholar of Christ's. B.A. from St John's, 1529. Fellow, 1537. B.D. 1543. Edwardian canon of Westminster (restored, 1558). (Frankfurt.) Master of the Temple, 1560. (*D.N.B.*)

Thomas Becon (1511–67). B.A. 1531. Ordained, 1538. Edwardian chaplain to Cranmer; rector of St Stephen Walbrook. (Strasbourg, Frankfurt, Marburg.) Elizabethan canon of Canterbury. (*D.N.B.*)

John Cheke. *See under* King's.

Thomas Dannett. Matric. 1548. Cousin of William Cecil. Diplomat. (France.)

Christopher Hales. B.A. 1539. Fellow, 1539. (Frankfurt.)

Robert Horne (1519–80). B.A. 1537. Fellow, 1536. Hebrew Lecturer and B.D. 1546. Edwardian chaplain to the King; and dean of Durham. (Strasbourg, Zürich, Frankfurt, Basle, Geneva.) 1559, restored to Durham. Bishop of Winchester, 1561–80. (*D.N.B.*)

William Ireland. Matric. 1544. Former Benedictine. Fellow, 1547. (Frankfurt.) Elizabethan rector in Essex and Herts. Died, 1571.

William Jackson. B.A. 1531. Fellow, 1532. (Geneva.)

Roger Kelke (1524–76). B.A. 1544. Fellow, 1545. (Zürich, Basle.) Elizabethan Master of Magdalene. (*D.N.B.*)

Thomas Lakin. Matric. 1544. Fellow, 1548. (Strasbourg.) Elizabethan preb. of Southwell and York. Died, 1574.

John Lever. B.A. 1550. M.A. 1553. Sixth son of John L. of Little Lever, Lancs. (Frankfurt, Aarau, etc.) Elizabethan master of Tonbridge School. Died, 1574.

Ralph Lever. B.A. 1548. M.A. 1551. Fellow, 1549. Fifth son of John L. (Zürich, etc.) Elizabethan preb. of Durham and chaplain to Bishop Pilkington. Master of Sherborne Hospital, 1577–85. Died, 1585. (*D.N.B.*)

THOMAS LEVER (1521–77). Master, 1550–3. B.A. 1542. Fellow, 1543. Ordained, 1550. Second son of John L. (Strasbourg, Zürich, Geneva, Frankfurt, Wesel, Aarau.) Elizabethan archdeacon of Coventry (1560–77). Master of Sherborne Hospital, 1564. Preb. of Durham, 1564–7; deprived. (*D.N.B.*)

Richard Luddington. Matric. 1544. (Frankfurt.)

John Orphinstrange. Matric. 1544. *Fellow of Trinity,* 1546–55. (Padua.) Lawyer.

James Pilkington (1520–76). B.A. 1539. Fellow, 1539. B.D. 1551. Third son of Richard P. of Rivington, Lancs. (Zürich, Geneva, Basle, Frankfurt.) First Elizabethan Master and Regius Professor of Divinity. Bishop of Durham, 1561–76. (*D.N.B.*)

Leonard Pilkington (1527–99). Brother of James. Matric. 1544. Fellow, 1545. (Frankfurt.) Elizabethan Master and Regius Professor of Divinity. Canon of Durham, 1567–99. (*D.N.B.*)

Edwin Sandys. *See under* St Catharine's.

Robert Swift (1534–99). Matric. 1549. Fellow, 1553. (Louvain.) Elizabethan Chancellor of Durham. (*D.N.B.*)

Percival Wiborne (1534–1606). Matric. 1546. Fellow, 1552. (Geneva.) Returned to St John's, 1559. Ordained, 1560. Canon of Westminster, 1560–1606, and preb. of Rochester; often cited for nonconformity. (*D.N.B.*)

Thomas Wilson. Matric. 1544. Fellow, 1548–53. (Frankfurt.) Returned to St John's, 1559. Canon of Worcester, 1560–71; dean, 1571–86. Died, 1586.

TRINITY

Thomas Acworth. Matric. 1551. B.A. 1554. Younger brother of George A. (Frankfurt.)
John Banks. Fellow, 1551-4. *See under* Michaelhouse.
Matthew Carew. Matric. 1548. Fellow, 1551-3. From Westminster School. (Padua.) Died, 1618.
Roger Carew. Fellow, 1546-50. Brother of Matthew. (Padua.) M.P. for St Albans, 1563-7.
Henry Cockcroft. Fellow, 1547-54. *See under* Christ's.
Thomas Donnell. Fellow, 1546-53. *See under* Christ's.
James Haddon. Fellow, 1546-50. *See under* King's.
John Jefferay. Fellow, 1551-4. *See under* Michaelhouse.
John Orphinstrange. Fellow, 1546-55. *See under* St John's.
John Pedder. Fellow, 1550-3. *See under* Peterhouse.

TRINITY HALL

Christopher Southhouse. Matric. 1552. (Frankfurt, Basle.) Elizabethan preb. of Lincoln.

CAMBRIDGE RELIGIOUS HOUSES

John Scory. Dominican, *c.* 1530. Edwardian Bishop of Rochester and Chichester. (Emden, Wesel, Geneva.) Bishop of Hereford, 1559-85. (*D.N.B.*)
Bartholomew Traheron (1510-58). Franciscan. B.D. 1533. (*D.N.B.*)

OTHERS

Thomas Cottesford. Studied at Cambridge. Edwardian preb. of York. (Frankfurt.) Died, 1555. (*D.N.B.*)
Edmund Cranmer. B.A. 1514. M.A. 1520. Brother of Thomas. Archdeacon of Canterbury, 1535. Died, 1557.
Thomas Gibson. Studied at Cambridge. Physician. (Strasbourg.) Died, 1562. (*D.N.B.*)
Geoffrey Jones. B.C.L. 1537. London rector. (Emden.)
Thomas Mountain. Graduated from Cambridge. Rector of Milton, Kent, 1545-53. Tried for treason at Cambridge, 1554; complicity in Northumberland plot. (Duisburg.) (*D.N.B.*)
John Old. Probably educated at Cambridge. Edwardian canon of Lichfield. (Frankfurt.) Died, 1557. (*D.N.B.*)

William Pickering (1517–75). Cambridge pupil of John Cheke. Diplomat. (Paris, Italy.) (*D.N.B.*)

Michael Reniger (1530–1609). B.A. of Cambridge. Fellow of Magdalen, Oxford, 1546–53. (Zürich, Strasbourg.) Archdeacon of Winchester, 1575–1609. (*D.N.B.*)

Thomas Steward. M.A. 1514. (Frankfurt, Strasbourg, Geneva, Basle.)

Robert Wisdom. Cambridge B.D. (Frankfurt, Strasbourg.) 1560–8, archdeacon of Ely. Died, 1568. (*D.N.B.*)

PART II

THE PURITANS AND AUTHORITY

CHAPTER V

THE TRIBULATIONS OF AUTHORITY:
1559-1565

I

CARDINAL POLE, Chancellor of the University, died within a
few hours of Queen Mary, on 17 November 1558. Elizabeth was
proclaimed Queen on the same day; and on 20 November she
held her first council meeting at Hatfield.[1] On 21 November, by
a letter dated at Hatfield, Philip Baker was nominated Provost of
King's, in succession to Robert Brassie, who had died in the last
days of the previous reign. Baker was admitted on 12 December,
and was thus the first of the Elizabethan heads.

In the December of 1558 there were two further changes in the
Cambridge masterships. John Christopherson, Master of Trinity
and Bishop of Chichester, who had been imprisoned at the end of
November, died. Dr William Bill, physician to Henry VIII and
Edward VI, who had been elected Master of Trinity in 1551 only
to be forcibly ejected by some of his own Fellows in 1553, was
restored to the mastership. Secondly, Edmund Cosin, who had
succeeded Sandys as Master of St Catharine's in 1553, resigned
both the mastership and the office of Vice-Chancellor; to be
replaced as Vice-Chancellor by John Pory (Master of Corpus
since December 1557) and as Master by John May (who during
the reign of Mary had been bursar of Queens'). Cosin continued
to live in Cambridge, and in 1561 his friend John Caius gave him
rooms in Caius College.[2]

Caius had refounded Gonville Hall in September 1557. In
January 1559, the month in which the Act of Supremacy was

[1] Conyers Read, *Mr Secretary Cecil and Queen Elizabeth*, 119.
[2] W. H. S. Jones, *A History of St Catharine's College*, 180.

passed, he was persuaded to accept the mastership, in place of the amiable but useless Thomas Bacon. Caius (who was to be physician to Elizabeth as he had been to Mary) continued as Master until 1573: but he never took any stipend for the office. In January also, Thomas Redman was elected Master of Jesus, the Marian Master, John Fuller, having died in December.

In February 1559 the Vice-Chancellor and the Senate formally invited William Cecil to accept the chancellorship of the university.[1] Cecil was officially installed as Chancellor on the 21st.[2] In March there came the first dispute of his reign: a quarrel between some of the Fellows of Queens' and Thomas Peacock, who had been admitted President in the autumn of 1557. Cecil, being unable to visit Cambridge, referred the matter to the Vice-Chancellor. Fortunately, at the beginning of May Peacock resigned—with a handsome gift from the Fellows as a token of good will.[3] There was restored as President of Queens' William May, the brother of John, who had been President from 1537 to 1553. Peacock continued to live privately in Cambridge. William May was beginning most gratifyingly to pick up the threads of his own past career; a month after he returned to Queens' he was reinstated as Dean of St Paul's; and in August 1560 he was elected Archbishop of York—only to die on the very day of the election. At Trinity Hall, William Mowse had, like Peacock, resigned his mastership by May 1559. He was replaced by the ecclesiastical lawyer Henry Harvey.[4] The Master of Christ's was William Taylor, chosen by Cuthbert Scot as his successor in December 1556. In March 1559 Cecil wrote to Taylor warning him that his position was under consideration.[5] For three months Taylor defiantly lingered on in Cambridge. Then, at the end of June, he fled. Pory described the scene to Cecil in a letter on 27 June: the

[1] S(tate) P(apers) Dom(estic) Eliz(abeth), vol. II, no. 21 (Public Record Office).
[2] University Audit Book, 1545–1659, p. 140 (University Archives).
[3] W. G. Searle, *History of Queens' College: 1446–1560*, 266. J. H. Gray, *The Queens' College*, 102. [4] H. E. Malden, *Trinity Hall*, 99–100.
[5] Corpus Christi College, Cambridge, MSS. vol. 118, p. 407.

disordered rooms, the clothes strewn over the floor, the rushes all untidy, and the college papers scattered.[1] In accordance with Pory's recommendation, Cecil immediately wrote to the Fellows of Christ's advising them to elect Edward Hawford, one of their number, to succeed Taylor.[2] This they did; and Hawford was admitted as Master on 23 July.[3]

Matthew Parker had returned to his beloved university at the end of 1558. For in spite of his concern at the miserable state of Cambridge at that time, it was still to him the town where 'of all places in England I would wish to bestow most time'. 'I had rather have such a thing as Bene't College', he wrote to Nicholas Bacon, 'than to dwell in the Deanery of Lincoln'.[4] Parker wrote to Cecil, a week after his installation as Chancellor, about the disordered state of some of the colleges, and the uneasy feeling concerning the anticipated changes.[5] Elizabeth had been Queen for over three months; there had been rumours in Cambridge of a general Visitation; followed by rumours that no such visitation was intended. Everyone was waiting to see which way the ball would bounce. The result was that this period appears as a sort of no-man's-land between two regimes. After the Act of Supremacy in January some heads of houses had seen that their time was up, for they knew they would be unable to take the oath. Yet they were still in residence at the end of February, 'about to resign to their friends chosen for their purpose, peradventure to slide away with a gain'. Parker reminded Cecil that Mary, with Gardiner as Chancellor, had in the first year of her reign looked very diligently to the state of the university, requiring a full report on the condition of every college. That was a wise precedent; and Parker sent copies of the Marian letters to the new Chancellor, being loath that 'in the first entry of your office colleges should sustain hurt

---

[1] S.P. Dom. Eliz. vol. IV, no. 66.   [2] *Ibid.* no. 67.
[3] J. Peile, *Biographical Register of Christ's College*, I, 28. The document of Hawford's presentation as Master is in the Cambridge University Archives: Registry Guard Books, vol. 92 (i), no. 6.
[4] Matthew Parker, *Correspondence*, 51.   [5] S.P. Dom. Eliz. vol. III, no. 3.

by any sleight, you not understanding the likelihood'. 'God grant', concluded Parker in this letter of 1 March 1559, 'so good luck of your election that the university may joy to be raised and restored.'

In a letter to Pory on 29 May,[1] acting under the instructions of a royal letter dated 27 May, Cecil (who had then been Chancellor for fourteen weeks) gave notice of an intended Visitation of the university. The commission was issued and the Visitors named on 20 June. The Visitors were Cecil himself, Parker, William Bill, Walter Haddon (sometime Master of Trinity Hall and Regius Professor of Civil Law), William May, Thomas Wendy (Fellow of the College of Physicians), Robert Horne (Dean of Durham), James Pilkington, and one non-Cambridge man, the Marian exile Sir Anthony Cooke. Of the nine Visitors, at least three must be present to visit the university and each and every college in head and members; to search out accused men and wrongdoers, the stupid and the idle, the guilty men, and 'those who obstinately and peremptorily refuse to subscribe to the newly resumed reformed religion'. They were to expel and remove those Masters, Heads, Presidents,, Fellows, lecturers and scholars unworthy of their position, not beneficial to their colleges, or to the commonwealth or to good letters; and those Masters and Fellows unjustly deprived for religion or any other cause were to be reinstated.[2] The Visitation took place in July 1559,[3] two and a half years, that is, after the Marian Visitation of the university. And, though thorough, compared with that last Visitation it was undramatic.

In only four of the fourteen colleges were any changes of Master made during or soon after July 1559. John Pory of Corpus and Andrew Perne of Peterhouse, both Marian Masters, continued in their offices without a break. And in the eight uneasy

---

[1] S.P. Dom. Eliz. vol. IV, no. 33.

[2] J. Lamb (ed.), Original Documents from the Library of Corpus Christi College, Cambridge, 276–7.

[3] The visitors were probably in Cambridge from the 7th (S.P. Dom. Eliz. vol. IV, no. 59) to the 23rd (S.P. Dom. Eliz. vol. V, no. 21).

Elizabethan months before the Visitors came to Cambridge, Baker of King's, Bill of Trinity and Redman of Jesus had become Heads because of the timely death of their predecessors; Hawford of Christ's because of the flight of his; and John May of St Catharine's, William May of Queens', Harvey of Trinity Hall, and John Caius, because of the resignation of theirs. That accounts for ten colleges. Now, direct changes of head were effected by the Visitors in only two colleges. On 20 July Edmund Grindal was admitted Master of Pembroke in succession to John Young, the Marian Regius Professor of Divinity, and James Pilkington was admitted Master of St John's, succeeding George Bullock, the Marian Lady Margaret Professor. These proceedings were conducted with a courtesy which was more than nominal. According to Thomas Baker, Bullock and the ejected Fellows of St John's in 1559 'were civilly entertained by the college, a respect that had not been shown by these men, when it was in their power to show such favours as they now had occasion for'.[1] And when the Fellows of Pembroke wrote to Grindal to offer him the mastership, they went out of their way to speak in high terms of Young.[2] A week after his admission at Pembroke Grindal was elected Bishop of London; he resigned the mastership in May 1562, having rarely resided. Bullock, who was succeeded as Lady Margaret Professor by Robert Beaumont, Fellow of Trinity, went abroad, and died in Antwerp in 1580. Young also died in 1580—after twenty years' imprisonment in England, first in the Fleet, then at Wisbech. Two colleges remain unconsidered. Richard Carr of Magdalene, who had been one of the three Edwardian Masters to carry on into the reign of Mary, lingered until November, when he was replaced by Roger Kelke. And Thomas Bailey, who had been elected Master of Clare in 1557, remained at the college until the summer of 1560,[3] when he went abroad, to Louvain and then to Douai, where he became a right-hand man of William Allen. Earlier in

[1] T. Baker, *History of St John's College*, I, 144.   [2] A. Attwater, *Pembroke College*, 42.
[3] Bailey was still Master in May 1560. J. R. Wardale, *Clare College*, 50.

1560—in February—the unsatisfactory Thomas Redman of Jesus, who had been Master for over a year but had never resided, was succeeded by Edward Gascoyne.

By the summer of 1560, then, there were eight men alive who had been Masters of Cambridge colleges under Mary and who were merely private citizens under Elizabeth: Bailey, Carr, Taylor, Mowse, Peacock, Bullock, Cosin, and Young. But only two, Bullock and Young, had been 'deprived'. There were, certainly, eleven 'Elizabethan' Masters. Three of them had been Marian exiles: Kelke, Pilkington, and Grindal. (Robert Beaumont was to become Master of Trinity on the death of Bill in July 1561.) But most of the other heads of houses could hardly satisfy the deeper requirements of the pure and reformed brethren. Baker and Caius were both to run into trouble for 'popery'; Harvey and Gascoyne had been Marian ecclesiastical administrators; John May and Hawford had been resident dons under Mary, taking the oaths and subscribing to the articles; Pory and Perne had been Marian Masters, and Perne Vice-Chancellor. The winds which blew from Geneva had hardly extensively purified the Masters' Lodges of Cambridge.

Of the changes on the Fellows' Tables, it is impossible to be at all certain. The only thing which can be said is that there was nothing like the spasm of expulsions and resignations occasioned by the death of Edward VI and the proclamation of Mary. At Corpus, for instance, at the beginning of Mary's reign, Matthew Parker and two of the eight Fellows had departed, and had been immediately replaced. The two new Marian Fellows—Richard Kitchen and William Birch—were certainly no longer in the college by 1564; but they were not expelled, and there was only one new Fellow of Corpus elected at the beginning of Elizabeth's reign. At Christ's there were no fellowship elections during 1559; however, 'owing to the rapid succession of Fellows about this time',[1] three dons elected in the last months of Mary's reign were

---

[1] Peile, *Biographical Register*, I, 51.

the senior Fellows by 1564. The rapid succession had been due to uncertainty and doubt, perhaps, but not to expulsion. No Fellows left Trinity in 1559: five did so in 1560, three of them being Marian admissions. The exports, so to say, were few; but the imports were large—no new Fellows were elected at Trinity in 1559, but nearly twenty in 1560. At St John's, about twenty Fellows had left the college at the beginning of Mary's reign— there were twenty-one new admissions in 1554. In all, fifty men were admitted Fellows of St John's during that reign: only six of them were still Fellows in 1564. Yet after the Visitation of July 1559 there were only three new Fellows admitted: Richard Longworth, Richard Sherman, and Thomas Locke. There were fifteen admissions in April 1560 (including Thomas Cartwright); and thirteen in 1561. Such statistics are merely negative, uncertain hints and pointers. But one thing they do show. There was no suggestion of a 'clean sweep' about the Visitation of 1559.

II

In one way, however, the first decade of the reign of Elizabeth did mark a 'new beginning', or at the least a reawakening, in the university. At Trinity, as we have seen, twenty new Fellows were admitted in 1560.[1] By 1564 there were forty-seven Fellows in the college; by 1573, sixty. Thus, for the first time for twenty years, it had become possible for the college to fill the available statutory fellowships. At St John's there were forty-three Fellows in 1564 and fifty-one in 1573; at Pembroke seventeen in 1564 and thirty in 1573. A similar increase can be traced in most colleges: at Clare the figures for the two years were eight and twelve; at Christ's eleven and thirteen; at Queens' fifteen and nineteen; at Peterhouse ten and fifteen; at Caius eight and ten. In some colleges, new fellowships were founded: Parker endowed four at Corpus in

[1] H. M. Innes, *Fellows of Trinity College*, 20.

1569. In all, between 1564 and 1573 there was an increase of about one-third in the numbers of Cambridge dons.[1]

Now, most of these dons were 'new men', men, that is, who had come up to Cambridge during the reign of Elizabeth. A man who came up to the university in 1559 would commence bachelor in 1563; and it is interesting to note that at St John's there were sixteen Fellows admitted in 1563, as against five in 1562 and three in 1564. There can never have been a period in the history of Cambridge in which there were so many young dons. A study of the lists of Fellows drawn up for the royal visit of 1564 shows this clearly. Of the eleven Fellows of Christ's seven had commenced bachelor since the accession of Elizabeth; and the three senior Fellows had been elected in the spring and summer of 1558. Six of the eight Fellows of Corpus had been elected in the new reign, and three had matriculated in it. Only two of the forty-three Fellows of St John's had been elected before 1558; seventeen of them had matriculated in 1559 or later. Of the forty-three, less than ten could have been more than twenty-five years old in 1564: Richard Curteys, the President and senior Fellow, was about thirty. At Trinity, under Beaumont, there were seventeen minor Fellows, all elected after 1562, and twenty-nine major Fellows, only four of whom had been elected before 1560.

Thus the 1560's might well be called the Decade of the Regents: a regent being a master of arts of up to three years' standing, who by the Elizabethan Statutes of 1559 was given considerable authority in the university. The unprecedented increase in the number of such young masters of arts in the 1560's (the younger sort of regent, complained the heads in 1571, 'doth daily increase more and more')[2] led to a lack of balance in the whole structure of power in the university. Especially as the regents—so the authorities also argued—had become 'not only younger in age,

[1] The figures in this section for 1564 are from the University Library, Cambridge, Baker MSS. vol. 'B', pp. 103–25. Those for 1573 are from John Caius's *Historiae Cantabrigiensis Academiae* (1574): in the edition of his *Works* by J. Venn and E. S. Roberts.
[2] Corpus Christi College, Cambridge, MSS. vol. 118, no. 44.

but more youthful and intractable at this day, than they were wont to be in times past'.[1] It was such inordinate exercise of their statutory powers by the young dons of the 1560's which led Whitgift to draw up in 1570 new university statutes in which their powers were considerably curtailed.

III

During the early 1560's there were, of course, changes within the college chapels. In Mary's reign the Edwardian 'reforms' had been, so far as possible, reversed. For example, the Crucifix and figures had been restored to the rood loft in Great St Mary's;[2] three altars were placed back in position at Queens';[3] and at St John's, under Bullock, a joiner was paid 2d. for 'setting up the rood' and a carpenter and his three assistants 4s. 1d. for restoring the altars, for one of which 'a table of the passion of Christ' was bought for £1. 13s. 4d.[4] At the beginning of the new reign the carpenters and joiners received further commissions. In 1562 the rood loft of Great St Mary's was again denuded, and partially dismantled, though the screen remained.[5] The loft was finally pulled down in 1569. At Jesus seven shillings were paid for a wooden communion table; and in 1562 a table of the Ten Commandments, costing 2d., was pasted up in the Chapel;[6] five years later the college bought the 'Genevan psalms in metre'.[7] The high altar at Queens' had been removed again in June 1559. The college accounts of St John's for 1559 are very full.[8] They record the purchase of two communion books and twelve English psalters from Baxter the stationer, also 'xii papers containing the Lord's Prayer'. (In 1563 Baxter was also to provide ten Genevan

[1] *Ibid.* no. 46.
[2] W. D. Bushell, *The Church of St Mary the Great*, 54.
[3] R. Willis and J. W. Clark, *Architectural History of the University of Cambridge*, II, 38.
[4] *Ibid.* 292.   [5] Bushell, *op. cit.* 54.
[6] Willis and Clark, *Architectural History*, II, 142.
[7] A. Gray, *Jesus College*, 74.
[8] Willis and Clark, *Architectural History*, II, 292–3.

psalters and the Ten Commandments in English.) John Waller and his apprentice had a heavy day's work at St John's 'pulling down the High Altar and carrying it away'; for which they were paid 1s. 8d.—with an extra 4d. to 'a poor fellow which helped to carry away the stone of the altar'. At the same time a glazier was busy setting up panes of plain glass in the chapel windows. In 1561 Waller worked for nine days 'whitening the Chapel', and 'plastering it in many places'. In 1560 the altar in John Fisher's chantry chapel was taken away; and the room over the little chapel was 'turned into a chamber for the advantage of the Master'.[1] That was one way of respecting the great Chancellor and benefactor. Another was to be demonstrated at Christ's, where in 1570 the vestments, copes and altar cloths, some of them bequeathed to the college by the Lady Margaret, were sold for £15;[2] though it is only fair to add that the prudent Hawford had hidden away many of the college treasures.[3]

Only one chapel escaped changes—because it was largely Elizabethan. Building had begun on the chapel of Trinity ten years after the foundation, in 1556. In that year three thousand loads of material were carried across from the old Grey Friars' site, at a charge of 3d. per load.[4] Stone was also to be brought from Ramsey Abbey, Huntingdonshire, where the bursar of the college supervised the destruction of the buildings.[5] The stonework was finished in 1565; and in that year the windows were glazed, mostly with plain glass or heraldic devices.[6] But in 1566 there was a sinister charge of 16d. in the college accounts for 'repairing of the places which were broken forth in all the windows wherein did appear superstition'.[7]

[1] C. C. Babington, *The Infirmary and Chapel of St John's*, 11.
[2] Willis and Clark, *Architectural History*, II, 207.
[3] J. Peile, *Christ's College*, 71.
[4] Willis and Clark, *op. cit*, II, 562.
[5] *Ibid.* 567. cf. *V.C.H. Hunts*, II, 192.   [7] *Ibid.*
[6] Willis and Clark, *op. cit*, II, 572.

IV

In September 1561, when Henry Harvey was Vice-Chancellor, Robert Beaumont wrote to the Chancellor deploring the lack of discipline in Cambridge. A stricter hand was needed: 'then should licentious youth be kept in awe, learning flourish, and pure religion take better root, to the confusion of our epicures and careless worldlings'.[1] Beaumont went on to recommend a few discreet changes in the masterships. If only William Day, Fellow of Eton, could replace Baker at King's; or if Francis Newton, Fellow of Trinity, might succeed Gascoyne at Jesus. Pembroke, nominally governed by Grindal, needed an effective resident Master: such as John Robinson, Fellow of the college, or Matthew Hutton, Fellow of Trinity. At St John's, James Pilkington had been for six months combining the office of Master with that of Bishop of Durham; why could not Leonard Pilkington take over the mastership? A month after Beaumont's letter, Leonard Pilkington was in fact admitted Master of St John's. Hutton, having replaced Beaumont as Lady Margaret Professor in December 1561, succeeded Grindal as Master of Pembroke in May 1562; by which time William Day had become Provost of Eton. John Robinson was to be President of St John's, Oxford, in 1564, and Francis Newton Dean of Winchester in 1565. It is worthy of note that, apart from Pilkington, all these men recommended by Beaumont had remained in Cambridge during the reign of Mary. Day had been a proctor.

Cecil, no less than Beaumont, was worried about the state of affairs in Cambridge. So much so that in June 1562 he wrote to the Vice-Chancellor announcing his wish to resign.[2] 'I am troubled to hear', he wrote,

how in that university a great part of the colleges be now of late become full of factions and contentions, and are like to increase: the

[1] S.P. Dom. Eliz. vol. XIX, no. 54.
[2] University Library, Cambridge, Baumgartner Papers, vol. X, no. 14 (i).

redress whereof cannot come from me, as it ought to do from a Chancellor, because I have neither skill to judge of the controversies, being risen upon questions of laws and private statutes, nor can come thither to subdue the same with my presence.

To the end of his days Cecil never lost the uneasiness (part shyness, part irritation) of a man of worldly affairs in the presence of scholars: 'I am not meet for the office, having no learning to judge of men learned.' Also, he had other things to do: 'I have no leisure to hear the causes, and less leisure to promote them, and consequently no opportunity to end them.' He ended this letter of June 1562 with a sharp paragraph about the Masters of Colleges:

I cannot find such care in the Heads of Houses there, to supply my lack, as I hoped for, to the ruling of inordinate youth, to the observation of good order, and increase of learning and knowledge of God. For I see the wiser sort that have authority will not join earnestly together, to over-rule the licentious parts of youth in breaking of orders, and the stubbornness of others, that malign and deprave the ecclesiastical orders established by law in this realm.

The heads hastened to persuade Cecil to remain in office. Perhaps they were not very surprised when they succeeded. They took the Chancellor's admonitions a little to heart, and began to try to see the Cambridge contentions in some perspective. They did not have to look far: at the bottom of most of the troubles were the 'untamed affections' of the regents. In January 1564 a letter was sent to the Chancellor from Cambridge suggesting that the powers of the regents, as detailed in the 1559 statutes, should be pruned.[1] This letter was the first step towards the new statutes of 1570; among those who signed it was the Lady Margaret Professor of Divinity, a Fellow of Peterhouse named John Whitgift.

Cecil, created Lord Burleigh in 1571, continued as Chancellor until his death in 1598: a reign of forty years, a fitting counterpart

[1] Lansdowne MSS. vol. VII, no. 70 (British Museum).

to those thirty-five years at the beginning of the century when Cambridge had enjoyed the protection of Fisher. Any study of Elizabethan Cambridge must bear witness to his moderate, wise and unselfish guidance: he is so often the hero of the story. Cecil, like Parker, loved his university and his college above most things of this world:

whereof although I was once but a simple, small, unlearned and low member, yet have I as great plenty of natural humour of love towards the same, as any other, that hath by Degrees been rewarded, to be in the highest place of that body.[1]

The point there is that Cecil left St John's in 1541, at the age of twenty-one, without taking a degree. In May he was entered at Gray's Inn, and in August he married Maria, the sister of John Cheke, whom he had met at the house of Cheke's parents in the parish of Great St Mary's. A son was born to the couple nine months after marriage: a year later Maria was dead and buried. This was the end of Cecil's youth, and, so far as history is concerned, the end of his private life.[2] In 1550 he became principal secretary to Edward VI and began the most brilliant public career of Tudor England. But at Cambridge he had made his friends—Cheke, Ascham, Thomas Smith—and courted his wife: it had, at the least, a double claim upon his affections. And in spite of the triviality, the pettiness, the pedantry, and the lack of consideration, Cambridge to Cecil was never to lose its spell.

In 1564, the year in which Calvin died at Geneva, the university enjoyed its greatest social event of the century: the visit of the Queen in August. As Cecil signalled to the trumpeters to play out, and Elizabeth rode slowly from Queens' to the west door of the chapel of King's, down the street where 'stood, upon both sides, one by one, all the university',[3] Cecil could surely rejoice in his authority as Chancellor and hope that the next years might see peace in Cambridge.

[1] Baumgartner Papers, vol. x, no. 14 (i).   [2] He married again in December 1545.
[3] C. H. Cooper, *Annals of Cambridge*, II, 186.

V

But hopes of peace were to be disappointed. In January 1565, soon after Robert Beaumont became Vice-Chancellor, a fellow commoner of Corpus called George Withers, inspired by the official removal of some of the stained glass in the windows of the Schools, preached a notorious sermon calling for the destruction of all the 'superstitious' painted glass in the university. In March Parker wrote to Cecil about this 'racket stirred up by Withers' for 'the reformation of university windows';[1] and the young man, bouncing with over-confidence, was called up to Lambeth.[2] But there was more at stake than stained glass. In January also the Queen had written to Parker demanding a 'uniformity of order' in every church 'according to the order and appointment of such laws and ordinances as are provided by Act of Parliament': this was to apply 'as well in both our universities as in any other place'.[3] In February Beaumont wrote to the Archbishop to give details of the situation in Cambridge:

upon the receipt of your letters containing the Queen's Majesty's pleasure for uniformity in doctrine, rites and apparel, I called all the Heads of colleges together, upon consultation with whom, after diligent and reverent perusing of the said letters, it was thought good that every Master should upon diligent enquiry made within his own college advertise me within eight days so that I might safely and truly write unto your grace accordingly. Now many of them have written, some by mouth advertised, and some sent me word, that all things touching the said three points are in good order; save that one in Christ's College, and sundry in St John's, will be very hardly brought to wear surplices. And two or three in Trinity College think it very unseeming that Christians should play or be present at any profane comedies or tragedies. But touching the substance of religion generally agreed upon, I know none that impugneth any part thereof, unless it be two or three suspected papists which yet lurk in one or two colleges,

---

[1] Lansdowne MSS. vol. VIII, no. 2.   [2] *Ibid.* no. 4.
[3] Parker, *Correspondence*, 226.

and shall I trust be revealed ere it be long. I do for the maintenance of orderly apparel what I can: but God knoweth I obtain of some more for fear of punishment than for love of good order.[1]

Beaumont was in fact nervously over-optimistic. Two days before, a young Fellow of St John's called William Fulke had preached in Great St Mary's. His sermon had caused a sensation, and Beaumont had ordered him to write a précis of it, to be sent to the Chancellor for his verdict. In this sermon Fulke had inveighed against 'popish trumpery': 'dehorting all men from the use of the same when as in no good sense they might be used among Christian men, and that the users thereof were reprobates and damned'.[2] This was the cloud no bigger than a man's hand.

Like Thomas Lever (who was to be deprived of his canonry at Durham by Bishop Pilkington in 1567) Fulke believed that the surplice and the cap 'serve not to edification, decency or order, but to offence, dissension and division in the Church of Christ, and as garments or rites belonging to the popish priesthood in the Church of Antichrist'.[3] Lever's fellow-exile Anthony Gilbey, incumbent of Ashby-de-la-Zouch in Leicestershire, made the same point, denying that 'a true minister of Christ ought to use and allow all those dregs of popery that yet do remain in our church, but that he must labour diligently by doctrine and example to root forth such manifest superstitions and corruptions of religion'.[4] And in October 1565 a complaint was sent to Gilbey from Cambridge about the conduct of Robert Beaumont as Vice-Chancellor.

Beaumont explicitly denied that an exile must of necessity be an extremist:

I say, that as I never judged, either at Geneva or elsewhere, anything in the last Book in King Edward's time appointed to be superstitious

---

[1] Corpus Christi College, Cambridge, MSS. vol. 106, p. 627.
[2] S.P. Dom. Eliz. vol. xxxviii, no. 7.
[3] Lever; in A. Peel, *The Second Part of a Register*, I, 54–5.
[4] Gilbey to Cartwright; *ibid.* I, 139.

and wicked, even so do I think, that a surplice prescribed by the same Book (all opinion of holiness, necessity, and worship set apart) may be worn without turning back to superstition.[1]

It must be worn, in fact, because it was ordered by the Supreme Governor; and Beaumont, as local agent of the Supreme Governor, could not evade his duty of seeing that others wore it too.

I wear the cap and surplice, the which if I refused to do, I could not be suffered to preach. I wish with many more godly brethren, that they may speedily be taken away: the which should shortly be brought to pass, if I were the public person for such matters lawfully authorised. But now my hands are tied.[2]

To some of the brethren at Cambridge it seemed that Beaumont's position as Master of Trinity and Vice-Chancellor (not to speak of his ministry at Little St Mary's) did in fact make him a public person lawfully authorized—authorized, in their opinion, to ignore the patently unjust and damnable vestment regulations of the national Church and to reveal himself as a prophet of the reign in Cambridge of all purity and virtue. The complaint was sent to Gilbey by a young bachelor of arts of Trinity, Thomas Wood, who had gone up to the college as a sizar in 1561. Wood mentioned that the Chancellor had written to Beaumont earlier in 1565, which had made the Vice-Chancellor 'very earnest' about 'cap matters'—'to the great grief and misliking of the godly'. The consequent orders of the Vice-Chancellor, Wood lamented, 'hath been stomached even of the poor little boys'. The poor little boys, in retaliation, resorted to a rag. One day Beaumont 'rode with his foot-cloth' to Great St Mary's to preach; and 'while he was at his sermon, certain of the boys clipped off all the hair of his horse's tail and top, and made him a crown, like to a popish priest'.[3] The following Sunday the joke was carried further. Before Beaumont went in procession to church the young bloods 'cut all the hair of his horse, taken before, in short pieces;

[1] University Library, Cambridge, Baker MSS. vol. XXXII, p. 427.
[2] *Ibid.* pp. 429–30.   [3] *Ibid.* p. 430.

and strewed it in the way as he went (instead of a carpet) from his chamber to the Church'. This was regrettable: but whom was the Vice-Chancellor to satisfy—his Sovereign or his friends? He could in fact only make 'many protestations of his good will and meaning towards all, and that it was against his conscience to hurt any, save for his duty towards the magistrate'.[1]

Spurred by Wood's sad story, the vicar of Ashby-de-la-Zouch wrote a letter of rebuke to the Master of Trinity. Beaumont replied in January 1566. The charges brought against him were indeed grave:

The first report is, that I am turned back again to the toys of popery and puddles of superstition for the pleasure of man, cloaking my doing with the name of obedience. The second, that I am vain-glorious, setting up my bristles against God's faithful servants, in a cause which I myself would promote, if I durst for displeasure. The third, that I ride with my foot-cloth far from mine old manners, and the ancient custom of the university, but furthest from the example of Christ, his Apostles, Mr Calvin, etc. The fourth, that I am cold in God's business and hot in the urging of man's traditions.[2]

Of these charges, the third was the most trivial, and the most easily answered:

I ride still as homely as you do, or at least as homely, as you have seen me ride in Leicestershire in all points. For ever since that time, I had none but the same horse still, until his tail was cut, within the college walls, between twelve and three o'clock in the night. And presently I ride on one worse than he. I was brought up in my tender years with haverbread, thin drink, cold milk, hanged beef and bacon, etc. For three or four years in Cambridge I never spent above fourpence the week; and after was forced to leave the university and teach abroad, for want of necessaries.[3]

The other charges were countered by a catalogue of Beaumont's services to the Reformation in Cambridge:[4] he had rid Trinity

[1] Ibid. p. 431.   [2] Ibid. p. 427.
[3] Ibid. p. 428.   [4] Ibid. p. 429.

College of its copes 'and of other monuments of superstition'; he had purged the windows in the Schools of popish glass; he had engineered a university grace of September 1565 for the sale of the vestments, censers, cruets, candlesticks and altar cloths still remaining in the university vestry;[1] he had sold the university Cross, and divided the profits between the colleges.[2] Moreover, in November he had petitioned the Chancellor not to enforce the vestment regulations in Cambridge—though this petition was also signed by the Lady Margaret Professor, John Whitgift. Further, Beaumont claimed that he was over-charitable almost in his execution of the regulations: 'I deprive none, I punish none that refuse them. Nay, my purse, my pen, with all the counsel and means that I can use (see how foolishly I brag) doth and shall help them.'[3]

The bragging was a little uneasy; and perhaps the Master protested too much. 'Indeed I can hardly escape the execution of the decree made with the Queen's authority, when the time of deprivation cometh.' It was, all in all, an uneasy position. Gilbey was ten years older than Beaumont, certainly; but for a self-appointed *primus inter pares* he seems to have caused commendably agonizing heart-searching in the Vice-Chancellor of his Alma Mater.

[1] *Grace Book Δ* (1542–1589), 191. The inventory of university vestments and ornaments in 1562 is in the University Archives; box labelled 'Vice-Chancellor's Court: File of Exhibita: 1559–74'.
[2] H. P. Stokes, *The Chaplains and Chapel of the University* (Camb. Antiq. Soc. Pubn.), 37.
[3] University Library, Cambridge, Baker MSS., vol. XXXII, p. 428.

CHAPTER VI

TROUBLES AT ST JOHN'S: RICHARD LONGWORTH AND WILLIAM FULKE

I

THE disturbances at St John's inspired by William Fulke took place during the Michaelmas term of 1565. At that time the strength of the college was nearly 290: forty-seven Fellows and about 240 young men.[1] The Master, Richard Longworth, like Thomas Lever and the Pilkingtons, was a Bolton man, one of the long and distinguished succession of Tudor dons generally hymned by a Stuart poetaster:

> Lancashire gave him breath
> And Cambridge education.[2]

Longworth had entered the college at the age of sixteen in 1549, when William Bill was Master; during the reign of Mary he had been a Fellow of Queens'; and on 27 July 1559, after the Visitation, he became a Fellow of his old college. In May 1564 he was admitted Master, succeeding Leonard Pilkington. It was later claimed by his enemies within the college that the election had been unconstitutional—'he procured himself to be elected within one hour after the vacation'.[3] 'Procured' is the operative word, as it seems probable that his swift rise to power was due to a final flourish of string-pulling by Leonard Pilkington, the majority of the Fellows having at first wanted Roger Kelke.[4] The President of the college was a considerably more attractive figure than the Master. Richard Curteys had matriculated from St John's a year

---

[1] Figures given by Curteys in December 1565. S(tate) P(apers) Dom(estic) Eliz(abeth), vol. xxxviii, no. 16 (i), fol. 104-5 (Public Record Office).
[2] E. E. Kellett (ed.), *A Book of Cambridge Verse*, 35.
[3] S.P. Dom. Eliz. vol. xxxviii, fol. 63.   [4] J. Strype, *Life of Parker*, I, 391.

after Longworth, and had been admitted Fellow in March 1553, among the last group of dons elected under Lever. He had remained at the college during Mary's reign; and in 1565, at the age of about thirty, he was senior Fellow—the only one surviving from the reign of Edward VI. (He had scored a distinct success at the royal visit of 1564 with his unusually eloquent orations.)[1] In the present story Curteys appeared as the leader of the anti-Puritan party among the Fellows, the lieutenant of Cecil in the college. William Fulke himself was five years younger than the Master and three years younger than the President, being just twenty-seven. He was educated at St Paul's (where his school-mates included Edmund Campion), and he had come up to St John's at the age of seventeen in 1555. He left the university before commencing bachelor, however, and returned to London to study law at Clifford's Inn. In 1562 he came back to Cambridge 'where he not abiding orderly for to go forward in the degrees of schools procured forthwith by his friends to be made of a sophister a Master of Arts, never being Bachelor'.[2] In March 1564 Leonard Pilkington secured Fulke's election as Fellow of St John's, and his appointment as 'Preacher of the House, without further assent of the seniors or any probation of his worthiness beforehand, and also before he had any licence to preach'.[3] Fulke was a volatile and genuine scholar, with a sharp legal mind, a love of astronomy, mathematics and oriental languages, and a reputation as a musician and an amateur naturalist. He combined scholarship with verve and an eye for the main chance; and with a capacity for taking pains which, while it did not amount to genius, gave to his undoubted talents an air both of ability and brilliance.

From the moment when he was elected Fellow, Fulke left his square cap to gather dust, and wore a hat. He also made himself the natural leader of a group of Fellows—Geoffrey Johnson, Edward Buckley, John Dakins, Edward Hansbie, Oliver Carter,

[1] T. Baker, *History of St John's College*, I, 161.
[2] S.P. Dom. Eliz. vol. xxxvIII, no. 7, fol. 11.　　　　[3] *Ibid.*

John Linsey, Lawrence Riley—whom he persuaded 'to reject their caps, gowns and surplices'.[1] More important, he was the especial favourite of the new Master. The balance of power was made quite obvious to the college when, in the summer of 1564, Fulke appealed in a college sermon for 'the taking away of the stairs' at the east end of the chapel:[2] an operation which was performed the very next day.

Matters were brought to a head in a series of sermons—four in number—preached by Fulke in the college chapel in the summer and early autumn of 1565. One sermon was an attack on the use for the Communion of unleavened bread, which Fulke called 'starch and paste'; the second made mock of kneeling for the receiving of the Sacrament; the third was against the wearing of cope or surplice by the minister at the Communion; and the fourth 'against the use of surplices generally'.[3]

The effect was electric. After the first sermon Longworth 'commanded common bread to be brought in for the communion then in hand'. The second had the immediate result that all the company save a few received the Communion 'some standing, some sitting in their stalls': 'The Minister going all along in his gown scantly with such reverence as holy bread was dealt in popish time, to the great offence of many there present, and withdrawing of them from communicating at the same time.' After the third sermon it became for a little time the custom of the college that either the priest or his server should have no surplice: but eventually 'they waxed so hot' that the surplice was completely abandoned by both. Moreover, Fulke's mentioning of copes reminded some of the Fellows that the college had a fine collection stored away. Indeed James Pilkington had received an offer of over £40 for them when he was Master; that offer had been rejected as too small. Now, however, they were cavalierly disposed of for £14, the Master, Fulke and five other Fellows

[1] Ibid.
[2] Ibid. no. 11 (ii), fol. 67.   [3] Ibid. no. 7, fol. 11.

making themselves 'both merchants and chapmen' in their zeal.[1]

Fulke's fourth sermon, preached to the college on 8 October 1565, 'was so vehement and earnest against surplices that he wished amongst other things that if God would not, the Devil might take them away; adding further, have I then preached against these white coats and will they never amend?' The Master was listening to this sermon from his gallery, a long study above the ante-chapel, looking down into the choir: the result of Fisher's structural alterations to the original chapel of the Hospital of St John.[2] And Fulke's eloquence so moved him that he 'came down without his surplice amongst the Fellows having their surplices on, and so received the communion'.[3]

October 8 was a Monday. Term, by statute, began on the 10th. The so-called 'St John's Incident' occurred on the following Saturday, the 13th, at evensong. Immediately the chapel bell began to toll, a number of the undergraduates (including Fulke's own thirteen pupils) quickly assembled themselves in the chapel without their surplices; then, as they had plotted, they 'hissed at such as came with their surplices on, by the which they were forced to retire, and either to absent themselves or else to enter in without surplices'.[4]

On that rowdy evening the Master was absent from college. When he returned, much to the horror of some of the more responsible Fellows, he openly condoned the whole incident. Speaking before the assembled college Longworth complimented those who had rejected the surplice, but advised them to walk warily. 'We are in this our doing singular', said the Master, 'and therefore shall be sure to have many that will be glad to find fault with us; yet I do not doubt but that God will maintain us in our

[1] S.P. Dom. Eliz. vol. xxxviii, no. 7, fol. 11 b.
[2] C. C. Babington, *The Infirmary and Chapel of St John's*, 22, and plan 2. Willis and Clark, *Architectural History*, ii, 281 and iii, plan 21.
[3] S.P. Dom. Eliz. vol. xxxviii, no. 7, fol. 11 b.
[4] *Ibid.* fol. 11 b–12.

singularity, having the right on our part.'[1] After this extraordinary speech many waverers decided to join with the rebels.

Three weeks later, on the morning of 1 November—the beginning of his last month as Vice-Chancellor—Beaumont preached in Great St Mary's an attack on 'the rash and unlawful attempts of them, which being private men, would by making public reformation thrust themselves into the office of the magistrate'.[2] Bitter experience during his year of office had led Beaumont to put his finger precisely on the implications of the situation; only a week or two earlier Thomas Wood had sent from Trinity to Ashby-de-la-Zouch his complaint about the Vice-Chancellor's intolerable strong line in matters vestiarian. In the afternoon of 1 November Fulke retaliated with a vigorous attack on the Vice-Chancellor from the pulpit of St John's.

For over six weeks after the beginning of term neither the Chancellor nor the ecclesiastical commissioners took notice of the disturbances at St John's. During those weeks a majority of the college, at the daily morning and evening prayer, consistently and continuously gave up the wearing of the surplice. The Johnian rebels were strong in their own estimation: they had acted of 'conscience', right was on their side, the heavens fought for them. How strong were they in fact? Of the forty-seven Fellows, at least eight, led by Fulke, were genuine Puritan rebels, and not mere camp-followers; and at least eight, led by Curteys, and including William Baronsdale, John Twidall, Humphrey Bohun, Robert Holgate, Rowland Ayer and John Daubney, were opponents of the Master. Unfortunately, the eight Puritans had between them nearly ninety pupils, and the eight conformists only forty. However, a sixth of the college, at least, stood out against the rebels. The claim of the Master, that 'all his company, accounting them three hundred in number, had thrown off surplices',[3] was exaggerated, misleading, and intended to mislead. So far as the

---

[1] *Ibid.* fol. 12.
[2] S. P. Dom. Eliz. vol. xxxviii, no. 10 (i).   [3] Strype, *Parker*, iii, 128–31.

undergraduates were concerned, the situation was complicated by the fact that there had been a record number of entries in the autumn of 1565,[1] and many of the boys remained unprovided with surplices throughout the Michaelmas term. Also, during the past seven years the college had developed the custom of 'the tolerating of certain gentlemen's children in the House, who at any time never used any surplice'.[2] For an undergraduate to appear without surplice was not therefore of necessity a sign that he had left it behind in his chamber as a deliberate act of rebellion. And of the forty Fellows who at first clung to Fulke's coat-tails, many at the least did so because they feared a hissing, or, more positively, because they liked a fight.

At the end of November Beaumont, dreading above all things a general disturbance in the university, made a gesture of appeasement. On the 26th he and Longworth signed a letter from Cambridge to Cecil: the other subscribers were Roger Kelke of Magdalene, Matthew Hutton of Pembroke, and the Lady Margaret Professor, John Whitgift, Fellow of Peterhouse. The letter asked the Chancellor not to enforce the national vestment regulations in Cambridge[3] 'for the avoiding of greater inconvenience, which then, as it seemed, could not otherwise have been repressed'.[4] This proved a false move. Cecil was extremely annoyed. His temper was not improved when William Fulke came to see him on 28 November, with an apologia for the disturbances at St John's, written by Longworth. How it grieved me, said Cecil, 'to behold such men of reputation, being Heads in an university, governors of societies, preachers to the people, to subscribe suddenly some lusty fellows' device, in writing to me, the Chancellor! I cannot express it without utterance of some passion, mixed with sorrow.' Cecil sat on the matter for a day or

---

[1] There were 239 undergraduates in residence in December 1565; S.P. Dom. Eliz. vol. xxxviii, fol. 104–5. In August 1564, at the time of the visit of the Queen, there had been 140; Harleian MSS. (British Museum Baker MSS.) 7033, fol. 114.
[2] S.P. Dom. Eliz. vol. xxxviii, fol. 112.
[3] Letter in Strype, *Parker*, iii, 125–6.   [4] *Ibid.* i, 387–8.

two; and then conferred with Parker and Grindal. After this discussion, seven weeks after the 'Incident', Cecil wrote an angry letter to the Master of 'my dear college of St John's', ordering him instantly to come to London: 'I must confess, truly no mishap in all my service did ever plunge me more grievously'; but 'because I mean either to reform this disorder, or rather to leave the authority for some that can agree with such as you—I have thought best to leave reasoning and to command you to repair hither to me, upon sight of this letter'.[1]

So, at the beginning of December, the internal affairs of a Cambridge college had assumed national importance. Longworth was to remain in London until 18 December. During the three weeks of the Master's absence, Fulke continued to incite the Johnians. In an especially violent sermon of 8 December he 'called all such as he did not like of, asses, dogs, beasts, and devils: so describing at that time some of the company, that the least and youngest boy in the auditory could mark him unto whom he meant'.[2] In the same sermon he significantly 'diminished the laws of the realm, referring all things to conscience'. To the boys it was all very stimulating, though rather confusing, and hardly edifying.

On that same day Parker wrote to Cecil to whet what seemed to be his almost blunted purpose.[3] The Archbishop did not wish the Johnian situation to become a high commission matter: 'I do not like that the commissioners' letters should go to private colleges, especially after so much passed.' But all the same, 'execution, execution, execution of laws and orders must be the first and the last part of good governance: although I yet admit moderation for times, places, multitudes etc.'. 'We mar our religion,' Parker argued, 'our circumspections so variable (as though it were not God's cause which He will defend) maketh

---

[1] Letter printed in *The Eagle* (St John's College Magazine), xxvIII (1907), 141.
[2] S.P. Dom. Eliz. vol. xxxvIII, no. 11 (ii), fol. 67.
[3] Lansdowne MSS. (British Museum), vol. vIII, no. 49.

cowards thus to cock over us.' In Cambridge the majority of men were ready to execute the Chancellor's orders: 'excepting a few Catalines: who by sufferance will infect the whole'. Thus, Parker concluded (with some asperity), if 'you their Chancellor, of the Privy Council, and in such place and credit as you be, will suffer so much authority to be borne underfoot by a bragging brainless head or two, in mine opinion your conscience shall never be excusable'.

The blow went home; and Cecil saw the Queen on 9 December, to discuss the Cambridge situation. Elizabeth ordered him 'to use all severity expedient to punish the authors and maintainers' of disorder.[1] The Chancellor, however, throughout his forty years of office, was a brake on the severity of others. And he wrote to Beaumont on 10 December pressing the quality of mercy as well as that of justice: 'I think it good, that as many as will voluntarily, or upon gentle admonition, reform themselves, ought to be gently used and borne withal: for that I think many were carried with the course of the stream of a hasty company.'[2] Longworth had exaggerated the extent of the Johnian rebellion; and now Cecil, more precisely informed by Curteys, knew that the situation was not beyond control. He also knew that the 'lewd leprosy of libertines' had not affected the other colleges. True, an undergraduate of King's had appeared in chapel without surplice: but the cause turned out to be that he had pawned it to a cook 'with whom he had run in debt for his belly'.[3] There had also been trouble in Trinity, where 'the inordinate walkers' had been spurred on by Thomas Cartwright: but Beaumont felt himself to be in full control of the situation there.[4]

On 10 December, two months after the initial 'Incident', Cecil

[1] Cecil to Beaumont, Strype, *Parker*, III, 128–31.
[2] *Ibid.*
[3] Strype, *Annals of the Reformation*, II, 162.
[4] S.P. Dom. Eliz. vol. xxxviii, no. 10, fol. 59. Paule, in his *Life of Whitgift* (1612), confused the Trinity disturbances with the 'incident' at St John's, and placed them under the mastership of Whitgift; 1699 ed. 11–12.

ordered Fulke to come up again to London; and entrusted the government of St John's to Richard Curteys.

The departure of Fulke considerably eased the situation. Curteys, writing to Cecil on 12 December, was quite optimistic. Having 'taken a very good and needful order' the President did 'nothing doubt to reform all, but such as hope that the Master's return shall either reverse all that is done in his absence, or at the leastwise shall bear out and colour their doings, as heretofore was accustomed'.[1] With this letter Curteys enclosed a series of articles: thirty-four against the Master[2] and thirteen against Fulke.[3]

The complaints against Longworth were a mixed assortment; taken with the further series of articles concerning him, prepared by Bohun and Smyth at the end of the month,[4] they set forth a picture of incompetence, corruption, and general violation of the college statutes. Throughout his year and a half of office the Master had preferred 'the unlearned and evil mannered'—unlearned bachelors, that is, 'before learned masters of art'—to 'lectures and chambers in the house'. He had given favoured treatment to such men as John Linsey (Fellow since 1558), who as master of the bakehouse had underweighed the bread, and as bursar had swindled the college out of nine loads of coal. We are very much in the badlands of college gossip: there is talk of illicit loans from the bedell and the college barber, of fraudulent leases of college farms, of scandal in the bakehouse and chicanery with the firewood. The Master was not averse to a little blackmail. He won the allegiance of John Dakins by informing him 'he should have no preferment except he would give in all points as he would, and in so doing he would make him a man'. He influenced the undergraduates by 'giving sundry fires in the Hall since Michaelmas, and feasting in the Hall and in his chamber'. In general, 'he maintaineth master Fulke, and others that inveigh

---

[1] S.P. Dom. Eliz. vol. xxxviii, no. 11, fol. 61.   [2] *Ibid.* no. 11 (i), fol. 63–6.
[3] *Ibid.* no. 11 (ii), fol. 67.
[4] *Ibid.* nos. 1 and 2. Humphrey Bohun and Richard Smyth.

against order, and the favourers thereof, and such manner of men doth he only privately encourage, and openly reward with the preferments of the House'. The varied articles were pulled together by indignation at the conduct of the Master during the present crisis: his pretended intimacy with Cecil, saying 'he knew better your honour's mind than any in England did'; his smear campaign against Curteys—'hearing and fearing lest the President in his absence should go about to redress this disorder' he had 'solicited men particularly to beware of business, and what they did at the motion of any, meaning the President'. The articles were permeated by a sincere conviction of the Master's private inadequacy for his public office: 'he doth never study, and preacheth so negligently, that both he is an offence unto his hearers, and also great disworship to the person and place he sustaineth'.

The conduct of Fulke provided even more food for righteous indignation to feed on. As lecturer he 'sharply and extremely useth such scholars whose tutors he misliketh', and 'keepeth the youth in such awe that neither by words or by deeds they dare show themselves contrary to his manifold fantasies'. With Carter and Riley and their respective pupils Fulke and his boys formed a group—about fifty in number: Fulke had thirteen pupils, Carter nineteen, and Riley seventeen—which 'both in their chambers and in Hall use to sing the Geneva psalms in tunes made for most wanton and light ballads'. Fulke 'traineth up his younglings in all these disorders, who upon his exhortations do complain Christian liberty to be taken away by the binding of men unto the wearing of a surplice'. The charges were serious; though it is permissible to read into some of them the natural but regrettable irritation of the respectable at the appalling popularity of a brilliantly iconoclastic young don. (The corruption of youth is an easy charge to fling at a teacher: it is implicit in the nature of the profession.) Finally, Fulke 'keepeth in his chamber conies, dogs, rats, birds, virginals: and useth to go a birding with his boys, to the great reproach of the ministry'. No wonder the boys liked him.

These Articles were taken down to London on Wednesday 12 December by Bohun and Smyth. The next day, the Chancellor wrote three letters,[1] perhaps jogged by the fact that on the Wednesday Parker had again dryly commented on the apparent lack of action in Cambridge, and the 'strange delay among the wiser sort'.[2] One letter was to Curteys, urging him to carry on the fight by 'the best ordinary means that you can', with 'the advice and assistance of the seniors and others of that college'. The second was to the new Vice-Chancellor, John Stokes, President of Queens', to tell him that if all else failed 'I am determined to resort to the authority of our sovereign Lady the Queen's Majesty, in whose power, by prerogative, the government of all manner of subjects doth belong'. The third was to Bishop Cox of Ely, Visitor of St John's: 'Nothing is more requisite than speed and severity, for surely, my Lord, I am inwardly afraid that if fear shall not stay this riotous insolency, these rash young heads, that are so soon ripe to climb into pulpits, will content themselves with no limits either in the Church or in the polity.' These were sharp letters, unusually so for Cecil. And all three were inspired by 'the earnest desire which I have to redress and quench this wild fury broken loose in that college of St John's, which I do and ought to esteem as my nurse'. Everything depended on how the college would respond to the authority of the President.

Curteys wrote to Cecil again on Monday 17 December. During the Saturday and Sunday, there had been 254 members of the college in residence (thirty-three being away); of these, 147 had come to chapel in surplices.[3] 'In years the eldest,' commented Curteys, 'in continuance the ancientest, in degree of schools the highest, and in all kinds of learning the forwardest, have only upon your honour's favour reformed themselves, without any manner of compulsion.'[4] But the imminent return of the Master

---

[1] S.P. Dom. Eliz. vol. xxxviii, no. 13, fol. 71–4 (drafts of the three letters).
[2] Lansdowne MSS. vol. viii, no. 50.
[3] S.P. Dom. Eliz. vol. xxxviii, fol. 105.   [4] *Ibid.* fol. 102.

made the situation uneasy. For 'whereas divers of the younger sort told me of their own accord that they meant to come in again with surplices', they changed their minds on the return to the college of William Hodgson, a rather elderly undergraduate who had ridden up to London with Longworth: 'they suddenly altered their purpose, some pretending necessary occasions to go forth, some lack of surplices, and some said plainly they durst not for fear of displeasure—I could not hear of whom'. As for the more recalcitrant members, 'some talk that they mean not any reformation before the Master's return: neither then, I believe'.[1] Curteys knew very well the dangers of partial success. If disorder 'be smothered for the present time by fair words (whereof some have great plenty) it will no doubt burst out into a more perilous flame, when such as dare withstand shall be either won, or removed, or discomforted'.[2]

II

Longworth returned to St John's at two o'clock on the afternoon of Tuesday 18 December. In his pocket was an apology which Cecil had prepared for the Master to deliver in the college hall. This apology Longworth duly read to the assembled Fellows and students in the evening. But he made nonsense of it: by omitting many phrases, inserting innuendoes against the conformists, and permitting himself such gratuitous observations as 'I wish I could as well have answered for you as I did for myself'; 'Mr Secretary took not the letters sent him from you so heavily as some bare you in hand he would'; 'you must not think that you shall hereafter so boldly talk in assemblies as heretofore you have done'. The reading over, he called Curteys, Bohun and Smyth on to the dais, and before the whole college 'severally and particularly' charged them 'with the doings before your honour, and at home in his absence, with such gesture and countenance that the disordered were much emboldened and the residue much discomforted'.

[1] S.P. Dom. Eliz. vol. xxxviii, fol. 102.   [2] *Ibid.* fol. 102b–103.

And the next morning in chapel, at the five o'clock prayers, 'whereas the greater part was come in with surplices he caused the other to come into the choir without'.[1]

Longworth wrote two letters to Cecil at this time: one on the Tuesday, the second on the Thursday. In the first[2] he described his obedient reading of the apology (!) and his hope that 'very many' of the college would now be 'persuaded to conform', as against the previous 'very few'. He also asked Cecil 'whether we may still retain the common bread in the ministration of the sacraments' and whether he himself, when he preached privately in the chapel, might do so without surplice. In the second he spoke of the events of the two days since his return: claiming that he had done what he could

by all kind of persuasions to reform all such things as were given me in commandment so to do: and this present Thursday, being the 20th of December, all the Fellows that were at home (saving one or two, who have promised speedily to conform themselves) came into the chapel at evening prayers with their surplices and hoods.... And almost all the scholars with their surplices, and many of the pensioners in like manner.[3]

But in fact the return of the Master did nothing to lessen the divisions in St John's. There seemed to be a general slackening of discipline; made less bitter only by the absence of Fulke, who was at this time expelled from the college. Fulke lived privately in Cambridge for over a year, claiming that Cecil had allowed him to do so, though Stokes refused to believe this.[4] The story goes that he lodged at the Falcon Inn in Petty Cury and lectured there with some success. He was re-admitted to his fellowship at St John's in March 1567. But of the forty-five Fellows in residence in December 1565, only about ten were staunchly behind Curteys; about fifteen were active supporters of the Master, and the floating vote, as it were, tended to be in the Master's favour. After ten

[1] Account by Curteys, *ibid.* no. 29, fol. 136.
[2] *Ibid.* no. 19, fol. 110. [3] *Ibid.* no. 20, fol. 112.
[4] S.P. Dom. Eliz. vol. xxxix, no. 67, fol. 178.

uneasy days Curteys wrote to Cecil once more. The Master's supporters, he claimed, had threatened and even beaten the pupils of their opponents.[1] It was true that all the resident Fellows came into chapel wearing surplice and hood: but the Master's supporters had developed a system both of cutting services, and of attending only for a few minutes the services which they did not boycott. The boycotted services were those on holy days, of which there had been five in the period described by Curteys. Longworth had been present at none of these—though he afterwards claimed that he had been watching from his gallery.[2] Only about eight Fellows had been present for the entire service on those days, and about fifty or sixty undergraduates. The Master and the two deans had punished no one for being absent on those occasions; nor had they objected when Fellows and students on ordinary days had not come into the upper chapel, but loitered 'in the nether chapel, the Hall and the kitchen'. Moreover Curteys, during Longworth's absence, had caused the 'Te Deum, Benedictus, Magnificat, Nunc Dimittis or the other Psalms joined with them to be sung according to the Book of Common Prayer, with a Psalm in metre in the end of the service'. When Longworth returned, he sent word from his gallery that the entire service should be sung in metre. In short, the Master 'reversed everything done in his absence by me with the consent either of the seniors or Fellows, ever picking one quarrel or other'.[3]

Curteys ended this account of the ten-day 'truce' by reporting an offensive sermon preached by Longworth in Great St Mary's on Thursday 27 December. The Master had taken the opportunity to address the university about 'such as had of envy and malice told and written lies'. He also said:

how little faults were made great, and great little, as if a man offend in external matters, which is nothing, then is he called and accounted a rebel, but if he is absent from his benefice or other living where he

[1] S.P. Dom. Eliz. vol. xxxvIII, no. 29, fol. 137b.
[2] *Ibid.* no. 20, fol. 112.　　　　　[3] *Ibid.* no. 29, fol. 137.

is bound by word of God, and hired by the world not to preach quarterly or monthly *sed quantum in ipso est*, that is counted no fault.

He wound up by attacking the Vice-Chancellor 'in such sort that every man knew whom he meant, and as Mr Vice-Chancellor took it himself'. The offence Stokes had apparently committed was that of suffering 'a black Sanctus to be sung in the stead of godly psalms' in St Bene't's. When this curious charge was later investigated, it was discovered that the strange noises in that church had been occasioned by the scholars of Corpus beginning another psalm in the choir after a town blacksmith had begun one in the nave.[1]

So the St John's disturbances dragged on. The second set of articles against Longworth was sent to Cecil at the end of December, with a petition appealing for more exact observance of the college statutes, and the appointment of reliable college officers: those recommended were John Twidall and John Becon as deans, Humphrey Bohun and John Daubney as bursars, William Baronsdale as master of the bakehouse, and Oliver Carter as steward.[2] But after Christmas Curteys became more and more unhappy. In January he decided to leave the college for ever,[3] to join the household of Sir Henry Cheney.

However, he did not do so. Cecil wrote him a comforting letter urging him to stay at his post. But there was a difficult year ahead. Longworth vetoed the re-election of Curteys as President at the annual meeting for the appointment of college officers at the beginning of 1566. Curteys was loath to lose the office; and the constant insults and upbraidings of the Master were wearing down his nerves.[4] In addition, by October rumours of such an unpleasant and slanderous nature had been spread about him—he was accused of having 'unlawfully kept a woman at Barnwell'— that Curteys brought an action for defamation against one Thomas Longworth. Longworth, though not a member of the college, was a man 'having some acquaintance with the Master and some

[1] *Ibid*. fol. 137b.   [2] Petition printed in *The Eagle*, xxviii, 259-60.
[3] S.P. Dom. Eliz. vol. xxxix, no. 14, fol. 45.   [4] *Ibid*. no. 19, fol. 59.

of the Fellows of St John's', a hanger-on and unofficial spy of the Johnian Puritans, primarily employed to keep the college authorities informed of any visits paid by the young men to the brothel area of Barnwell. This case, heard in the Vice-Chancellor's court, was the last straw.[1] Curteys made quite clear to Cecil that he could no longer stay in Cambridge; and in November he was appointed Dean of Chichester, where he was installed in March 1567, the very month in which Fulke returned to St John's.

During 1566 Baronsdale and Thomas Drant came to the fore as persistent opponents of Longworth. In May Longworth had asked Baronsdale to submit some accounts, and had received from him a distinctly dusty answer: 'after many contentious, contumelious and very unseemly words, he said that I was no Master, neither did he take me for any'.[2] (The fact that Baronsdale had been admitted Fellow of the college three years before Longworth, though he was three years younger, was hardly an adequate excuse for this sort of thing; though it may, of course, be an explanation.) At about the same time Drant refused to revoke a college commonplace which the Master had disliked.[3] In fact Longworth was finding it difficult to enforce his authority at all. Did this not mean, he asked Cecil in May, that 'it will not be my case only, but of all the Masters in the university, if Fellows and young scholars may in such wise or like sort contrary to all good order prevail against the Master'?[4] John Wells, a Fellow of Clare, wrote to Cecil in June that the quarrels in St John's, however much they may have been matters of principle nine months before, were now the result of 'private grudge and displeasure':

I am sure that some of the quietest sort, because of the strife that is nourished among them, and like daily to increase, will shortly depart the House, if they may be well provided for in other places. Some of

---

[1] There are ten papers relating to this case in the University Archives, Registry Guard Books, vol. 4, no. 22; and a letter about it in the box labelled 'Vice Chancellor's Court, Documents from the file of Exhibita, 1559–74'.
[2] S.P. Dom. Eliz. vol. XXXIX, no. 84, fol. 204.
[3] S.P. Dom. Eliz. vol. XL, no. 8, fol. 20.   [4] S.P. Dom. Eliz. vol. XXXIX, no. 84.

them with whom the Master is offended do know (they say) no other cause of grudge except it be they were diligent to give you understanding, when disorder for apparel and surplices was in the House, which is not yet quite reformed.[1]

There was to be one unexpected turn of the screw. After his return in the spring of 1567 Fulke became the leader of the party in opposition to the Master; and finally Longworth was expelled by the Bishop of Ely in November 1569. In April 1570, when he was thirty-eight, Curteys was elected Bishop of Chichester. As Bishop, he continued to be a prey to rumours spread by men less ineffective than he, being 'commonly held to be dishonest and a drunkard'.[2] However that may be—and perhaps there was some confusion between Richard Curteys and his brother Edmund, a canon of the cathedral who was deprived for drunkenness and witchcraft in 1579—the Bishop died in debt.[3] That was in 1582, three years after the death of Longworth, and four years after William Fulke, chaplain to the Earl of Leicester, had been elected Master of Pembroke. Fulke's successor as Master was the efficient college treasurer, Lancelot Andrewes: both Andrewes and his next successor as Master, Samuel Harsnet, were to occupy Curteys's see of Chichester.

The troubles at St John's continued. The college had developed a proud tradition of faction; and men were not lacking to uphold it under Longworth's successors—Nicholas Shephard, thirteenth Master of the college, described by Thomas Baker as 'a slug',[4] John Still, and Richard Howland. It was under William Whitaker, however, admitted Master in 1587, that the tradition once more bore fruit in a manner which concerned both university and national politics.

But the tangled story of the troubled reign of William Whitaker must be left for a later chapter.

[1] S.P. Dom. Eliz. vol. XL, no. 8.
[2] P. M. Dawley, *John Whitgift and the Reformation*, 104.
[3] Inventory of his goods in Lansdowne MSS. vol. LIV, no. 44.
[4] Baker, *History of St John's College*, I, 168.

135

CHAPTER VII

THE PURITAN ASSERTION

THE old attacks against the abuses of the Church of Rome were continued against the reformed Church of England by those to whom the establishment seemed a 'crooked halting betwixt two religions'.[1] 'This halting in religion for policy', wrote Anthony Gilbey to Thomas Cartwright, 'driveth away the true fear of God';[2] and the course of the English Reformation had been effectively dammed—'in the stead of the old beast popery that is wounded to death by God's word, we raise up this second beast policy, to do all that the other beast did before'.[3] Thus, prophesied the vicar of Ashby-de-la-Zouch, 'religion shall wax cold and become an outward hypocritical show, only for custom and policy'.[4]

The spirit, in other words, was once again displaying its regrettable tendency to be smothered by the letter. The indignation was, like that of Latimer, a protest of the deeply shocked against things 'whereby the glory of God was obscured'. Moreover, there was still an 'unpreaching prelacy'; the hungry sheep still looked up, and were not fed. John Rudd of Christ's, preaching in Great St Mary's in 1597, declared that 'not the tenth part of the ministers of this our Church of England are able ministers or teachers, but dumb dogs'. A curate, he continued, 'not being a preacher, is no minister; nor doth edify more than a boy of eight years old may do'.[5] John Millen, also of Christ's, had made the same point in the same church a quarter of a century before. The clergy of England, Millen claimed in 1573, 'do not only not advance and set forward the edifying of the Church, but as much

[1] A. Peel (ed.), *The Second Part of a Register*, I, 142.
[2] *Ibid.* 140.   [3] *Ibid.* 141.   [4] *Ibid.* 140.
[5] University Archives, Registry Guard Books, vol. 6 (i), no. 25.

as lieth in them they do deface, hinder and pluck down the same'. 'Twelve diligent men', he asserted, 'would do more good in England than all the preachers that now be.'[1] The assertion led to Millen's expulsion from the university.

The Cambridge Puritans attacked with especial vehemence those ministers who 'tarry in their College, and lead the lives of loitering losels'.[2] Good-for-nothing, these non-resident pluralists 'live in ease and pleasure amongst us, as spots and blots of the university, suffering their flock in the mean time to wander in the mountains, notwithstanding they hear continually the contrary out of the Word of the Lord'.[3] Charles Chadwick of Emmanuel more precisely announced that 'thousands of souls were murdered by the non-residents of the university'; by a private process of mystical mathematics he had arrived at an accurate calculation—'between thirty or forty thousand, to be murdered by computation'.[4] Another attack on the same lines came from Francis Johnson and Cuthbert Bainbrigg, both Fellows of Christ's, in sermons preached in Great St Mary's in January 1589. The latter stated that 'we have an Amazia amongst us, which forbade Amos to preach at Bethel, and that these do not exhort to feed but stay them that would feed'.[5] The former declared:

our ministers are not like unto Moses and Jeremy, that refused to take a charge upon them when it was offered. For they seek it and speak for it, and procure others to speak for them, and pay money for it, and pay money aforehand. And by this means they bring disgrace unto themselves; and if they be publicly disgraced or reproved for the same, they have deserved it.[6]

Cartwright, in his literary controversy with Whitgift in the 1570's, had also taken the Cambridge non-residents to task: 'pernicious examples of riotous feasting, and making great cheer

---

[1] Lansdowne MSS. vol. XVII, no. 81.
[2] W. H. Frere and C. E. Douglas (ed.), *Puritan Manifestos*, 31.
[3] Peel, *op. cit.* II, 186.   [4] J. Strype, *Annals of the Reformation*, V, 722.
[5] University Archives, Registry Guard Books, vol. 6 (i), no. 1.
[6] *Ibid.* no. 6.

with the preys and spoils which they bring out of the country'.[1] Whitgift defended the parson-dons as 'sober, honest, wise, quiet men, faithful and learned preachers'. They did indeed reside in Cambridge for 'the necessary good of the college and public utility'; but 'that time of absence which is given unto them by statute they do carefully bestow in their cures, and other places where there is need, according to their duty and conscience'.[2] Furthermore, said Whitgift, in the fifteen years between the beginning of the reign of Elizabeth and 1573, the University of Cambridge had bred at least 450 preachers: and there were 102 preachers 'now in this University'.[3] More particularly, the prosperity of Trinity was to a great extent due to

the gravity, the honesty, the wisdom, the learning, the discreet government of those whom you call 'non-residents': whom not I, but the noble founder's statutes, ratified by the Queen's Majesty's authority, and allowed by the wisdom of the realm for most just consideration, even for the better government of the college, being otherwise full of youth, have licensed... to continue in their Fellowships with one living besides.[4]

The classic picture of the Puritan conscience face to face with Elizabethan Cambridge is found in a letter written to the Chancellor in November 1570 by Edward Dering of Christ's.[5] The non-residents came under the most intensive fire: 'while they are clothed in scarlet their flocks perish for cold, and while they fare deliciously, their people are faint with a most miserable hunger. This fault is intolerable, and such as God abhorreth.' John Milton, a later alumnus of Christ's, was hardly to do better than this. Dering's letter breathed the spirit of Righteousness; and, in the things of the Spirit, 'the unconscious assumption of effortless superiority'. 'I carry the testimony of a true conscience', he informed the Chancellor: 'I fear the breach of my faith, which

[1] J. Whitgift, *Works*, III, 395. [2] *Ibid.* 396.
[3] *Ibid.* I, 313. [4] *Ibid.* III, 396.
[5] Lansdowne MSS. vol. XII, no. 86.

in a good cause had been afraid to tell a man of his sin; the grief of conscience, which cannot be cured again with any Prince's favour; the displeasure of God, which is weighty to crush in pieces both me and you.' Gregors Werle would have 'got along famously' with Edward Dering. Dering went on to remind Cecil of his impotence before God—as Grindal was to remind Elizabeth of hers. The Chancellor, he assumed, could never have seen 'the horror of sin'. But, in the curious dispensations of Providence, even a Chancellor might be granted grace, to 'regenerate you with a mighty spirit, that you may tread under foot all worldly vanity, and lift up pure eyes to see and pity the estate of His Church'. Dering, of course, could hardly hope for a Canossa.

The Puritan, certainly and precisely, could love righteousness and hate iniquity because 'the glory of the great God was set up in my heart, as the square and rule of each and every particular practice'.[1] The walk with God, the vision of Truth: and the consequent and obvious duty—to return, like a philosopher-king, to the cave, there without compromise to copy the visionary archetype, first (in Plato's phrase) 'scraping the canvas clean'. William Charke of Peterhouse 'thought something to be wanting' whereby 'our Church, lately rescued from darkness, might come nearer to' the 'original pattern',[2] the pattern, that is, of the best reformed Churches. The 'Idea' of the authors of the 'Second Admonition to Parliament' was 'a platform out of God his book (where it is described at full) according to his will in the same revealed, and the examples of the best Churches beyond the seas, as Geneva, France, etc'.[3] If the Puritans came into conflict with the lesser spiritual sensibilities of authority, they were the more convinced of their infallibility. The Vice-Chancellor, Thomas Nevile, found the road to sensible discussion with Bainbrigg and Johnson blocked by their conviction that 'God had herein revealed that unto them which he had not done before unto any

[1] T. Goodwin, *Works*, v (1704), xiv. [2] J. Strype, *Life of Whitgift*, i, 90.
[3] Frere and Douglas, *Puritan Manifestos*, 94.

others, and that that which had long before lain hid in darkness should now by them be brought into light'.[1] What could even a future Master of Trinity do with men so at ease in Zion?

This spiritual calculus had been applied by the early Cambridge reformers to questions of ecclesiastical abuses, or of the theology of justification and of the Eucharist. In the 1560's it was applied by the Cambridge Puritans to the 'dregs of popery'. And in 1570, with his Cambridge lectures which 'marked a new point of departure in the history of Puritanism',[2] Thomas Cartwright, Lady Margaret Professor, applied it to the whole question of Church government. The certain and unchangeable form of Church government commanded in the Scriptures was, he argued, the Presbyterian system. Thus the names and functions of Archbishops and Bishops should be suppressed; the Church should rid itself of ecclesiastical chancellors and other such officials; ministers should be in charge of one congregation, and no more, and they should reside there; ministers should be elected by the congregation, not created by the Bishop.[3] When challenged, he defended himself with the plea that his teaching involved no sedition: 'I do not deny that I have taught that our ministry has deviated from the ministry of the ancient and apostolic church:... but I said all this quietly and calmly.' He further denied the charge that he was a 'stirrer of new things'—his cause, he said, was precisely 1570 years old. He appealed to the Puritan imperative and demanded that the Chancellor translate it into action: 'If the cause be just, if it be indispensable to the Church, if without it the commonwealth would dissolve, its parts falling asunder in turn (which event, without discipline, is unavoidable), then the cause is worthy.'[4] 'But if the cause be not just....'

[1] Lansdowne MSS. vol. LXI, no. 8.
[2] A. F. S. Pearson, *Thomas Cartwright and Elizabethan Puritanism*, 33.
[3] From the six articles by which Cartwright was condemned in 1570; Strype, *Whitgift*, III, 19–20.
[4] Translated from S.P. Dom. Eliz. vol. LXXI, no. 40, printed in Pearson, *Cartwright*, 424–8.

Cartwright's teaching was never improved upon in Elizabethan Cambridge, nor were any important additions made to his arguments. Lesser men echoed his voice. In the same year of 1570 there were flanking movements by Edmund Chapman of Trinity, who preached that to hold more than one living was unlawful, and by Robert Some of Queens', who denounced Bishops, non-residents, and ecclesiastical courts.[1] Nicholas Brown of Trinity, in two sermons preached in Great St Mary's in June 1572, 'uttered doctrine and reasons tending to the infringement of the order and manner of creating or electing ministers, or the regiment now used in the Church of England'.[2] In 1573 John Millen in turn asserted that 'the ordering and making of ministers now used in the Church of England is a horrible confusion, and contrary to the word of God'; that 'ignorant ministers were no ministers, because they were not chosen by God'; that 'it is not lawful to admit him into the ministry which cannot preach'; and that 'a minister not being rightly called by the congregation is no minister'.[3] But the most effective of Cartwright's immediate Cambridge disciples was William Charke, who preached to the university in December 1572 that Bishops and Archbishops had been introduced into the Church by Satan, and that no minister in God's Church ought to have superiority over any other.[4] Charke had aroused 'the great expectation of many long before his sermon, raised, as may probably be thought, by some speech given out by him concerning those things whereof he would entreat'.[5] Eventually sentence was pronounced against Charke by the Vice-Chancellor and eleven heads of houses.[6]

Twenty years later the mixture was as before. The offending points of Francis Johnson in 1589 included: 'that the Church of God ought to be governed by elders'; 'that this form of government is prescribed and commanded by the word of God' and 'no

[1] Strype, *Annals*, II, 373. [2] Lansdowne MSS. vol. XVII, no. 65.
[3] *Ibid.* no. 81. [4] Lansdowne MSS. vol. XV, no. 64.
[5] Lansdowne MSS. vol. XVI, no. 34.
[6] University Archives, Registry Guard Books, vol. 6 (i), no. 19.

other form of government is to be allowed'; 'that neglect of this commanded government hath been the cause of ignorance, idolatry and all disobedience'; 'that there ought to be an equality amongst ministers and elders'.[1] And among the battle cries of the clever young men of the 1590's was the not very novel assertion that 'the beauty of our Church in the government thereof, is far from that of the Presbytery &c, in the time of the Apostles &c'.[2]

One development there had been in those twenty years: an increased suspicion of the magistrate. For the Puritan placed the magistrate where Dering placed Cecil—in the framework of 'the commonwealth where Christ is truly preached'. After one term of lectures from Cartwright, his predecessor as Lady Margaret Professor, William Chaderton, had put his finger on the implications: 'to overturn and overthrow all ecclesiastical and civil governance that now is, and to ordain and institute a new found Policy'.[3] The elaboration of the position by Cartwright in his controversy with Whitgift in the following years is well known. Civil magistrates, he said, must be governors of the Church:

But it must be remembered that civil magistrates must govern it according to the rules of God prescribed in His word, and that as they are nurses so they be servants unto the Church, and as they rule in the Church so they must remember to subject themselves unto the Church, to submit their sceptres, to throw down their crowns before the Church, yea, as the prophet teacheth, to lick the dust off the feet of the Church.

Otherwise, Cartwright succinctly concluded, God is made to give place to men, heaven to earth. Whitgift advised his readers to note these words of Cartwright especially well: 'for they contain the overthrow of the Prince's authority both in ecclesiastical and civil matters'.[4]

And so there was always in Puritan thinking, implicit or explicit, the theme of rebellion through conscience. It was

[1] University Archives, Registry Guard Books, vol. 6 (i), no. 1.
[2] Lansdowne MSS. vol. LXII, no. 42.
[3] Pearson, *Cartwright*, 28.   [4] Whitgift, *Works*, III, 189.

obvious, as Robert Some pointed out in 1570, that 'the Queen's
Majesty's laws did permit many detestable, devilish, and damnable
things'.[1] In 1565 William Fulke had significantly 'diminished the
laws of the realm, referring all things to conscience';[2] and
conscience did not make cowards of them all, those men who
believed that 'if we examine every thing done in this Church of
God in England by the word of God, and hold that which is good,
though the laws be offended, that law is to be reformed, and not
we to be punished'.[3] Naturally, in the published theory, it was
'her Majesty that by her princely authority should see every of
these things put into practice'.[4] But conscience and the word
could not wait for ever, and both the Puritans and the authorities
were aware that they were here on the fringe of the century's
'most controverted point in political philosophy',[5] the question
of the right of resistance. When Robert Beaumont was Vice-
Chancellor he had condemned 'the rash and unlawful attempts
of them, which being private men, would by making public
reformation thrust themselves into the office of the magistrate'.[6]
And, argued the ecclesiastical commissioners at the examination
of Cartwright in 1591, we know from whom you draw your
ideas of government: from John Knox and Christopher Goodman
and John Ponet—and is not the aim of their writing to encourage
a 'further reformation against the Prince's will by force and arms'?[7]
What would happen, Bancroft demanded, 'if the Gospel should
wrest the sword, out of any civil magistrate's hand'?[8] It was
perhaps the crucial question of Elizabethan debate, a question on
which the comment of authority was clear enough: 'they shall
not need to expect either Prince or Parliament, but may throw

---

[1] Strype, *Annals*, II, 373.
[2] S.P. Dom. Eliz. vol. XXXVIII, no. 11 (ii), fol. 67.
[3] 'Second Admonition', Frere and Douglas, *Puritan Manifestos*, 93.
[4] *Ibid.* 130.
[5] G. H. Sabine, *History of Political Theory*, 357.
[6] S.P. Dom. Eliz. vol. XXXVIII, no. 10 (i).
[7] Lansdowne MSS. vol. LXVIII, no. 50.
[8] R. Bancroft, *A Survay of the Pretended Holy Discipline* (1593), 14.

down and set up, as great builders do, whatsoever shall be most agreeable to the mutability of their own affections'.[1]

From the pulpits of Elizabethan Cambridge this theme of the opposition between the law of Christ and the law of the prince intermittently but dangerously crackled and flickered. The most revealing words of Cuthbert Bainbrigg in 1589 were those in which, interpreting 'fire to be the word of God preached, he said that there were some that had a bar to stand between them and that fire, and to strike that fire out of their hands that did bring it; and this bar he said to be our statutes of the university and positive laws'.[2] And the popular themes of the Cambridge pulpit in the late 1580's were these: 'any sentence given by a judge is to be examined of every private man, by the word of God'; 'it deserveth not obedience, if by them it be not found to be thereunto agreeable'; 'the godly and zealous in these times are ordinarily persecuted by the authority of the superiors'. There was a message of comfort too: 'the young ones in God's school are not to faint, or to be discouraged by such tyranny'.[3] That was negative comfort: but it implied a positive programme.

To those in authority, the statutes of the university were a part of the universal godly order: they were, moreover, 'both established by her Majesty and likewise to be justified by the word of God'.[4] So the Puritans were called before the Consistory Court of the Vice-Chancellor and heads, and ordered to read their retractations. These retractations are upon occasion a most convenient handbook of Anglican apologetic. That prepared for Francis Johnson may serve as an example:

I do not think that there is set down by the word of God any precise form of eternal regiment of the Church which must of necessity be observed in all times and places without exception; but am persuaded that for the better government of particular congregations, her Majesty

[1] Bancroft, *Daungerous Positions* (1593), 140.
[2] University Archives, Registry Guard Books, vol. 6 (i), no. 6.
[3] Lansdowne MSS. vol. LXII, no. 42.   [4] Lansdowne MSS., vol. LXI, no. 8.

may establish such orders, as by her godly wisdom with the advice of her godly and learned prelates she shall find to be most expedient for the state of her country, according to her Majesty's pre-eminence in church government established by the laws of this realm, and expressed in her most just title, which is both agreeable to the word of God, and conformable to the example of most ancient churches, which have been ruled by Christian magistrates.[1]

Johnson could not stomach this Anglican assertion. He left for the Low Countries.

Exile was a desperate remedy. But in the late 1580's there were a lot of rather desperate dons. Hugh Gray of Trinity College, preaching in 1590 on the theme of the Christian rebel, said:

that as the Jews did excuse themselves for not building the Temple, that being once forbidden by Darius it was dangerous for them to go forward without some warrant from him lest they should be accounted rebels, so do we in these times pretend the same excuse why we proceed not in the building of the spiritual Temple.

Christ's coat, he picturesquely added, 'is not to be rent, because it was without seam; yet is it not to be made of linsey wolsey'. Gray was brought before the Vice-Chancellor, the chief informer against him being the son of John Knox—Eleazor Knox, Fellow of St John's. Before the Vice-Chancellor, Gray expressed the chagrin of those Elizabethan Puritans of the last decade of the reign who almost lost heart when they thought of the hopes of the first decade. This was the ground bass of the developed Puritan assertion:

these thirty years we have neither added any thing which might further, nor took away anything which might hinder, the building of God's Temple among us: but that our proceeding therein is like to the journeys of the Israelites in the wilderness, which went but eleven days' journey in forty years.[2]

Could that wilderness ever blossom as the rose?

---

[1] University Archives, Registry Guard Books, vol. 6 (i), no. 18.
[2] *Ibid.* no. 39, section 9.

CHAPTER VIII

PURITANISM AND AUTHORITY IN ELIZABETHAN CAMBRIDGE

I

IN the autumn of 1568 there were complaints of 'divers mis-demeanours as well in manners as in doctrine in the society of Bene't College'.[1] For one thing, some of the eight Fellows of Corpus objected to the Latin form of the liturgy which colleges had been given permission to use in 1560; and they had gone 'contemptuously out of the chapel whilst the Master was reading, saying "Latin service is the Pope's dregs"'.[2] (The 'chapel' was either the chamber south of the choir of St Bene't's, or the room above it, at the north end of the gallery between St Bene't's and the Old Court.) For another thing, at the opposite end of the scale, a Fellow of the college named Marmaduke Pickering was at that time preaching 'popishly' on justification and original sin, condemning Calvin as a heretic, and calling priests' wives whores and their children bastards.[3] The Master of Corpus, John Pory, was an exact contemporary of Parker, having gone up to the college with him in 1520. But age had withered his efficiency—age combined with frequent absences from his lodge: and during the 1560's Corpus had come to be notorious for its lack of order and good government.

So at the end of 1568 Parker wrote to the Vice-Chancellor, Young of Pembroke, to redress and order the schisms in the college by virtue of the authority of the ecclesiastical commission.

[1] Parker to Cecil, Lansdowne MSS., vol. x, no. 48, fol. 152. Corpus Christi was familiarly known as Bene't College until the building of the New Court in the 1830's.
[2] Quoted from Harleian MSS. vol. xx (British Museum Baker MSS.) by Masters (ed. Lamb), *History of the College of Corpus Christi and the Blessed Virgin Mary*, 121.
[3] *Ibid.* 318–19.

This was not a very tactful move. Six years before, in October 1562, the ecclesiastical commissioners, empowered in the Act of Supremacy with the delegated authority of the supreme governor, had attempted to interfere in the case of John Sanderson, a Fellow of Trinity expelled by Beaumont for the teaching of 'superstitious' doctrine. The attempt had produced a proud and stinging rejoinder from the then Vice-Chancellor, Provost Baker:

I am moved by consent of heads of colleges in the name of the university to notify unto your honours that the said cause is depending in the said Court of the Chancellor. And that the said Chancellor hath the cognizance of all causes as well ecclesiastical as civil by special privilege and charter granted by the Queen's Majesty and her progenitors: as your honours, brought up in the said university,...can remember.[1]

In the same way, in 1568, the Vice-Chancellor did not execute Parker's commission, because he feared it might prejudice the privileges of the university.[2]

In January 1569 Parker, Grindal, and two other commissioners wrote to Cecil, who had been informed of the Corpus deadlock, to make clear that 'the Queen's Majesty's Commission for causes ecclesiastical doth extend and may be executed upon persons resident within either of the universities, or within any other privileged place within the realm'. This was not to ignore the liberties of the university, said Parker. If the Vice-Chancellor carried out the commission, it was to show his 'obedience unto the authority of the Queen's Highness committed to the said commissioners':[3] that and no more. But in spite of the reassurance, the Vice-Chancellor still 'proceeded not to the execution of our said commission'.[4]

In face of this obstruction, Parker decided directly to investigate the state of affairs in his old college, by calling the

[1] Corpus Christi College MSS. vol. 106, p. 545.
[2] Lansdowne MSS. vol. x, no. 48, fol. 152.
[3] *Ibid.* fol. 153.　　　　　　　　　　　　[4] *Ibid.* fol. 152.

Fellows down to Lambeth for discussions. All the eight Fellows appeared—except one. That one was the chief troublemaker: Thomas Stallar, a bachelor of arts in his early twenties, who had matriculated from Corpus as a sizar in 1562, and had been elected Fellow in 1567. Parker wrote to Young ordering him to see that Stallar was sent to Lambeth. When Young received this order, he bluntly told Stallar on no account to appear before the commissioners. Also, Parker had instructed Young to supervise a search in Corpus for 'suspected books', the actual searchers being appointed by the commissioners. The Master of Pembroke carried out these orders by forcibly ejecting the official agents from Corpus, and causing 'a search to be made by such, and in such manner, as he devised, unsealing the door that we for that purpose caused to be sealed'. In his letter of self-justification the Vice-Chancellor told the Archbishop that he had 'never heard that any extraordinary and foreign authority had intermeddled to call any from the university'. (An allegation, commented Parker, which 'we marvel not a little at'.[1])

The story of that particular commotion at Corpus must unfortunately be left in mid-air. The documents relating to the end of the affair have disappeared. But Stallar continued in his fellowship until 1570, when, rather surprisingly, Parker made him his chaplain: he later became archdeacon of Rochester.

One thing, however, was quite clear: Pory, now nearly seventy, was a liability. For two or three years Parker had been gently trying to persuade his old friend to resign the Mastership. He was 'always very loath to do so'; until the Christmas of 1569, when the Archbishop finally won him over. His resignation took place in February 1570.[2] From that moment, Parker sadly commented, 'his joy is gone'.[3]

At this point Parker made a great mistake: he imported a

[1] Lansdowne MSS., vol. x, no. 48, fol. 152.
[2] Corpus Christi College Bursary MSS., vol. of 'Miscellaneous Documents: 1430–1700', no. 50.
Lansdowne MSS. vol. xii, no. 35, fol. 82.

member of Trinity as Master of Corpus. This was Thomas Aldrich, senior proctor for the year, who had commenced bachelor of arts from Trinity under Beaumont in 1562 (although he had matriculated from Corpus in 1558). The old Archbishop was full of enthusiasm for his promising 'find', not yet turned thirty. He wrote to Cecil in March 1570 about Aldrich's honesty, his skill in Greek, Latin and Hebrew, his fluent French and Italian —a man to be trusted: 'like to do service in the realm hereafter'.[1] Unfortunately, the protégé proved a sad disappointment. Within six months of his admission as Master Aldrich was signing petitions in favour of Thomas Cartwright; and by the beginning of 1573 he had made it strikingly clear to Parker that he was 'an head precisian in despising of the degrees of the University'.[2]

Strikingly clear: in January 1573 Aldrich refused to proceed to the degree of bachelor of divinity, which by the college statutes he was bound to do at that time, being three years after his election.[3] Perhaps, like the authors of the 'Second Admonition to Parliament', he despised the 'ostentation and outward glory'[4] of academic degrees. (A violently bitter irritation against gowns and hoods and the whole ritual of the Cambridge hierarchy was in later years to be displayed by at least one undergraduate of Corpus at this time: Robert Browne.) When Aldrich announced his decision to the twelve Fellows of Corpus (four fellowships had been founded in 1569, two of them by Parker) he set in train a long series of violent college arguments on the exact interpretation of the college statute. Parker himself had drawn up those statutes during his mastership (1544–53): they had come into force in 1549, and were not to be superceded until 1861. And in February Aldrich and the Fellows wrote to Parker to refer the question of interpretation to him.[5]

Aldrich had gambled on the good will of his patron. But

[1] *Ibid.*   [2] Lansdowne MSS., vol. xvii, no. 35.
[3] Edwardian statutes of the college, chapter 3.
[4] W. H. Frere and C. E. Douglas, *Puritan Manifestos*, 98.
[5] Lansdowne MSS. vol. xvii, no. 39.

Parker had lost patience with the 'troublous precisian': his government, so promising at first, had turned out to be 'evil'; and there had been many 'grievous complaints made against him'.[1] The exercises and discipline of the college had been neglected; college estates (such as the manor of Wilbraham) had been leased out to his own friends, though there had been better terms offered by others; the Master treated 'the Society with contempt and insolence, whilst he made himself too much acquainted with the gentlemen of the country'.[2] So Parker advised Aldrich 'to depart quietly',[3] and to instruct the Fellows to elect as his successor the President of the college, Robert Norgate, the oldest member of the high table. Norgate was thirty.

The Master and his party among the Fellows received this directive very badly. Aldrich, cutting across the authority of the Archbishop, appealed directly to the Queen, some of the Fellows going down to the court to obtain letters of dispensation from the letter of the college statute. To nip this plot in the bud, Parker wrote to Elizabeth in June about the iniquity of Aldrich, who now 'saith he will stand utterly against me', and about the ingratitude of some of the Fellows of Corpus: 'They say in jest, that I am Pope of Lambeth and of Bene't College, and that I am out of all credit and of no reputation, and that they will sue to some great man of the Council to accept him as chaplain, to outface me and to beard my authority.'[4] Aldrich therefore received no comfort from the Queen. And in July Parker and the ecclesiastical commissioners wrote to the Vice-Chancellor, Thomas Byng of Clare, 'requiring and commanding you in the Queen's Majesty's name' to have Aldrich 'bound with sufficient sureties to make his personal appearance here before us, and other our colleagues at Lambeth, immediately upon the receipt of these our letters'.[5]

[1] Lansdowne MSS. vol. xvii, no. 55.   [2] Masters, *Hist. of Corpus Christi Coll.* 127.
[3] Lansdowne MSS. vol. xvii, no. 55.
[4] *Ibid.* no. 35 (enclosure).
[5] University Archives, box labelled 'Letters of Elizabeth I', no. 55.

This letter once again raised the question of the authority of the ecclesiastical commission in relation to the privileges of the university. Upon its receipt, Byng and the heads immediately appealed to Burleigh. They had, they said, already taken bond and surety of the Master of Corpus to appear before them from time to time, 'to answer all objections in any matter'; and further-more, the controversy between him 'and certain of the Fellows' being about the breach of a college statute, it was surely a matter for decision by the Chancellor, 'forasmuch as we are fully per-suaded that to send him thither by such authority should be against the privilege of this university'.[1]

On 14 July a petition was sent from Corpus[2] which more precisely revealed the internal balance of power in the college. The petition was in favour of the Master, and it was signed by five Fellows: Henry Aldrich, younger brother of Thomas, who had been elected Fellow in 1569, on one of the new Parker foundations; Thomas Robardes, the bursar; and three men elected Fellows under Aldrich—Adam Longworth, John Scot and Henry Lewis. The other seven Fellows were Norgate, Robert Swett, Joseph Bird, Thomas Gooch, Richard Willoughby, Robert Sayer and the elegant Richard Fletcher, later Bishop of London and future father of John Fletcher (who was to go up to Corpus in 1591): these men had all been elected at the end of Pory's reign, and it may be assumed that they were all opponents of the present Master.

The appeal of the Vice-Chancellor to the Chancellor occasioned a letter from Parker to Burleigh on 15 July. The Archbishop was certain that it would have been better for the Corpus disputes to have been resolved by himself 'in commission, for I do know more than the whole university doth, whose privileges yet I did not mean to hurt'. The real danger, as Parker saw it, was not the possible threat to the liberties of the university by the com-missioners, but the fact that the jurisdiction and authority of the

[1] Lansdowne MSS. vol. XVII, no. 69.   [2] Ibid. no. 70.

151

commissioners, and therefore the prerogative of the Crown, were too 'daintily looked on'. This irresponsibility in the end would be detrimental to the university as a whole; and it would be 'the utter undoing of that poor college'. Aldrich, of course, was beneath contempt: 'his insolency is too great, the childish maliciousness of his vain tales, and his with his brother's ingratitude to me, besides their manifest precisianship, is too intolerable'.[1] Parker's feeling for Corpus is the moral core of the whole story. 'I do not care who hath the hearing of the controversy', he wrote to Burleigh three days later, if 'the college be saved, and lewd and monstrous governance escape not away unreformed.' The salvation of Corpus, rocked by controversy, by envy hatred malice and all uncharitableness, might be difficult. But Parker was confident that all but one of the Cambridge heads disapproved of the Master; which compensated in some measure for that 'state of war' which the Archbishop, with great sadness, saw in his 'old nurse the college'.[2]

In an attempt finally to settle this 'factious matter', the Archbishop and the Chancellor decided to compromise with the university. Burleigh wrote to the heads from Theobalds on 18 July. He admitted that the commissioners' calling of the Master to Lambeth was perhaps unfortunate, as the deciding of all university disputes 'should appertain unto me as your Chancellor, which I would have taken upon myself or else committed to some other to be ordered if I had been made acquainted with the same in time'. But now in fact the matter was before the commissioners, and they had worked on it. So

I have conferred with my Lord of Canterbury touching the cause, and moved him, to the end that as well her Majesty's prerogative as your privileges might be saved upright, that the matter might be heard and determined jointly by his Grace and others of the commissioners, and by some of your university.[3]

---

[1] Lansdowne MSS. vol. xvii, no. 38.   [2] *Ibid.* no. 39.
[3] University Archives, 'Letters of Elizabeth I' (box), no. 204.

Parker wrote to the Vice-Chancellor on the same day to give more details of the arrangements:

your Chancellor hath appointed you with two senior Doctors or Bachelors in Divinity to attend upon us here to hear the cause and controversy betwixt Mr Aldrich and certain Fellows of Corpus Christi College. This is to pray you to make your repair up hither, so soon as you may, for that I have appointed myself with as much convenient speed as I can to purpose my journey to Canterbury, to attend upon her Majesty in her progress. I have sent you the copy of the words of the college statute, which may direct you for such as shall come up unto us. Mr Aldrich likewise is to be willed to come up accordingly. And when you be come to my house, we shall then signify unto you how we shall proceed.[1]

As it happened, Byng was away from Cambridge at the time. The letter was delivered to the deputy Vice-Chancellor, Andrew Perne. Perne read it with mounting irritation. He called a hurried meeting of those of his colleagues in residence; including Aldrich, who firmly said that 'he in no case will come before my Lord of Canterbury, but only before my Lord Burleigh'. After the meeting Perne sent Parker's letter on to Byng, after scribbling at the foot of it an almost illegible note[2] suggesting an emergency meeting with the Chancellor at Theobalds in two or three days' time: 'Mr Vice Chancellor, all the heads of the colleges which be at home desire you to come to my Lord Burleigh's upon Wednesday at night, when Dr Hawford and I will meet with you to wait upon my Lord Treasurer to desire him to have further conference of our privileges.' Perne was so indignant that he apologized for not suggesting an earlier meeting: 'I hear that Lord Burleigh will remain at Theobalds this week: we should have come before, but Dr Hawford can get no horses before.' That was on the 19th. On the 21st the Master of Peterhouse and the Master of Christ's set off on horseback for Hertfordshire.

[1] *Ibid.* no. 161.   [2] *Ibid.*

153

The meeting at Theobalds probably took place on the 22nd: for on the 23rd Parker received a letter from Burleigh in which the Chancellor expressed fresh doubts about 'whether all and singular these matters must be heard by the Chancellor or Vice-Chancellor, and only within the university'. The Archbishop, irritated by this new check, was not prepared to go further than he thought strictly necessary in respecting a scruple of this sort: 'I would be glad to attend upon you: if no prejudice or hurt to our commission might grow, in yielding to them of the university more than is needful: whose privileges yet I would be as glad to maintain as any of them.'[1] So the Chancellor and the Archbishop met once more. And at the end of July they decided to refer the case exclusively to the Vice-Chancellor, who was to try it with the heads in the Consistory Court at Cambridge.

Thus, at the beginning of August, Byng called before him the Master and Fellows of Corpus to discuss the exegesis of the college statute. This meeting was completely inconclusive; and—such is the irony of the whole affair—the heads, having won their constitutional point, now decided to let the decision rest with Parker![2]

Parker gave Aldrich one choice: he could either resign or be deprived. He promised Parker to resign. But the Archbishop at first did not believe that he would: 'burnt child dreadeth the fire: and therefore I cannot tell how to take him'.[3] But Aldrich for once kept his word; and on 22 August 1573 Robert Norgate was admitted Master of Corpus. As a consolation for his disappointed hopes in Corpus, Aldrich was made a canon of Westminster. He died three years later, in 1576, at the age of only thirty-six. Norgate celebrated his election by marrying the daughter of Parker's half-brother. But he too was to have an uneasy reign, being involved in disputes with the Fellows about the cost of the new chapel.

[1] Lansdowne MSS. vol. XVII, no. 40.
[2] *Ibid.* no. 76.   [3] *Ibid.* no. 44.

The only sympathetic figure in the case was Parker. To be called Pope of Lambeth in the 'Admonition to Parliament' in 1572 was bad enough; but not so bad as to be called Pope of Bene't College by senior members of Corpus in 1573, and to be defied by men such as Henry Aldrich who 'hath and do live off my purse daily'.[1]

But Parker was over seventy, and a sick man. Two years later he was dead.

II

The Aldrich affair is a story of Cambridge Puritanism: but so involved with the conflict of college personalities, with the peculiar authority of Parker in Corpus, with the differences of opinion between Archbishop and Chancellor, and with the constitutional issues of the royal prerogative (as exercised by the ecclesiastical commissioners) in relation to those liberties and franchises and privileges of the university which had been confirmed by the Elizabethan charter of April 1561[2]—so involved with such considerations that it is difficult to see the wood for the trees. Throughout the reign of Elizabeth the relationship between the commissioners and the university was uneasy. The friction was intensified because the commissioners were becoming more and more a Commission, with professional procedure and the formalities of a court, at the time when the Vice-Chancellor was given more specific statutory powers in the trial of religious disputes.

The case was depending, Provost Baker had written to the commissioners in 1562, in the court of the Chancellor, who 'hath the cognizance of all causes as well ecclesiastical as civil by special privilege and charter':[3] depending, that is, in the Consistory

---

[1] *Ibid.* no. 39. Henry Aldrich died in 1593, and left £40 to his college, to provide charcoal for the hall fire during the thirty days following Candlemas (W. H. Burgess, *John Robinson*, 33).

[2] C. H. Cooper, *Annals of Cambridge*, II, 165–8.

[3] Corpus Christi College MSS., vol. 106, p. 545.

Court of the Vice-Chancellor. This court met weekly during term, the Vice-Chancellor sitting with some of the heads (usually six) and one doctor of civil law, with the registrary or a clerk acting as secretary. The powers of the court dated from a charter of Edward I, confirmed by Richard II, and in turn confirmed in the Elizabethan charter, which also made the Consistory a court of record—a court whose proceedings were recorded and were valid as evidence. These provisions of 1561 were confirmed by Act of Parliament in 1571; and thus the authority of the court was placed beyond challenge. The procedure of the Consistory Court was in accordance with the civil law, not the common law; it sat in private; the accused was tried without jury and without counsel —the procedure was the same as that of the Court of Star Chamber, or of the court of the ecclesiastical commissioners. In his court, the Vice-Chancellor heard both criminal and civil cases in which a university man of the status of master of arts or higher was concerned. 'Clerks' of less than the degree of master were called before the court of the commissary: Thomas Legge was commissary from 1579 to 1605. Thus cases of debt, or defamation, or of injury, were heard in the Consistory. More important, by the charter of Richard II the university had been authorized to exercise ecclesiastical jurisdiction, and the Consistory Court in the sixteenth century had an 'essentially ecclesiastical power'.[1] The important development in Elizabethan Cambridge, so far as the relations of the Puritans and authority were concerned, was clause 45 of the new university statutes of 1570.

By this clause, any man preaching or lecturing 'anything against religion, or any part of the same as received and established by public authority' could be ordered by the Vice-Chancellor 'with the assent of the majority of the Heads of colleges' to 'recant and publicly confess his error or rashness, which if he shall have refused to do, or not done humbly, in the manner in which he is ordered, he shall, by the same authority, be for ever expelled

[1] J. R. Tanner, *Historical Register of the University* (1917), 65.

from his college and banished the university'.[1] This authority was expressed in the Consistory; and in 1571—the year of the statutory confirmation of its powers and procedure—a room on the east side of the Schools Quadrangle was fitted out as a court.[2] A succession of offenders, from Thomas Cartwright to Peter Baro and John Overall, was to feel the force of this discipline in Elizabethan Cambridge. Suppose the power were abused? Well, the commissioners were in the background, and the Archbishop, and the Chancellor: each of them a potential *deus ex machina* for a don in trouble, ready to complain of unjust treatment by the university.

The stresses and strains of these various levels of authority were sharply and dramatically illustrated in the case concerning Francis Johnson and Cuthbert Bainbrigg, both Fellows of Christ's College, in 1589.

At the beginning of January, Bainbrigg and Johnson preached sermons which seemed to be against the 'religion established by public authority': Bainbrigg's sermon was on the 5th,[3] and Johnson's on the 6th.[4] They were both called before the Consistory Court. But the interviews were unsatisfactory and matters came to a standstill. Into the uneasy hush there burst, on 19 January, a letter from Archbishop Whitgift and five ecclesiastical commissioners. Although, they said,

by our authority we might convent persons so offending before us, and deal with them according to their demerits: yet for that we do greatly tender the privileges and dignity of that place, we have rather thought good to commend the matter unto you, as a thing of good consequence and worthy to be redressed. Not doubting but you will take such order therein as appertaineth.

So the authority of the Consistory Court and the 1570 statute was to be reinforced in this case by the somewhat back-handed good-

---

[1] Translated from J. Heywood and T. Wright (ed.), *Cambridge University Transactions during the Puritan Controversies*, I, 37.
[2] R. Willis and J. W. Clark, *Architectural History of the University of Cambridge*, III, 22.
[3] University Archives, Registry Guard Books, vol. 6 (i), no. 6.   [4] *Ibid.* no. 1.

will of the ecclesiastical commission, and by the practical advice of the commissioners. The letter ended sharply:

we will, require and authorise you by virtue of her Majesty's commission for causes ecclesiastical to us and others directed, that forthwith upon the receipt hereof you call the said Bainbrigg and Johnson before you, and them to examine upon such points and portions of their sermons as were offensively taken, and further to deal with them, as you in your discretions shall think convenient.[1]

If the two offenders refused to accept the jurisdiction of the Vice-Chancellor, they were to be called before the commissioners.

The Vice-Chancellor was Thomas Nevile of Magdalene. When he received this letter he called Bainbrigg and Johnson once more before his court, on 22 January. The usual procedure in this sort of case was for the substance of the offending sermon to be determined and decided by the depositions of a half dozen or so of the auditors. Nevile maintained that in this instance that was impossible. There 'were witnesses ready to have been produced, but by threatening words they were terrified'.[2] And so Bainbrigg and Johnson were ordered orally to deliver, on oath, the contents of their own sermons. This they would not do: 'our only stay is, that in this our case, having preached publicly, we be not constrained under our oath to give matter of accusation and proof against ourselves (if any crime were committed): it being contrary to the word of God and law'.[3]

Thus this episode of Cambridge Puritanism was involved with the constitutional question of the oath so-called 'ex officio mero', imposed by prerogative authority 'by virtue of its office', and unknown to common law. Defendants—and this was the objection —were compelled 'upon their own oaths to accuse themselves'.[4] The objectors, like the later authors of the fifth amendment to the Constitution of the United States of America, believed

[1] University Archives, Registry Guard Books, vol. 6 (i), no. 23.
[2] Lansdowne MSS. vol. LXI, no. 12.   [3] Ibid. no. 4.
[4] A complaint of 1593, quoted in J. R. Tanner (ed.), Tudor Constitutional Documents, 572.

it to be intolerable that any person should 'be compelled in any
criminal case to be a witness against himself'.[1] The Roman law
procedure of the oath 'ex officio', first used by the Marian
ecclesiastical commissioners, had been revived by Whitgift in
1584, in spite of Burleigh's dislike of it as 'too much savouring of
the Romish Inquisition'.[2] The supplicants to Parliament in 1586
had objected that the oath 'to a conscience that feareth God is
more violent than any rack, to constrain him to utter that he
knoweth, though it be against himself and to his most grievous
punishment'.[3] Cartwright, before the High Commission in
October 1590, was also to refuse to take the oath: 'I esteemed it
contrary both to the laws of God and of the land, to require such
an oath, especially of a minister.'[4]

For their refusal to take such an oath in January 1589, Bainbrigg
and Johnson were imprisoned in the Tolbooth, the town jail;
where they were to remain, bail not being granted, for six
months.

Burleigh at first approved of this decision of Nevile's. In fact
he thought that the Vice-Chancellor had not gone far enough, but
ought also to have deprived them of their fellowships.[5] Nevertheless, the two prisoners knew that he was, so to say, the charitable
link in the chain of authority, and among their petitions and
appeals and complaints from the Tolbooth many were addressed
to him. 'May it please your Lordship to understand', they wrote
in May,

that we were not committed for anything uttered by us in our sermons:
but only because we did not yield to take a corporal oath to deliver the
truth, the whole truth, and nothing but the truth of that we spake in
our public sermons, and thereby to accuse ourselves (whereas the whole
audience afforded sufficient witness) if in anything we had offended.[6]

[1] Amendments to the Constitution, Article V.
[2] Tanner, *Tudor Constitutional Documents*, 374.
[3] A. Peel (ed.), *The Second Part of a Register*, II, 82.
[4] Lansdowne MSS. vol. LXIV, no. 22, fol. 67.
[5] University Library, Cambridge, Baker MSS., vol. XXX, p. 373.
[6] Lansdowne MSS. vol. LXI, no. 10.

Their sermons had lasted for an hour and a half—how was it possible for them to recall everything they had said?: 'it is unconscionable to tie the conscience of a man to take the holy name of God in witness of that which himself knoweth before he speak he cannot perform'.[1] Burleigh reacted in the expected manner. He wrote to Nevile to say that the imprisonment now seemed to him 'a very hard course'.[2] Nevile agreed with him. But he claimed that 'the university without this course is hardly to be governed'; and that the procedure hath been 'according to law both established by her Majesty and likewise to be justified by the word of God'.[3] In order to establish this legality the more effectively, a committee of seven Cambridge lawyers, with Thomas Byng in the chair, considered the question whether Bainbrigg and Johnson were bound by law to answer on oath. The committee unanimously decided that they were.[4]

Yet the fact was that the months went by, and the situation remained exactly as before. What was to be done? In June the Vice-Chancellor attempted to satisfy Bainbrigg and Johnson by requiring the oath of them 'after another manner'. But the two men, even though they had now been in prison for more than twenty weeks, protested that though the method might be different, the end was the same: 'under oath to give matter of accusation and proofs against ourselves'. And they could not 'with a good conscience take it, taking warrant in the word of God to the contrary'.[5] So the spring had passed into summer, and summer was fading into autumn, and Bainbrigg and Johnson assumed more and more the aura of martyrdom as the weeks and the months went by.

On 13 September they were released on bail. This decision had been made at a meeting on 9 September of the Vice-Chancellor and six heads: John Still of Trinity, Humphrey Tyndall of

---

[1] Lansdowne MSS. vol. LXI, no. 12. [2] Ibid. no. 8. [3] Ibid.
[4] University Archives, Registry Guard Books, vol. 6 (i), no. 5.
[5] Ibid. no. 16. (In Johnson's hand.)

Queens', John Copcot of Corpus, Thomas Byng of Clare, Thomas Legge of Caius, and Lancelot Andrewes of Pembroke.[1] It had been there decided that the examination by oath would be dropped; but that Bainbrigg and Johnson must be tried by authority of clause 45 of the statutes. Retractations were drawn up for them, to be publicly delivered at the beginning of the Michaelmas term.[2]

As might have been expected, Bainbrigg and Johnson, now living in the comparative comfort of Christ's, took heart to object in turn against this decision. They wanted time to deliberate; they had not offended against the university statutes; the retractations which the heads had drafted for them were both unconstitutional and inaccurate, being drawn up without their being consulted, and by men most of whom had not heard the original sermons.[3] So the beginning of the Michaelmas term went by, and nothing was done.

Eventually, late in October, Bainbrigg was ordered to read his retractation in Great St Mary's on 14 December.[4] He did so: and he was to remain at Christ's as a Fellow until 1620. Johnson, however, refused to retract; and on 30 October the Vice-Chancellor and heads, by authority of the statute, expelled him from the university.

As a final gesture of defiance, Johnson remained in Cambridge and appealed against the decision. By chapter 48 of the 1570 statutes he had the right to do so, the appeal to be heard by three judges. On 18 December Johnson heard in the Consistory Court that his request for an appeal had been refused. He still remained in Cambridge, however; and so he was once more taken into custody and imprisoned in the Tolbooth. Now, he had appealed against his expulsion partly on the advice of the Chancellor. In a letter to Burleigh on 22 December Johnson told the story of his failure:

I requested the Proctor to present my appeal, and to procure delegates to be chosen according to statute, which was all I could here do. And

---

[1] *Ibid.* no. 15 (a).   [2] *Ibid.* no. 19.   [3] *Ibid.*   [4] *Ibid.* no. 14.

now not only have I profited nothing, but being called before Mr Vice Chancellor and the Heads the 18th of this present month, I was there (for any thing I heard) by the sole authority of the Vice Chancellor charged the next day to depart the university, except I would there desire some longer respite for the ridding away of my stuff. Whereunto I making answer that I waited the issue of my appeal made to the university, which depending, I was by law to remain in state as before, I was again required to answer whether I would the next day depart the university, or ask respite for the removal of my stuff. Whereunto I answering that I was not so much minded to let fall my appeal, was by the Vice Chancellor committed to close prison without bail or mainprise, until such time as I would yield to let fall my appeal, and give over my title to the university and to my Fellowship; where I did lie and continue three days in the Tolbooth, in a close and cold corner, straitly kept that none of my friends might come at me, nor comfort come to me from them; and now because of the extremity of the weather am removed to the bailiff of the Tolbooth his house, with most strait charge that none at all be suffered to come unto me.[1]

Perhaps Francis Johnson was rather a barrack-room lawyer, and a little too fond of his assumed role as 'a poor prisoner overthrown by the power of mine adversaries in a just cause'.[2] But the great stir he provoked in the university is tribute to the changed position since the days of Aldrich. Then, the question of university privilege had been posed in terms of over-powerful central administration and liberal and courageous Vice-Chancellors: now, it was rather a matter of autocratic Vice-Chancellors and heads impeding those liberties which any subject of the supreme governor had the right to enjoy. 'I beseech your Lordship to consider', continued Johnson to Burleigh, 'whether that withal the sovereign authority of our gracious Queen (whom God long continue among us with much glory) be not impugned by making themselves (without, nay against, law and statute) supreme judges and governors, not to be appealed from.'[3] The petition with sixty-eight signatures sent from Cambridge on

---

[1] Lansdowne MSS. vol. LXI, no. 15.   [2] *Ibid.*   [3] *Ibid.*

23 December (comparing Johnson to Jeremiah, the prophet cast
into prison, and hinting that Burleigh should be the delivering King
Zedekiah) made the same point: 'The privileges granted to our
whole body of this university' are 'violently pulled from us by
those who ought to go before us all in maintaining them': 'We
doubt not but your Lordship soon perceiveth how unequal it is,
that the parties from whom the appeal was made should be judges
whether the appeal was lawful or not.'[1]

However, Johnson's appeal was not allowed; and he next
appears to history as chaplain to the English congregation at
Middelburg. But the case continued to worry thoughtful and
moderate Puritans. William Whitaker, Master of St John's,
writing to Burleigh a few weeks after the shouting had died down,
expressed their fear: 'The liberty of appeals being now of late
utterly lost, whereby one member is already cut off, not the
worst: the inconvenience hereof will appear, as may be justly
feared, more hereafter; not in one or two, but in as many as
shall utter anything, though in never so good thought, contrary
to the liking of a few.'[2]

III

This fear that those speaking in 'good thought', if they did so
'contrary to the liking of a few', might invite arbitrary and
unjust treatment, had been in the minds of thinking men in the
university for twenty years; that is, since the introduction of the
new statutes of 1570.

These statutes were largely the work of John Whitgift, Master
of Trinity. Their occasion was the controversy about the lectures
of the Lady Margaret Professor, Thomas Cartwright. The cause
lay deeper.

The growing demands of the Cambridge Puritans in the 1560's
were related to, and intensified by, the increasing numbers in the

---

[1] *Ibid.* no. 16.   [2] Lansdowne MSS. vol. LXII, no. 41.

university. This increase found its most influential constitutional expression in the greater numbers of junior Fellows: young men in a hurry. Masters of arts of up to three years' standing were regents, or teaching masters.[1] After three years they became non-regent masters. The Senate, or common assembly of all resident members of the university of the degree of master and above, was divided into two houses: a 'lower' house, consisting of the non-regent masters; and an 'upper', the regent house, consisting of the regents and the doctors of the university. The Senate was, as it were, the 'Body of the University'. The Head, the *Caput Senatus*, was a presiding committee of six men: the Vice-Chancellor, three doctors, one non-regent and one regent master. Now, by the first Elizabethan statutes, of 1559, the regent masters possessed decisive power in the university. For instance, the Vice-Chancellor was elected by a majority of the regents.[2] This authority, moreover, tended to be abused, and made for disorder. There were increasing complaints during the 1560's about 'the younger sort of regents': 'the which younger sort doth daily increase more and more'.[3]

The statutes of 1570 gave more power (or, as in the case of the Consistory Court, a more strictly defined power) to the Vice-Chancellor and the heads of houses. So, the objectors to the statutes claimed, power passed from the Body of the University to the Head. Certain ancient privileges, the objectors claimed, 'derived from the body of the university', have passed to the Masters of colleges and have therefore been abrogated: the election of the Vice-Chancellor and other officers of the university; the choice of the *Caput Senatus*; the power to veto the proctors and taxors; the freedom of appeals; and 'the absolute jurisdiction of the negative voice in all public and private affairs both at home and abroad'. All these things, it was claimed, were once ours,

[1] University Statutes of 1559, XVIII.
[2] *Ibid.* XXIX.
[3] Corpus Christi College, Cambridge, MSS., vol. 118, no. 44, fol. 1a.

and now they are theirs: the new statutes have established 'an unreasonable jurisdiction'.[1]

The Vice-Chancellor was now effectively chosen by the heads of houses, who nominated two candidates, one of whom the majority of the regents and non-regents must choose. This, argued the heads, was to avoid 'the former contentions and labours by factious regents, for unmeet and unfit men'.[2] More, the term of regency was extended from three years to five—this, Whitgift presumably thought, would make the body of regents slightly older and much wiser. The *Caput Senatus* had been by the statutes of 1559 elected by the whole Senate, from nominations made by the Vice-Chancellor and the proctors. Now, election was by the heads and doctors only; the *Caput* remained in office for a whole year and not for just a single congregation; and each of the six members had an absolute veto on any grace submitted—therefore no grace could be put forward in the Senate without the unanimous approval of the *Caput*. Most of the *Caput*, protested the objectors, are Masters of colleges:

whereby it falleth out that nothing can pass all the whole year whereof they mislike, or any one of them. Insomuch that experience hath already proved, that some one of the Head, minding to further some unworthy, stayed by others, has nipped all graces for that congregation, and threatened to continue so the whole year unless he were preferred.[3]

University lectors, once nominated by the Vice-Chancellor and proctors, were now nominated by the heads, and two names given to the non-regents and regents, one of which they must elect: 'by these means', argued Whitgift, 'the intolerable labour and partiality in the preferring of unmeet men, and the corruption of officers, is taken away'.[4]

Especially important were the Vice-Chancellor's power of imprisonment, the authority of the heads in interpreting the

[1] *Ibid.* no. 45, fol. 4.
[3] *Ibid.* no. 45, fol. 2.
[2] *Ibid.* no. 46, fol. 2.
[4] *Ibid.* no. 46, fol. 3.

university statutes, and the liberty of appeal. By the 1559 statutes, the Vice-Chancellor had been unable to commit any resident member of the university to prison 'without the consent of the greater part of Masters of Colleges'. The new statutes, it was objected, gave him 'absolute authority to send Masters of Arts to prison at his pleasure. And therefore the first word now commonly is, To the Tolbooth with him: as by divers examples is to be proved.'[1] The right of interpretation was given in 1570 to the Chancellor and a majority of the heads, whereas it had previously been the right of a majority of the regents and non-regents. The heads argued that the new interpreters, by their wisdom and experience, were more able than 'the younger sort, who hath commonly greater will than judgement in such things'.[2] Thirdly, with regard to the choice of the delegates for hearing appeals, in the 1560's the proctors had named delegates, who were then approved or disallowed by the 'body'. Now, the delegates were chosen by the *Caput*, which was chosen by the heads, who were usually parties in cases of appeal: those from 'whose unjust sentence appeal is made'. So when the heads 'offer wrong' they 'themselves appoint judges to redress that wrong'.[3]

Finally, the 1570 statutes increased the powers of the heads within the colleges. This, said the objectors, was 'an intolerable injury to establish the Masters' tyranny'.[4] This, replied the heads, had been done to check those Fellows 'so far from flattering their Masters that they forget good manners and dutiful obedience'.[5] All the changes in 1570 had been made 'for the advancement of virtue and learning, and the maintenance of good order, set forth by the Queen's Majesty's authority'.[6]

The statutes were dated 25 September 1570. During 1571 lengthy objections to them were prepared; these, together with the replies of the heads, were judged in May 1572 by Parker,

[1] Corpus Christi College, Cambridge, MSS., vol. 118, no. 45, fol. 5.
[2] *Ibid.* no. 46, fol. 5.   [3] *Ibid.* no. 45, fol. 2.   [4] *Ibid.* fol. 3.
[5] *Ibid.* no. 46, fol. 4.   [6] *Ibid.* fol. 1.

Grindal, Sandys and Cox, who thought that 'the statutes as they be drawn up may yet stand, and no great cause why to make any alteration'.[1]

Early in November 1570 Whitgift and the heads, in thanking the Chancellor for 'the procuring of the late statutes', mentioned that 'the younger sort for the restraint of their liberty much murmur and grudge at them'.[2] From November 1570 to November 1571 the murmurs were subdued, for Whitgift himself was Vice-Chancellor. But in the Michaelmas term of 1571 there was an organized campaign against the statutes, led by the proctors for the new academic year—Arthur .Purefye of Peterhouse and John Becon of St John's (who was also public orator); abetted by Degory Nichols (one of the taxors) and by Lancelot Browne of Pembroke. The explosion began in the Master's Lodge at Corpus. Aldrich was consulting with the Vice-Chancellor and most of the heads, and some other university officials, when Browne took it upon himself to make a bitter attack on the statutes. This caused a certain amount of embarrassment. Much more than embarrassment was felt later, when Becon made an oration in the Regent House 'to the defaming of the Queen's Majesty's Statutes, and to the great discrediting of the heads of colleges, using such insolence against them as the like has not been heard'. Spurred on by this official audacity, 'the inferior sort' were much 'encouraged and emboldened both to speak and to set themselves against their seniors and Heads'. Richard Fletcher, 'a busy regent of the proctor's faction', went so far as to abuse Thomas Gooch, another Fellow of Corpus, in the Regent House: 'saying that if he were served according to his deserts he should have his hood plucked over his ears'.[3] Amidst the disturbances a petition went the rounds, objecting in detail to the new statutes. This was presented to the Chancellor in May 1572. It was signed

---

[1] *Ibid.* no. 39.   [2] S.P. Dom. Eliz. vol. LXXIV, no. 29.
[3] Corpus Christi College MSS., vol. 118, no. 48.

by 164 Fellows of colleges—that is, by half the total number of dons in the university.[1]

These 'grievances of the body of the university for the alteration of the ancient privileges and customs' were of course expressed in terms of the constitution, of the old natural and acquired rights of the university. But the opposition was also the product of religious enthusiasm. Edward Dering of Christ's, in the full force of his outraged Puritan conscience, condemned the new statutes as 'unrighteous';[2] and attacked the personal character of the heads who had produced them—Whitgift, Perne, Harvey of Trinity Hall, and Thomas Ithell of Jesus. For, of the fourteen Masters, four or five—and those the authors of the statutes—'do always what they list'; and these four or five were 'either enemies unto God's gospel or so faint professors that they do little good in the Church'. Four or five, but especially one: John Whitgift. When Whitgift was Vice-Chancellor,

men dare not give their voices according to their conscience for fear of displeasure: and not without cause, for Doctor Whitgift in a scrutiny, some giving their voices simply and freely, was exceedingly moved, and called for pen and ink to write their names, thinking that with so terrifying of them, they would for fear give as he would have them.

In the past, Dering had both liked and respected the Master of Trinity. But 'yet he is man': and a man whom 'God hath suffered to fall into great infirmities'. 'So forward a mind against Mr Cartwright, and other such, betrayeth a conscience that is full of sickness. His affections ruled him, and not his learning, when he framed his cogitations to get more statutes.'

And yet the statutes of 1570 remained in force until 1856. It may therefore be said that the history of the university for three centuries was vitally influenced by the policy of Whitgift as Master of Trinity, *primus inter pares*, in the ten years after 1567.

[1] Corpus Christi College MSS., vol. 118, no. 38. Signatures at pp. 633-4. Of the 164 names I have traced with certainty only 131.
[2] Dering to Cecil, November 1570. Lansdowne MSS., vol. xii, no. 86.

IV

John Whitgift matriculated from Pembroke in 1550 at the age of eighteen.[1] Nicholas Ridley was Master of the college, and the young Yorkshireman's tutor was John Bradford. (In 1567, when Whitgift, on the recommendation of Grindal, was elected to succeed Matthew Hutton as Master of the college, the Fellows expressed their thankfulness that the tradition of Ridley was in safe hands.[2])

During the reign of Mary, Whitgift remained in Cambridge as a Fellow of Peterhouse, under the protection of Andrew Perne, who personally nursed him through a serious illness—the Marprelate tracts were later to brand him as 'Perne's boy'.[3] In 1560, when he was twenty-eight, he was ordained by Cox of Ely, and presented to the living of Teversham, three miles outside Cambridge. In 1563 he was elected to the Lady Margaret chair—twelfth in succession after Erasmus. The manuscript of his Lady Margaret lectures on the Book of Revelation is preserved in the Cambridge University Library.[4] He transferred to the Regius professorship of divinity in 1567; and resigned it in November 1569.[5] Thomas Cartwright, Fellow of Trinity, attended some of Professor Whitgift's lectures. He did not think as highly of them as most: 'You are better acquainted', he told Whitgift some years after, 'with the names of logic and philosophy, than with any sound or substantial knowledge of them.'[6] Whitgift, stung by the taunt, replied:

Touching my reading in the Schools (which you here opprobriously object unto me) though I know that the university had a far better

---

[1] Whitgift was probably born in 1532; P. M. Dawley, *Whitgift*, 2. He seems to have gone up first to Queens', but quickly moved to Pembroke.

[2] Strype, *Whitgift*, III, 7.   [3] Dawley, *Whitgift*, 44.

[4] University Library, Cambridge, MSS., vol. Ff/2/36. There are two autograph stipend receipts of Whitgift as Lady Margaret Professor in University Archives, Registry Guard Books, vol. 39 (i), no. 2.

[5] University Archives, Box labelled 'Mandates of Elizabeth I', no. 224.

[6] Whitgift, *Works*, I, 144.

opinion of me than I deserved, and that there were a great many which were in all respects better able to do that office than myself, yet I trust I did my duty and satisfied them. What logic I uttered in my lectures, and how I read, I refer to their judgements; who surely, if they suffered me so long to continue in that place, augmented the stipend for my sake, and were so desirous to have me still to remain in that function (reading so unlearnedly, as you would make the world believe I did), may be thought either to be without judgement themselves, or else to have been very careless for that exercise.[1]

The year 1567, when he became Regius Professor, marked Whitgift's unusual success. He preached before the Queen, who took to him at once, made her little pun about 'White Gift', and appointed him a royal chaplain; he was elected Master of Pembroke; after three months there he resigned, to succeed Robert Beaumont as Master of Trinity.

In 1567 Whitgift was thirty-five. For the next ten years the policies of the university were swayed by his hand. He was throughout that decade a member of the *Caput Senatus*, and he was twice Vice-Chancellor. In 1568 he was also appointed a canon of Ely—a preferment which he resigned in June 1571 on becoming Dean of Lincoln. During the last six years of his mastership he spent some months of each year in Lincoln, and during the last year of it he was also prolocutor of the lower house of Convocation. In all these appointments Whitgift fought to the top of his strength 'pro Ecclesia Dei'. The authority of the Church was like that of the State and the University and the Master of Trinity, a reflection of the authority of God, a power ordained by God, and all were spiritual charges. From the beginning there was no doubt where authority lay in Trinity. 'A Master of a college', he was to remind Cartwright,

(the which example also Master Calvin doth use) hath a perpetual office: he is chief governor of that society; and all the members thereof owe duty and obedience unto him, as to their head: he hath authority

---

[1] Whitgift, *Works*, I, 64.

to punish and to see laws executed: neither do I think that either archbishop or bishop claimeth greater authority and jurisdiction over their provinces and diocese than is due to the Master within his college.[1]

Thus he would not suffer those with whom he had to do to 'disquiet the university or college with false doctrine and schismatical opinions'; he could not 'suffer them openly to break and contemn those laws and statutes which they are sworn to observe, and I to execute'.[2] His rule in Trinity was such that five years after he had succeeded Beaumont, he was able to write of the college as 'never in better quietness, never replenished with more toward scholars, never fuller of students of all degrees... than it is at this present'.[3]

Whitgift was the archetypal public school headmaster: efficient, devoted, an administrator in mind and soul and body, with a public conscience which sometimes seemed ruthless and more often than not unattractive, and a private conscience which he rarely allowed himself to reveal. He lacked the robust sensitivity of Parker, and the spiritual subtlety of Grindal. Matthew Parker, full-faced, kind, moderate, comes down to us in his portraits and his letters as a likeable English pastor. Edmund Grindal made a stand for spiritual values which makes him immediately sympathetic to post-Tractarian generations. But Whitgift is a withdrawn figure: the sad eyes, dominant nose and rather contemptuous mouth of the National Gallery portrait keep a modern sensibility at a safe distance; the shell of a shy man perhaps, but who knows? He had more power than either of his predecessors, and so he is a lonelier figure. One thing, however, can be said: in exercising that power, Whitgift was always just and often, especially in his dealings with the university, very charitable.

Giles Wigginton, who went up to Trinity in 1564 under 'that blessed man of God Dr Beaumont', left a bitter account of the

[1] *Ibid.* II, 279–80.
[2] *Ibid.* III, 395.
[3] *Ibid.* 396.

policy and tactics of the new Master.[1] Whitgift made 'diligent enquiry after such scholars and boys as durst be bold to reprove sin and to call for reformation', calling them 'saucy boys, busy bodies and meddlers with matters of estate'. Young Giles caught the Master's eye as especially saucy. Whereupon he 'looked narrowly into my life', countenanced an accusation that he 'danced once (which was when I was a child), and did not wash my hands often enough', and said he would use 'short arguments with me', meaning 'the rod'. There was an especially unfortunate incident in 1568. Wigginton returned to his chamber to find that one of his fellow pensioners had just committed suicide by hanging. He in fact arrived in the room at the same time as a servant of the Master (Whitgift being at work on the floor below) who had been angrily sent to reprimand Wigginton for the noise.

Wigginton became a Fellow in 1571. And for the next six years

at sundry times and in sundry sorts I suffered many like injuries at his hands and at the hands of his chief adherents, scholars and friends, procured and encouraged by him to molest and trouble me, namely for wearing my hat instead of a square cap, and for not wearing of a surplice when I went to the chapel, for speaking against non-residents, stage plays, and popery or prelacy and such like matters. They also called me unsociable, while he kept me from all the offices and pre-ferments which should have fallen to me, treating me as no Master had ever been known to treat Fellow.

Obviously Wigginton was the prize college bore, with a developed persecution complex. He left Trinity in 1578 to be vicar of Sedbergh, and continued, in his own estimation, to be hounded by Whitgift. In 1586 he was imprisoned at Lambeth for refusing to take the oath 'ex officio'. 'My old adversary the Archbishop', he wrote from prison, 'hath treated me more like a Turk or a dog than a man or a minister of Jesus Christ.'[2] Two years later he was

[1] Peel (ed.), *Second Part of a Register*, II, 241–3.
[2] Quoted in C. H. and T. Cooper, *Athenae Cantabrigienses*, II, 320.

again in prison, suspected of complicity in the Martin Marprelate organization.

So Whitgift ruled Trinity, a lean, severe, and awe-inspiring presence. Eating in hall with the boys, 'as well to have a watchful eye over the scholars, and to keep them in a mannerly and awful obedience, as by his example, to teach them to be contented with a scholar-like college diet'.[1] Himself acting as tutor to some pupils,[2] including Francis Bacon, who became a fellow commoner of Trinity in April 1573 at the age of twelve years and three months. (Francis's father, Sir Nicholas, was a Corpus man, a contemporary of Parker: his mother was the sister of Burleigh's second wife, the former Mildred Cooke.) Whitgift never missed the college disputations and prayers: 'chiefly for devotion, and withal to observe others' absence, always severely punishing such omissions and negligences'.[3] At least one Fellow found himself in the Tolbooth because of excessive Puritanism.[4] But, as the Master was to remind Cartwright, 'I never expelled any of degree since my first coming to Trinity College, but two: the one for pertinacy, the other for perjury'.[5] The pertinacious Fellow was Walter Travers, of whom Whitgift wrote: 'I did elect him Fellow of Trinity College, being before rejected by Dr Beaumont for his intolerable stomach: whereof I had also afterwards such experience, that I was forced by due punishment so to weary him till he was fain to travel, and depart from the college to Geneva.'[6] The Fellow expelled for perjury was Cartwright himself.

[1] G. Paule, *Life of Whitgift* (1699 ed.), 23–4.
[2] Whitgift's accounts with his pupils, in his own hand (Lambeth Palace MSS.), were printed in 1847–8 by S. R. Maitland, *British Magazine*, vols. XXXII and XXXIII.
[3] Paule, *op. cit.* 23.
[4] John Browning, Fellow, 1563–83.
[5] Whitgift, *Works*, III, 507.
[6] Quoted in Walton's Life of Hooker; in Hooker, *Works*, I, 30.

V

The clash between Whitgift and Cartwright in 1570 was the most dramatic and far-reaching of the disputes between the Puritans and authority in Elizabethan Cambridge. Cartwright was two or three years younger than Whitgift; yet they had commenced bachelor together in 1554, Cartwright having been a scholar of St John's under Thomas Lever. In 1556 Cartwright left the university to study law in London, as William Fulke was also to do. He returned to Cambridge in 1560 as a Fellow of Trinity under Beaumont, but he soon went up the street to a fellowship at St John's, where he became junior dean in 1562; after three months of this onerous office, however, he was once more elected Fellow of Trinity, where he remained until the end of 1565. He spent 1566 in Ireland, as chaplain to the Archbishop of Armagh, Adam Loftus, himself a Trinity man. In 1567 (Whitgift's great year) he took up his fellowship at Trinity again, and became university preacher. It was said that he filled Great St Mary's so full that 'the sexton was fain to take down the windows, by reason of the multitudes that came to hear him'.[1] And in November 1569, when William Chaderton, Lady Margaret Professor, was recommended by Cecil to the Regius chair which Whitgift had resigned because of pressure of work in Trinity, Thomas Cartwright was elected to succeed Chaderton. He was deprived almost exactly a year later, in December 1570.

The first official complaint came from William Chaderton. He wrote to the Chancellor on 11 June 1570 giving details of Cartwright's teaching, and complaining also of the complementary sermons of Edmund Chapman of Trinity and Robert Some of Queens'.[2] On 24 June, in the course of an angry letter, Edmund Grindal (who had been installed as Archbishop of York on the 9th) recommended to Cecil that he order the Vice-

[1] Samuel Clarke (ed.), *Lives of Thirty-two English Divines* (1677), 17.
[2] S.P. Dom. Eliz. vol. LXXI, no. 11.

Chancellor to veto the grace for Cartwright's doctorate of divinity, due during the Commencement at the beginning of July.[1] Cecil was moved to action. On 26 June he wrote to the Vice-Chancellor, Dr John May of St Catharine's, recommending that if any of

this sort shall be appointed to receive any degrees at this Commencement, I think it good and necessary that they be forborne and respected, until some further proof be made of them. For to bestow credit or reputation upon such, is to minister to them weapons to wound our mother the university of study and piety, and to rend asunder the seemly garment of concord.[2]

And so on 29 June there came the long-remembered meeting of the Senate in the Regent House, on the north side of the Schools quadrangle: the swan song of the old regime, the end of the power of the regents. At the election of the members of the *Caput Senatus* the supporters of Cartwright vetoed the names of every one of the candidates proposed; so that 'none could be admitted to be in the same Head for passing of graces, but only such as were known to favour Cartwright's cause'.[3] Dr May bravely retaliated by vetoing the grace for Cartwright's degree. 'For which my doing,' he wrote to the Chancellor that evening, 'I have suffered this day no small troubles at his and his favourers' hands, and am like to sustain more, unless by your honour's authority I may be in my lawful doings assisted.'[4]

July was a month of attack and counter-attack. Petitions were sent down from the university, some in favour of Cartwright, others against him; Cartwright himself wrote at length to the Chancellor; Grindal and Parker made themselves always on call to give advice to Cecil; and Cecil remained calm in the storm. At the beginning of August the Chancellor showed that he was unwilling to rush into dogmatism. 'How far Mr Cartwright hath herein proceeded,' he wrote to the heads on 3 August,

[1] E. Grindal, *Remains*, 324.
[2] University Library, Cambridge, Baker MSS., vol. XXIX, p. 367.
[3] S.P. Dom. Eliz. vol. LXXI, no. 27.   [4] *Ibid.*

'I cannot certainly determine.' So far as he could see, the Lady Margaret Professor did not seem to have 'any arrogancy, or intention to move troubles, but as a reader of the Scriptures to give notes by way of comparison betwixt the order of the ministry in the time of the Apostles, and the present times now in this Church of England'. However, he had ordered Cartwright 'not to deal any further in these kinds of questions in his readings or sermons or any otherwise', until there had been a conference about the matter some time in the Michaelmas term; and Cartwright had agreed to these conditions. This, said the Chancellor, was a provisional move:

For the further determination of these new questions, as well for common order as for the truth of the controversy, I shall gladly receive your advices and opinions, meaning thereunto to conform myself for the credit I have in your wisdom and great learnings, and the love that I trust you bear to the true and common quietness.[1]

Whitgift was extremely irritated by this letter. 'I think your Honour doth not fully understand Mr Cartwright's opinions', he wrote from Trinity on 19 August. He urged the Chancellor to more violent action; and announced that, for the good order of the university, especially after the disgraceful scenes at the Commencement, he had prepared (with Perne, Ithel and Harvey to help him) the draft of a new code of university statutes.[2] From this point, things moved quickly. The statutes received the royal assent five weeks later, on 25 September; and in November, under the new regulations, Whitgift was himself elected Vice-Chancellor.

During the first weeks of Michaelmas term there took place the conferences with Cartwright suggested by Burleigh in August. They were not satisfactory. 'The more favourably he is dealt with,' the heads wrote to Cecil on 7 November, 'the more

[1] University Library, Cambridge, Baker MSS., vol. XXIX, p. 364.
[2] Strype, *Whitgift*, III, 16–17.

untractable we find him.'[1] The Day of Judgement came for Cartwright on 11 December, when he was summoned before a meeting of the Consistory Court in the Master's Lodge at Trinity: the nine heads present were Whitgift, Perne, Harvey, Ithel, Byng, May, William Chaderton, Hawford, and Roger Kelke of Magdalene.[2] Cartwright was shown a summary of his teaching in six Latin articles, a summary which had been drawn up in November. He acknowledged the document to be a fair précis of his opinions; and the heads agreed among themselves that it was against the religion 'received and established by public authority'. In accordance with clause 45 of the new statutes, the Lady Margaret Professor was ordered to 'recant and publicly confess his error'. This Cartwright refused to do. He was therefore deprived of his professorship and forbidden to preach in the university. And 'there was no appeal tendered'.

Cartwright went to Geneva, and returned to Cambridge in April 1572: only to be deprived of his fellowship at Trinity in the summer. Whitgift wrote to Parker in September:

I have pronounced Mr Cartwright to be no Fellow here, because contrary both to the express words of his oath, and a plain statute of this college, he hath continued here above his time not being full minister. Which truly I did not know until now of late; for if I had known it before, I might have eased myself of much trouble, and the college of great contention. Hitherto (I thank God) it hath been as quiet a college as any was in all Cambridge. Now it is clean contrary marvellous contentious, which I can ascribe to no cause so much as to Mr Cartwright's presence here.[3]

A month later, in October, the Master of Trinity completed his 'Reply to the First Admonition to Parliament'; in May 1573 came Cartwright's 'Answer' to this 'Reply', and Whitgift immediately began work on his 'Defence'. In December,

[1] *The Eagle* (St John's College Magazine), xxx, 12.
[2] Report of the meeting in University Archives, Registry Guard Books, vol. 6 (i), no. 30.
[3] Quoted by A. F. S. Pearson, *Thomas Cartwright and Elizabethan Puritanism*, 429.

Cartwright was summoned to appear before the ecclesiastical commissioners, and he fled the country. The two parts of his 'Second Answer' appeared in 1575 and 1577. A petition to the Archbishop from prison in January 1592 was to be the last footnote to their literary exchanges.

It was an odd business, this prolonged and public literary warfare between two Cambridge contemporaries, the one a Master, the other a sometime Fellow whom that Master had deprived. 'You and I', wrote Whitgift to Cartwright in the early 1570's, 'have not been long nor much conversant together; and yet surely I suppose that I know you both touching your religion, conversation and affection, as well as if I had been twenty years companion in your chamber with you.'[1]

In June 1577 Whitgift, then aged forty-five, preached for the last time in Trinity College Chapel. On 21 August he had been consecrated Bishop of Worcester by Grindal, Horne, Aylmer, and Curteys. He took his text from the thirteenth chapter of the second Epistle to the Corinthians: 'Finally, brethren, farewell. Be perfect, be of good comfort, be of one mind, live in peace; and the God of love and peace shall be with you.' The sermon was appropriately received by the college: 'it so moved their affections, that they burst out into tears, insomuch that there were scarce any dry eyes to be found amongst the whole number'.[2]

The next day, with great style and affection, John Whitgift was escorted from the university.

VI

Of course, all the acts of university authority were in theory those of the Chancellor. And the nature of authority in Elizabethan Cambridge was coloured by the character of Burleigh: paternal, careful, and perhaps—so Whitgift thought in the summer of

[1] Whitgift, *Works*, I, 519.   [2] Paule, *Whitgift*, 26.

1570—a little slow in coming down firmly against the rebels. Whitgift was an impatient administrator in those days: 'It is time to awake out of sleep, and to draw out the sword of discipline, to provide that laws, which be general, and made for uniformity as well of doctrine as ceremonies, be generally and universally observed.'[1] But Burleigh asked for the truth, and was determined to stay for an answer; remaining calm or undecided amidst a hail of petitions and letters from sincere but contradictory groups. He had an obvious and open-minded charity. He wrote to the heads, for example, in 1572, to ask that William Charke, suspended for a sermon in favour of Cartwright, be restored to his fellowship at Peterhouse:

Forasmuch as the said Charke hath been with me, and partly wisely extenuating his fault, partly very honestly acknowledging, that he committed the same by overmuch vehemency of his spirit, and faithfully promising never hereafter to deal therein again, or with like that may be offensive, hath showed some good parts of nature and good gifts to be in him, the which in mine opinion it were great charity and good wisdom by gentle using and persuasion rather to reduce to be profitable in the Church of God, than by so sudden cutting him off from the course of his studies utterly to lose.[2]

'Great charity and good wisdom.' But in this particular case Burleigh was mistaken. The heads, astonished, wrote a further account of Charke's contumacy.[3] Burleigh then drew back: he was sorry 'that he was not made privy of Charke's fancies'.[4] In fact he had been, three months before. The affair ended in March 1573: 'I have remitted Charke to be ordered as you shall think expedient; I have had less respect unto him, for that I found not that submission and conformity in him, whereof I had conceived some opinion at the writing of my letters to you in his favour.'[5]

[1] Whitgift, *Works*, I, 122.
[2] University Library, Cambridge, Baker MSS. vol. XXIX, p. 373.
[3] Lansdowne MSS. vol. XVI, no. 34.
[4] Strype, *Annals of the Reformation*, III, 279.
[5] University Library, Cambridge, Baker MSS. vol. XXIX, p. 373.

Burleigh's sometimes rather blind fairness often made things difficult for the authorities in Cambridge. In Charke's case, the culprit, on being called before the Consistory, had refused to recant, saying that Burleigh had told him not to.[1] In the case of Bainbrigg and Johnson also the Chancellor was rather less forthright than the heads expected, once he had received appeals and begging letters from the prisoners. In April 1589, the heads asked Burleigh definitely to support their insistence on the procedure by oath: 'for that your Lordship hath not made any express mention of receiving their answers upon their oaths, they seem to take advantage, and make construction as though your Lordship would not have them sworn at all'.[2]

Such uncertainties and inefficiencies, and the fact that beyond university authority there were ecclesiastical commissioners and Visitors and Archbishops, and even the Queen herself—all of whom might be interested in a Cambridge dispute—prevented the government of the university from being that unrelieved tyranny which William Whitaker had feared. The trials before the Consistory, dons examining dons, were well mannered and fair. Even the tiresome Bainbrigg and Johnson were 'four or five times dealt withal, not in rigorous sort, but in civil and courteous wise with offer of conference, as of intent to persuade them and not to force them'.[3] By sixteenth-century standards, that was perhaps not too bad.

VII

The cases considered in this chapter have been spectacular affairs, not at all matters of the trivial round. The brushes between the Puritans and the authorities were of course not all of that stature. The Consistory Court was not always the scene of high drama. The case of William Perkins, Fellow of Christ's and friend of Bainbrigg and Johnson, will show in better proportion the week-

---

[1] Lansdowne MSS. vol. XVI, no. 34. [2] *Ibid.* vol. LXI, no. 6.
[3] *Ibid.*

by-week working of the discipline of the university in religious matters.

In January 1587, Perkins, then aged twenty-eight, preached at a Communion Service in the college chapel. A complaint about the matter of his sermon was made to the Vice-Chancellor, John Copcot of Corpus. Perkins had

noted this as a corruption in our Church, that the minister doth receive the bread and wine not at the hands of another minister, but doth take it himself; that to kneel when we receive the sacrament is superstitious and anti-Christian; and that another corruption is to turn ourselves towards the east.[1]

Six days after the event, Perkins was called before the Consistory: the Vice-Chancellor, sitting with six heads and one lawyer. He began by refusing 'to answer sufficiently until he might know his accusers'. This request was refused. But four members of Christ's, including Bainbrigg, were called: to answer on oath whether Perkins had in fact maintained the three opinions which had been complained of. The witnesses were unsatisfactory—they could not remember this, they had not arrived in time to hear him say that—and Perkins, being asked further to 'satisfy' the court, now said he was 'most willing with all my heart to do it'. He gave a lengthy explanation-cum-apology to the court. He denied that he had condemned the minister's communicating of himself as 'unlawful and a corruption in our church'; he had not said that kneeling was unlawful: but 'my opinion was this, that of the two gestures which are used, sitting and kneeling, sitting is more convenient, because Christ he sat, the Pope he kneeleth'; he held that turning to the east was a matter 'indifferent, and to be used accordingly'—that is, 'in things indifferent we must go as far as we can from idolatry'. His statement—taken down by a clerk— ended with the words: 'I confess most freely this thing, I did not

[1] The official minutes of the case, signed by Copcot, are in Corpus Christi College Bursary MSS. vol. of 'Miscellaneous Documents: 1430–1700', no. 51.

seek the disquiet of this congregation: yet that I might have spoken at a better time, more convenient.'

And that was that. The Vice-Chancellor and six Masters of colleges had had a busy morning, and learned once more that what some persons remember of other persons' sermons is not really very much to go by. Nothing had been gained, but nothing lost. In the story of the conflict between the Puritans and authority in Elizabethan Cambridge, this had been merely a minor skirmish: a matter of routine.

CHAPTER IX

MORE TROUBLES AT ST JOHN'S: WILLIAM WHITAKER AND HENRY ALVEY

I

RICHARD HOWLAND, sixteenth Master of St John's, was consecrated Bishop of Peterborough in February 1585. For two years he bore the double responsibility of the mastership and the bishopric; he then decided to resign the former, and in February 1587 Burleigh, Whitgift, Andrew Perne and Thomas Byng (acting Visitors of the college during the vacancy of the see of Ely) wrote to the President and Fellows[1] to recommend as his successor the Regius Professor of Divinity, William Whitaker, a Trinity man: 'a man of long time conversant among you, and of gravity, learning, discretion and zeal to the furtherance of godliness, well known unto us all, to be a person meet for such a charge as any other we know there'. The Visitors made clear that Whitaker could be imposed on the college by royal authority, 'without pursuing the ordinary manner and course of election': yet

for the desire we have to have him preferred rather by election, so as the statutes of the college and former usage might be observed so far as shall be requisite; as also that he might be placed there amongst you with the good concurrence and unity of all your consents: we have thought good to resolve of that course, advising and very heartily exhorting and requiring you, that upon the receipt hereof you would proceed to election, and incline to him with your good wills and voices, whereby, coming in with more full consent, he may have the more cause to entertain every of you with like good affection, and be the

[1] Letter dated 17 February 1586 (i.e. 1586/7) in University Archives, 'Mandates of Elizabeth I' (box), no. 200.

better able to retain you all in that good unity and concord, a matter of good consequence, and principally respected of us, for the better government of the house in generality.

That letter was sent from Greenwich on 17 February: and Whitaker was in fact admitted Master a week later, on 25 February. The details of the election are obscure, and Thomas Baker was to maintain that the Fellows voted against Whitaker.[1] The two favourite candidates had apparently been Andrew Downes, the new Regius Professor of Greek, elected Fellow of the college in 1571, and John Palmer, junior dean of the college, who had been admitted Fellow in 1573. Howland himself seems to have favoured as his successor Laurence Stanton, who had gone up to St John's in 1566, and was elected Fellow in 1572.[2] Another possible candidate was Anthony Watson, Fellow of Christ's; later to be Dean of Bristol and Bishop of Chichester. Whitaker, however, was senior to all these men: he had gone up to Trinity in 1564, under Beaumont, and was elected Fellow in 1569, under Whitgift. In 1578 he resigned the fellowship, on the occasion of his marriage to Susan Culverwell. Cecilia, Susan's sister, was the wife of Laurence Chaderton. (Susan died in 1589: in 1591 Whitaker was to marry Joan, the widow of Dudley Fenner.) Whitaker's uncle was Alexander Nowell, Dean of St Paul's: who has his memorial among the ungodly as a renowned angler (in which pursuit he instructed his nephew) and as the inadvertent inventor of bottled beer, but who is more properly honoured for his Latin Catechism, which William had translated into Greek in 1573. By 1587 William had achieved a high reputation as a champion of the Protestant cause. His controversial works against Campion, Sanders and Rainolds had already appeared, and he was now working on his refutation of Bellarmine and Stapleton. Also, like the Levers and the Pilkingtons and Richard Longworth, he was

[1] Thomas Baker, *History of St John's College*, I, 180.
[2] Strype, *Annals of the Reformation*, v, 642.

a Lancashire man,[1] which was a recommendation in St John's, if nowhere else. Eleven Fellows, headed by Downes, had previously written to Burleigh pressing the claim of Whitaker.[2] However, there were those in the university and in St John's who were very much opposed to him; Andrew Perne at one point was among them.[3] So the prospects for unity and concord in the college after the new Master moved in at the end of February were perhaps not so rosy as the Visitors had allowed themselves to hope.

The factions in St John's, intensified by two years of virtually absentee mastership, were even more pronounced in 1587 than they had been in the days of Longworth. This was in spite of the fact that in 1576, after complaints of 'factions and contentions'[4] in the college under John Still, new statutes had been prepared, which came into force in 1580, and which were to govern the college until 1849. The authors of these statutes included Burleigh, Whitgift and Cox: and their intention was to strengthen the powers of the Master. Whitaker determined to exercise that power; and, knowing that 'the statute hath set down absolutely, without support of seniors, any punishment',[5] in April 1588 the Master, by his sole authority, expelled a Fellow from the college. This was Everard Digby, who had been elected in 1573. The occasion was his sitting down to table without having paid his commons, in spite of four warnings, the last by Whitaker himself. The cause was his general irresponsibility and suspected popish

[1] William Whitaker was born in 1547 in the manor house of the estate of Holme, four miles south-east of Burnley, and four miles from the Yorkshire border; within ten miles of the moors now best known as the background of *Wuthering Heights*. His mother was a Nowell, the daughter of another prominent Lancashire family, from Read (ten miles from Holme). Her brother Laurence, of Christ's, a Marian exile, died in 1576: Alexander was to survive as Dean of St Paul's until 1602. The historian and topographer Thomas Dunham Whitaker, a descendant of William's eldest brother Robert, was to be born in the manor house of Holme in 1759; his valuable account of William Whitaker is in book VI, chapter I, of his *History of the Parish of Whalley*, published in 1801 (second edition 1806); he also gave a chart of the Whitaker family (1806 ed. pp. 337–8), a chart of the Nowell family (246–7) and a description of the estate of Holme (339).
[2] Strype, *Annals*, v, 643.   [3] Strype, *Whitgift*, I, 455–7.
[4] Grindal to Burleigh; Lansdowne MSS. vol. XXIII, no. 7.
[5] Lansdowne MSS. vol. LVII, no. 78.

sympathies. The detailed charges against Digby included his insulting John Palmer in the presence of the undergraduates, his going fishing at the time of chapel services, his attacks on the Calvinists in College disputations, and his blowing a horn and halloo'ing in the college court.[1] Both Leicester and his brother Warwick had written to Whitgift during the early part of 1588 to complain of Digby: the former called him 'a very unsound and factious fellow'[2] and the latter 'a seducer of youth in the college'.[3] But Whitgift was not convinced. He strongly disapproved of Whitaker's arbitrary action, which he thought was a 'private revenge'.[4] On 30 April he wrote to Burleigh about the Master's 'evil dealing':

Mr Whitaker, Palmer, and some others of St John's College deal very extraordinarily in this matter of Digby's, and (as I think) contrary to their own statutes, but I am assured contrary to the rule of charity, I might say of honesty also....I am sorry Mr Whitaker doth so far forget himself: but without doubt, it is the violence of Preciseness, which desireth a rule and government absolute without controlment, be it never so vehement and unjust.[5]

When the Archbishop and the Chancellor sat in judgement on the case, however, Whitaker successfully defended his action: and Digby was not re-admitted.

Within a year of his admission, then, the Master had run into trouble. And in September 1588 petitions were sent from the college to the Chancellor protesting about the sovereign statutory power of the Master, and the exercise of that power by Whitaker. The main complaint was that 'this absolute authority hath been

---

[1] A series of eighteen articles against Digby, with his replies, is in University Archives, Registry Guard Books, vol. 93, no. 6. Other documents relating to the case were copied by Baker, Harleian MSS. vol. 7039 (British Museum Baker MSS.), pp. 157–62. But the fullest account is Whitaker's detailed defence of his action; Lansdowne MSS. vol. LVII, no. 57, printed by J. Heywood and T. Wright, *Cambridge Transactions during the Puritan Controversies*, I, 507–21.
[2] Lansdowne MSS. vol. LVII, no. 47.   [3] *Ibid.* no. 70.
[4] *Ibid.* no. 72.   [5] *Ibid.* no. 70.

of late often used upon very small cause'.[1] It was also alleged[2] that Whitaker had ignored the counsel of the seniors in preferring such men as John Allenson, whom he made lecturer in Greek; Richard Harris, the new lecturer in Hebrew; and Brian Taylor, whom he had presented to a living in spite of his commonplaces containing 'undutiful and unreverend speeches of the bishops and other of the clergy'. Also, he had refused to punish Thomas Bernhere and William Peachy for not wearing the surplice. In all things he had sinned, in 'not making the seniors privy'; though they had 'divers times' put the Master 'in mind' of his true powers. There were also, it seems, other and perhaps less serious things amiss in St John's: 'there is much vessel yearly lost in the kitchen';[3] the Master had 'inhibited all manner of plays, and that comedy which was usually played to celebrate the Queen's day'.[4] But it especially rankled that Whitaker had so delighted to honour Henry Alvey: who had been a Fellow for ten years before Whitaker's admission and whose influence had grown steadily during that decade—until it was now intolerable.

Henry Alvey is a strangely neglected figure, being neither in the *Dictionary of National Biography* nor in the Coopers' *Athenae Cantabrigienses*. He had matriculated from St John's in 1571, a Nottinghamshire boy; at the time, that is, of the disturbances created by the supporters of Cartwright and the opponents of the new university statutes. Now, Alvey was born in 1554,[5] the son of a Robert Alvey. Was he a relation of Richard Alvey, canon of Westminster and sometime Fellow of the college, who was in his early forties at the time of Henry's birth, who went to Frankfurt with his wife in April 1555, and who died in 1584? Unfortunately there is no evidence on that point. Henry certainly had an elder brother, Edward, who was a pupil of William Fulke in 1565,[6] and

---

[1] University Library, Cambridge, Baker MSS. vol. XXVII, p. 83.
[2] University Archives, Registry Guard Books, vol. 6 (i), no. 35—a charge of 43 breaches of statute by the Master.   [3] *Ibid.* p. 6.   [4] *Ibid.* p. 3.
[5] His age was given as thirty-seven in 1591, in the Star Chamber depositions.
[6] S. P. Dom. Eliz. vol. XXXVIII, fol. 104b.

who was elected Fellow in 1570, becoming a Senior Fellow in 1575; but Edward had left the college by 1587. Henry Alvey was elected Fellow of St John's, with Richard Clayton and Nathaniel Knox, in 1577. He was thus an academic generation younger than Digby, Palmer, Stanton, Downes, or Daniel Munsay. Yet by the summer of 1588, barely a year and a half after the admission of Whitaker, Alvey had become 'the Master's right hand'.[1] It was alleged that Whitaker was completely dependent on Alvey's advice and counsel. Also, the Master's party at the Fellows' table openly maintained that Whitaker might 'lawfully watch opportunity to expel any, how honest, learned, sufficient soever, that in all opinions, elections and so forth do not consent and join with him' as Master—those, in other words, who 'cross his government'. Alvey 'boldly affirmed that he saw no reason why the Master should not watch his times and take all advantages, protesting that if he were in his place he would do it'.[2] And in January 1589 Alvey was admitted a Senior Fellow.

During the winter of 1589 Alvey campaigned in the university in favour of the imprisoned Francis Johnson of Christ's College. He led fifty Johnians through the streets to Peterhouse to force the proctor to arrange an appeal for Johnson; he non-placeted graces in the Senate, including that for the granting of a doctorate of divinity to Lancelot Andrewes, Master of Pembroke; and, with eleven other members of his college he signed the petition for Johnson in December.[3] The eleven were Daniel Munsay, Arthur Johnson, Robert Hill, Thomas Bernhere, Henry Briggs, William Hall, Ralph Furness, Richard Harris, Gregory Newton, John Allenson and Abdias Ashton. Of these, Alvey, Munsay and Johnson were bachelors of divinity: and they swayed the young men, Ashton, Bernhere, Briggs, Hall, Hill and Newton, all of whom were elected Fellows under Whitaker. Newton was the

---

[1] Petition printed in *The Eagle* (St John's College Magazine), xxxv, 267.
[2] *Ibid.*
[3] Lansdowne MSS. vol. LXI, no. 10.

youngest: he had matriculated from Christ's in 1582, and was therefore about twenty-three in 1589. Alvey was thirty-five.

Alvey was also suspected of complicity in the movement within the Church of England during the 1580's which expressed itself in the setting-up of those 'synods, assemblies or conventicles', the history and nature of which were investigated first in the high commission, and then in the Star Chamber, during 1591. The godly pattern of Church government described by Cartwright in his Cambridge lectures of 1570 had been set out as an aim of practical policy in the 'Second Admonition to Parliament' of 1572. The 'First Admonition' had recommended that there should be 'in every congregation a lawful and godly seignory'; and that to ministers, seniors and deacons 'is the whole regiment of the church to be committed'.[1] The Second provided the details: there should be pastors and teachers, responsible to the elders and the congregation;[2] every congregation should have a consistory, to admonish and excommunicate;[3] the congregations were to be bound into a national organization by means of provincial synods, headed by a general synod, the 'council of the whole land'.[4] The appeal to Parliament failed. Thus, 'as the Discipline required by petitions could not be publicly established by law, it was thought in conscience necessary to establish it and practise it privately'.[5] The strict theory—given permanent form in 1574 by a Latin treatise of Walter Travers—served to crystallize the earlier strivings after a godly discipline. There had been prayer meetings, and conferences, and prophesyings—these last being suppressed in 1574, the year before Parker died. There had been the London congregations of the late 1560's: the meetings at the Plumbers' Hall, the Privy Church of Richard Fitz; and the establishment at Wandsworth in 1572 of what can be called the first English presbytery. All this became more regular and inter-

[1] W. H. Frere and C. E. Douglas, *Puritan Manifestos*, 16.
[2] *Ibid.* 97.   [3] *Ibid.* 118-20.
[4] *Ibid.* 108-9.
[5] Richard Bancroft, *Daungerous Positions* (1593), 104.

dependent, until it was possible to talk of a Presbyterian movement within the Church of England, discussing at the parochial or *classis* level, consolidating at the provincial level (though the movement was entirely clerical and perhaps concerned in all no more than a few hundred men). In 1583 the University of Cambridge was linked in a striking way with the Presbyterian movement. In that year, the university appointed a printer: this was Thomas Thomas, who set up shop in the Regent Walk, opposite the west door of Great St Mary's.[1] But, as Sir Sydney Roberts has written, 'Cambridge printing was for many years continually harassed by two disturbing forces—theological suspicion and commercial jealousy'.[2] Both worked together in that very year: when the Stationers' Company seized and burnt all the copies of an English book of discipline published by Thomas. (This was probably an abridged version of Travers's treatise, in the translation by Cartwright.)

The details of those concerned with the Presbyterian movement are contained in the documents drawn up during the official investigation in the early 1590's. Of the known 'members' (or sympathizers) nearly forty were Cambridge men.[3] Cartwright and Travers were the most important of these: but there were others of the same generation—Thomas Barbar of St John's, Edmund Chapman of Trinity and John Knewstubb of St John's had petitioned in favour of Cartwright in 1570; George Northey of Clare and Laurence Chaderton of Christ's had petitioned against

[1] S. C. Roberts, *History of the Cambridge University Press*, 29. Five years later, in October 1588, the Master and Fellows of Trinity leased to John Legate, 'printer to the university', 'two shops late in the tenure of Thomas Bradshaw stationer, in the parish of Great St Mary's, next the market place, adjoining the west end of the parish church, builded upon the churchyard wall: the one at the north-west corner of the church, containing length 24 feet 3 inches, abutting upon the high street towards the west; the other at the south-west corner, in length 24 feet 3 inches as now builded: paying yearly 6s. 8d. at michaelmas'. (Trinity College senior bursar's muniments, Box 25 (ii).)
[2] S. C. Roberts, *op. cit.* 25.
[3] Names in the introduction to R. G. Usher, *The Presbyterian Movement in the reign of Queen Elizabeth as illustrated by the Minute book of the Dedham Classis, 1582–1589* (Camden Society 1905).

the new statutes in 1572. The father of the company was Percival Wiborne, who had gone up to St John's in the last year of the reign of Henry VIII. Other Cambridge men found some memorial here: Humphrey Fenn of Queens', William Negus of Trinity, Richard Rogers, John Udall, and George Johnson of Christ's, and four Peterhouse men, Stephen Egerton, William Charke, Dudley Fenner, and poor John Penry. The minute book of the *classis* at Dedham, in Essex, fifty miles from Cambridge, covering the years 1582 to 1589, has been published.[1] At the eighth meeting, in June 1583, it was agreed that delegates should 'crave the judgements of some godly men in Cambridge touching the question of the Sabbath'.[2] In June 1585 Edmund Chapman 'signified that there would be a meeting at Cambridge of divers godly men, where it were expedient that questions should be moved to them to have their judgement how far we might read in the Book of Common Prayer'; also to 'crave their advice how to prevent the mischief that is like to ensue by some that make a schism and rent from our Church'; and lastly 'whether we may use the Bishops and come to their Courts'.[3] Three weeks later it was regretted that the Dedham committee for drawing up the questions had not yet reported. But it was decided that when the brethren did get around to putting something definite on paper, the document should be taken to Cambridge by Knewstubb.[4] In general, the minute book of the Dedham *classis* bears ample witness to the ineffectiveness of the Presbyterian movement in the 1580's.

Alvey was among the small group of resident Cambridge dons whose names were connected with the movement; others in the group were Thomas Brightman of Queens' and William Perkins of Christ's. During the late 1580's provincial synods of the local brethren were held in Cambridge during September, at the time of Stourbridge Fair. There had been one such meeting in 1587,

[1] By R. G. Usher, *ibid.*
[2] *Ibid.* 30.
[3] *Ibid.* 50.
[4] *Ibid.* 51.

dominated by Cartwright, where the godly discipline was discussed; those present included Laurence Chaderton, Master of Emmanuel, Knewstubb, and Thomas Barbar. There had been another Cambridge meeting in 1589. William Perkins was present: and his description of the 1589 assembly, given on oath in 1591, has been preserved.[1] Perkins said:

that Mr Cartwright and Mr Snape,[2] two of the deponents in this case, have met together and have treated and debated whether the rules and methods of this said Book of Discipline called *Disciplina Ecclesiae* were agreeable to the Word of God or not: and this deponent saith that the same meeting or conference was had at St John's College in Cambridge about this time two years, as this deponent remembereth, and that in the chamber of a student there, who was then absent, and whose name this deponent for his conscience sake forbeareth to set down. And this deponent being examined who else besides the said Mr Cartwright and Mr Snape or this deponent have been in the said assembly (which as this deponent saith was all the assembly he was at) this deponent thereto saith again that this deponent himself was present in the same assembly, and none else of the deponents to this case, saving he said Mr Cartwright and Mr Snape. But whom or how many else besides were there in the same assembly, this deponent dareth not to express.

Further examined, Perkins continued:

in the said assembly in St John's College in Cambridge as aforesaid there was a Moderator who propounded the questions there debated of, and noted every man's opinions and reasons upon the same. And this deponent being examined who hath been so chosen, he saith not any of the deponents in this case, and who else was, he dareth not to tell for the reasons before mentioned.

In answer to a later question, Perkins said:

that, in the said assembly or meeting had at Cambridge as aforesaid (which was all this meeting that this deponent had with any of the now deponents in this case) this question and no other was treated and

[1] Public Record Office, Star Chamber Depositions: Star Chamber, 5: A: 49/34.
[2] Edmund Snape, an Oxford man, incorporated M.A. at Cambridge in 1586.

debated of in scholastical manner: viz. whether that the sacrament ought to be received at the hands of unpreaching ministers or not. And some held and agreed that they were not, and others said that they were; but not by any subscribed unto, to this deponent's knowledge.

On one point Perkins was quite firm: 'he doth not know, nor hath credibly heard, that any of the deponents in this cause have practised or put in use this authority or power of an eldership or presbytery or any part thereof'.

Now, another of the witnesses in August 1591 was Henry Alvey. His evidence immediately follows that of Perkins in the bundle of Star Chamber depositions preserved in the Public Record Office. Alvey began by maintaining that he did not know Snape at all; and that he knew Cartwright 'by his face and no otherwise'. He had certainly never 'had conference with them'. Neither had he 'been present in any assembly or assemblies with any of the deponents in this case, or with any other person or persons, where any such or like matters as be mentioned in this interrogatory were concluded, ordered, treated, or debated of'. He did not know that any of the matters mentioned in any of the interrogatories had been determined or subscribed to by anybody 'in any classical, or general assemblies, or in any other meetings whatsoever'. More particularly, 'he doth not know of, nor was present at, any assembly or meeting of any ministers at any time within the town or county of Cambridge to confer or treat of any such matters as be mentioned in the xxvth interrogatory, or any matter tending that way, or about any other matters'.

And that was as much as the Star Chamber could determine about the assembly in St John's College in the autumn of 1589. Alvey came out of the investigation as a completely innocent party, and his evidence was so unexciting that it was not used in Bancroft's surveys of the Presbyterian movement published in 1593, nor has it ever been reprinted. Yet the fact remains that, in 1595, the anti-Puritan party among the Fellows of St John's precisely and carefully said that in September 1589, in the absence of Whitaker, Alvey had 'suffered a conventicle of Mr Cartwright and his complices to be gathered in our college': more, they accused Alvey of 'keeping our Master's lodgings, where they then met'.[1]

However greatly those charges of 1595 are minimized, however unfairly 'loaded' (to use a neat Americanism) a word such as 'conventicle', however wary one must be in evaluating an accusation brought against a man at one stage in his life concerning the events of another—however fair, that is, one tries to be to Alvey, the fact remains that the signed indictment of many responsible and presumably informed men contradicts his earlier testimony, given under oath. It is perhaps impossible and unnecessary to do more than to bring against both parties a verdict of 'not proven'.

II

Whatever the nature and proceedings of the meeting in St John's in 1589, the line between the study group and the unlawful cell, between the conforming and the factious Puritan, was wavering ominously, and there was ample factual basis for rumour, especially when, during 1590, the government investigation into 'dangerous seditious factions' was intensified. Materials were at hand for an informer with an eye to the main chance; and the perpetual problem arose—'how to protect the innocent citizen from getting pinched between the reality of the threat and the epidemic fear of it'.[2]

Cartwright was arrested and imprisoned in October 1590. And in that same month a rumour about Alvey and his supporters was circulated within St John's: a rumour that he had set up in the college a secret 'eldership or presbytery', a church within the church. The rumour began with the senior dean, John Palmer.

Now, Palmer was a thoroughly unreliable character. In 1580,

[1] Lansdowne MSS. vol. LXXIX, no. 61.
[2] Alistair Cooke, *A Generation on Trial: U.S.A. v. Alger Hiss* (New York, 1950), 341.

when he was about thirty, he had acted the title role in the Latin play *Richard III*, performed in St John's, and written by the Master of Caius, Thomas Legge (by origin a Corpus man). According to Thomas Fuller he thus 'had his head so possessed with a prince-like humour, that ever after he did what then he acted, in his prodigal expenses'.[1] Whatever the reason, the prodigality was certainly evident. In 1587, when he was senior bursar of the college, he came before the Vice-Chancellor's court on a charge of debt, the sum named being £120.[2] Two years later, in 1589, he was before the court again, this time as the plaintiff in a defamation case. A certain lady with the curiously appropriate name of Agnes Vixen, to whom Palmer was in debt, had blazed into the court of St John's one May morning and informed all and sundry, 'very loud', that Palmer was 'an hypocrite' and 'a discredit unto all learned men and to the Master and Fellows of the college'.[3] But Whitaker liked him, and in September 1589 he was appointed senior dean. Palmer, as Dean of Peterborough, was to die in prison for debt in 1607, under suspicion of stealing the lead from the roof of his own cathedral.

The rumour of October 1590 began in this way. Palmer had a conversation with Daniel Munsay, President of the college, and firm friend of Henry Alvcy. 'I think', said Palmer, 'you have a presbytery among you.'[4] 'What if we have', replied Munsay. 'You censure men at your pleasure', continued Palmer. 'Some censures', growled Munsay, 'be good.' Munsay, it must be admitted, was a tactless ass. The petitioners against Whitaker in 1588 had claimed that Munsay was 'known and accounted by all the House to be the only indiscreet and foolish man among all the seniors,[5] and in that very month of October 1590 Eleazor Knox

[1] Fuller, *The Worthies of England*, II, 491.
[2] University Archives, Registry Guard Books, vol. 7, no. 49.
[3] *Ibid.* vol. 6 (ii), no. 62.
[4] Conversation reported in a letter from Whitaker to Burleigh dated 26 October 1590; bought by St John's in 1948, and now in the library.
[5] University Archives, Registry Guard Books, vol. 6 (i), no. 35, p. 1.

wrote that 'he is known to be a fool, and cannot conceal, but must tell truth'.[1] Palmer at any rate agreed with the latter part of this charitable observation, and took Munsay's somewhat non-committal replies as an acknowledgement of the truth of the original remark. He told another senior Fellow about it—Simon Robson, a contemporary and friend of Palmer. And soon the story was all over the college.

In the middle of October the Master called together the fourteen or so senior Fellows to examine the matter, and to question the other dons. Munsay, to Palmer's face, completely denied the rumours. A lively meeting followed; in which it became obvious that the affair was yet another excuse for the Puritan and anti-Puritan parties in the college to abuse and accuse each other, and for the opponents of the Master (led by Eleazor Knox, and including Andrew Downes, Laurence Stanton, Simon Robson and Richard Clayton) to score a decisive point. The party lines in 1590 were the same as they had been in 1588. This meeting was the more ridiculous because no one knew exactly what was meant by a presbytery, in the context of college gossip. Was it a formal body, with officers and fixed meetings and definite acts, the much feared 'new form of church government by Doctors, Pastors, Deacons and Elders with a new devised form of common prayer and administration of sacraments'?[2] Alvey and the Puritans rested themselves 'upon the word and definition, upon *genus* and *differentia* of a presbytery: and flying and refusing to answer whether they had any assembly which might in some proportion answer unto it'.[3] Knox and the anti-Puritans claimed 'that it might be, though they had no presbytery in such manner as they desired, yet it was like they had something answering unto it'.[4] 'Something answering unto it' might of course mean almost anything. Bancroft in 1584 had placed as supreme among the

[1] Letter of Eleazor Knox, 20 October 1590; bought by St John's in 1948 and now in the library.
[2] A phrase from the 1591 inquiries; S. P. Dom. Eliz. vol. CCXXXVIII, no. 102.
[3] Letter of Knox, St John's Library. [4] *Ibid.*

'dealings of the precisians' their 'private conferences for the better agreeing in their opinions';[1] and with this criterion the most informal meeting, study group, or 'unit' of the puritanically inclined could be seen as having the nature of a presbytery. Given the general background of the national scare in 1590, the facts of the 1589 assembly at St John's, and the strong Puritan sympathies of a majority of the Fellows, Palmer's rumour could hardly fail to be an effective spark. Whitaker, in the chair, saw the danger of a conflagration. He knew where an ill-defined dispute, 'proceeding from the root of envy and discontent',[2] might lead. And he put his foot down, protesting 'before the living God that I know of nothing that hath any analogy or resemblance to this imagined presbytery'.[3] (Did he, one wonders, know about the meeting of September 1589?)

The rumour (helped on its way by an indiscreet sermon about Church discipline by Daniel Munsay) spread beyond the college, and beyond Cambridge, to the ears of the ecclesiastical commissioners, at that time busy with the examination of Cartwright. Burleigh asked the Vice-Chancellor about it; and on 20 October the Vice-Chancellor and some heads wrote to the Chancellor declaring that 'none of us did ever hear any fame or speech in the university of any such presbytery or any such like disorderly meetings there before this present, and we are persuaded there is no such matter'.[4] On the same day thirty-five of the fifty Fellows of St John's also wrote to Burleigh, testifying that 'we do not know that there is amongst any of our said college any such presbytery as hath been reported'.[5] This letter was not signed by Knox: nor by Downes, Stanton, Palmer, Robson, Robert Booth, Roger Morrell, Clayton, or Anthony Higgins—eight seniors who had been elected Fellows before Whitaker became Master. Of the thirty-five, eighteen had petitioned for Francis Johnson, or

---

[1] A. Peel (ed.), *Tracts ascribed to Richard Bancroft*, 12.
[2] Letter of Whitaker, St John's Library.   [3] *Ibid.*
[4] Lansdowne MSS. vol. LXIII, no. 91.   [5] *Ibid.* no. 92.

were to support Alvey in 1595; and twenty were men who had been elected to fellowships since Whitaker's accession. The seniors who signed the letter were Alvey, Munsay, Arthur Johnson, John Bois and Henry Nelson.

As a result of the doubts and the dangers, Whitaker was called down to London. By 24 October he was lodging there, in the house of his uncle, the Dean of St Paul's.

The Master was in a difficult position. The previous May there had been a 'rumour' spread at court that he had forbidden the delivering of a loyal oration in St John's: a report proceeding, Whitaker had then said, 'from some envious body, God knoweth who'.[1] And now Burleigh had received from St John's an anonymous but detailed list of over twenty charges against Whitaker's policy as Master. Whitaker was worried, for it was only two years since the complaints of September 1588. He wrote to Burleigh on 24 October:

I will not complain to your Lordship of those that have complained of me, who seeing me resolved to come up about my necessary defence, and fearing that the complaint made concerning a presbytery would be easily disproved, have devised other matters, which either touch me not at all or else are most frivolous, and yet being thus heaped together, seem to be of some weight. And although I partly foresee the inconvenience of a new visitation, which is the only thing that they shoot at, yet I fear not any course of justice whatsoever.[2]

Burleigh had also received a letter from Eleazor Knox, written on 20 October.[3] The letter was permeated by an almost pathological dislike and suspicion of Whitaker 'and his favourers'. The two men were certainly on very bad terms. After the college meeting in the middle of the month Knox had accused Whitaker of being too lenient to the college Puritans, and threatened to report him to the ecclesiastical commissioners. At this, the Master

---

[1] Whitaker to Burleigh, 14 May 1590; *ibid.* no. 86.   [2] *Ibid.* no. 93.
[3] Letter of Knox, St John's Library.

198

'first scoffed and then threatened, saying: Complain if you dare for your ears'. But Knox could not claim that the report of the presbytery was proved: 'For the matter itself, what truth is in it, I know not.' His case rested—if it is examined—entirely on the evidence of Palmer. But he did claim, as the petitioners of 1588 had claimed, that there was an inner ring in the college: 'some over-ruling authority which determineth and ordereth causes, before they come to the hearing of the Seniors'. And, on behalf of 'all here that favour the present estate', he asked for a visitation of the college by the ecclesiastical commissioners—the thing, he thought, which the Master most feared: 'for he justly and greatly feareth the strict examination of the High Commission as such as he knoweth to be fully acquainted with the deceitful and deceiving nature and conditions of those men, and which know their starting holes, and can therefore fox and ferret them out, how closely soever they convey themselves'.

On 26 October Whitaker wrote a long reply to the charges against him,[1] charges 'so untrue, that the author or authors were ashamed to set their names thereunto'. The report of the presbytery was 'incredible'. 'Who are the officers?' Whitaker asked: 'Where have been their meetings? When have they met? What have they done?' The rumour, like the charges, seemed to the Master to have sprung from the 'poison of papistry'—the spirit of Digby in arms. He was sad, though not vindictive, about those Fellows, 'skilful at telling smooth tales', who had made life difficult for him; especially his former protégé, John Palmer.

Mr Palmer never received at my hands any measure but good, as the whole college and himself knoweth. For favouring of him I have sustained displeasure both at home and abroad. What his offence deserveth I leave it to the Lord Treasurer to judge. My desire is not to hurt him. What his drift hath been therein, I leave it to God and his own conscience. Only I may say he hath in this showed himself more unkind than I looked for.

[1] Letter of Whitaker, St John's Library.

In general, Whitaker, surveying his reign of almost four years, felt himself able to conclude: 'We have been, through God's blessing, very quiet a long time: now these troubles have arisen about a presbytery, that is to say indeed, about nothing. The parties that are grieved are not many, and I have endeavoured by all kindness and gentleness to content them, but I see it will not be.'

The supporters of the Master within the college were out for blood. Their victim, not surprisingly, was Palmer. They complained to Burleigh; and in November Palmer was compelled for his own safety to write to the Chancellor denying that he had invented the rumour about the presbytery:[1] 'it is known and acknowledged, who did publish this report, and yet (I know not how) they whom it concerneth, are so transported by affection, that all their displeasure is bent towards me and as I hear such a course is intended as...will be my great trouble and undoing, having no other state of maintenance than my place in that college'. Palmer protested that he was 'far from seeking the slander of the college, to which I am so much bound'. Nor had he intended the 'discredit of our Master, who I verily think is ignorant of this thing'. Here, certainly, is one of the clues to the tangled skein. Whitaker was a scholar, and a busy one: how much did he in fact know about what was happening in St John's? After Whitaker's death some of the Fellows were to complain that he had given 'himself over wholly to his study'; that he was 'by nature quiet and tractable'; and that power in St John's had passed to 'some others, who contrary to his mind suffered conventicles in our college of Cartwright and his associates'.[2] Palmer claimed that for the Master's peace of mind 'we did all offer ourselves to do whatever we were able, if it would have pleased him to accept it'. Was Knox referring to Whitaker in his letter of 20 October, when he urged strong measures 'lest the simplicity and ignorance of some be hurtful to the Church, and bring damage to this society'?

[1] Lansdowne MSS. vol. LXIII, no. 95.   [2] Lansdowne MSS. vol. LXXIX, no. 69.

In November, Whitaker was back in St John's, discouraging 'violence and extremity towards any'.[1] The whole affair, like so much else in the history of Elizabethan Cambridge, ends not with a bang but a whimper. There was not in fact a visitation of the college; and the situation was eased eight months later, in July 1591, by the death of Eleazor Knox, at the age of thirty-three.

Henry Alvey was once more to appear at the centre of a quarrel during the mastership of Whitaker. That was in December 1591, at the yearly election of officers. The Master wished Alvey—'a man singularly well deserving of the college'[2]—to be the next President. However, only three of the seniors present in the chapel were in favour of Alvey; one of the three was Alvey himself; the other two Munsay and Henry Nelson. The other five, including Richard Clayton and Robert Hill, were opposed to Alvey: they suggested Simon Robson or Anthony Higgins. Whitaker, however, ruled that Alvey be elected. The five opponents swept out of the chapel, threatening to appeal to the Queen. The issue resolved itself into a constitutional question of the powers of the Master; and the Master, of course, carried the day.

The sinister fact was that Henry Alvey had climbed yet one more rung of the ladder of power.

III

Whitaker died on Thursday, 4 December 1595, at the age of forty-seven; leaving his widow with child, but without funds.[3]

[1] Letter of Whitaker, St John's Library.

[2] Harleian MSS. (British Museum Baker MSS.), vol. 7039, p. 163. Whitaker described the scene to Burleigh in a letter of 15 December; pp. 163–4.

[3] Letter of Alexander Nowell, Lansdowne MSS. vol. LXXX, no. 11. When the baby, a boy, was born in 1596, Joan decided upon the name of Jabez, 'because I bore him with sorrow' (Cooper, *Athenae Cantabrigienses*, II, 197). Whitaker is said to have had eight children by his two wives. Only Jabez, Samuel and Alexander are known by name; there was also one daughter, who went to Virginia in 1624. The other four children are not traceable: although it is possible that Thomas Whitaker, born about 1578 (who went up to Trinity in 1594 and became a schoolmaster in Burnley until his death in 1626) was a son of William, by Susan; and that William Whitaker, born about 1592, who entered St John's in 1609 and was a Lincolnshire parson from 1620 to 1642, was a son by Joan.

Almost immediately a dozen anti-Puritan Fellows wrote to Burleigh:[1] William Pratt, Otwell Hill, William Billingsley (son of the next Lord Mayor of London), Owen Gwyn (to be Master of the college, 1612–33), George Buddle, George Gouldman, Christopher Powell, William Mottershed; and four Fellows elected during or after 1591, Edward Abney, Peter Bindless, Valentine Wood, and Valentine Carey (later Master of Christ's and Dean of St Paul's). They wrote to complain of the growth during the reign of the late Master of what might be called the 'Alvey Party'. Those men whom Whitaker had entrusted with power had so transformed St John's since the departure of Howland 'as is incredible to be told': 'the college is so full of such like men, as they are the greater number of the society, and so if the new Master be chosen by them we must needs greatly fear what they will do'. The anti-Puritan party was in a slight minority. Within a fortnight of Whitaker's death two petitions were sent from the college to Burleigh in support of Henry Alvey,[2] signed in all by twenty-nine Fellows, out of a total number of about fifty. There was no doubt that Alvey was the candidate the Puritans had in mind as Master. And his opponents wrote again to Burleigh on 14 December making the serious charge that 'Mr Alvey for the space of seven or eight years last past, hath in all elections and bringing young students to the House ambitiously contrived a plot for the Mastership'.[3]

The funeral of William Whitaker was on 10 December. It was a very elaborate affair.[4] The chapel, hall and court of the college were hung with mourning drapes, shields, and memorial verses; the coffin was carried to Great St Mary's in full procession of the whole university, and was met outside the west door by the mayor and aldermen in mourning. The funeral sermon was preached by the Vice-Chancellor, Dr Roger Goad, Provost of King's. The

[1] Lansdowne MSS. vol. LXXIX, no. 69.   [2] Ibid. no. 68.
[3] Ibid. no. 61.
[4] Description by Thomas Fuller, History of Cambridge, 287.

procession and the coffin then returned to St John's, where, after a Latin oration by John Bois, the corpse was laid to rest in the college chapel. There followed a banquet of sweetmeats. Finally, there was another Latin oration, this time in Great St Mary's, by the public orator.

The election of a new Master was due on Wednesday 17 December. During the week after the funeral Alvey was campaigning heavily. But on Friday the 12th Thomas Nevile of Trinity and Humphrey Tyndall of Queens' (Whitaker's greatest friend in Cambridge) wrote to the court pressing the claims of Lawrence Stanton.[1] Meanwhile, Burleigh had asked the Vice-Chancellor and heads for their opinion; but on Saturday the 13th they tactfully replied that they preferred to leave the matter 'to your Lordship's own wisdom, who far better knoweth what is most fit'.[2]

And there hovered over the whole election the threat of royal displeasure. On Sunday the 14th, Elizabeth told Whitgift to tell Burleigh that she wished Lawrence Stanton to be elected.[3] Whitgift wrote a letter of confirmation later in the day: the recommendation, he said, 'must be urgent and in the nature of a commandment, otherwise I doubt the event'.[4] Before this news had reached Cambridge, two letters were sent to the Chancellor, dated Monday the 15th. One was from Goad and the heads, to warn Burleigh that the Fellows of St John's, still debating strongly, had not yet been able to agree on a compromise candidate.[5] The second was from twenty-four Fellows of the college, suggesting possible candidates.[6] Their list included Alvey, but not Stanton. It also included Roger Morrell, John Knewstubb, John Ireton (a Fellow of Christ's who had matriculated from St John's in 1565), John Reynolds (the Dean of Lincoln) and Richard Clayton,

[1] Lansdowne MSS. vol. LXXIX, no. 59.
[2] Ibid. no. 60.
[3] Cecil Papers (Salisbury MSS. Hatfield House), vol. XXXVI, no. 79.
[4] Ibid. no. 80.   [5] Lansdowne MSS. vol. LXXIX, no. 63.
[6] Ibid. no. 62.

who for the past two years had been Master of Magdalene. On this same Monday Burleigh wrote to the President of St John's:

Although I have by my former letters ordered that her Majesty's commandment should be given unto you to forbear from all manner of proceeding in the election of a Master there, until her Majesty might be better informed what were meet to be done in that election for the benefit and quiet of the House: which her Majesty's commandment (she being not only the foundress of that college, but supreme governor in all causes and over all persons in her dominions, as well ecclesiastical as civil) she looketh to have obeyed by you all, and every of you in the College; which I doubt not, but being notified unto you, you will obey. Yet being newly again by her Majesty expressly reiterated to be signified unto you by me her councillor and your Chancellor I do...reiterate her royal commandment unto you, charging you upon pain of your deprivation and her Majesty's indignation to forbear to proceed to any election...until her Majesty's royal pleasure shall be signified unto you.[1]

So the election did not in fact take place on Wednesday the 17th.

During the week the Queen heard that Stanton was married; and her enthusiasm for him rather waned. The claims of the bachelor Richard Clayton now came to the fore. Of all the suggested candidates, he was the only one likely to be approved, more or less, by both parties in the college. So, on Friday Burleigh wrote to the Vice-Chancellor to signify the royal pleasure.[2] The letter arrived in Cambridge on Saturday the 20th. Goad was instructed to summon before himself and the heads 'the President of St John's College, and some convenient equal number of the Fellows that appear to be divided in opinion'. He was to tell them that 'if they will have the choice of their Master by an election, it shall be free for them to choose one of these two, Doctor Clayton or Mr Stanton'. If they refused this liberal concession, the election was to be postponed until the Queen decided specifically upon the next Master.

[1] Lansdowne MSS. vol. CIII, no. 83.   [2] Ibid. no. 84.

On Monday the 22nd, two and a half weeks after the death of Whitaker, Richard Clayton was elected and admitted Master of St John's.

IV

Clayton was a mild but efficient man, fair to both sides. He ruled for seventeen years, until his death in 1612—a reign longer than that of any save one of his seventeen predecessors. (Also, he succeeded the unfortunate John Palmer as Dean of Peterborough in 1607: a balanced appointment, for Palmer had succeeded Clayton as Master of Magdalene in 1595.) During his rule, the energies of the college were canalized into quarrels about such topics as the building of the second court, the foundation stone of which was laid in October 1598. (Constructional and aesthetic matters offer a harmless but comparatively effective outlet for academic passions.) Indeed, Thomas Baker was to write that the Fellows were 'so overjoyed or so overbusied with architecture, that their other studies were intermitted and the noise of axes and hammers disturbed them in their proper business'.[1] Clayton, moreover, unlike Whitaker, encouraged amateur theatricals. At Christmas 1598 there was performed in St John's 'The Pilgrimage to Parnassus', the first part of a trilogy which constituted 'the most brilliant product of the Tudor University stage'.[2] The characters of this satirical and topical entertainment included one Stupido, an arch-precisian despising secular learning and 'diabolical ruffs and wicked great breeches full of sin', and described as a 'plodding Puritan', an 'artless ass, and that earth-creeping dolt'. The 'Frivolity' was an enormous success; and sequels were acted in the college in 1601 and 1602.

In October 1601 Henry Alvey was elected provost of Trinity College, Dublin, succeeding Walter Travers. During his five years under Clayton he had been a quiet man, though Hacket was

[1] Baker, *History of St John's*, I, 190–1.
[2] F. S. Boas, *University Drama in the Tudor Age*, 346.

to ascribe to his influence the opposition in the college to the young John Williams, who commenced bachelor in 1603.[1] His energies, however, had found less dangerous outlets than formerly; for in 1600 Alvey led the Johnian deputation to Whitgift concerning the bitter disputes with Trinity about the enclosure of Garrett Hostel green.[2] Alvey, who never made himself completely at home in Dublin, resigned the provostship in 1609, but remained at the college until 1612 as Vice-Chancellor.[3] He then appears to have returned to Cambridge, where he had property, and where he died in 1627 at the age of seventy-three. In his will he gave 100 marks to his college library, as well as many books, and some money to be given to a scholar, preferably a Nottinghamshire one. He also bequeathed £10 for a long table, or for covers for the two Fellows' tables, to be used at feasts: given 'as a poor remembrance of my tabling there many years as a member, and not seldom since on invitation'.[4]

But the college in which Alvey dined as guest was in one respect different from the college he had known as Fellow and President. By 1611, the year of the centenary of the foundation Charter, 'the feuds between Anglican and Puritan had well nigh died out'[5] in St John's.

[1] J. Hacket, *Scrinia Reserata* (memorials of John Williams) (1693), 10.
[2] *The Eagle*, XVI, 464–75.
[3] G. D. Burtchaell and T. U. Sadleir, *Alumni Dublinenses* (1924), 12.
[4] A. F. Torry, *Founders and Benefactors of St John's*, 35.
[5] J. B. Mullinger, *St John's College*, 96.

CHAPTER X

THE CAMBRIDGE PURITANS

I

A COMMENT made by Archbishop Mathew on the Laudian revival in Cambridge applies equally to the Puritan tradition in the university: 'it was not the numbers that adhered to the movement which counted, but rather its impact upon a cloistered academic life'.[1] Of course, the words, 'movement' and 'member' are deceptive. They assume a strictly definable character, and a nicely calculable trend; they suggest the party card. The words 'puritan' and 'puritanism' can never be used so definitely. The church historian may know a Puritan when he sees one, but if he is pressed to give reasons, to define with precision the nature of the pigeon hole into which his Malvolios have been popped, he is likely to cut a very uncertain figure. Again, we may know the Puritan leaders of Elizabethan Cambridge: the vocal, the troublemakers, those who have left their mark. But their influence can never be precisely plotted, either within the university, or—and more important—upon the parishes of England. In any case, leaders are perhaps not the most significant part of the story.

> Far back, through creeks and inlets making,
> Comes silent, flooding in, the main.

There are some lists. We know the names of the dons who petitioned for Cartwright in 1570; those who protested against the new statutes in 1572; the supporters of Francis Johnson in 1589; the opponents of William Barrett in 1595; and those (some dons, some not) who were implicated in the *classis* organization. These

[1] David Mathew, *The Age of Charles I*, 201.

lists are rewarding to analyse. But with one qualification: they are not a ready-made roll-call of the extremer Cambridge Puritans. One might have petitioned for Cartwright as a liberal tribute to learning and piety; against the statutes because of devotion to the old laws and customs of the university; in favour of Johnson because of resentment at bad treatment of a colleague; against Barrett because of irritation at a young theological iconoclast. Some of those in the presbyterian *classes*, certainly, were Puritans of the extremer sort: Wiborne, Cartwright, Penry, Travers. But others were much concerned with conformity to the establishment: Laurence Chaderton, Richard Greenham, William Perkins.

The three petitions for Cartwright in July and August 1570 contained the names of thirty-three Fellows; including six from Trinity, six from St John's, and the Master of Corpus. Of these thirty-three, nine also petitioned two years later against the new statutes: Hugh Booth, Osmund David, Christopher Kirkland, John Knewstubb, Alan Parr, John More, Edmund Rockrey, Lawrence Washington and Robert Willan. John Knewstubb of St John's was also to be named in the inquiries into the *classis* movement; as were three other supporters of Cartwright: Thomas Barbar of St John's, Richard Greenham of Pembroke, and Edmund Chapman of Trinity. Knewstubb indeed was a regular Johnian Puritan, though he was left fairly undisturbed in his Suffolk parish from 1579 to 1624. But not all the petitioners for Cartwright can be branded, from the Anglican point of view, as guilty men. Richard Howland of Peterhouse was to be Master of Magdalene from 1576 to 1577, and then Master of St John's until 1587; John Still of Christ's was to succeed Cartwright as Lady Margaret Professor and Whitgift as Master of Trinity. Bartholomew Dodington of Trinity had already been Regius Professor of Greek for eight years, and was to continue to be so for another fifteen.

The petition against the statutes, a year and a half later, was a much bigger affair. John Caius, in his history of the university,[1] gave figures for 1573 which may be applied to the events of 1572. There were, according to Caius, about 320 dons in Cambridge. One hundred and sixty of them petitioned against the statutes— a remarkably high figure. They included twenty-two of the sixty Fellows of Whitgift's Trinity. The largest proportionate contribution came from St John's: out of fifty dons, twenty-nine signed the petition. Corpus came next, with seven out of twelve; five of the seven were to oppose the puritan Aldrich in 1573—Thomas Gooch, Robert Sayer, Joseph Bird, Richard Willoughby (who later became a papist), and Richard Fletcher (the future Bishop of London). Jesus contributed five out of ten; Christ's six out of fifteen (including Edmund Barwell, later Master, and Laurence Chaderton); Caius four out of ten; Queens' seven out of nineteen, including Rockrey; Peterhouse five out of fifteen, including Richard Perne, nephew of the Master; St Catharine's two out of six; Pembroke six out of thirty, including Thomas Lorkin, the Regius Professor of Physic; and Trinity Hall two out of ten. These men were a varied group. Some were destined to be Bishops: Fletcher, Robert Bennett of Trinity, Godfrey Goldsborough of Trinity, and a young master of arts of Jesus called Richard Bancroft. Then there were the moderate men, loyal to the university: Chaderton, Barwell, Hound, Legge, Tyndall —all to be heads of houses. And there was the lunatic fringe: Ambrose Copinger of St John's, Willoughby of Corpus, and Humphrey Cartwright of Christ's, who ended his days as a Jesuit.

The petition for Francis Johnson, in December 1589, had sixty-eight signatures. St John's was again the most prominent contributor, with twelve Fellows, headed by Munsay, Arthur Johnson, and Alvey. Next came the contingent from Emmanuel —a new star in the university firmament, founded in 1584. Eleven Fellows of the 'pure house of Emmanuel' signed for Johnson, including John Richardson, who was later to be Regius

[1] *Historiae Cantabrigiensis Academiae* (1574).

Professor of Divinity (1607), Master of Peterhouse (1608), and Master of Trinity (1615–25). Richardson was by origin a Clare man: so was William Branthwaite. Four of the eleven Emmanuel men were transfers from Trinity—John Duke, Robert Houghton, William Jones and Lawrence Pickering. John Cocke was from Magdalene, John Gray from Queens', Richard Rolfe from St John's; and Charles Chadwick and Nathaniel Gilbey were by origin Christ's men. Eleven Fellows of King's signed the petition, including Dr Edward Lister, royal physician. There were six Fellows of Trinity (led by Hugh Gray and Thomas Harrison); and six from Johnson's own college of Christ's—Bainbrigg, Perkins, George Downham, Thomas Gray, Thomas Mourton, and Thomas Laughton. Nine men from Clare and three from Queens' completed the list.

Five of these 1589 petitioners were connected with the *classis* movement: Alvey, Harrison, Perkins, Thomas Brightman of Queens' and Robert Sparke of King's. And nine of them were to appear six years later as opponents of William Barrett; including Alvey, who in 1595 led a contingent of eighteen Johnian Fellows (in a petition with fifty-six signatures); among them were John Allenson, Abdias Ashton and the mathematician Henry Briggs, three men who had also supported Johnson.

The importance of ring-leaders, and of the continuity of such leaders, is apparent.

It was the claim of the petitioners for Cartwright that, though few, they spoke for many.[1] Certainly the bare names at the foot of a petition give little indication of the universal commotion which these 'causes célèbres' occasioned in the university. During 1571, as a result of the campaign of the anti-statute party, 'the peace and study of the whole university' was 'disquieted, the inferior lightly regarding their duties now at home through the expectation of some innovation'.[2] The two proctors and some of

---

[1] S.P. Dom. Eliz. vol. LXXI, no. 35; Pearson, *Cartwright*, 423.
[2] Corpus Christi College MSS. vol. 118, no. 48.

their supporters among the young regents indeed threw their
bonnets over the windmill, not to mention their caps. They did

not only go very disorderly in Cambridge, wearing for the most part
their hats, and continually very unseemly ruffs at their hands, and great
galligaskins and barrelled hose stuffed with horse tails, with scabilonians
and knit nether socks, too fine for scholars; but also most disguisedly
they go abroad, in wearing such apparel even at this time in London.
... A great sort of godly men, and such as bear good will to the
university, are greatly offended, to see such unseemly going of scholars,
and especially of proctors and ministers (through whose lewd ensample
and behaviour, the university is evil spoken of, and poor scholars less
respected).[1]

The great petition against the statutes was in May 1572. Six
months later, in December, William Charke of Peterhouse
preached in the university, and thereby added his contribution
to the disorder. The heads summed up the situation in a letter to
Burleigh:

since Charke hath broached these untimely contentions, others have
ventured to continue the same, whereby the minds of some are so
incensed, that in many colleges they study and devise only how to
molest and disquiet their governors; their drift, as it is well known,
being nothing else but to procure to themselves a licentious liberty.

They concluded with a sinister reflection: 'What poison lieth hid
in popularity, cannot be unknown to your singular wisdom.'[2]

The next great university disturbances were in 1589; when the
supporters of Bainbrigg and Johnson were 'no small number'.[3]
One of the villains of the piece, as in 1571, was the proctor,
Richard Betts of Peterhouse. There was first a plot during
November, at the time when Nevile had relinquished the office
of Vice-Chancellor and his successor had not yet been appointed.
Betts was to attempt to block Nevile's sentence of expulsion
against Johnson. This attempt failed. Then, when Johnson

[1] Ibid.
[2] Lansdowne MSS. vol. XVI, no. 34.   [3] Ibid. vol. LXI, no. 8.

appealed against the sentence to the new Vice-Chancellor (Thomas Preston of Trinity Hall), the Johnsonians tried to have men of their own persuasion chosen as delegates for the hearing of the appeal. This move also failed. Next, when the Vice-Chancellor was away from Cambridge, Henry Alvey moved into the fray. The story was told by some of his colleagues:

Mr Alvey gathered together his complices of our house and the town, to the number of three score, whereof the greater part was thought to be of our house, where he like their captain going before them led them, all being in their hoods, to the Proctor at Peterhouse, to enforce him to call a Congregation for the accepting of Johnson's appeal.[1]

This tumultuous assembly would have prevailed: 'had not the keys of the Regent House door been carefully withheld by Master Dr Still and Tyndall, who heard of and perceived the violence they intended'.[2] Thus foiled by the Master of Trinity and the President of Queens', the malcontents 'laboured to make a general uproar in the university and to stay all things in the Congregation',[3] by non-placeting the university graces—including that for the bestowing of the degree of doctor of divinity on the Master of Pembroke, Lancelot Andrewes. This 'confederacy'[4] was in turn defeated. Finally—as Preston wrote to Burleigh in January 1590—

their fifth device was, and is still continued, by a certain liberty of speech in the pulpit, either to discourage the magistrate, as far as by words they may, from the doing of his duty in the repressing of them, or by animating the younger sort against lawful authority, by the liberty and strangeness of their positions, to bring the governors there into contempt; being agreeable to that course which hath been lately taken for the overthrowing of the present estate, as your Lordship better knoweth, and is the ready way to confusion in that common nursery of learning, as our experience teacheth.[5]

[1] Lansdowne MSS. vol. LXXIX, no. 61. [2] Ibid. vol. LXII, no. 42.
[3] Ibid. vol. LXXIX, no. 61. [4] Ibid. vol. LXII, no. 42.
[5] Ibid.

Some of the noise of course had been due as much to the desire for a little unacademic amusement as to the serious call of virtuous indignation. But the petition for Johnson in December had alarmingly shown that the minority movement was not to be despised, either in strength or in distinction.

The authorities made a great point always of the 'youth' of such malcontents; that is, their junior status on the university ladder. The dangerous group in the 1560's, as we have seen, had been 'the younger sort of regents'.[1] Parker and Grindal, in 1572, agreed with the heads that 'these younger men have been far overseen to seek their pretended reformation by disordered means'.[2] In view of these aspersions, which came so naturally to the lips of Elizabethan administrators—'You are unlearned, and but boys in comparison of us, who have studied divinity before you, for the most, were born'[3]—it is salutary to investigate the ages of those dons who signed petitions against authority.

The men who petitioned for Cartwright, and who might, with 'the youth of the university', have attended his lectures, included the Regius Professor of Greek, the Master of Corpus, a prebendary of Norwich (Edmund Chapman), the Vice-Provost of King's (Alan Parr), one proctor (Reuben Sherwood), and two university preachers (Simon Buck and George Slater). None of the petitioners had matriculated later than 1561: and the two who did so in that year, Hugh Booth and John Knewstubb, were twenty-five or -six in 1570, masters of arts of a year or two's standing. Many had matriculated in 1559 or 1560: including Robert Some. John Still was twenty-seven; and Richard Greenham thirty-five—the same age as Whitgift. The senior petitioner was Parr, who had gone up to King's in 1546 and must have been

[1] Corpus Christi College MSS. vol. 118, no. 44.
[2] *Ibid.* no. 39.
[3] This was Whitgift's comment to a Puritan delegation in 1583 (Peel, *Second Part of a Register,* I, 217). The reply was obvious: 'We acknowledge our youth, my Lord, neither make we any account to have an opinion of learning; we hold ourselves sufficiently learned if we know and can teach Christ Jesus, sincerely, according to His word and the plainness of it.'

about forty. Three had matriculated under Edward VI: Dodington, William Pachet of Queens' (later Fellow of Pembroke), and Edmund Sherbroke of St John's; and seven under Mary, including Aldrich and Howland. Of the twenty-eight Cartwright petitioners whose matriculation dates are known, and whose age can therefore be roughly guessed, eleven were over twenty-eight. All but two of the thirty-three petitioners had been Fellows for five years or more.

The petition against the statutes in 1572 was certainly a rather younger affair, a gesture by the more vociferous regents. Of the 130 men whom I have precisely identified, nearly half had been admitted master of arts in 1570 (twenty-three) or 1571 (thirty-four). Six, indeed, were the newest of possible M.A.'s, and all six, significantly, were Johnians. Twenty-one dated as M.A.'s from 1569, and seventeen from 1568. The youngest petitioner was probably Nicholas Browne, who had gone up to St John's in 1568, and could not have been more than twenty. Twenty-five of the petitioners had matriculated in 1564, when the vestment controversies were beginning. In all, seventy-four had come up to Cambridge after 1561; and a further forty or so in the first three years of the reign. But, here again, there were older men. Alan Parr once more: and two Regius professors—Thomas Lorkin (Physic) and Thomas Legge (Civil Law). Other older men were Robert Lansdale of Jesus, who had matriculated from Christ's in 1552, and William Ward, a future Regius Professor of Physic, who had gone up to King's in 1550.

The Johnson petition of 1589 bridged the gap between the generations. It included three men who had gone up to Cambridge at the time of the statute disturbances: Henry Alvey, Laurence Ley of Trinity, and Philip Agmondesham of King's. (Agmondesham was born in 1554 and was therefore thirty-five at the time of the petition.) Arthur Johnson of St John's, like Munsay, Alvey, Hugh Gray and Thomas Harrison, was a bachelor of divinity. He had matriculated in 1573, with Harrison, who was to be a Fellow of Trinity until 1621. Daniel Munsay had been a Fellow of St John's since 1572, having matriculated under Longworth in 1564: he was the senior petitioner in 1589. Twenty-five of the sixty-eight men had matriculated after 1580, including George Downham, who was about twenty-four, and probably the youngest. But the most representative section was provided by those fifty men who had matriculated between 1575 and 1580: including William Perkins, who had been a master of arts for over five years, and who was then twenty-nine. We may take this as the average age and status of the Johnson petitioners.

It would therefore not be wise to interpret the disturbances connected with the expulsions of Cartwright and Johnson, and the battles around the new statutes, as merely revolts of young men against old men. The truth is not so simple as that.

II

But the Cambridge contribution to English Puritanism was not wholly dependent on the Fulkes and the Cartwrights and the Alveys; any more than on the Smyths, the Brownes and the Robinsons. This book is concerned with university and college disputes, which are fun, and which are the dramatic high-lights of the story. But they are not the whole story, for they reveal only in a perverted fashion the beliefs and actions of Christian men. The cacophony of quarrels becomes tiresome. There are moments when T. S. Eliot's reminder might usefully be matter for reflection:

> You are not here to verify,
> Instruct yourself, or inform curiosity
> Or carry report. You are here to kneel
> Where prayer has been valid.

That was said, of course, of Little Gidding. And Isaac Walton praised those clergy who visited the household of Nicholas Ferrar in the 1630's as being 'more inclined to practical piety, and devotion, than to doubtful and needless disputations'.[1] The point now to be illustrated is that many of the Puritan 'godly pastors' nurtured by the University of Cambridge, however closely some of them may have skirted nonconformity, were, as country parsons, in the same tradition of pastoral devotion to which Andrewes and George Herbert belong. 'The Anglican Church', Canon Roger Lloyd has written, 'is essentially and fundamentally pastoral. It cannot be said too often for nobody will ever understand Anglicanism who ignores this basic fact.'[2]

The most attractive 'godly pastor' was Richard Greenham of Pembroke, rector from 1571 to 1591 of Dry Drayton, five miles from Cambridge. Greenham matriculated in May 1559, two months before Grindal was admitted Master of the college; he was Fellow from 1566 to 1570 and he petitioned in favour of Cartwright; he was later among those who attended meetings of the Cambridgeshire *classes*. He felt deeply about the pastoral abuses in the Elizabethan Church. Of non-resident ministers he said 'methinks they should see written on everything they have, *Pretium sanguinis*—"This is the price of blood"'.[3] But he was a moderate and charitable man, ready to reprove 'the younger sort' from the pulpit of Great St Mary's for their preoccupation with points of ecclesiastical controversy. Summoned before the Bishop of Ely on a detail of conformity, he gave a good answer to the question where lay the onus of discontent: 'it might lie on either side, or on neither side: For (said he) if they loved one another as they ought, and would do all good offices each for other, thereby maintaining love and concord, it lay on neither side.'[4] It is one of the little ironies of Elizabethan history that his household at Dry Drayton was to include the pathologically prickly Robert Browne.

Dry Drayton became a model parish for the conforming

[1] Walton, *Life of Herbert*, in *Lives* (World's Classics ed.), 311–12.
[2] R. Lloyd, *The Church of England in the Twentieth Century*, II, 23.
[3] T. Fuller, *The Church History of Britain*, v, 192.
[4] Samuel Clarke (ed.), *The Lives of Thirty-two English Divines*, 13.

Puritan; and it was the first of its kind. During his twenty years' ministry Greenham rose, summer and winter, at four, to administer the verbal bread of life to his rural parishioners. After the morning sermon, he tramped the fields of his parish, chatting with his parishioners at the plough. On Sundays he preached twice; and catechized the children before Evensong. He was a very practical Good Shepherd. Under his direction, the farmers laid down corn and barley when stocks were plentiful; when the lean time came, the villagers bought from the granary at four groats the bushel, when the price on Cambridge market was ten groats. When he rode past the Castle at Cambridge, he seldom failed to distribute alms to the prisoners. Nor was he self-concerned enough to ensure that charity began at home. His wife was often forced to borrow money to gather in the parson's harvest. And, though he was a fine preacher and a generous friend, it was as a spiritual director that Greenham made his mark. 'It is a greater thing in a Pastor', he wrote, 'to deal wisely and comfortably with an affected conscience, and soundly and discreetly to meet with an heretic, than to preach publicly and learnedly.'[1] Thomas Fuller, whose father was an acquaintance of Greenham, was in turn to write of him: 'his masterpiece was in comforting wounded consciences. For, although Heaven's hand can only set a broken heart, yet God used him herein as an instrument of good to many, who came to him with weeping eyes, and went from him with cheerful souls.'[2]

Greenham had no children (though his wife, a physician's widow, brought her children to Dry Drayton). But the household was none the less a family affair. For long or short visits came Cambridge dons, or country parsons such as Richard Rogers of Essex. It was a Puritan Academe, with a touch of Little Gidding. The atmosphere must often have been like that of Charles Simeon's Friday evening conversation parties for under-

[1] R. Greenham, *Works* (1599), chapter 54, 'Of Prophecy and Preaching', p. 322.
[2] Fuller, *Church History*, v, 192.

graduates in nineteenth-century Cambridge, or the Holy Club of the Wesleys in eighteenth-century Oxford.

At the end of his ministry in Cambridgeshire, the story of Greenham became oddly moving. Nearly sixty years old, looking back on his years of prayer and fasting and good works, he could not avoid despondency and loneliness. He saw no good wrought by his ministry at Dry Drayton, but on one family. Dry Drayton remained, in spite of his tears and his preaching, ignorant and obstinate. And so Greenham left the village to spend the last three years of his life in London.

He died of the plague in 1594. But the good which he did lived after him. Five years after his death, his Works were collected by Henry Holland; and Holland's Preface is 'possibly the earliest of the long series of spiritual portraits of Puritan divines and others of the elect which were to play so important a part in Puritan propaganda'.[1] In that series, most of the great names were Cambridge men. This Cambridge Movement, like the Oxford Movement, found its most intense and attractive expression in the life and work of the parish parson.

Many of the Puritan 'saints' whose lives were later to be collected and edited by Samuel Clarke lived and died in parishes within easy reach of Cambridge. Even John Cotton, at Boston from 1612 to 1633, was within seventy miles of his adopted college of Emmanuel. Norfolk, Suffolk and Essex were dotted with godly pastors. Ipswich was sixty miles from Cambridge; but Samuel Ward of St John's, who was lecturer there from 1603 to 1635, was also lecturer at Haverhill, less than twenty miles from the university. Barnardiston was also about twenty miles away: Samuel Fairclough of Queens' went there in 1623, and stayed for six years, before moving two miles south to Kedington, where he remained until 1662. From 1628 to 1651 the incumbent of Great Wratting, five miles from Kedington, was Richard Blackerby of Trinity. Previously Blackerby had run a household seminary on

[1] W. Haller, *The Rise of Puritanism*, 26.

Dry Drayton lines at Ashdon, near the Hertfordshire border, twelve miles from Cambridge. William Bedell of Emmanuel, later Bishop of Kilmore, went to Bury St Edmunds in 1602; from 1616 to 1627 he was rector of Horningsheath, three miles south-west of Bury. The other Suffolk incumbent who played a large part in the Puritan historical legend was John Carter of Clare, who moved to Bramford, four miles from Ipswich, in 1583. He remained there until 1617. Essex was further afield. But when Richard Rogers of Christ's, lecturer at Wethersfield from 1572 to 1618, set out from his parish to visit Dry Drayton, he had a journey before him of less than thirty miles.

The primary function of the godly pastor was defined by John Cotton: 'To discover the mind of God, and therewith the sentence of judgement, in matters too hard for inferior judges.'[1] The better to bear this burden, they imposed upon themselves a firm discipline of study and private prayer. Hugh Broughton of Christ's, rector of Washington, Durham, from 1583, was said to spend from twelve to sixteen hours a day in study and prayer.[2] They were all hard-reading men, and they were up betimes. William Gouge of King's, who was at St Anne's, Blackfriars, first as curate, then as rector, from 1608 to 1653, rose at four because 'he was much troubled that any should be at the works of their calling, before he was at his';[3] and each morning at six Richard Sedgewick of Peterhouse led in prayer the husbandmen of Wapping.[4] John Carter prayed for five or six hours a day in his study, 'very loud and mostly very long' to give an example to his children.[5] (These spiritual exercises reaped their reward: Blackerby 'knew eighteen persecutors taken away remarkably upon his fasting and prayer'.[6]) Much of the prayer was devoted to self-examination. 'O! those penitent, unbowelling confessions, earnest deprecations, petitions, panting-longings, and sighings

[1] Clarke (ed.), *Thirty-two Divines*, 225.
[2] Samuel Clarke (ed.), *The Lives of Sundry Eminent Persons in this later Age*, 2.
[3] Clarke (ed.), *Thirty-two Divines*, 243.   [4] *Ibid.* 158.
[5] *Ibid.* 135.   [6] Clarke (ed.), *Eminent Persons*, 63.

after God, and his Grace'[1]—that was an Emmanuel man, Samuel Crook, a Somerset parson during the first half of the seventeenth century. William Perkins, in a treatise published in 1591 concerning the practical application of the doctrine of reprobation, advised the Christian to 'diligently try and examine himself whether he be in a state of damnation or a state of grace'.[2] The Puritan followed the workings of grace in his heart with a fearful exactitude and a scrupulous casuistry. Thus, with the prayers, went the diaries, the Puritan substitute for the confessional. These are not always entirely spiritual; that of John Rous of Emmanuel, for instance, a Suffolk rector from 1623 to 1642, was a hotch-potch of gossip and political news and doggerel.[3] But the aim of most of them was that of John Carter: to 'cast up his accounts with God every day'.[4] The best known of the Puritan diaries is that which Richard Rogers kept from 1586 to 1590.[5] It is an excellent example of the technique of looking diligently to oneself: 'to know mine own heart better, where I know that much is to be gotten in understanding of it, and to be acquainted with the divers corners of it and what sin I am most in danger of and what diligence and means I use against any sin and how I go under any affliction'.[6] For it was possible, in experience if not in dogma, to fall out of the hands of the living God: 'I cannot be comforted with any grace from the Lord, but I am soon carried to lightheartedness, and so to lose it again, yea and worse.'[7] Thus life for Rogers was a continual fret. He studied for ten hours a day, but worried about 'what heavenly books lie by me unoccupied and unsearched'.[8] He was anxious because he felt unwell, or because he craved inordinately for his wife, or because of the bad weather, or because he had avoided those parishioners 'whom

---

[1] Clarke (ed.), *Thirty-two Divines*, 208.   [2] Perkins, *Works*, I (1616), 361.
[3] John Rous, *Diary* (ed. E. Green, Camden Society, 1856).
[4] Clarke (ed.), *Thirty-two Divines*, 141.
[5] Printed by M. M. Knappen, *Two Elizabethan Puritan Diaries* (1935).
[6] *Ibid.* 62.   [7] *Ibid.* 70.
[8] *Ibid.* 84.

I perceive to be fallen from grace'.[1] Yet though the way of perfection was corrupted, the pilgrim errant and uncertain, his progress surely led to the comprehension of the will of God. The reward, for those elected by God and loved by Him, was a full assurance: godly consideration of the heart led in the end to a 'sweet, pleasant and unspeakable comfort'. 'I have had a comfortable and sensible feeling of the contempt of the world and in study, good company, and other peaceable thinking, of the liberty and happiness in Christianity.'[2] The absurd side of the search for the signs of election or reprobation in the soul needs no emphasis: it is easy to remember Thomas Goodwin of Christ's, the Commonwealth President of Magdalen, found in his latter days with half a dozen night-caps on his head, asking each apprehensive visitor whether he was of the number of the elect.[3] Ultimately, however, one may say of most of the Puritan pastors what Fuller said of John Dod of Jesus: that he 'made to himself a cabin in his own contented conscience'.[4]

Nor did the Puritan pastor for ever wrestle with his conscience in his closet. He was usually a great family man. He married seriously and carefully, into kindred stock. Dod, for example, married the step-daughter of Richard Greenham. The strain of an unworldly husband and a ceaseless succession of children told on the women; some of the godly pastors, such as Thomas Gataker of St John's, buried as many as four wives. John Dod, himself the youngest of seventeen, bred a family of twelve. So the private devotion was consummated in household piety. The home of John Carter was described by his son as 'a little Church'; the father, with his air 'sober, grave, and very religious', gathered around him thrice daily his wife, children and servants, and read to them from the Scriptures. The effect upon visitors was such that 'all that came to his house would say, they had seen Adam and Eve, or some of the old patriarchs'.[5] This was typical; and it

---

[1] *Ibid.* 87.   [2] *Ibid.* 65.   [3] G. F. Browne, *St Catharine's College*, 119.
[4] Fuller, *The Worthies of England*, I, 279.   [5] Clarke (ed.), *Thirty-two Divines*, 135.

was constructed on text-book rules. From Erasmus to the Civil War, a feature of English literary taste was the succession of books devoted to domestic case divinity. William Perkins, refusing (like a good Christ's man) to praise a fugitive virtue, said that 'God's graces may as well be exercised in the family as in the cloister',[1] and after his death there was published at Cambridge his course of sermons on *Christian Oeconomie: or, a short Survey of the right Manner of erecting and ordering a Familie according to the Scriptures.*[2] For Perkins, as for Aristotle, the family was a natural institution, 'the seminary of all other societies',[3] though 'the only rule of ordering the family is the written word of God'.[4] By this rule he laid down the essentials of domestic justice: with particular chapters on the duties of husband and wife and son, and on the relation of master and servant. This tradition of practical divinity was continued in William Gouge's seven-hundred-page treatise *Of Domesticall Duties,* published in 1622, and dedicated to his parishioners at Blackfriars.

In the Greenham tradition, the pastors kept open house. Richard Blackerby at Ashdon had not only the sons of local folk— gentry, yeomen, and tradesmen—to live with him but also students such as Samuel Fairclough of Queens'. With him, they followed the discipline of the Puritan day, relieved perhaps by a scholarly walking party. They studied divinity for half the week, the humanities for the other half; and on Sunday there were six sessions of preaching and reading and catechizing. There was no nonsense. 'He (in good earnest) made it his business to live with God, and to His glory'[5] and his pupils would do the same. Many Cambridge students stayed with Cotton at Boston or Gataker at Rotherhithe. The parlour of Gataker was said to be 'one of the best schools for a young student to learn divinity in; and indeed his house was a private seminary for divers young gentlemen of

---

[1] Perkins, 'A Reformed Catholic', *Works,* I, 586.
[2] In *Works,* III (1618).   [3] *Ibid.* Dedicatory Epistle.
[4] *Ibid.* 669.   [5] Clarke (ed.), *Eminent Persons,* 60.

this nation, and far more foreigners, who did resort to, and sojourn with him'.[1] Rogers too kept young men as boarders. One of them married his daughter.

So, in their fashion, the Puritan pastors were great entertainers. John Dod always invited a dozen friends to dinner on Wednesdays and Sundays ('besides his four or six constant widows')[2]: and the habit was general. The diet was of course wholesome and the table talk edifying. Samuel Crook was by nature a witty man, but he 'abhorred froth, and babbling'; the object of his talk was to instruct as well as to cheer, 'without biting sarcasms, or unbeseeming scurrility'.[3] They were stewards in their Master's house: and they never forgot it.

In their parishes they served God seven whole days, not one in seven. William Gouge lectured every Wednesday morning at his Blackfriars' Church. Men came from the City and the Inns of Court to hear him; and 'when any country ministers, and godly Christians came to London about their affairs, they thought not their business fully ended, unless they had been at Blackfriars' lecture'.[4] The tradition of the Order of Preachers was in worthy hands there. Gouge celebrated the Holy Communion monthly; preceded the evening before by a general visitation of the parish to note and examine prospective recipients. Also, during his ministry of nearly half a century at St Anne's, Gouge supervised building operations in the church and the rectory, and laid out the churchyard afresh. He was a happy man: and 'the height of his ambition was to go from Blackfriars to heaven'.[5]

The weekly mid-day lecture or sermon was an essential part of the Puritan ministry. John Cotton lectured at Boston on Thursdays; he also preached in the early morning on Wednesdays and Thursdays, and on Saturday afternoons.[6] Many Cambridge dons rode the seventeen miles to Kedington to hear Samuel Fair-

---

[1] Clarke (ed.), *Thirty-two Divines*, 256.
[2] *Ibid.* 177.
[3] *Ibid.* 210.
[4] *Ibid.* 239.
[5] *Ibid.* 238.
[6] *Ibid.* 220.

clough's Thursday lecture. But it was the Sabbath that was 'the Market Day of thy Soul'—the phrase was John Dod's. The example of Thomas Wilson, a contemporary of Milton's at Christ's, and rector of Maidstone during the Commonwealth, will show the Puritan Sunday at its most conscientious. On Saturday, Wilson meditated and prayed until midnight. He then slept: but for three hours only. At three he rose to continue his private prayers; in which at seven he was joined for two hours by his family. At nine came the morning service in church. This lasted for two and a half hours, and included with the Old Testament lesson an hour of exposition—Wilson kept an hour glass on his desk—followed by the sermon, also lasting an hour. After church, at about noon, there were more family prayers. At dinner, Wilson ate sparingly, and retired to his study before the meal was over. Then there was godly singing and more religious exercises in the family circle. The afternoon service in church followed the morning pattern; but the lesson was taken from the New Testament. There was again an exposition, and a sermon. After this service, friends and neighbours gathered in the rectory, for an informal question-and-answer quiz, in which the points of the two Lessons were elaborated and driven home. This was followed by prayer. Supper was served at the house of a neighbour, and took the form of a spiritual *salon*, where the Lessons and the sermons were again discussed. At about ten the godly retired to bed with more prayers and a psalm. For Wilson it had been a twenty-hour day. We may take at its face value the comment of a visiting judge of assize, who remarked that in all his circuit he never saw the Sabbath more strictly observed.[1]

Thus the Puritan vision of the godly Church, where 'in every parish they may have a preaching pastor'[2] (the 'Gospel preached' being the 'ordinary means to beget faith'[3]) was in some circum-

[1] Clarke (ed.), *Eminent Persons*, 24.
[2] 'Second Admonition to Parliament', in Frere and Douglas, *Puritan Manifestos*, 95.
[3] Perkins, 'A Golden Chain', *Works*, I, 71.

stances realized. (But a Puritan survey of Essex in 1586 had noted 'sufficient, painful and careful preachers'—such as Richard Rogers —in only thirty-eight of the 335 parishes.[1]) Preaching meant 'plain preaching, which is God his plain order'.[2] 'It is a by-word among us', wrote Perkins, '"It was a very plain sermon". And I say again, "the plainer, the better".'[3] In his treatise on the art of preaching, published at Cambridge in 1592,[4] Perkins laid down rules for the preparation and delivery of sermons. They should not be written but spoken 'by heart';[5] in the delivery there must be 'a speech both simple and perspicuous, fit both for the people's understanding and to express the majesty of the Spirit'[6]; there should be 'gravity in the gesture of the body'—'the trunk or stalk of the body being erect and quiet'.[7] In short:

The Order and Sum of the sacred and only method of Preaching.

1. To read the text distinctly out of the canonical Scriptures.

2. To give the sense and understanding of it, being read, by the Scripture itself.

3. To collect a few and profitable points of doctrine out of the natural sense.

4. To apply (if he have the gift) the doctrines rightly collected, to the life and manners of men in a simple and plain speech.[8]

The Puritan style was plain, but teaming with homely imagery. Dod had 'an excellent gift in similitudes',[9] and so had Perkins.

---

[1] Peel, *Second Part of a Register*, II, 163.

[2] 'Second Admonition to Parliament', *op. cit.* 115.

[3] Perkins, 'Commentary on Galatians', *Works*, II, 222.

[4] *Prophetica, sive de sacra et unica ratione concionandi*; translated by Thomas Tuke, *The Arte of Prophecying, or, a Treatise concerning the sacred and onely true manner and methode of Preaching* (1606). Reprinted in *Works*, vol. II (1617).

[5] *Works*, II, 670.　　　　[6] *Ibid.*　　　　[7] *Ibid.* 672.

[8] *Ibid.* 673. Professor W. S. Howell has taken Perkins's method of division and subdivision as 'a contribution to the cause of Ramism in England', and shows that Perkins used some of the arguments of Ramus's *Dialecticae Libri Duo* (an edition of which by William Temple of King's was published in 1584). Yet, as Professor Howell himself points out, Perkins did not mention Ramus in his 'bibliography' to *Prophetica*. (W. S. Howell, *Logic and Rhetoric in England: 1500–1700*, 206–7.) It would appear that the importance of the influence of the language and method of Peter Ramus on the Cambridge Puritans can be exaggerated.

[9] Clarke (ed.), *Thirty-two Divines*, 173.

Dod 'could not endure that ministers should use hard and unusual English. He said, that most ministers in England usually shoot over the heads of their hearers'.[1] And so he 'took great care to speak to the meanest capacity, and to feed the lambs'.[2] The care was rewarded: for two hundred years after his death 'The Worthy Sayings of Old Mr Dod' were found pasted on cottage walls, and they were sold in cheap pamphlet form until at least the end of the eighteenth century.[3] (Dod's *Plain and familiar Edition of the Ten Commandments* earned him the nickname of 'Decalogue Dod'.) 'He was excellent for practical divinity, and living by faith';[4] and the final tribute of his biographer is very fine:

His ministry was so spiritual, and yet so plain, that poor simple people that never knew what religion meant, when they had gone to hear him, could not choose but talk of his sermon. It mightily affected poor creatures to hear the mysteries of God (by his excellent skill that way), brought down to their own language and dialect.[5]

Such a comment provides a little of the answer to the question posed by Father Philip Hughes at the end of his survey of the English Reformation: 'And in all this, where is the mind and heart of the ordinary man?'[6]

The Puritan pastors led their flocks into 'the green pastures of solid, and savoury truths'.[7] In these green places the pastors lived, and had their being, and died. The death was often painful and the life dogged by ill health. Samuel Crook (who 'fed not his flock with airy dews of effeminate rhetoric', nor 'with the jerks, and quibbles of a light spirit, which he ever abhorred as the excrementitious superfluities of frothy brains, and unhallowed hearts'[8]) was so weak and sickly that he preached his own farewell sermon many times. The last hours of William Gouge, a lifelong

---

[1] Clarke (ed.), *Thirty-two Divines*, 176.   [2] *Ibid.*
[3] Haller, *The Rise of Puritanism*, 59.
[4] Clarke (ed.), *Thirty-two Divines*, 176.   [5] *Ibid.* 177.
[6] Hughes, *The Reformation in England*, III, 404.
[7] Clarke (ed.), *Thirty-two Divines*, 206.   [8] *Ibid.*

martyr to asthma and the stone, were a frightful agony—though he did survive until the age of seventy-nine. Gataker, in spite of perpetual headaches, lived to be eighty. John Dod died in great pain, when he was ninety-six. Most of them, like Thomas Hill of Emmanuel, the Commonwealth Master of Trinity, confessed on their deathbeds their 'great comfort, and joy in God's discriminating electing-love'.[1] Others made a worse end. Paul Baynes of Christ's died in Cambridge in 1617, with 'many doubts and fears';[2] it was the last recorded phase of his pilgrimage in grace.

A description of Gataker might be applied to many of his fellow Cambridge men in the parishes of England: 'a faithful shepherd, and a fit mirror for pastors, as well as an exact pattern for people'.[3] Their success survives even the enthusiastic exaggeration of their biographers. Fairclough's church at Kedington, we read, was

so thronged, that (though, for a village, very large and capacious, yet) there was no getting in, unless by some hours' attending before his exercise began; and then the outward walls were generally lined with shoals and multitudes of people, which came (many) from far, (some above twenty miles), so that you could see the Church yard (which was likewise very spacious) barricaded with horses, tied to the outward rails, while their owners were greedily waiting to hear the word of Life from his mouth.[4]

The 'multitudes' included the Cambridge Puritans of the 1620's and 1630's.

Like the Tractarian parish priests over two centuries later, these men passed easily into non-conformity: that is, they did not scrupulously use the Book of Common Prayer or conform to the regulations about vestments and ceremonies. In 1584 sixty Suffolk ministers were suspended, for their objections to the

[1] *Ibid.* 233.   [2] *Ibid.* 24.
[3] *Ibid.* 260.   [4] Clarke (ed.), *Eminent Persons*, 187.

Order of Baptism: they included John Carter and John Knew-stubb.[1] Two years later twenty-nine ministers of Essex were in turn suspended, for their refusal to wear the surplice: Richard Rogers and John Ward were among them.[2] Such men remained in the Church not only because they thought separation unreasonable, but because they were prepared to tarry until the Church was in fact reformed. 'I have a longing desire', said John Carter, 'to see, or hear of the fall of Antichrist: But I check myself, I shall go to Heaven, and there news of it will come thick, thick, thick.'[3] The proudest boast of Carter's son about his father was this: 'He was always a non-conformist, one of the good old Puritans of England. He never swallowed any of the ceremonies against his conscience: So that he was often troubled by the Bishops, but God raised him up friends that always brought him off, and maintained his liberty.'[4] Their friends were certainly influential. The story of Puritanism in Suffolk owes much, for example, to Sir Nathaniel Barnardiston, the patron of Fairclough, with whom he worked in a Gelasian harmony: 'the magistracy and ministry joined both together and concurred in all things for the promoting of true piety and godliness'.[5] The path of the non-conforming minister was not a lone one. It could, however, be heroic. Arthur Hildersham of Christ's commenced bachelor in 1584: from the early 1590's until his death in 1632 he was incumbent of Ashby-de-la-Zouch. During that period he was suspended at least seven times, sometimes for long periods, once imprisoned, and once heavily fined. Such a tradition was to flower under the Laudian regime. For John Cotton the world, in 1633, seemed worse than ever it was. So, on the advice of John Dod, he left Lincolnshire for Massachusetts. It was to flower more fruitfully under the Commonwealth: when Thomas Gataker and Thomas Goodwin were to sway the Westminster

[1] Peel, *Second Part of a Register*, I, 243.　　[2] *Ibid.* II, 260–1.
[3] Clarke (ed.), *Thirty-two Divines*, 136.　　[4] *Ibid.* 134.
[5] Clarke (ed.), *Eminent Persons*, 169.

Assembly, when Henry Burton of St John's returned to St Matthew's, Friday Street, and when William Gouge refused the provostship of King's.

Other Cambridge Puritans found more attractive the spirit of John Dod:

> A Grave Divine; precise, not turbulent;
> And never guilty of the Church's rent.[1]

The tone was expressed by an Emmanuel man, William Bradshaw: 'in matters not doubtful, and controversial, at least to conform ourselves to such outward fashions as are generally used in those times, and that Church wherein we live'.[2] That begged almost all the questions. But it does make clear that many of the Puritan pastors can claim a rightful, if uneasy, place in the Anglican tradition. The spirit of Richard Greenham was still abroad in the land: it was nobly expressed by Samuel Fairclough: 'if a man lives holily, and walks humbly with God, I shall ever love him, notwithstanding his conformity; and if he be proud, contentious and profane, I will never think well of him for his non-conformity'.[3] Under the Commonwealth, Fairclough lived on quietly as Pastor of Kedington, refusing the mastership of Trinity. He was deprived in 1662; and his successor was a promising young Cambridge man called John Tillotson.

In 1651 Anthony Tuckney, reproaching his former pupil Benjamin Whichcote, now Provost of King's, for too great a devotion to natural philosophy, reminded him:

how richly useful a spiritual plain powerful ministry would be in the university; I need not tell you why: but that in former times, when the question was, why Cambridge men were accounted more profitable preachers than Oxford men; Mr Baynes said, the reason was, that God had, from the first reformation, blessed Cambridge with exemplary plain and spiritual preachers.[4]

---

[1] *Memorials of John Dod* (ed. J. Taylor, 1875), inscription under frontispiece.
[2] Clarke (ed.), *Thirty-two Divines*, 57.   [3] Clarke (ed.), *Eminent Persons*, 190.
[4] 'Eight Letters between Whichcote and Tuckney', printed with Whichcote, *Moral and Religious Aphorisms* (ed. S. Salter, 1753), 37.

THE PURITANS AND AUTHORITY

(It is fitting to add that this liking for the 'plain and practical sermon' was shared by George Herbert.[1])

'A marvellous good neighbour', said Costard of the curate, 'and a very good bowler.' There was, at any rate, more to the godly pastors than that.

III

The interconnection of the godly pastors was remarkable. Like the interrelated intellectual aristocracy of England in the nineteenth century, and after, analysed by Noel Annan,[2] they formed almost an exclusive tribe, promoting by pedigree an apostolic succession of plain living and high thinking. 'Here's to us and all like us!' The genealogies of the great Puritan families, such as the Rogers's and the Culverwells, illustrate the point.

John Rogers was a Chelmsford carpenter in the reign of Henry VIII. His son Richard, who went up to Christ's in 1566, was the diarist of Wethersfield, a country parson until his death in 1618. Richard Rogers married twice. By Barbara, his first wife, he had two sons: Daniel and Ezekiel. Both boys went to Christ's, Daniel commencing bachelor in 1596 and Ezekiel in 1605. Daniel became a Fellow of the College (1600–8) and succeeded his father at Wethersfield, where he died in 1652 at the age of eighty. Ezekiel emigrated to New England in 1638 from his living of Rowley St Peter (Yorkshire) and founded Rowley (Massachusetts); he died in 1661. Richard's second wife was Susan, the widow of John Ward, rector of Haverhill. Susan brought three children with her to Wethersfield: Samuel, John and Nathaniel. Samuel Ward matriculated from St John's in 1595, was elected one of the first Fellows of Sidney Sussex in 1599, and became lecturer at Haverhill and Ipswich from 1603 until 1635,

[1] The words are from his first sermon at Bemerton. Walton, *Lives* (World's Classics ed.), 295.
[2] In his *Leslie Stephen* (1951); and in his essay on the intellectual aristocracy in *Studies in Social History* (ed. J. H. Plumb 1955).

when he was suspended. John Ward, admitted to Emmanuel as a sizar in 1596, was also suspended in the 1630's. Nathaniel Ward, the most famous of the three brothers, had been born at Haverhill in 1578, and went up to Emmanuel in 1596. After graduating, he studied law in London and travelled in Europe, before he was ordained in 1618. In 1628 (after two years as curate of St James's, Piccadilly) Nathaniel was presented to the living of Stondon Massey in Essex, from which he was suspended in 1633. He then sailed to Massachusetts, and was chosen minister of the church at Ipswich (or—to use the Indian name—Agawam). His legal training proved useful in the late 1630's, when he was asked to draw up a code of laws for the colony; a compilation which was issued in 1641 (after being debated and amended by the General Court) as the 'Body of Liberties'. But Nathaniel Ward is best known for his trenchant and exuberant *The Simple Cobbler of Agawam*, which was published in London in 1647, after his return to England. Nathaniel died, an Essex parson once more, in 1652. His son John, born at Haverhill in 1606, had been instituted in 1641 as pastor of Haverhill (Massachusetts). Now, John Rogers the carpenter produced another son besides Richard. That was a junior John, who passed his life in Chelmsford, as a cobbler. His son, 'roaring John' Rogers, went up to Emmanuel in 1588 (being financially supported by his uncle Richard) and took his B.A. degree in 1592; from 1605 until his death in 1636 he was lecturer at Dedham. Roaring John's most noteworthy son was Nathaniel Rogers, born at Haverhill, who was an Emmanuel sizar in 1614, and who emigrated from his Suffolk rectory in 1636. Nathaniel Rogers succeeded Nathaniel Ward as pastor of Ipswich (Massachusetts) and died in 1655. His son, the fourth John, graduated from Harvard in 1649, and was to be President of the college in the 1680's.[1]

The Culverwell family displays an even more interesting succession, in its satisfactory combination of an interest in city

[1] S. E. Morison, *Harvard College in the Seventeenth Century* (1936), 442.

trade and colonial expansion, with Puritan piety and a Cambridge education. Nicholas Culverwell, a London merchant-haberdasher, made the money. In the early 1580's the son of another City haberdasher had married Judith Culverwell, who was probably Nicholas's niece. This young man, just down from Oxford, was Thomas Smith. During the lifetime of his wife, Smith was to become involved with the Russia and Turkey Companies; but Judith, dying young and without issue, was never to see Thomas at the height of his power in the first years of the reign of James I: knighted, Governor of the East India Company, and Treasurer of the Virginia Company. Nicholas Culverwell himself had three sons and four daughters. The eldest boy, Samuel, went up to Christ's in 1568. (Nicholas had a great affection for Christ's, and was to leave £200 in trust to the Haberdashers' Company to endow a 'Mr Culverwell's Preacher'—the poorest graduate divinity student in the College.) Samuel was ordained in 1578, and became a 'godly pastor' in Yorkshire until his death in 1613. Ezekiel Culverwell, a year or two younger than Samuel, was first educated at Oxford, but—it never being too late to mend—crossed to Cambridge in 1578 and was incorporated M.A. In 1578 also Nicholas junior went up to Christ's at the unusually early age of twelve. Doubtless Ezekiel and Nicholas were taking prompt advantage of the fact that the family now had a *pied-à-terre* in Cambridge; for in 1577 William Whitaker had forfeited his fellowship at Trinity to marry their sister Susan. Another of the Culverwell daughters married Arthur Dent, born in 1553, who went up to Christ's in 1571, was rector of South Shoebury, Essex, from 1580 until his death in 1601, and author of such edifying works as *The Ruin of Rome*, edited after his death by his brother-in-law Ezekiel 'for the daunting of papists, seminary priests, and all that cursed rabble'. Elizabeth Culverwell became the wife of Thomas Gouge, of Stratford, Middlesex, who was later to be a member of the Virginia Company: a son was born to them in 1578—this was William Gouge, whom we have seen as one of the Puritan 'saints', and who was, in time, to have strength of mind enough to refuse the provostship of King's.

By Susan Culverwell, William Whitaker had two sons. They both died in 1617. But the manner of their death could hardly have been more different. Samuel Whitaker, born in 1587 (the year of his father's appointment to the mastership of St John's) progressed from Eton to King's, became Fellow of his college in 1608, passed away quietly in his bed at Cambridge, and was buried in the chapel. Alexander Whitaker was born in 1585, and went from Eton to Trinity in 1602: his college contemporaries included John Cotton and John Winthrop. He was ordained priest in 1609 and took a living in Yorkshire. But after less than two years Alexander—in the words of his friend William Crashaw— 'without any persuasion (but God's and his own heart) did voluntarily leave his warm nest, and to the wonder of his kindred, and amazement of them that knew him, undertook this hard, but in my judgement, heroical resolution to go to Virginia, and help to bear the name of God unto the Gentiles'.[1] Alexander Whitaker landed at Jamestown in May 1611. The first settlement had been founded there precisely four years before, and Robert Hunt, an Oxford man,[2] had been chaplain to the colonists, celebrating the first recorded Holy Communion on American soil on 21 June 1607 (the third Sunday after Trinity). But Hunt died in 1608. And it is Whitaker who assumes the title of 'Apostle to Virginia'—the first effective Anglican missionary on the North American continent. He became minister of the new settlement of Henrico, nearly fifty miles up-river from Jamestown,

---

[1] William Crashaw, epistle dedicatory to Alexander Whitaker's *Good Newes from Virginia* (1613). See H. C. Porter, 'Alexander Whitaker: Cambridge Apostle to Virginia', *The William and Mary Quarterly*, Third Series, vol. XIV, no. 3 (July 1957).

[2] Hunt, formerly Vicar of Reculver (Kent) and then of Heathfield (Sussex) was probably a graduate of Magdalen, Oxford. He was certainly not a member of Trinity Hall, Cambridge, as Venn (following Cooper) stated in the *Alumni*. (C. W. F. Smith, 'Chaplain Robert Hunt and his parish in Kent', *Historical Magazine of the Protestant Episcopal Church*, March 1957.)

THE PURITANS AND AUTHORITY

about fifteen miles below the later site of Richmond. Here he had 'his parsonage, or Church land, some hundred acres impaled, and a fair framed parsonage house built thereupon'.[1] From 1612 he ministered also to the settlement of Bermuda Hundred, five miles away, founded where the Appomattox joins the James. And in 1612 (the year in which his uncle Laurence Chaderton became a member of the Virginia Company) Whitaker sent home his sermon *Good Newes from Virginia*, which plainly and pithily pointed out the abundance of the harvest and the paucity of the labourers (with some charming final pages devoted to a description of the beauty and riches of Virginia) and which was printed in London in 1613. In the spring of 1614 Alexander's constant prayers for a powerful and effectual ministry to the Indians were strikingly (almost melodramatically) answered by his successful instruction in the Christian verities of the nineteen-year-old Princess Pocahontas, whom he also baptized. This frontier career was cut tragically short. For in the spring of 1617 Alexander Whitaker was drowned in the James River, at the age of thirty-two.

Seven years later there died in Virginia Alexander's half-brother Jabez, the posthumous child of William Whitaker by his second wife, Joan. Jabez was also connected with the mission to the Indian. At the age of twenty-three, with the rank of lieutenant and newly married, he was sent out to the colony by the Company in the autumn of 1619, in charge of tenants for one of the plantations known as the College land; that is, the acres set aside for the endowment of an Indian college 'for the training up of those infidels in true religion, moral virtue and civility'.[2] Jabez' plantation prospered, he was promoted to captain, begat a child, and became a member of the Virginia Assembly. When he died, in 1624, he was twenty-eight. The last appearance of the name

---

[1] Ralph Hamor, *A True Discourse of the present estate of Virginia* (1615), 31.
[2] Quoted from an order of November 1618 by W. F. Craven, *The Southern Colonies in the Seventeenth Century* (1949), 132.

of Whitaker in the records of the Virginia Company was in 1625:
'there came into this Colony a sister of Mr Whitaker's who made
enquiry after the goods of her deceased brother but found that he
left little of value behind him'.[1]

Cecilia Culverwell, the fourth daughter of the city haberdasher,
married Laurence Chaderton (a Lancashire man, like William
Whitaker) in 1576. Laurence and Cecilia had only one child—
a daughter, Elizabeth. Elizabeth was to marry Abraham Johnson,
who went up to Emmanuel in 1591. (He was the son of Archdeacon Robert Johnson, the founder of Oakham and Uppingham
schools, and a former Fellow of Trinity.) Abraham and Elizabeth
had three boys. Samuel, the eldest (born in 1605) went to
Emmanuel in 1620 and was rector of Ashdown, Essex, from 1640
until 1658; Ezekiel (who was to be Master of Uppingham)
followed Sam to Emmanuel in 1622; and Francis, the youngest,
went to the college in 1633. Now, Elizabeth Chaderton was
Abraham's second wife. His first wife had borne him a son,
named (of course) Isaac. Isaac Johnson matriculated from
Emmanuel in 1614, and was ordained priest in 1621. Much to the
annoyance of father Abraham (but to the delight of his grandfather the archdeacon) Isaac won for his wife the Lady Arbella
Fiennes, daughter of the third Earl of Lincoln. Isaac and Arbella
sailed to Massachusetts in 1630 with their friend John Winthrop.
But Arbella, sickened by the voyage, died at Salem in August:
and Isaac survived her by less than a month. In his will Isaac
Johnson bequeathed 'to my reverend grandfather Mr Doctor
Chaderton as a testimony of my thankfulness for my education
under him five pieces of two and twenty shillings a piece and the
like sum to my worthy grandmother his wife'.[2] Cecilia Chaderton
gained nothing by the gift, for she herself died in 1631.

[1] *Records of the Virginia Company* (ed. S. M. Kingsbury), IV, 511. Many of the papers
relating to Jabez Whitaker in these printed records (I, 370, 508; II, 50; III, 226, 441–3,
571; IV, 585) are from the Ferrar collection at Magdalene College, Cambridge.
[2] *Winthrop Papers*, II, 53.

IV

Such brief family chronicles provide a bird's eye view of a century and more of English religious history. But is the main theme the influence of the parents, the tradition of the native heath, or the training of the university? In most cases, an intertwining of all three. Yet often it was the influence of Cambridge which was the greatest. Laurence Chaderton, for instance, came of a Lancashire Roman Catholic family: and his father felt compelled to send him this stern letter in 1565: 'If you renounce the new sect which you have joined you may expect all the happiness which the care of an indulgent father can secure you; otherwise I enclose in this letter a shilling to buy a wallet with. Go and beg for your living.'[1] The new sect: that is, the Puritans of Christ's.

The importance of Christ's College as a seed plot of Puritanism was not positively due to its Elizabethan Masters: Edward Hawford (1559–82) and Edward Barwell (1582–1606). From the Puritan point of view neither was particularly satisfactory. Hawford was an orderly administrator of the Perne type, whose support of Whitgift in 1570 had aroused the ire of Edward Dering. He quarrelled with Dering and the more extremely puritanical members of his Fellows' table; and at least one of these disputes—that with Hugh Broughton—was in the great tradition of college faction. Barwell was more promising, for he had signed the petition against the statutes in 1572. Perhaps because he sympathized a little, but not too much, with the college Puritans, the factions in Christ's gathered force during his mastership. At one point order was restored only after the intervention of the Master of Corpus, an administrator of such efficiency and officiousness that the whole college united against him. Yet the fact that there was only one change of Master during the reign meant that tradition could quietly grow. Of the fifty-seven Masters of Elizabethan Cambridge, Hawford and Barwell had

---

[1] W. Dillingham, *Life of Laurence Chaderton*, 4.

long reigns. Not so long as that of Goad, Provost of King's for forty-one years; or Perne, at Peterhouse for thirty-six years; or Chaderton, for thirty-eight years Master of Emmanuel. But steady reigns—compared with St John's, which had eight Masters in forty years.

Puritanism at Christ's owed its rise not to the Masters but to the Fellows. Cambridge Fellows were then 'tutors', *in loco parentis*, to an extent unknown today. A don might have anything from one to twenty pupils, boys who lived with him, and directly paid him, and were entirely controlled by him. (Of the forty-seven Fellows of St John's in 1565, forty-two had pupils: twenty had five or more, and three fifteen or more.)[1] Thomas Fuller's description of John Preston, a tutor at Queens' from 1609 to 1622, was applicable in lesser degree to many Elizabethan dons: 'He was the greatest pupil-monger in England in man's memory, having sixteen fellow commoners (most heirs to fair estate) admitted in one year in Queens' College, and provided convenient accommodation for them.' It was said that 'every time when Master Preston plucked off his hat to Doctor Davenant the college master, he gained a chamber or study for one of his pupils'.[2] When Preston succeeded Chaderton as Master of Emmanuel in 1622, he took his pupils with him. One of them was called Chambers, a fact which inspired what was probably Fuller's worst joke.

Now, Elizabethan Christ's, a college of fifteen Fellows, was extraordinarily fortunate in the quality of its dons. Edward Dering was Fellow from 1560 to 1571. Laurence Chaderton entered the college under him; and he himself became a Fellow in 1568. Other Fellows elected during the 1560's were John Still, William Tabor, Walter Allen, Robert Holland and John More— all to be petitioners for Cartwright; John Millen, expelled the university in 1573; and Barwell. Richard Rogers matriculated in

[1] S. P. Dom. Eliz. vol. xxxviii, no. 16 (i), fol. 104-5.
[2] Fuller, *Worthies*, ii, 517.

1566, Arthur Hildersham went up to the college in 1570 and William Perkins in 1577, when Chaderton was about to leave because of his forthcoming marriage. Francis Johnson matriculated in 1579 and George Downham in 1581. Johnson and Perkins were elected Fellows in 1574, a year later than Cuthbert Bainbrigg.

Perkins was a Fellow until his marriage in 1595. For eleven years, therefore, his was the great name in the college; and in those years there came up John Smyth, Sam Ward, Paul Baynes, Richard Bernard and William Ames. Ward, even when he was twenty-four, a bachelor of two years' standing, confided to his diary his pride in his former tutor: 'May 23, 1595...Of my thought of pride in Mr Perkins' chamber. The good will that Mr Perkins shewed me.'[1] Ward thanked God 'that he selected me out of my brethren to come to Cambridge, as that I came to this college, and that in Mr Perkins' time'.[2] The year in which Perkins left the college for a private house in Cambridge, John Smyth was elected Fellow; and the first years of the new century, the last of the mastership of Barwell, saw as Fellows Ames, Daniel Rogers, Baynes and Thomas Taylor. And when Thomas Goodwin went up to the college in 1614 he was much affected by the thought that he might go to Heaven with the Fellows of Christ's; or at least with those half dozen 'that were great tutors, who professed religion after the strictest sort, then called Puritans'.[3] Eight years later John Milton entered the college.

In 1589 half a dozen of the Fellows of Christ's had signed the petition for their persecuted colleague Francis Johnson. But by that time there was a new candidate, with its eleven petitioning dons, for the honour of being the prime Puritan stronghold—Emmanuel.

The founder of Emmanuel, Sir Walter Mildmay, like the first Master, Laurence Chaderton, was a Christ's man. The deed of foundation was dated May 1584; and the admissions of pensioners

[1] M. M. Knappen (ed.), *Two Puritan Diaries*, 104.
[2] *Ibid.* 119.   [3] T. Goodwin, *Works*, v, vi and ix.

are recorded from November.[1] The foundation number of Fellows was seven. The aim of the foundation was succinctly expressed by Mildmay himself:

the one object which I set before me in erecting this college was to render as many as possible fit for the administration of the Divine Word and Sacraments; and that from this seed ground the English Church might have those she can summon to instruct the people and undertake the office of pastors, which is a thing necessary above all others.[2]

Thus it was most fitting that the site of the college—bought by Mildmay in 1583 for £550[3]—was that of the old priory of the Preaching Friars. And as building operations began once more in Preachers' Street, under the supervision of Ralph Symons, the old church became the new hall.

Laurence Chaderton, who resigned the mastership of Emmanuel in 1622 at the age of eighty-six, was the grand old man of the Puritan movement in Cambridge. He had been a member of the Puritan delegation to the Hampton Court Conference in 1604, which suggested, among other things, that the use of the surplice be made optional. By that time it had been brought to official notice that the Book of Common Prayer was disregarded in Emmanuel in favour of 'a private course of public prayer', and that the surplice was not worn in the college chapel.[4] (Ten years later the nephew of Chaderton, Alexander Whitaker, writing from Virginia to his cousin William Gouge, expressed surprise that 'so few of our English ministers that were so hot against the surplice and subscription[5] come hither where neither is spoken of'.[6]) It

---

[1] E. S. Shuckburgh, *Emmanuel College*, 4.   [2] *Ibid.* 23.

[3] Willis and Clark, *Architectural History of the University of Cambridge*, II, 688.

[4] Harleian MSS. 7033 (British Museum Baker MSS.), vol. VI, p. 85; quoted in Willis and Clark, *Architectural History*, II, 700–1.

[5] That is, the ordination oath required by the Canons of 1604, to affirm that the Book of Common Prayer 'containeth in it nothing contrary to the word of God, and that it may lawfully so be used: and that he himself will use the form in the said book prescribed, in public prayer, and administration of the sacraments, and none other'.

[6] Ralph Hamor, *A True Discourse* (1615, first issue), 60. This passage was omitted in a second issue of Hamor's book, later in 1615. See H. C. Porter, 'Alexander Whitaker: Cambridge Apostle to Virginia', *William and Mary Quarterly*, July 1957.

had also been reported that the members of Emmanuel received the sacrament 'sitting upon forms about the Communion Table';[1] to this charge Chaderton replied that there were 'sitting communions in Emmanuel College; which he said was so, by reason of the seats so placed as they be, yet that they had some kneeling also'.[2] The new *Constitutions and Canons Ecclesiastical* of 1604 ordered that Masters, Fellows, scholars and students should communicate 'kneeling reverently and decently upon their knees according to the order of the Communion Book'; that the surplice and (in the case of graduates) the hood must be worn in chapel; and that 'the order, form, and ceremonies shall be duly observed as they are set down and prescribed in the book of common prayer, without any omission or alteration'.[3] This restatement of the basic discipline which had been in theory obligatory for over forty-five years occasioned much searching of conscience in Emmanuel. Sam Ward, Fellow of the college, noted in his diary that Wednesday, 18 January 1605, was the fell day when 'the surplice was first urged by the Archbishop to be brought into Emmanuel'[4]—twenty years, that is, after the founding of the house. Yet Chaderton was a conforming Puritan. He knew that those 'who dislike the government of the Church by bishops will substitute something far less beneficial both to Church and State'.[5] And the personal piety and integrity of the Master averted much wrath. When it was pointed out to James I on his visit to Cambridge in 1615 that the chapel of Emmanuel faced north and the kitchen east, he remarked with his usual sound sense: 'God will not turn away his face from the prayers of any holy and pious man, to whatsoever region of heaven he directs his eyes. So, doctor, I beg you to pray for me.'[6] It was at that visit that

---

[1] Willis and Clark, *op. cit.*

[2] Barlow's narrative of the Hampton Court Conference, in E. Cardwell, *History of Conferences* (1840), 212.

[3] Canons XXIII, XVII, XVI.

[4] Knappen (ed.), *Two Puritan Diaries*, 130; i.e. January 1604/5.

[5] Dillingham, *Life of Chaderton*, 10.

[6] *Ibid.* 11.

Richard Corbett made his well-known comment on the celebrations:

> But the pure house of Emmanuel
> Would not be like proud Jezebel,
> Nor show herself before the King
> An hypocrite, or painted thing:
> But, that the ways might prove all fair,
> Conceiv'd a tedious mile of prayer.[1]

After his resignation in 1622, Chaderton lived privately in Cambridge for another eighteen years. The last great moment of his life was in 1640, when Lord Finch, Keeper of the Seal, walked in procession into the college with his former tutor, now over a hundred years old. William Dillingham was present at this tender ceremony, and recorded the gracious speech which Finch made before the Fellows and students of the college: 'Here I hold by the hand the first master of your college, my own ever-to-be-honoured tutor, the father of my soul.... The great seal is proud to be carried before you, sir, before you quit this world.'[2] At the banquet which followed, Chaderton was the guest of honour; and after it, the Lord Keeper escorted the old man down the street to his house. Chaderton died within the year.

Two years before that banquet at Emmanuel—that is, in May 1638—it had been decided by the General Court of the colony of Massachusetts Bay that Newtown (founded on the Charles River in 1630) be newly named Cambridge; and perhaps the most important contribution of Emmanuel to Puritan history lies in the fact that of the hundred or so Cambridge men who braved the Atlantic crossing to New England between 1629 and 1640 (as against only thirty-two from Oxford) thirty-three were Emmanuel bred.[3] The Emmanuel exiles included two former Fellows of the college, Thomas Hooker and John Cotton; Isaac Johnson; Nathaniel Ward and his son John; Nathaniel Rogers;

---

[1] 'To be sung to the tune of "Bonny Nell"'; E. E. Kellett, *A Book of Cambridge Verse*, 21.
[2] Dillingham, *op. cit.* 20. Finch was the new High Steward of Cambridge.
[3] S. E. Morison, *The Founding of Harvard College*, Appendix B, 359–410: 'English University Men who migrated to New England'.

Samuel Stone, who was born at Hertford in 1602, and after whose birthplace the settlement of Hartford (Connecticut) was to be named; Thomas Shepard, minister at Cambridge, 'the most noted evangelist of early New England';[1] Richard Saltonstall, who sailed in the Winthrop fleet from Southampton in 1630 with his father Sir Richard, a Clare man who was one of the original patentees of the Bay Company and who founded one of the most famous families in Massachusetts—a Saltonstall represents that State as Senator in the Washington of the 1950's; and Simon Bradstreet, future governor of the colony, sometime steward to Theophilus, fourth Earl of Lincoln (brother of Lady Arbella Fiennes), and husband of Anne, daughter of another of the earl's stewards. Anne Bradstreet—whose gorge rose at first when faced with the 'new world and new manners' of Massachusetts—was to express, in her poetry and (more especially) in her prose 'Meditations', much of the best of the religious life of seventeenth-century New England.[2] 'New England must include a new Emmanuel'[3], and in September 1638 John Harvard, who had gone up to Emmanuel under Preston in 1627, made himself immortal by dying of consumption in Charlestown at the age of thirty, and leaving half his estate to the college which had opened at Cambridge in the summer. The General Court decided in March 1639 that 'the college agreed upon formerly to be built at Cambridge shall be called Harvard College'.[4]

During the September of 1640—less than two months before the death of Chaderton—William Mildmay, great-grandson of the founder, was admitted fellow commoner of Emmanuel. He went in 1644 with his tutor to New England, where he took his A.B. degree from Harvard, class of 1647.

[1] *Ibid.* 400.
[2] Thomas Jefferson Wertenbaker, *The Puritan Oligarchy*, chapter 3, 'The Puritan Spirit in Literature'. There is a brief selection from, and appeciation of, Anne Bradstreet in Perry Miller (ed.), *The American Puritans, their Prose and their Poetry*.
[3] Morison, *op. cit.* 107.   [4] *Ibid.* 221.

V

The great migration across the Atlantic was the climax to the history of Elizabethan and Jacobean separatism. That history effectively began with a Corpus man, Robert Browne of Rutlandshire, 'the father of English congregationalism', who was a student at the college under Thomas Aldrich, commencing bachelor in 1573. At Cambridge Browne was 'known and counted forward in religion'; and he left the university without proceeding to the degree of master. During the 1570's, earning his living as a schoolmaster, he 'fell into great care, and was sore grieved while he long considered many things amiss, and the cause of all, to be the woeful and lamentable state of the Church'. This anxiety resulted in his dismissal. At the end of 1578 Browne returned to Cambridgeshire, to live with Richard Greenham at Dry Drayton. Although he had decided not to submit himself to ordination, and although he had no preaching licence (when he was given one, he threw it into the fire) Browne began to preach in the villages around Cambridge. His success was such that 'certain in Cambridge' asked him to minister in the town. For some six months he preached in St Bene't's, the church adjoining his old college; here he quickly became notorious as the self-styled 'witness of that woeful state of Cambridge, whereunto those wicked prelates and Doctors of Divinity have brought it'. To the especial amazement of the Master of Trinity, he preached against 'the calling and authorizing of preachers by bishops'.[1]

Art thou the Church of Christ, when thy stars be not in His hand, but the fists of thy bishops do pull them down from thee? Yet is the Church of England the pillar and ground of truth. For the bishops override it. They are the truth, and it is the ground. It is the beast, and they are the riders. It stoopeth as an ass for them to get up. The whip of their

---

[1] The quotations in this paragraph are from Browne's own autobiographical account; 'A True and Short Declaration' (1584), *The Writing of Harrison and Browne,* ed. Peel and Carlson, 397–404.

spiritual courts, and the spurs of their laws, and the bridle of their power, do make it to carry them.[1]

The parishioners of St Bene't's were most impressed, and some of them collected a stipend and asked him to take full charge. This he refused to do, 'for that he saw the parishes in such spiritual bondage, that whosoever would take charge of them must also come into that bondage with them'. In the winter of 1580 Browne fell ill: and he was on a sick-bed when the news was brought him that he had been forbidden to preach in the diocese. The bearer of this news was the young chaplain to Bishop Cox of Ely, Richard Bancroft.

In the spring of 1580 Browne left Cambridge for Norwich, to join Robert Harrison. Harrison had matriculated from the St John's of Richard Longworth in 1564, but he had gone to Corpus later, and commenced bachelor from the college in 1568, just before Browne entered it. Browne now convinced Harrison that 'we are to forsake and deny all ungodliness and wicked fellowship, and to refuse all ungodly communion with wicked persons', because 'God will receive none to communion and covenant with him which as yet are at one with the wicked'.[2] By 1581 the two Corpus men had formed at Norwich a regular separatist Church with a covenant of subscription, and an order of prayer and discipline. Browne also became well known in the diocese of Norwich as a preacher, attracting congregations of a hundred and more in private houses and conventicles. In April 1581 he was arrested; and for the next nine months he was in prison, either at Bury St Edmunds or in London. In the spring of 1582 Browne and Harrison and their congregation gathered together again; and 'they all agreed and were fully persuaded that the Lord did call them out of England'.[3]

So they crossed to Middelburg in Zeeland. But the two years which Browne spent there were not conducive to happiness in

[1] Browne, 'Treatise on Matthew, chapter 23', *ibid.* 207.
[2] 'Declaration', *ibid.* 412.   [3] *Ibid.* 424.

Zion. For one thing, Cartwright arrived in Middelburg shortly afterwards, and quarrelled with Browne about whether the Established Church was to be reformed from within, or forsaken as irreformable. For another, Browne fell ill again, and became a prey to nervous depression. Even some of his former followers turned against him, on one occasion threatening to turn him out of the house. Browne so resented Cartwright's defence of the Church of England as a true Church, though corrupt, that he was driven in his writings to an invective shrill to the point of lunacy. The invective sprang from a shocked incomprehension of those who 'play mock-holiday with the service of God'.[1]

They are all turned back after babbling prayers and toying worship, after priestly preachers, blind ministers, and canon offices, after popish attire and foolish disguising, after fastings, tithings, holy days, and a thousand more abominations: and their feet do stick fast in the mire and dirt of all popery, that they cannot get out.[2]

The ministry of the Church of England would become holy only if 'all the dumb ministers were hanged up in the churches and public assemblies for a warning and terror to the rest'.[3] For the usual preaching in England was a mere excuse for men to show 'their university degrees, and how well they become their hoods, or their scarlet gowns, and what standing in Cambridge'.[4]

Even Middelburg was no place for an uninterrupted flow of this sort of thing. And in the autumn of 1583 Browne sailed for Scotland with the four or five families which had remained faithful to him. Within a month of arrival he had been imprisoned by the Edinburgh Kirk.

In 1585 Browne's effective career ended. In that year, as Robert Harrison lay dying in Middelburg, worn out by his quarrels with Browne's wife and the other exiled Englishwomen, Browne was examined by Whitgift and signed a submission to the

[1] *Ibid.* 415. [2] 'Treatise on Matthew', *ibid.* 205-6.
[3] 'Answer to Cartwright', *ibid.* 452. [4] 'Treatise on Matthew', *ibid.* 173.

Supreme Governor. Six years later, in September 1591, he was at last ordained deacon and priest; and presented to the living of Achurch-cum-Thorpe Waterville, Northamptonshire. For the next forty-two years Robert Browne lived as a country parson. While he ministered more or less quietly to his flock, the self-styled Brownists waned and waxed in England at large, and in Holland. How many people, when they used the epithet Brownist, knew the whereabouts of its founder? Thomas Fuller, as a boy, knew the crotchety rector of the parish a mile from his home: 'He was of an imperious nature, offended if what he affirmed but in common discourse were not instantly received as an oracle.... He had in my time a wife, with whom for many years he never lived, parted from her on some distaste: and a church wherein he never preached, though he received the profits thereof.'[1] So Robert Browne is remembered as a half-mad eccentric, a 'common beater of his poor old wife'. He certainly continued his capacity to flout authority. From 1616 to 1626 he was excommunicated. And at the age of over eighty, in a sudden passion, he struck the parish constable. He was trundled by cart, on a feather mattress, to Northampton goal, where he died in 1633. It was a fitting end. There had been quiet, sunny periods for Browne: in the court of Corpus, or the rectory at Dry Drayton; and he loved to teach music to his children, his son accompanying the psalms on the viol. But his main boast was that he had been in thirty-two prisons: 'and in some of them he could not see his hand at noon day'.[2]

Separatism may have been for Browne a god that failed. But he had written, in 1582, 'A Treatise of Reformation without Tarrying for Any.' That was the battle cry for many spirits in successive generations of Cambridge men. It came to be so for Francis Johnson of Christ's, who after his expulsion from the university at the end of 1589 went to Middelburg as minister in the English Church of the Merchant Adventurers. He returned

[1] Fuller, *Church History*, v, 68–9.   [2] *Ibid.* 67.

to England in 1592 as chaplain to the London congregation of Barrowists: 'just at the moment when a new leader was most needed to inspire the flagging energy of the persecuted separatists'.[1] Within the year the Separatist movement was given its martyrs: Henry Barrow of Clare, John Greenwood of Corpus, and John Penry of Peterhouse. The executions and the terror split the ranks of the brethren; and in the spring of 1593, after the passing of the 'Act to retain the Queen's Majesty's subjects in their due obedience', the migration of the London Church to Holland began. Johnson himself was arrested. He remained for nearly five years in the Clink prison, Southwark, where he married, in 1594, a rich and genteel widow, Mrs Thomasine Boyes. The Privy Council arranged for his release in 1597, intending him to be exiled on the Magdalen Islands, in the Gulf of St Lawrence. But the weather was bad, the ship returned to harbour, and in September Johnson slipped away to Amsterdam.

So began the comedy of

> ...the holy brethren
> Of Amsterdam, the exiled saints.[2]

Within two weeks of Francis Johnson's arrival a house had been hired on the south bank of the Amstel, near the Muntplein. The amiable Henry Ainsworth of Caius, who had been in Amsterdam for three or four years already, became teacher of the now newly organized English congregation, with Johnson as pastor. The congregation began to flourish exceedingly: by the turn of the century there were three hundred communicants, under their efficient pastor and calm teacher, their ruling elders, their deacons, and their one elderly and rather irritable deaconess. But the Church was not long without its troubles. The first discords were occasioned by the sartorial and other flippancies of Mrs Thomasine Johnson, known to the impious of Amsterdam as the 'bouncing

---

[1] C. Burrage, *The Early English Dissenters*, I, 136.
[2] Ben Jonson, *The Alchemist* (1610).

girl'. It was objected by the stricter brethren (led by Francis's brother George, also a Christ's man) that she laid abed on the Lord's Day until nine o'clock; that she was suspiciously addicted to wine bibbing; and that 'she stood gazing, bracing or vaunting in shop doors. Contrary to rules of modest behaviour in the daughters of Zion.' The main fire of criticism was directed against her attire. For Thomasine wore 'a long busk, after the fashion of the world, contrary to Romans xii. 2'; she displayed five or six gold rings, a great deal of lace, excessive ruffs, a tucked apron, and whalebone in her petticoat; she wore 'a long white breast, after the fashion of young dames, and so low she wore it, as the world call them codpiece breasts'. Most offensively, she possessed splendid hats, 'immodest and toyish in a Pastor's wife'.[1] Francis's father joined George in denouncing these rags. Francis's answer was simple. He flung at them the charge of anabaptistry, and excommunicated them both.

There followed a kind of peace, until the arrival in Amsterdam at the beginning of 1608 of an old pupil of Francis Johnson: John Smyth. Smyth had gone up to Christ's in 1586, and was Fellow from 1594 to 1598. He was always in trouble at Cambridge; in 1597, for instance, he was called before the Consistory after a college commonplace against the burial service, the surplice, and the churching of women.[2] In 1600 he became a lecturer and preacher at Lincoln, where he also ran into difficulties, on one occasion being suspended—though he was reinstated after an appeal. In about 1605 he moved a little north-west of Lincoln to officiate in the separatist congregations at Gainsborough (Lincs.) and Scrooby (Notts.).[3] At Scrooby, between Retford and Doncaster, the brethren met in the manor house, where there lived an old Peterhouse man called William Brewster. Smyth left England with some of his flock at the end of 1607.

[1] Burrage, *Early English Dissenters*, I, 160–1.

[2] University Archives, Registry Guard Books, vol. 4, no. 2.

[3] For Scrooby, which is known to American historians as 'the cradle of Massachusetts', see H. M. Dexter, *The England and Holland of the Pilgrims*, book III, chapter 2.

Within a year of arriving in Amsterdam he had quarrelled with the hierarchy of the existing English congregation, and set up a purer, more reformed Church, elsewhere in the city: 'the brethren of the separation of the second English Church at Amsterdam'. Smyth, like Jonson's Ananias, believed 'all's heathen but the Hebrew'; that is, he objected to written translations of the Bible as 'not part of spiritual worship, but rather the invention of a man of sins'.[1] More important, the whole pattern of pastor, teacher and elders had come to seem to him an unspiritual perversion. He had also meditated much on baptism. And as a result of his musings, one day in 1609 he unchurched his old Church, renounced his former ministry and rebaptized himself and his forty faithful followers. The story that he stripped from the waist upwards, waded into the Amstel, and sluiced himself with water[2] is, though picturesque, probably false. The scene was more likely the room usually used for worship, where Smyth dipped his hand in the water in a bowl, and poured it over his own forehead.[3] However, the theory that only the pure can initiate the pure had received its *reductio ad absurdum* at the hands of John Smyth of Christ's, henceforth known to history as the 'Se-baptist'.

Smyth's saga was not yet over. His doctrines became increasingly crazy and soon he was excommunicated by an effective minority of his own congregation. Shaken but unbowed, he set up quarters with the rest of his flock in the back room of an Amsterdam bakehouse. But his changes of heart and mind made his last years lonely and troubled. Fortunately they were few. He died of consumption in August 1612, and was buried in the Nieuwe Kerk in September.

John Robinson had arrived in Amsterdam shortly after Smyth. He was born at Sturston, five miles from Gainsborough; and he went up to Corpus as a sizar in 1592 at the age of sixteen, when

[1] H. M. Dexter, *The True Story of John Smyth*, 7.   [2] *Ibid.* 30.
[3] Dexter, *England and Holland of the Pilgrims*, 456.

John Jegon was Master, and Thomas Jegon a tutor. He became a Fellow of Corpus in 1598, and in 1600, for one year, he held the office of dean. He resigned his fellowship when he married in 1604. Perhaps he would have resigned in any case. For at this period Robinson was meditating deeply on light and darkness, on the children of God and the children of Satan. After a short time in Norwich he became convinced that to remain within the Church of England would be a betrayal of that truth 'in my heart as a burning fire shut up in my bones':[1] 'because we know that not anti-Christ, but Christ, shall be our judge, we are bold upon the warrant of his Word and Testament' to 'proclaim to all the world separation from whatsoever riseth up rebelliously against the sceptre of his kingdom; as we are undoubtedly persuaded the communion, government, ministry, and worship of the Church of England do'.[2] So he went home, to Gainsborough and Scrooby. And in 1608 he in turn arrived with a party in Amsterdam, after three abortive attempts to cross the North Sea by night from Boston or Grimsby, attempts cut short by betrayal, pursuit, and imprisonment.

But Robinson's congregation maintained its unity, and did not worship with the existing English churches in Amsterdam. In May 1609, tiring perhaps of the squabbles of their compatriots, they moved south to Leiden.

In 1610 there came the last and most disastrous of the schisms in Amsterdam: the departure of Henry Ainsworth. Johnson and Ainsworth quarrelled about the powers of the congregation in relation to those of the elders. Ainsworth, insisting that the authority of the elders was not sovereign but delegated, moved with his 'congregationalists' to another house two doors down the street. The rival groups had become known as the Franciscan and the Ainsworthian Brownists; and the latter began a lawsuit for the possession of the original property. They may have won it, for soon afterwards Francis Johnson went to Emden. He

[1] J. Robinson, *Works*, II, 52.   [2] *Ibid.* III, 406.

returned to Amsterdam only to die: which he did in 1618, at the age of fifty-five.

When Johnson died, Ainsworth re-united the shattered English Church under his direction until his own death in 1623. But some members of Johnson's flock preserved their integrity. In the winter of 1618, having obtained a patent for a plantation from the Virginia Company of London, they sailed across the Atlantic, a hundred and eighty of them, insufferably crowded in a small ship. The food supply failed, there was an outbreak of dysentery, the vessel was driven from its course, and the captain died. Less than fifty of the passengers survived the voyage. Such was the pathetic epilogue to the story of Johnson's Church at Amsterdam.

News of this disaster reached the Church of Pastor John Robinson and Elder William Brewster at Leiden in the summer of 1619. But it did not discourage those in the congregation for whom Holland was not quite the Promised Land, those who were increasingly inclined to lift their eyes unto 'those vast and unpeopled countries of America, which are fruitful and fit for habitation, being devoid of all civil inhabitants, where there are only savage and brutish men which range up and down'.[1] As early as 1617 the Leiden community had expressed the desire 'to live as a distinct body by themselves under the general Government of Virginia',[2] and they began the search for a sponsor. Negotiations were first begun with the Virginia Company (a leading promoter of which, Sir Edwin Sandys, was the son of the lord of Scrooby manor, where Brewster's father was bailiff). Robinson and Brewster wrote to Sandys in December 1617: 'We are knit together as a body in a most strict and sacred bond and covenant of the Lord, of the violation whereof we make great conscience, and by virtue whereof we do hold ourselves straitly tied to all care of each other's good and of the whole, by every one and so mutually.'[3] However, though permission was obtained

[1] William Bradford, *Of Plymouth Plantation*, 25.
[2] *Ibid.* 29.   [3] *Ibid.* 33.

to settle in the vast domain of 'Virginia', attempts to obtain a specific grant of land, or financial support, were for some time frustrated. Eventually the prospective pilgrims formed a partnership with a group of London gentlemen and merchants led by Thomas Weston, who was looking for a good speculation and who had himself been granted a patent for land from the Company. The terms of the partnership were drawn up in July 1620. Weston and his English associates contributed money shares, and agreed to charter and fit out a ship and provide the initial food, clothing and supplies; the adventurer-planters who were to cross the Atlantic as colonists made their contribution either in money or provisions; and the members of the Leiden church who sailed with them contributed 'themselves and their capacity for hard and profitable work'.[1] After two false starts the twelve-year-old and overcrowded *Mayflower* put to sea from Plymouth on 6 September—'about the worst month, on an average, for a westerly passage under sail'.[2] Of the hundred and one passengers, thirty-five were from the Leiden congregation, under the leadership of Brewster.

Robinson continued as pastor of the two hundred remaining brethren of Leiden. At the end of July he had preached to the volunteer pilgrims on the eve of their departure to the port at Delft, whence they were to sail to Southampton on the *Speedwell*, a vessel they had bought with their own money.

So a New England was called into being to redress the spiritual balance of the Old; and John Robinson, sometime dean of Corpus

---

[1] C. M. Andrews, *The Colonial Period of American History—The Settlements*, 1 (1934), 265. The pilgrims bought out their London partners in 1626 by an arrangement which has been called 'the earliest example of Yankee business acumen'; W. W. Sweet, *Religion in Colonial America*, 80; cf. Andrews, *op. cit.* 284–6.

[2] S. E. Morison, 'The Saga of Mayflower I', *The New York Times Magazine*, 14 April 1957, 12. The voyage to the site of Provincetown in New England took sixty-six days: 'The old Mayflower was not too slow, as is proved by the fact that she sailed home in only thirty days, and with a short crew at that; but she was no speed queen, even for 1620' (*ibid.*) The *Mayflower* rounded Cape Cod, and anchored, on 11 November; on 11 December the exploring party landed at Plymouth (on the rock); and the *Mayflower* sailed into Plymouth harbour on 16 December.

Christi College, who lies buried as 'Predicant van de Engelsche Gemeente' in the Pieterskerk at Leiden, has gone down to history as the pastor of the Pilgrim Fathers.

William Brewster was the only Cambridge man on the *May-flower;* and of all the Cambridge graduates who took part in the exodus to New England before the Civil War, he was the senior, having gone up to the Peterhouse of Andrew Perne in 1580. Until he died in 1644 at the age of seventy-seven Brewster was elder of the Plymouth Church. Indeed, for almost ten years after the pilgrims' anchor had been dropped in Cape Cod Bay, Brewster was the supreme governor of the Plymouth congregation. For four years the little colony had no pastor. Brewster conducted the services and preached, but there was no baptism and no Lord's Supper, and marriages were performed by the civil authority—the civil marriage ceremony was in fact to be usual in New England (and not infrequent in Anglican Virginia[1]). In 1624 the London Company sent out a clergyman: one John Lyford, who celebrated Communion and baptized at least one child, but according to the Book of Common Prayer, for which indiscretion he was driven from the colony a few months after his arrival. The Plymouth Church did not have a regularly admitted pastor until 1629, when Ralph Smith of Christ's came to this township on the hill, with its three hundred inhabitants, its two streets lined by well-constructed houses of hewn planks, its meeting house with six cannon carefully and significantly erected on the roof. Poor Smith in turn was a failure, 'being of very weak parts'.[2] He resigned, amidst a universal lack of protest, in 1635. His successor was a Magdalene man, John Rayner.

Ralph Smith had crossed to New England on the *Talbot,* the other passengers of which included Francis Higginson of Jesus,

---

[1] W. F. Craven, *The Southern Colonies in the Seventeenth Century,* 274.
[2] Plymouth Church Records for 1629; *Publications of the Colonial Society of Massachusetts,* XXII (1920), 64.

who had been deprived of his living for nonconformity in 1627, and Samuel Skelton of Clare (whose luggage included a library of fifty-five volumes). This voyage of 1629 was promoted by the Massachusetts Bay Company, which had bought territory surrounding the Charles River from the short-lived New England Company in March 1628, and had sent out one of its members, John Endecott, to the struggling and tiny community of Salem in September. Higginson and Skelton arrived at Salem in July 1629, where they were promptly instituted and ordained respectively teacher and pastor of the Church. Now, when the *Talbot* had passed Land's End in May, and passengers had crowded to the stern for a glimpse of the last of England, Higginson had taken occasion to address the group:

> We will not say as the separatists were wont to say at their leaving of England, Farewell Babylon! Farewell Rome! But we will say, Farewell dear England! Farewell the Church of God in England, and all the Christian friends there! We do not go to New England as separatists from the Church of England; though we cannot but separate from the corruptions in it: But we go to practise the positive part of Church Reformation, and propagate the Gospel in America.[1]

And the confession of faith and the church covenant drawn up at Salem in August were intended to preserve—albeit in an elusive manner—a union with the Established Church at home.[2]

Meanwhile, in March 1629, the Massachusetts Bay Company had received its royal charter. In July, at the Commencement, there was a meeting in Cambridge of 'many reverend divines' to discuss plantation matters.[3] Isaac Johnson, who was in Sempringham at the time, regretted that John Winthrop could not be present. But Winthrop returned to his university in August, when the famous meeting was held in Cambridge which was to inspire 'a

---

[1] Quoted from Cotton Mather's *Magnalia* in Andrews, *Colonial Period of American History*, I, 377.

[2] J. D. Phillips, *Salem in the Seventeenth Century* (1933), 54.

[3] Letter of Johnson to Emmanuel Downing; *Winthrop Papers*, II, 103.

new experiment in colony building'.[1] This meeting consisted of twelve leading members of the Bay Company, including Sir Richard Saltonstall, Johnson, Winthrop, and a fellow Trinity man, John Humphrey. These men there bound themselves and their families to 'inhabit and continue in New England'; a crossing of a three-thousand-mile Rubicon which was to be undertaken on one condition—that the charter and the 'whole government' of the company be 'legally transferred and established to remain with us and others which shall inhabit upon the said plantation'.[2] In other words, the proposed colonial community was to be separate and self-governing, free of any dependence upon authority in England: the whole incorporated company would move itself across the Atlantic. This Cambridge decision was approved by the General Court of the company a few days later; the transfer of the charter was legally effected in September; and in October Winthrop was elected governor of the company, with Humphrey as his deputy.

At about this time Winthrop prepared a justification of the intended plantation in New England. 'This land', he wrote, 'grows weary of her inhabitants.' But in God's providence Massachusetts could be 'a refuge for many whom he means to save out of the general calamity'. It was in Old and not in New England that the true Church was an alien in a strange land. One of the marks of this truth was the state of the universities:

The fountains of learning and religion are so corrupted as (besides the unsupportable charge of their education) most children (even the best wits and of fairest hopes) are perverted, corrupted, and utterly overthrown by the multitude of evil examples and the licentious government of those seminaries, where men strain at gnats, and swallow camels, use all severity for maintenance of caps, and other accomplements, but suffer all ruffian-like fashions, and disorder in manners to pass uncontrolled.[3]

[1] Andrews, op. cit. 393.
[2] Proceedings of the Massachusetts Historical Society, LXII (June 1929), 279–80.
[3] Winthrop Papers, II, 139.

Winthrop's own Cambridge career had been brief. He had gone up to Trinity, from Groton in Suffolk, in December 1602, when he was not yet quite fifteen. But he fell seriously in love rather early and left the college to be married in April 1605. Fortunately for his spiritual well-being he 'married into a family under Mr Culverwell his ministry in Essex'[1]: that is, Ezekiel Culverwell. Here he began to seek 'a better assurance by the seal of the spirit'; and was much exercised in 'reading of Mr Perkins'.[2] His first son was born in 1606.

Governor Winthrop with the company and the charter sailed from Southampton in March 1630. The leading vessel of the fleet of four ships was the *Arbella*: so named in honour of the wife of Isaac Johnson, the former Lady Arbella Fiennes, who was on board with her husband. The little fleet anchored at Salem in June, after a voyage of seventy-seven days. Winthrop automatically superseded Endecott as governor of the colony. But there were difficulties at Salem—lack of water for one thing—and Winthrop soon went a little farther south, to the Charles River. Then he crossed the bay: and in September 1630 Boston was founded and named. The first teacher of the Boston Church, chosen at Charlestown in August,[3] was John Wilson of Eton and King's, sometime Fellow.

Winthrop's party was greeted on the miniature peninsula by one white inhabitant. For on what was later to be called Beacon Hill, nicely settled in a cottage with an orchard, trading amicably with the Indians, there lived—of all things!—an Emmanuel man: William Blackstone. Blackstone had gone up to Cambridge in 1614, had been ordained, and had crossed to New England in

---

[1] *Ibid.* I, 155. Winthrop's own spiritual autobiography, written in 1637.
[2] *Ibid.* 156.
[3] *Ibid.* II, 267. Winthrop's journal for 27 August 1630: 'We of the congregation kept a fast, and chose Mr Wilson our teacher;...we used imposition of hands, but with this protestation by all that it was only as a sign of election and confirmation, not of any intent that Mr Wilson should renounce his ministry he received in England.' The covenant of the first church in Boston (drawn up at Charlestown in July) was signed by Winthrop, Dudley, Johnson, and Wilson; *ibid.* 308.

1623, a member of the ill-fated expedition organized by Sir Ferdinando Gorges. He was not to find the first Bostonians much to his taste. 'I came from England', he said, 'because I did not like the Lord Bishops, but I cannot join with you because I would not be under the Lord Brethren.'[1] So he moved south in 1635 to a more desolate and congenial atmosphere in what was to become the colony of Rhode Island. It has been well said of this Cambridge clerical Crusoe: 'having constituted for several years the entire white population of the capital of New England, he has a symbolic value, and deserves his eccentric place in the annals of his university'.[2]

Blackstone was not the only Emmanuel man to become restless in Massachusetts in 1635. Thomas Hooker, pastor of Newtown—who had been suspended from his lectureship at Chelmsford in 1629, had spent three years in Rotterdam and Delft, and had arrived in Boston with John Cotton in September 1633—also felt the pinch. What depressed Hooker were the cramped conditions, the lack of opportunity, the poor soil—'the reasons that were to urge pioneers westward throughout American history'.[3] In 1636 he went a hundred miles south-west, with his congregation of a hundred families, to Hartford, on the Connecticut River. That was a voluntary migration. But the most famous exile from Massachusetts was a banished man: Roger Williams of Pembroke, expelled from the Colony by Winthrop and the General Court in October 1635. Williams, 'a maverick among the intellectuals of New England'[4], was the greatest of the Cambridge contributors to the American tradition and the American 'myth'—in which (however naïvely) he is the 'irrepressible democrat', 'the first great liberal, the champion of toleration and democracy in an

[1] L. B. Wright, *The Atlantic Frontier*, 112.
[2] Jocelyn Gibson, 'Cambridge: Nurse of a Nation', *Cambridge Journal*, vol. IV, no. 5 (February, 1951), 313. Blackstone died in 1675.
[3] *Ibid.* 306. Winthrop to Sir Symonds D'Ewes, July 1635: 'the people and the cattle are so increased as the place will not suffice them' (*Winthrop Papers*, III, 200).
[4] Perry Miller, *Roger Williams* (1953), 32.

intolerant and oligarchical age'.[1] In fact he was cranky, puzzling, excitable, unpredictable, a sort of New England Robert Browne: someone called him 'divinely mad'. Williams was born in the year Queen Elizabeth died; a protégé of Sir Edward Coke, he graduated from Pembroke in 1627. In 1629 he became chaplain in the household of Sir William Masham in Essex, and soon after his arrival there he married one of the maids, having been rejected by one of the ladies. Exactly one year after his wedding, in December 1630, he sailed from England with his wife and arrived at Boston in February 1631. The Boston Church craved his pastoral services; but he refused, because the congregation had not explicitly or irrevocably separated from the Church of England. Circumstances prevented his accepting an invitation from the Salem Church to succeed Higginson, and he went to Plymouth, where he assisted Ralph Smith, 'occasionally preaching but not officially ordained'.[2] He went to Salem as pastor in 1634. There followed over a year of bickering: in which the main issue was that of separatism, and the most important of the minor issues Williams's denial of the validity of the land grants in the company charter—were not the Indians, Williams argued, the rightful owners of the territory? Thus in the bitter, snowy January of 1636 Roger Williams set off fifty miles south through the 'wilderness' (a favourite word of his), to the Narragansett Bay, in search of the lost Zion. In the summer he negotiated a land deal with the Indians, founded a settlement, and called it Providence. When he returned on a visit to England in 1644 he obtained a charter uniting the several townships, which by then had been established, into the colony of Rhode Island, the third New England state to be founded by a Cambridge graduate, a colony committed to the proposition that church should be separate from state: where—as the General Assembly was to remind the governor and General Court of Massachusetts in 1658 when the question arose of the expulsion of Quakers—'freedom of

[1] Gibson, *loc. cit.* 307.   [2] Miller, *op. cit.* 19.

different consciences, to be protected from enforcements, was the principal ground of our Charter,...which freedom we still prize as the greatest happiness that men can possess in this world'.[1]

Finally, there had been two further involuntary exiles from Massachusetts, in 1637: Mrs Anne Hutchinson, the kindly, but intolerable, unofficial spiritual adviser of Boston, and her brother-in-law, John Wheelwright of Sidney Sussex College. Mrs Hutchinson went to Rhode Island, where she was massacred by Indians in 1643. Wheelwright sailed north, up the Atlantic coast to the settlement of Portsmouth (New Hampshire), and then a few miles down one of the rivers of the bay to land obtained by deed from the Squamscott tribe: where he founded Exeter. This Sidney man deserves to be remembered for much. But in the folk-lore of Old, as well as of New England he is picturesquely but pettily recalled to mind chiefly as the bachelor of arts who tripped up at football a sportive young fellow commoner of his college called Oliver Cromwell.

These disturbances should not turn attention from the fact that the great migration from England in the 1630's was a 'surprisingly close-knit, almost cosy, family affair'.[2] And the influence of the nucleus of Cambridge men—itself large—was out of all proportion to its size. Of the hundred Cambridge emigrants, six had been Fellows: Thomas Hooker and John Cotton of Emmanuel; John Knowles of St Catharine's; John Wilson of King's; and Thomas Rashleigh and Charles Chauncey of Trinity. (Chauncey was to be President of Harvard from 1654 to 1672.[3] His predecessor, the first President, was a Magdalene man, Henry Dunster. Nathaniel Eaton of Trinity was head of the college from its foundation in 1636 until 1640, but the title of President cannot properly be applied to him.)

For our story, it should also be pointed out that nine of the

[1] *Records of the Colony of Rhode Island* (ed. J. R. Bartlett), I (1856), 378–9.
[2] Gibson, *loc. cit.* 304.
[3] Morison, *Harvard in the Seventeenth Century*, 320–39.

Cambridge New Englanders had matriculated in the reign of Elizabeth: Higginson, Cotton, Nathaniel Ward, Robert Peck of St Catharine's, John Philip of Emmanuel, Emmanuel Downing of Trinity Hall, Peter Saxton and Ralph Partridge of Trinity, and William Brewster—that 'wise, discreet, and extraordinarily gentle man'.[1]

VI

Because of the pervading Cambridge tinge of the first generation of emigrants to New England, William Perkins, William Ames, Richard Sibbes and John Preston became 'the most quoted, most respected, and most influential of contemporary authors in the writings and sermons of early Massachusetts'.[2] Thus the sermons preached to Cambridge congregations by Perkins in the 1580's and 1590's, published in book form both during his lifetime and after his death, moulded the piety of a whole nation. The Puritan tradition, in the first and last resort, must be assessed in terms of the Pulpit.

On Sundays in Cambridge, the whole university was required to attend both the morning and afternoon sermons in Great St Mary's. If the preacher was a doctor or bachelor of divinity, he was escorted from his college to the church by the esquire bedell. Matthew Stokys, who was esquire bedell from 1557 to 1585, left details of the ceremony in writing.[3] For a bachelor, the little bell of the church was rung; for a doctor, the 'great bell'.[4] By the statutes of 1570, in addition, each regent was required to preach twice in Great St Mary's, once in English, once in Latin. (Stokys could remember the time when the white canons sat in Great St Mary's, in the fourth stall on the south, and the monks

[1] G. F. Willison, Saints and Strangers (1945), 43.
[2] Perry Miller, 'The Marrow of Puritan Divinity', Publications of the Colonial Society of Massachusetts, XXXII (1935), 257. This valuable essay was reprinted in Miller, Errand into the Wilderness: quotation at p. 59.
[3] Printed by Dean Peacock as an appendix to Observations on the Statutes of the University.
[4] Ibid. xviii.

in the fourth stall on the north.[1]) The town came to the church as well. An order of the corporation 'for the better frequenting of sermons' in 1576 ordered that all householders and servants in Cambridge 'shall come to the sermon, either in the church where they dwell, or else to the sermon in St Mary's'.[2] Great St Mary's must have been full to overflowing then; for the present galleries were not built until the eighteenth century. On special occasions (such as the Commencement) wooden tiers were erected on scaffolding round the church for the students. The masters of arts sat on movable benches, the bachelors either stood or squatted on stools or on the floor. If a mere bachelor or undergraduate too closely approached the chairs of the mayor and corporation, or the stalls reserved for the dignitaries of the university, he was to be 'openly corrected in the common schools with the rod'.[3] There were also in the church some box pews, eight feet high, which were much criticized during the Laudian revival.[4] The pulpit was set in the middle of the nave; and the stirring and the gossip before the sermon began must have gone to make a scene which Rowlandson would have enjoyed.

At the Commencement sermon of 1620 Symonds D'Ewes of St John's College could find a seat only on the highest tier of the scaffolding, behind the pulpit: indifferent for hearing, but 'very commodious'.[5] This was disappointing, for Symonds was a pious youth. He had already heard one sermon that day, in his college chapel, and he was later to hear, in a town church, another. James Duport, a Fellow of Trinity in the 1650's, drew up a list of rules for his students which might have been issued at any time during the previous century.[6] The boys were to be diligent in their attendance at morning chapel; they were to read books of

[1] *Ibid.* xix.
[2] Cooper, *Annals*, II, 345. [3] *Ibid.* 430.
[4] W. D. Bushell, *The Church of St Mary the Great*, 152.
[5] J. Marsden (ed.), *College Life in the Reign of James I* (extracts from the unpublished diary of Symonds D'Ewes), 105.
[6] Printed by G. M. Trevelyan in *The Cambridge Review*, no. 1575 (May 1943).

practical divinity, such as those of Richard Sibbes; they were to be 'constant at St Mary's Church every Lord's day, forenoons and afternoons, and take notes of the sermon'. (Also, 'if you be with company on the Lord's day, let your discourse be of the sermon'.) If this was the ideal, then John Tillotson, who was at Clare from 1647 to 1655 under Ralph Cudworth, was a model undergraduate. He was noted as 'a very attentive hearer of sermons, of which at that time there was both great and good store, he generally hearing four every Lord's day, besides the weekly lecture at Trinity Church on Wednesdays'.[1]

The lecture at Holy Trinity had been instituted by the town in 1610; and additional galleries were built into the church to cope with the crowds. The first lecturer appointed was Richard Sibbes, Fellow of St John's, to 'whose ministry, besides the townsmen, many scholars resorted'.[2] Sibbes's successors were John Preston (1624), Thomas Goodwin (1628), and Benjamin Whichcote, Fellow of Emmanuel (1636). The lectureship lapsed in 1750—thirty years before Charles Simeon became vicar of the church. Puritan dons played a great part in the life of others of the fourteen parishes of Cambridge. Chaderton was for fifty years lecturer at St Clement's, a post which he resigned in 1618 at the age of seventy-nine—in spite of a spate of letters from the parishioners begging him to remain.[3] The object of Chaderton's preaching at St Clement's was 'not to tickle his hearers' ears with an empty jingle of words, but to insinuate the most salutary truths into their hearts in a pleasant manner'.[4] It may have been the congregation of St Clement's which, after a sermon of two hours which Chaderton wished to draw to a close, begged him to continue: 'For God's sake, sir, go on, we beg you, go on.'[5]

From the point of view of the university, these town lectureships were far too popular with the young men. About 1620 the

[1] Quoted from Birch's life of Tillotson in Charles Smyth, *The Art of Preaching*, 98.
[2] Clarke, *Thirty-two Divines*, 143.   [3] Dillingham, *Life of Chaderton*, 14.
[4] *Ibid.* 12.
[5] *Ibid.* 13–14. Dillingham obtained this story from Fuller; *Worthies*, II, 208.

Sunday lecture at Holy Trinity at one o'clock was declared out of bounds, for the students had been neglecting their duties at Great St Mary's in order to hear Sibbes. John Preston—to whose sermons in Queens' townspeople and members of other colleges flocked, 'so that the outward chapel would be often full before the Fellows came'[1]—decided to fill the gap by preaching himself on Sunday at three in St Botolph's, immediately after the sermon in Great St Mary's. His sermons 'occasioned such a throng and crowd as was incredible'.[2] But one Sunday afternoon Dr Newcome, the commissary of the Chancellor of the diocese, made it his business to be in the congregation; and as Preston mounted the steps into the pulpit, Newcome stepped forward to forbid him to preach. This occasioned a minor riot in the church, and Newcome left in a huff. While Preston preached, Newcome was galloping to Newmarket to consult Bishop Lancelot Andrewes. The King also heard the story, and advised Andrewes to order the university to call Preston before the Consistory. There was a great deal of angry discussion in Cambridge, and much string-pulling at court. At length, Preston was ordered by the Vice-Chancellor to read a recantation in St Botolph's. This he did: but he followed it by a sermon on grace of such vehemence and persuasion that the scoffers went silent home. Meanwhile the politic Preston had revenged himself on the commissary by preventing the marriage of his daughter, Jane Newcome, to the most attractive young man in Queens'. And soon he was preaching before the King at Hinchingbrook, with such success that many days were spent in making fair copies of his sermon for distribution amongst the court. Before the winter was out John Preston had been appointed chaplain to Prince Charles.[3]

Preston was the most popular preacher in Cambridge from 1609, when he left King's to become a Fellow of Queens' at the age of twenty-two, until his death as Master of Emmanuel in

[1] T. Ball, *Life of Preston*, 40.   [2] *Ibid.* 43.   [3] *Ibid.* 42–69.

1628. Yet even he could not rival the fame of the great William Perkins, who was born in the first year of Elizabeth's reign and died in the last. For over fifteen years Perkins preached in St Andrew's Church, opposite Christ's; and this, no less than his teaching in Christ's, and the flow of his printed sermons and treatises from the University Press after 1590, made his influence unique in his generation.

Between 1590 and 1618 John Legate and Cantrill Legge printed nearly 210 books at Cambridge: of these, over fifty were works by Perkins. Before Perkins's death in 1602 Legate had printed over twenty of his works, beginning with *Armilla Aurea* in 1590; and some of them had run into three editions. A one-volume collected edition of Perkins's works appeared in 1600. After his death the flow continued: until there came from the Cambridge Press in 1616 to 1618 a revised three-volume edition, containing nearly forty separate titles. Some of these were translations of Latin treatises: 'A Golden Chain' (the English version of *Armilla Aurea*) by Robert Hill, Fellow of St John's; *The Art of Prophesying*, translated by Thomas Tuke; the treatise on predestination (to which Arminius wrote a reply), by Tuke and Francis Cacot; *Christian Economy*, by Thomas Pickering. Thomas Pickering was a Fellow of Emmanuel, who edited Perkins's three books of *Cases of Conscience*, first published in 1606. Perkins's other posthumous editors were Thomas Taylor, Fellow of Christ's, one of his 'ordinary hearers in Cambridge',[1] who saw through the press the *Sermons on Jude* in 1608; William Crashaw, Robert Hill, Ralph Cudworth, and Thomas Pierson. William Crashaw was a Fellow of St John's, best known to history as the father of Richard Crashaw, who was born in 1613. William had gone up to the college as a sizar in 1588, aged sixteen, when William Whitaker was Master; he was elected Fellow in 1594.[2]

[1] Preface to Perkins's commentary on Jude, in *Works*, III (1618).

[2] Crashaw was to serve as chaplain to the Virginia Company, before whom he preached a famous sermon in 1610: *A New-yeeres Gift to Virginea*. In 1611 he arranged for his friend Alexander Whitaker to be sent to the colony and in 1613 wrote the prefatory epistle to

With Pierson of Emmanuel he had heard Perkins's course of sermons on Hebrews, 'and wrote it from his mouth'[1]: they published it in 1608. Crashaw also edited the *Exhortation to Repentance* (an exposition of the second chapter of Zephaniah), which appeared in 1605. In the preface to this work,[2] Crashaw took occasion to 'humbly praise the Lord of heaven, who gave me my time in the university, in those happy days, wherein (besides many worthy men of God, whereof some are fallen asleep and some remain alive unto this day) this holy man did spend himself like a candle, to give light unto others'. The sermons on repentance, said Crashaw, were 'in my hands, and not delivered to me from hand to hand, but taken with this hand of mine from his own mouth.' And they completed the argument of that treatise on repentance which Perkins had published in 1593, being his sermons preached in the early 1590's to 'that great and general assembly at Stourbridge Fair'. Robert Hill, though a Fellow of St John's, was a Christ's man: he had gone up to the college in 1581, the year in which Perkins commenced bachelor. Hill published the *Combat between Christ and the Divell* in 1604: of it he wrote:[3]

This copy it was brought into my hand, I have conferred with another, I have perused it at the press, I heard divers of the sermons, I have added nothing of mine own:...By his life had I much comfort, and I will seek to honour him after he is dead: I was twenty years acquainted with him: I at his request made the first fruits of his labours to speak English.

That is, the English *A Golden Chain*, first published in Hill's translation in 1591. Cudworth, like Crashaw, was to be the father of a more celebrated son: Ralph was born in 1617. The

Whitaker's *Good Newes from Virginia.* (H. C. Porter, 'Alexander Whitaker: Cambridge Apostle to Virginia', *William and Mary Quarterly*, July 1957.) It may also be noted here that in 1620 an anonymous benefactor gave two gifts of books to the colony, for the prospective Indian college: the books were Augustine's *City of God*, and the three-volume Cambridge edition of Perkins's works; *Records of the Virginia Company* (ed. S. M. Kingsbury), I, 421.

[1] 'Commentary on Hebrews', title page, Perkins, *Works*, III.
[2] *Works*, III.   [3] *Ibid.*

father had gone up to Emmanuel in 1589, and progressed to a fellowship. He published Perkins's *Commentary on Galatians* in 1604. This was Perkins's last work: he had written it out in his own hand after preaching the sermons from memorized notes—this was unusual, for his normal procedure, according to Cudworth,[1] had been to have his sermons 'taken by some diligent auditors and perused by himself'. The *Commentary on Galatians* was a course of Sunday sermons which had extended over three years. 'There were some places in the original copy', wrote Cudworth,

to which the author would (no doubt) have given some review and correction, if God had drawn out the line of his life but a little longer: which I have filed and polished according to my poor skill, though very sparingly, in such places only as were obscure, or had any phrase of doubtful construction, or otherwise seemed to be mistaken: pointing and interlining the rest, to fit it for the press.

Thomas Pierson had gone up to Emmanuel a year after Cudworth, in 1590. The most important of Perkins's works which he prepared for the printers was the *Treatise of Man's Imagination* (1607). 'For my furtherance in the publishing of this', wrote Pierson, 'I had the author's own draft of the platform of it; besides two perfect copies of all his sermons.'[2] When the first edition of Volume Three of the collected *Works* appeared in 1609, Pierson explained that some of Perkins's early sermons were not included: 'They were of the first fruit of his labours, which if he had intended for the press, he would no doubt have revised long since, as he did some other things which then he handled and published.'[3] He also appealed to

those that have unprinted copies in their hands, to use them for their own private benefit: but if any rest not satisfied herewith, I would yet intreat thus much of them, that before they put hand to work for the press, they would acquaint M. Perkins' executors with their reasons

---

[1] *Works*, II.   [2] Preface to the Treatise, *Works*, II.
[3] Note at the beginning of *Works*, III.

that move them thereunto; from whom I doubt not, but they shall receive either sufficient satisfaction for their stay, or good leave to proceed in their intended course. Which thing I do the rather advise, because the executors have a general inhibition out of his Majesty's Court of High Commission, prohibiting the publishing of any his works without their consent.

Perkins's executors were Laurence Chaderton, Edward Barwell, James Montagu (Master of Sidney Sussex), Richard Foxcroft, and Perkins's brother-in-law, Nathaniel Cradock.

Thus the publishing of the works of William Perkins was for some of the Cambridge Puritans almost a local industry. These bibliographical details throw light not only on Perkins himself, but on the methods of editing and printing in England at the turn of the century. To round them off, it remains to be stated that in 1611 a one-volume Latin edition of Perkins's works was published at Geneva, followed by a fuller edition in two volumes, published in 1618 and 1624; and that various separate works were translated into Spanish, Dutch, Irish and Welsh. In fact, William Perkins of Christ's was the first of the Cambridge best-selling authors.

When Thomas Goodwin went up to Christ's ten years after Perkins's death, Cambridge was still 'filled with the discourse of the power of Mr Perkins his ministry, still fresh in most men's memories'.[1] Many of the future Puritan saints had been his diligent hearers: Henry Burton and John Cotton among them. But he did not appeal exclusively to a Puritan audience. John Williams, who went up to St John's in 1598, was his 'constant auditor'—'so early', commented Hacket, 'his well-kneaded judgement took delight in clear and solid divinity'.[2] Moreover, like Greenham, Perkins won renown as a spiritual adviser, ministering the word in due season to the weary: 'the which most weighty duty of the ministry was so familiar unto him', wrote Thomas Taylor, 'that he made it his holy days' exercise (as his

[1] T. Goodwin, *Works*, v, ix. [2] Hacket, *Scrinia Reserata*, 9.

recreation) to resolve cases of conscience'.[1] Thus Thomas Fuller, who took Perkins as the pattern for the faithful pastor, commended him as an 'excellent surgeon' at 'jointing of a broken soul, and at stating of a doubtful conscience';[2] and his books of *Cases of Conscience* have been called by a recent writer on casuistry 'the first sustained attempt in English to present the subject in an orderly and comprehensive manner'.[3] Fuller's tribute to the plain preaching of Perkins is deservedly well known: 'He would pronounce the word *damn* with such an emphasis, as left a doleful echo in his auditors' ears a good while after; and when catechist of Christ's College, in expounding the commandments, applied them so home, able almost to make his hearers' hearts fall down, and hairs to stand upright'. His sermons 'were not so plain but that the piously learned did admire them, nor so learned but that the plain did understand them'. And Fuller could pay no greater compliment than this: 'our Perkins brought the schools into the pulpit, and, unshelling their controversies out of their hard school terms, made thereof plain and wholesome meat for his people.'[4]

When Perkins died in October 1602 at the age of forty-three, other men besides Sam Ward, sometime student of Christ's and now Fellow of Emmanuel, must have thought the world almost at an end: 'Consider the great blow given unto the gospel of Christ by the death of Mr Perkins, who by his doctrine and life did much good to the youth of the university, of whom he was held in great reverence, and who likewise did exceeding great good by his advice and direction to many ministers in the country, who did resort to him from everywhere.' Perkins's deathbed was a painful one, for he was 'in great extremity by reason of the stone'. Nevertheless he was quiet and patient; and when, as he put out his hand, he was asked what he wanted, he answered: 'Nothing but mercy.' His death, Ward concluded, 'is likely to be an

---

[1] Preface to Commentary on Jude, Perkins, *Works*, III.
[2] Fuller, *Holy State*, 81.
[3] Thomas Wood, *English Casuistical Divinity during the Seventeenth Century*, 34.
[4] Fuller, *loc. cit.*

irrecoverable loss and a great judgement to the university, seeing there is none to supply his place'.[1]

But to John Cotton, a seventeen-year-old sizar of Trinity, the death of Perkins came as a blessed relief. The boy had been tortured by the religious reflections which the sermons of Perkins had aroused in him, and which seemed to be 'an hindrance unto him in his studies'. Then, 'as he was walking in the fields, he heard the bell tolling for Master Perkins who lay a dying, whereupon he was secretly glad in his heart, that he should now be rid of him who had (as he said) laid siege to, and beleaguered his heart'.[2] But three years later he was converted to a true and lively faith when he heard a sermon by Richard Sibbes, who was then twenty-eight. And in turn, in 1610, when Cotton, now a Fellow of Emmanuel, had returned to his room after preaching what he thought was a fruitless sermon, he heard a knock on his door. It was John Preston, a young don of Queens', who 'coming in, acquainted him with his spiritual condition, and tells him how it had pleased God to work effectually on his heart by that sermon'[3] —almost as Bilney had worked on the heart of Latimer ninety years before; and as Preston was to work on the hearts of many, as tutor of Queens' and Master of Emmanuel.

VII

Such men naturally formed within the university an inner circle of Puritan piety and learning: a world within a world. Professor Haller, tracing the lines of personal friendship, has written of the 'spiritual brotherhood' of Cambridge divines.[4] The brotherhood assumed the characteristics of all such formative movements, whether in religion, politics or art: the inbreeding, the cross-fertilization, the canalization into training and tradition, the

---

[1] Knappen, (ed.), *Two Puritan Diaries*, 130.
[2] Clarke (ed.), *Thirty-two Divines*, 218. [3] *Ibid.* 219.
[4] W. Haller, *The Rise of Puritanism*, chapter 2.

proliferation of lesser works imitative of the masters, 'the liability to be unduly dominated by the influence of a man of striking personality or highly individual style'.[1] But one point needs to be made: being a university brotherhood, it was not rigidly exclusive. The dons spoke with their colleagues at the gate. As Canon Smyth has written, one 'of the definite advantages of being a Fellow of a college is that a man in that position finds himself a member of a co-operative Society'.[2] The meetings in the Cambridge of the 1580's for the exposition of the Scriptures, like those of the 1520's for the study of Luther, were scholarly; and Lancelot Andrewes joined with Laurence Chaderton and John Knewstubb and other of the godly brethren to study the original languages, the grammatical interpretation, the logical analysis, the 'true sense', and the 'doctrines' of the Bible: all of them 'eloquent men, and mighty in the Scriptures'.[3]

With that reservation, the Puritan spirits gravitated naturally together. The friendships significantly outlasted their university days. Richard Rogers was much edified in the late 1580's by a visit to Wethersfield by John Knewstubb, rector of Cockfield: 'These three days we two had very comfortable and profitable companyings in prayer and conference together.'[4] Rogers himself rode frequently to Felstead, to visit Ezekiel Culverwell, or to Braintree and Coggeshall, where the incumbents were both Cambridge men. When John Preston lay dying in 1628, a mile from the parish of Fawsley, he called John Dod to him, 'and desired him to speak to him of death and heaven, and heard him with patience and thankfulness'.[5] Dod prayed with him to the end.

Thomas Goodwin confessed in later years his debt to 'the several holy youths in Christ's College, who had made known unto me the workings of God upon them'.[6] Nearly forty years

[1] Thomas Bodkin, *Flemish Paintings* (Faber Gallery), 4.
[2] Smyth, *The Art of Preaching*, viii.   [3] Clarke (ed.), *Thirty-two Divines*, 133.
[4] Knappen (ed.), *Two Puritan Diaries*, 95.
[5] Clarke (ed.), *op. cit.* 172.   [6] Goodwin, *Works*, v, vi.

later Thomas Wadsworth, another Christ's man, associated himself with 'an honest club of scholars, of his own, and other
colleges': who were 'not only daily conversant in philosophical
exercises, but did frequently meet to promote the great business
of real godliness, and growth in grace, and to make experiments
on their own hearts of that religion when they should be called
to impart to others'.[1] The fruits of such spiritual experimentation
were severely practical. At the end of Elizabeth's reign Thomas
Gataker, William Bedell and Abdias Ashton had developed a
scheme of preaching in parishes near Cambridge where the
pastors seemed by Puritan standards incompetent.[2] Gataker
preached regularly at a village in Bedfordshire where the incumbent was rumoured to be over 130. Gataker was a young don
of Sidney Sussex at the same time as his friend William Bradshaw;
and when Bradshaw died, Gataker paid a moving tribute to the
continuity of their friendship—'the knot once knit, from the first
to the last, continued firm and inviolate, never loosed nor
slackened, so long as God was pleased to lengthen out the line of
his life'.[3]

The knots had been knit, firmly and naturally, in undergraduate
days at Cambridge:

> Where once we held debate, a band
> Of youthful friends...

VIII

In the saga of the Puritan heroes, stylized in the hagiography of
their juniors, the climax was the point of conversion. 'A sinner
in the very first act of his conversion', wrote Perkins, 'is justified,
adopted and incorporated into the mystical body of Christ.'[4]
There was usually a moment of shock from which the conversion

[1] Clarke (ed.), *Eminent Persons*, 177.
[2] Life of Bedell by his son; ed. T. W. Jones (Camden Society, 1872).
[3] Clarke (ed.), *Thirty-two Divines*, 31.   [4] Perkins, *Works*, I, 637.

was dramatically dated: for Perkins, it was when he heard himself called 'drunken Perkins' in a Cambridge street; John Dod's spiritual renewal was occasioned after he had been unjustly accused of fraud by the bursar of Jesus;[1] for Richard Blackerby, a hearer of Perkins in the nineties, the moment came when he was 'riding alone upon Newmarket Heath, bemoaning his sad condition before the Lord'.[2] As biography, such pin-pointing may be suspect: as psychology it rings true enough. As T. S. Eliot has observed, we do not like to look out of the same window, and see quite a different landscape. But when we do, the spiritual story can begin.

The autobiography of Thomas Goodwin[3] was the most detailed working-out in personal terms of the Calvinist theology of conversion, and of the relations of grace and will. Grace worked upon him from the time when, as a child of seven, he heard from his grandfather of the dangers of hell fire. Compared with the later *coup de grâce* these stirrings were, however, 'lighter impressions and slighter workings', though Goodwin as a schoolboy thought himself 'not only to have grace, but more grace than my relations, or any inhabitant of the town that I knew of'. At Cambridge he passed much time in self examination, cataloguing the signs of grace, using the catechism of Ursinus to 'set myself to discover whether I had grace or not'. But on one occasion his tutor, worried by Goodwin's extreme youth—he was not yet thirteen when he went up to Christ's, 'little of stature, the least in the whole university then, and for divers years'—forbade him to receive the Sacrament. This was a great disappointment, because for a month before this particular Communion Service he had prepared for it by attending the sermons of Sibbes, and, intense on his stool, by reading the works of Calvin while the congregation awaited the preacher. The boy was so shaken, in fact, that he left off saying

---

[1] Clarke (ed.), *Thirty-two Divines*, 168.   [2] Clarke (ed.), *Eminent Persons*, 57.
[3] Goodwin (ed.), *Works*, v. The quotations in the following section are taken from pp. v–x. Goodwin went up to Christ's in 1614.

his prayers. Worse, he attended the brittle sermons in Great St Mary's, 'the great wits of those times striving who of them should exceed each other'. As a result of this returning 'into the lusts and pleasures of sinning, but especially the ambition of glory and praise' he was elected a Fellow of St Catharine's in 1619.

Then, on Monday 2 October 1620, on his way to a reunion at Christ's, Goodwin heard the funeral bell of a town church. Curiosity compelled him to attend the service, though, he wrote—slightly over-playing his part perhaps—'I was never so loth to attend a sermon in my life.' The preacher was Dr Thomas Bainbridge, Fellow of Christ's, who discoursed on the theme that 'every man had a time, in which grace was offered him; and if he neglected it, 'twas just with God, that it should be hidden from his eyes'. Goodwin forgot the meeting at Christ's and returned dazed to St Catharine's. 'I thought myself to be as one struck down by a mighty Power.' He was then nineteen and the pattern of his life was clear; the knot was unknotted, the crossed uncrossed, the crooked made straight.

> There is a tide in the affairs of men,
> Which, taken at the flood, leads on to fortune;
> Omitted, all the voyage of their life
> Is bound in shallows and in miseries.

That was the key to the Universe of Grace.

PART III

THE UNIVERSE OF GRACE

CHAPTER XI

GRACE ABOUNDING

THE third part of this essay on Tudor Cambridge is a detailed study of the theological disputes within the university in the 1590's. Much of the story, to some, may seem unsympathetic; but it would be a failure of historical and human sensibility to ignore it, to pass by on the other side—even though that other side is thronged with a great crowd of historical witnesses. (Those historians repelled by theological controversy might find an incentive to studying it in the story told by Senator Saltonstall of the staunch old Republican who attended all the Democratic rallies: 'I just go to their meetings', he explained, 'so's to keep my disgust fresh!') The story is in essence about grace—and the history of the doctrine of grace is indeed forbidding. Shelves and shelves of bulky, unread volumes, the stifling importance of great authors, the intricacies and confusions of scandals and controversies, have laid upon the theology of grace that inverted form of the Midas touch which kills all interest as dead as a door nail. The articles, the canons, the decrees, the points, the propositions—all these are distilled conclusions, without life, without passion. Yet the doctrines of grace and predestination, reflecting, in their immense complication, simple convictions about the sort of being God is and the kind of creature man is, concern not merely theology but all aspects of the human condition: literature, psychology, politics, to mention no others. Such concern takes the student into a no-man's-land, where the tracks of theology, history, and criticism peter out, or merge—it is difficult to see which. The territory is dangerous and suspect—at least to Englishmen. It is a standing reproach against English literary critics, historians and theologians that we have no work comparable to Henri Bremond's classic *Histoire littéraire du sentiment religieux en*

277

France. Again, how many contemporary English writers for the theatre could echo this reflection of Henri de Montherlant?

If it happened to me one day to be thunderstruck by 'grace', I should put myself in the line that I am tempted to call the heart of Christianity, because I seem to see it running, like sap in a tree, through the heart of Christianity: it is a tradition that goes from the Gospel to Port-Royal by way of St Paul and St Augustine (and does it not skirt Calvin?). The motto I give is Bossuet's cry: 'Doctrine of the Gospel how severe you are.' And its form is that of the ever narrowing way.[1]

One tends to forget that Calvin, like Pascal, was a Frenchman.

The dilemma is eternal. If order has gone and chaos is come again, how many traces of the order remain, and how many of those traces can human beings hope to see, to feel, to know? The case of conscience is eternal too:

> Hell strives with grace for conquest in my breast:
> What shall I do to shun the snares of death?

The words are those of Christopher Marlowe, who went up to Corpus in 1580, two years after William Perkins entered Christ's. Christian pessimism is succinctly expressed in the limerick:

> Man made a hopeful beginning
> But then spoilt his chances by sinning
> We hope that the story
> Will end in God's glory
> But at present the other side's winning.

It springs, that is, from a dogmatic assumption, not based on experience, but confirmed by it. The same idea was expressed, at greater length and with more elegance, by Newman:

To consider the world in its length and breadth, its various history, the many races of man, their starts, their fortunes, their mutual alienation, their conflicts; and then their ways, habits, governments, forms of worship; their enterprises, their aimless courses, their random achieve-

---

[1] Quoted by J. Griffin, in the preface to his translation of *The Master of Santiago* (1951), 14. Mr Whittaker Chambers has popularized himself as 'an involuntary witness to God's grace'; *Witness* (New York, 1952), 6.

ments and acquirements, the impotent conclusion of long-standing facts, the tokens so faint and broken of a superintending design, the blind evolution of what turn out to be great powers or truths, the progress of things, as if from unreasoning elements, not towards final causes, the greatness and littleness of man, his far-reaching aims, his short duration, the curtain hung over his futurity, the disappointments of life, the defeat of good, the success of evil, physical pain, mental anguish, the prevalence and intensity of sin, the pervading idolatries, the corruptions, the dreary hopeless irreligion, that condition of the whole race, so fearfully yet exactly described in the Apostle's words, 'having no hope and without God in the world'—all this is a vision to dizzy and appal; and inflicts upon the mind the sense of a profound mystery, which is absolutely beyond human solution.

What can be said to this heart-piercing, reason-bewildering fact? I can only answer that, either there is no Creator, or this living society of men is in a true sense discarded from his presence;...*if* there be a God, *since* there is a God, the human world is implicated in some terrible aboriginal calamity.[1]

That is one Christian attitude. Here is a second:

Heaven and Earth was God's house,...He gave it me...From whence I clearly find how docile our nature is in natural things, were it rightly entreated. And that our misery proceedeth ten thousand times more from the outward bondage of opinion and custom, than from any inward corruption or depravation of Nature...Natural things are glorious, and to know them glorious.[2]

So wrote Thomas Traherne. It is another, and equally valid, Christian position. The chaos and the joy can of course be combined. They were by George Herbert:

> Then Sin combined with Death in a firm band
> To raze the building to the very floor:
> Which they effected, none could them withstand;
> But Love took Grace and Glory by the hand,
> And built a braver Palace than before.[3]

[1] Newman, *Apologia pro vita sua* (ed. M. Ward, 1946), 162–3.

[2] 'Shades of the Prison House', *Felicities of Thomas Traherne* (ed. A. Quiller-Couch, 1943), 25.

[3] Herbert, *The Temple*, no. 57, 'The World', in *Works* (ed. A. B. Grosart, 1891), 112.

Is grace a lightning flash into the dark abyss, a force contrary to nature, the unpredictable gift of a sovereign, just, but incomprehensible God to an insignificant creature, totally fallen and lost? Or does grace gently link God and man and all creatures in a cosmic harmony, a dance of joy? Is it finishing touch, or destroyer? The great Christian controversies—such as those which concerned Cambridge men in the last years of the reign of Elizabeth I—are worked out within such presuppositions. The Church of Rome, said Perkins, 'doth too much extol the power of man and his natural strength': it is 'an enemy to the grace of God'.[1] So, he thought, were Barrett and Baro and Andrewes and their school; and in the same way Anthony Tuckney was to attack the natural theology of his sometime pupil Benjamin Whichcote.

The power of God and the nature of man: why is there such difference of opinion about the relationship? Perhaps, at bottom, because there is a difference between what N. P. Williams has called the once-born and the twice-born Christian; between the man with a 'religious' consciousness, seeing grace as power, and the man with a 'moral' consciousness, seeing it as illumination.[2] Dante saw God as a point of light. And—so one is informed—those who are born in Boston have no need to be reborn. Whatever the explanation, if there be an explanation, the initial cast one way or the other gives to a man his 'world picture'. Some words of Albert Camus are suggestive: 'The great impulses of the human spirit bring with them a whole universe, sometimes splendid, sometimes miserable, for their passion lights up an entire private world, where they find once more their natural home. There is a universe of jealousy, and of ambition; of egoism or of generosity. A universe: that is to say, a metaphysic, an attitude of the mind and spirit.'[3]

[1] Perkins, 'God's Free Grace and Man's Free Will', *Works*, I, 718.
[2] N. P. Williams, *The Grace of God*, chapter I.
[3] Camus, *Le Mythe de Sisyphe*, 24 (my translation).

The theological controversies in Cambridge between 1595 and 1600 revolved round the nature of the 'comfortable certainty of true faith' and its connection with God's decree of election. William Barrett, by raising the issues of the possible loss of justifying faith, of the limits to the Christian assurance of salvation, and of the quality of justifying faith itself, struck at the heart of the Calvinist certainty; and the question of the loss of faith and grace was taken up by John Overall, Regius Professor of Divinity, and was also to be one of the points of the Arminians. These questions entailed the wider issues of election and reprobation: the Arminians were to go farther than the Cambridge men in discussion of the former, but Barrett and Overall were much concerned with the latter. Peter Baro, Lady Margaret Professor, widened the issue again by arguing the death of Christ for all men, and the will of God to save all his creatures. Overall supported him here; and it is on this point that the Cambridge Movement was most coincidental with the slightly later Arminian arguments. Baro also dealt with the problem of the nature and distribution of grace: and the Arminian assertion that grace can be resisted, that it is not overriding, finds many pre-echoes in the arguments of the Cambridge men of the 1590's.

Baro at least, with his concern for universal grace, for the universal saving will of God, and the death of Christ for all men, may be called (he died in 1596) an Arminian *avant la lettre*. He and his Cambridge supporters (of whom there were many: he began to lecture in 1574) were striking a blow for Christian humanism. If God's decrees are not absolutely immutable, if at least some of them are conditional, if He does not force his creatures but exercises His sovereignty by bestowing the power of choice, if the gifts of His Spirit can be lost by man's misuse of them—then the burden of the argument is on our human shoulders. If God is a Being whose Reason is reflected in our reason, whose laws are intelligible to creatures who, in spite of the Fall, are still in His image, still not quite exiles from the

Kingdom of Heaven, if God's grace does not work against nature but through it—then there is a harmony of Reason, Nature and Grace, a co-operation between God and man, a natural theology made perfect by the Divine Word. The rational 'vein of doctrine' which Anthony Tuckney was to attack in Benjamin Whichcote in 1651 goes back in Elizabethan Cambridge at least to the lectures of Baro. Thus the detailed Cambridge disputes of the 1590's take their place in the story of the movement 'from Puritanism to the Age of Reason'[1] in England: of 'the genesis of liberal theology'.

The quarrels must be thought of alongside the same story in Europe: the fights between Arminius and Gomarus[2] at the University of Leiden in the first years of the seventeenth century; the influence of the Italian Faustus Socinus, who went to Holland, at the age of nearly sixty, in 1597. Alongside the controversies about predestination in the Lutheran Church in the second half of the sixteenth century, which began at Strasbourg in the early 1560's with the disputes between the Calvinizing Italian Girolamo Zanchi and the moderate John Marbach, and which led to the Lutheran Formula of Concord in 1577, affirming that God wills all men to be saved, that reprobation is caused by God's foresight of our unbelief, and that therefore the interpretation of reprobation as a mere act of God's sovereign will is 'false, horrid and blasphemous'.[3] The Lutheran Saxon Visitation Articles of 1592 re-asserted these beliefs, with an appended list of the 'false and erroneous doctrines of the Calvinists':[4] these errors being that Christ died only for the elect, that God created the greater part of mankind for damnation, that the elect cannot fall from grace, and those not elect are necessarily damned, be they never so virtuous. Thus, to some successors of the early Cambridge reformers, the word 'Lutheran' became a term of abuse. John Rudd of Christ's,

---

[1] The title of Dr G. R. Cragg's Cranmer Prize essay (published 1950).
[2] Gomarus had studied at Cambridge in the 1580's.
[3] P. Schaff, *The Creeds of the Evangelical Protestant Churches*, 172. Schaff told the story of the Lutheran disputes in his *History of the Creeds of Christendom*, 302–40.
[4] Schaff, *Creeds of Ev. Prot. Churches*, 189.

preaching in Great St Mary's in 1597, attacked the 'papists and Lutherans in Cambridge'[1]; and before leaving the university in November 1595 to discuss doctrinal propositions at Lambeth, William Whitaker bade farewell to his brother-in-law the Master of Emmanuel thus: 'he promised Mr Chaderton, and thereupon gave him his hand, that he would stand to God's cause against the Lutherans'.[2] There had been earlier men in the reformed fold whose influence had been thrown on the side of 'humanism and rationalism' against 'Calvinism'. Men such as Castellio, whom Symonds D'Ewes of St John's was to bracket with Ochino, Socinus, Servetus and Erasmus as a reviver of the heresies of Pelagius.[3] Or the fantastic Spaniard Anthonio de Corro, a sometime monk of Seville who fled to France in 1558 and came to England ten years later as pastor of the Spanish Protestant congregation in London; during the 1570's he was reader at the Temple (where Richard Alvey attacked him for discoursing 'not wisely on pre-destination'), and also a lecturer in Divinity at Oxford (residing in Christ Church), where the Vice-Chancellor supposed him to be 'tainted with Pelagianism';[4] in the 1580's Corranus became in turn a canon of St Paul's and of Lichfield; and he died, aged sixty-four, in 1591. Corranus was to be paid the compliment—by Walter Travers—of being the spiritual predecessor of Richard Hooker,[5] his successor as lecturer at the Temple in the 1580's. Finally, the Cambridge quarrels were contemporary also with disputes about grace in the Church of Rome: occasioned by the 'over-pessimism' of Baius in the 1560's and the 'over-optimism' of Molina in the 1580's; quarrels about the nature and distribution of grace which led to the debates *de Auxiliis* at Rome in the 1590's, to be continued in the Jesuit Order after the publication of

[1] Cambridge University Archives, Registry Guard Books, vol. 6 (i), no. 25.
[2] Diary of Sam Ward; Knappen, *Two Puritan Diaries*, 125.
[3] D'Ewes, *Autobiography and Correspondence*, II, 64.
[4] A. Wood, *Athenae Oxonienses*. See also J. Foster, *Alumni Oxonienses*. William Barlow commented on a 1575 'excellent' lecture of Corranus; *Zürich Letters*, Second Series, 261–2.
[5] R. Hooker, *Works*, III, 558–9.

Lessius's treatise on grace and predestination in 1610. And Jansen, much influenced by the conflicts in his native Holland[1] which preceded the Synod of Dort in 1618, wrote during the 1630's his study of Augustine, which occasioned the most fascinating and perhaps the most influential of all the chapters in the history of thinking about nature and grace.

That history is as long as the history of the Christian Church. The historian, like the film director, must vary his angles. After the close-up, the long shot, the general panorama. What happened in Cambridge in the 1590's was a significant part of what happened in Europe in the late sixteenth and early seventeenth centuries. It was also a part of the general Christian tradition of dispute about grace, about the relation between the liberty of man and the power of God; about what has been called the 'optimism' or the 'pessimism' of grace.[2] The tradition takes in Augustine and the Pelagians, debating in the early fifth century about free will and the effects of sin; the 'semi-pelagians' of the fifth century, such as John Cassian, raising questions of the irresistibility of grace, the nature of reprobation, and of whether Christ died for each and every man—a question reaffirmed in the alternative by the Council of Arles in 473; those who denied the universal saving will of God—Isidore of Seville in the seventh century and Godescalc in the ninth; those who debated universal redemption in the France of the seventeenth century and the England of the eighteenth; and those who, in our own day, continue the (often angry) discussions about natural theology and reason and revelation.

Nor are these questions for professional theologians only. Dr Johnson, in a discussion with Mrs Knowles on Wednesday

---

[1] Cornelius Jansen was born near Leerdam in 1585.

[2] H. Rondet, *Gratia Christi*, 137. Père Rondet's book (1948) is the most recent Roman Catholic treatise on the doctrine of grace, and the novelty and interest of many of his observations (especially his remarks on St Thomas) make it most surprising that there has been no English translation. The other good book on the history of the doctrine of grace is Nigel Abercrombie's *The Origins of Jansenism*.

15 April 1778, took up a position which would have been sympathetic to William Barrett and which echoes the Council of Trent. The discussion was about the assurance of salvation.

MRS KNOWLES: The Scriptures tell us, 'The righteous shall have *hope* in his death'.

JOHNSON: Yes, madam; that is, he shall not have despair. But, consider, his hope of salvation must be founded on the terms on which it is promised that the mediation of our Saviour shall be applied to us,— namely, obedience; and where obedience has failed, then, as suppletory to it, repentance. But what man can say that his obedience has been such, as he would approve of in another, or even in himself upon close examination, or that his repentance has not been such as to require being repented of? No man can be sure that his obedience and repentance will obtain salvation.

MRS KNOWLES: But divine intimation of acceptance may be made to the soul.

JOHNSON: Madam, it may; but I should not think the better of a man who should tell me on his deathbed, he was sure of salvation. A man cannot be sure himself that he has divine intimation of acceptance; much less can he make others sure that he has it.

MRS KNOWLES: (seeming to enjoy a pleasing serenity in the persuasion of benignant divine light): Does not St Paul say, 'I have fought the good fight of life, I have finished my course; henceforth is laid up for me a crown of life?'

JOHNSON: Yes, Madam; but here was a man inspired, a man who had been converted by supernatural interposition.[1]

Johnson might then have thought well of Oliver Cromwell, who is said to have asked on his death bed, 'Is it possible to fall from grace; for I know that I was once in grace?'

The problems here are fundamentally theological; but they are pastoral too. John Overall, visiting his parish of Epping in the 1590's, found many of his flock troubled in mind, because 'they could not be persuaded that Christ died for them'. Overall therefore preached to them on II Corinthians v. 15: that Christ died

---

[1] Boswell, *The Life of Dr Johnson* (Everyman edition), II, 212.

for all. This comfort, however, aroused the wrath of some of the local clergy, who protested to the Bishop of London about his teaching.[1] The preaching of truth and yet the preaching of comfort: it was not always an easy matter, for the godly pastors who were also learned theologians, and the study of their problems touches the heart of the great mysteries of conscience and doctrine, of mercy and judgement. Does God wish all his creatures to be saved? St Paul said so: 'God will have all men to be saved' (Timothy ii. 4)—a text quoted by Whitgift against the Calvinists in 1572.[2] But, if so, how does this wish connect with the presumption (without which the Christian verities are naught) that all men are not saved? The Calvinists gave one attempt at an answer by interpreting the Pauline text to mean 'all kinds of men'. Another gloss on the text was that of St Thomas: 'antecedently, God wills that all men should be saved, but this is to will conditionally, not absolutely'.[3] The approach to the problem by way of a distinction in the will of God was made in Elizabethan England by Baro, Overall and Hooker. It was anathema to the Calvinists: to talk of the prerogative power of God as conditional was to deny the Divine Sovereignty. And, while the theologians debated, there awaited them in the pews the 'poor consciences that seek steadfast assurance of eternal life'.[4] Suppose they could not find it? John Randall of Christ's was neither the first nor the last to take his own life after musing on the scriptural doctrine of predestination.

The debate continues; for it is perpetual. Père Rondet has written: 'In their perpetual oscillation between semi-pelagianism and predestinarianism, the theology of grace and that of predestination have slowly established the bounds of the debate on the harmonizing of grace and liberty; but without ever succeeding

[1] University Library, Cambridge, MS. Gg/1/29, fol. 119a–122b.
[2] Whitgift, Works, III, 383.
[3] Summa, I, Q. 23, art. 4; in Nature and Grace (selections from the Summa, translated and edited by A. M. Fairweather), 107–8.
[4] Calvin, Institutes, 1/7/1 (tr. Thomas Norton, 1611 ed.), 20.

in eliminating the mystery.'[1] And it is important to emphasize that the story of the theology of the Elizabethan Church of England was that of a debate, and not of an unchallenged Calvinist oration. In the Cambridge of the 1580's one could have heard Whitaker and Perkins: one could also have heard Overall and Andrewes and Baro—indeed Andrewes had been preaching at Pembroke for three years when young Perkins was ordained. The 'veins of doctrine' ran side by side; and the disputes of the 1590's in the university must be interpreted not as a study of reigning and resplendent Calvinism challenged by upstart Arminianism, but as the rear-guard action of one important party on seeing another important party beginning to capture a little too much territory, upsetting, as it were, the theological balance of power. The rear-guard action in fact did little more than guard the rear. The Calvinists did not win the day in the Cambridge of 1595, nor did they do so in the English Church. The moderation of Archbishop Whitgift prevented their demanding or achieving unconditional surrender. The immediate future lay with Andrewes and Overall: and in many ways Benjamin Whichcote, who began to preach in the university in the 1630's, was their heir.

This third part of the essay therefore ends with a brief study of the theology of Whichcote; the central chapters are a detailed study of the Calvinist claim and its validity in 1595, and of the university disputes provoked by William Barrett, Peter Baro and John Overall; the section begins with a survey of the work of the most popular and the most impressive of the Cambridge preachers of the 1590's—that is, William Perkins of Christ's.

[1] Rondet, *Gratia Christi*, 168 (my translation).

CHAPTER XII

THE THEOLOGY OF WILLIAM PERKINS

In the long succession of great Cambridge preachers William Perkins is usually placed as the prominent practical divine; who, in the words of Fuller, brought academic controversies 'out of their hard school terms' and 'made thereof plain and wholesome meat for his people'.[1] He is remembered today, if at all, for his 'Case Divinity', especially for the three books of *Cases of Conscience*, published four years after his death: as 'the first English casuist',[2] at one with the medieval moralists and with such godly pastors as Lancelot Andrewes, George Herbert and Jeremy Taylor in the resolve 'to educate the individual conscience in the way of holiness and to educate the social conscience in the way of justice'.[3] William Ames, who was an undergraduate at Christ's in the 1590's, was to write in the 1630's:

I gladly call to mind the time, when being young, I heard worthy Master Perkins...amongst other things which he preached profitably, he began at length to teach, how with the tongue of the learned one might speak a word in due season to him that is weary...by untying and explaining diligently Cases of Conscience (as they are called)... left he many behind him affected with that study; who by their godly sermons (through God's assistance) made it to run, increase and be glorified throughout England.[4]

He was, then, the first of the casuists of Christ's. The practical Christian life was the important thing. 'If any will be curious to search further into this point'—he is discussing the manner of the generation of original sin—'let them know, that there is another

---

[1] T. Fuller, *The Holy State and the Profane State*, 81.
[2] W. E. Houghton, *The Formation of Fuller's Holy and Profane States*, 73.
[3] T. Wood, *English Casuistical Divinity during the Seventeenth Century*, x.
[4] William Ames, *Conscience* (1639), 'To the Reader'.

288

matter which more concerns them to look into. When a man's house is on fire, there is no time then to inquire how, and which way, and whence the fire came, but our duty is with all speed and expedition to use all good means to stay it.'[1] What is the practical application of the point of doctrine? What is the use of it? Yet this was an application, no less but no more. The basic thing was the doctrine, the revealed Truth of God: 'it resteth upon most certain and sufficient grounds, collected and drawn out of the very word of God';[2] unlike the case writing of the papists, which was prejudicial to the resolution of the conscience precisely because it sprang from false doctrine.[3] The comfort was administered in strict terms of Calvinist dogmatic. 'A Case of Conscience, the greatest that ever was: How a Man may know whether he be the Child of God or No': that was the title of a work Perkins published in 1592. His life's work—his short teaching life of less than twenty years—was to answer that question, in a specific manner: 'that I might clear the truth, that is (as they call it) the Calvinists' doctrine'.[4]

Perkins's first book was published at Cambridge by John Legate in 1590. He was then thirty-two, and had been a Fellow of Christ's for six years (he resigned his fellowship when he married in 1595). This book was *Armilla Aurea*. Legate published a second edition in 1591 (Perkins's preface was written in January); and in the same year, in April, came a translation, by Robert Hill of St John's, with the title *A Golden Chaine, or the Description of Theologie, containing the Order of the Causes of Salvation and Damnation, according to Gods Woord*. In 1592 there were published a third edition of the Latin version, and (in July) a second edition, much enlarged, of the translation, which was reprinted in 1595.

As printed in the collected edition, 'A Golden Chain' begins quite in the medieval manner, with a 'visual aid'—a chart, to be

---

[1] Perkins, 'Exposition of the Creed' (1595), *Works*, I, 162.
[2] Epistle by Thomas Pickering before Perkins's 'Books of the Cases of Conscience', in *Works*, II.
[3] *Ibid.*   [4] 'Treatise of predestination' (1598), *Works*, II, 605.

opened out, comprising a number of balloons joined by lines of varying thickness. The topmost balloon represents the Trinity. Beneath it come 'God's Foreknowledge: His Decree' and 'Predestination' ('Election' and 'Reprobation'); followed by 'Creation', 'The Fall of Adam', 'The State of Unbelief', and 'Christ the Mediator of the Elect'. (A compact bird's-eye view of the Calvinist version of predestination and the atonement.) Here the lines divide: to the left, 'The Order of Salvation from the First to the Last' (decree of election; love of God to the elect in Christ; effectual calling; justification; sanctification; glorification; life eternal); to the right, 'The Order of the Causes of Damnation' (God's hatred of the reprobate; no calling; ignorance and vanity of mind; hardening of the heart; a reprobate sense; greediness in sin; fullness of sin; damnation; death eternal in hell). The two chains of balloons converge near the bottom of the chart, the one revealing 'God's Justice and Mercy' and the other 'God's Justice'; and they combine for the final point—'God's Glory'. (Within the general design are subsidiary groups showing 'How Faith doth apprehend Christ and all his Benefits' and 'The Temptations of the Godly and their Remedies'.) The chart, as Perkins explained, may be shown 'instead of an ocular catechism to them which cannot read: for by the pointing of the finger they may sensibly perceive the chief points of religion, and the order of them'.[1]

The clarity and simplicity of the chart set the tone for the whole of this impressive treatise. Robert Hill was to write of Perkins: 'an excellent gift he had to define properly, divide exactly, dispute subtly, answer directly, speak pithily and write judicially'.[2] And these qualities of succinctness and simplicity—qualities common to all the Puritan godly pastors—were stressed and ordinately adorned in Perkins by his vivid and homely imagery.

[1] *Works*, I, 11.
[2] Epistle before 'Commentary on Revelation' (1604), *Works*, III. For the possible influence of Ramus on this proper definition and exact dividing see W. S. Howell, *Logic and Rhetoric in England: 1500–1700*, chapter 4, 'The English Ramists', especially pp. 206–7 (concerned with Perkins's *The Art of Prophesying*).

Like John Dod, he had 'an excellent gift in similitudes'.[1] No bare account of his theology can do justice to the power of his writing and preaching, the eloquence and the sheer picturesqueness of it.

In the fifty-eight chapters of *A Golden Chain* Perkins gave a panoramic view of his 'revealed truth'. His order could not be bettered for an outline of his theology. Passages from his later works are inserted in the following sketch, to complete or elaborate the argument.

He began by discussing God: discussing him not in terms of reason or nature (as Lancelot Andrewes had done in the chapel of Pembroke in the 1580's, or as Benjamin Whichcote was to do in the chapel of Emmanuel in the 1630's) but in terms of grace and will. 'The divine Nature, is especially in perpetual operation by three attributes, the which do manifest the operation of God towards his creatures. They are his Wisdom, Will and Omnipotency.'[2] 'The will of God', he wrote in 1598, 'is the cause of causes: therefore we must make our stand in it, and out of it or beyond it no reason must be sought for: yea indeed there is nothing beyond it.'[3] It follows that 'God is above all his laws, and not bound to them: he is an absolute Lord and lawgiver; and therefore his actions are not within the compass of moral laws, as men's are'.[4] Perkins's most developed statement about the nature of the will of God was made in the last work he published before he died: *God's Free Grace and Man's Free Will* (1602). The divine will is capable of division. There is first God's secret will, or the will of his good pleasure: and secondly his revealed, or signifying will. The secret will is his eternal decree, 'the first and principal working cause of all things'.[5] Man cannot criticize this will, cannot question the judgements of God 'when they sound

---

[1] Clarke, *Thirty-two Divines*, 173. F. P. Wilson, in his *Elizabethan and Jacobean* (1945), 49, praised the simplicity of Perkins's style. G. L. Kittredge, discussing the *Treatise on Witchcraft*, was especially attracted by Perkins's 'virile and methodical intellect' (*Witchcraft in Old and New England*, 1929, 290).
[2] *Works*, I, 12.   [3] *Works*, II, 610.
[4] *Works*, I, 160.   [5] *Ibid.* 15.

not with our reason, contenting ourselves with this, that we know
God to have a sovereignty in his will, to will at his pleasure, and
his will to be good'.[1] At this point is sighted the danger spot of
Calvinist dogmatic: does God will evil? Perkins affirmed that
'God permitteth evil, by a certain voluntary permission', for he
'forsaketh his creature, either by detracting the grace it had, or
not bestowing that which it wanteth'. (And we must not think
God 'unjust' in this, for it is his 'pleasure to bestow how much
grace, and upon whom he will'.)[2] It is, as it were, a negative
permission: 'when God suspends or withdraws sustentation and
government from the will, it cannot of itself but will amiss, as
the staff in my hand presently falls, when I do but pull back my
hand...: evil is not the effect of God's will; because God put
nothing into man's will to cause it to will amiss: but he only
ceaseth to confer unto it help and direction, which he is not bound
to confer'.[3] But there is a little more to it than this. 'God is not
only a bare permissive agent in an evil work, but a powerful
effector of the same'; not that he 'instilleth an aberration in the
action, nor yet supporteth the same': but that 'he most freely
suffereth evil, and best disposeth of it to his own glory'. To
explain this point Perkins brings in typical images: 'Let a man
spur forward a lame horse; in that he moveth forward, the rider
is the cause; but that he halteth he himself is the cause. And again,
we see the sun beams shining through a glass, where the light is
from the sun, the colour not from the sun but from the glass.'[4]
All things, after all, work together for good. 'The thing which in
its own nature is evil, in God's eternal counsel is respectively good,
in that it is some occasion and way to manifest the glory of God
in his justice and his mercy.'[5] It is therefore good that evil should
be. God's will 'is to forsake his creature, and not to hinder the
being of evil when he may'.[6] In summary of the question of God
and evil Perkins wrote this: 'whereas God foresaw it in his

---

[1] *Works*, I, 723. [2] *Ibid.* 16. [3] *Ibid.* 740.
[4] *Ibid.* 16. [5] *Ibid.* 15. [6] *Ibid.* 724.

eternal counsel, and yet willed not to hinder it when he might, in effect he willed the being of it in the world; though simply he wills it not'.[1] So much for the secret will of God. What of his revealed will? The fact is, says Perkins, that God 'conceals part of his will, and reveals part'. This is not to assume 'any fraud or double dealing in God. For he doth not speak one thing, and mind another, after the fashion of hypocrites': he does what he does 'not for the hurt of any after the manner of the deceivers, but for the good of men'.[2]

The fundamental decree of God, the great act of his will, is predestination. 'God's decree, inasmuch as it concerneth man, is called Predestination: which is the decree of God, by the which he hath ordained all men to a certain and everlasting estate: that is, either to salvation or condemnation, for his own glory.'[3] We are at Chapter Seven of *A Golden Chain*: or the third balloon. From now on, the theme of predestination is the motif of the work, the thread upon which hang the successive chapters: the vantage point from which the other features of Christian theology must be viewed.

Perkins went on to consider the Fall: its nature and results. Man 'by creation was made a goodly creature in the blessed image of God'.[4] God denied to Adam the gift of perseverance: that is, he gave him the grace 'to be able to will and do that which is good' but not the grace 'to be able to persevere in willing and doing the same': he 'confirmed him not with new grace'.[5] God did not then incline the mind of Adam to sin, 'he did not infuse any corruption, neither did he withdraw any gift, which he did bestow in the creation: only it pleased him to deny, or not to confer, confirming grace'.[6] Perkins was to express this idea in the following image:

A goldsmith intends to make a jewel of greatest value and price: he compounds it of gold, pearl, and precious stones: when he hath brought

[1] *Ibid.*   [2] *Ibid.* 726.   [3] *Ibid.* 16.
[4] 'Exposition of the Creed', *Works*, I, 153.   [5] *Ibid.* 160.
[6] 'Treatise of predestination', *Works*, II, 607.

it to perfection, he doth not put this condition to it, that if it fall, it shall not be bruised or broken. And God created Adam in all perfection, and gave him a power and ability to continue in the said perfection, if he would: yet did he not put into his nature this condition, that he should be unchangeable and unalterable, when it should be assailed by the force of outward temptation.[1]

Why did God not do so? Because, said Perkins, it 'was his pleasure, that this fact should be an occasion or way to exercise his mercy in the saving of the elect, and his justice in the deserved condemnation of impenitent sinners'.[2]

And so Adam sinned: and 'all his posterity sinned with him; as in a Parliament whatsoever is done by the burgess of the shire, is done by every person in the shire'.[3] By Adam's fall man 'lost' the image of God, and became 'a limb of the devil, a rebel and a traitor against God's majesty: And this is the state of everyone of us, by nature we are at enmity with God'.[4] This is the fact of original sin: 'which is corruption engendered in our first conception, whereby every faculty of soul and body is prone and disposed to evil'. (Original sin is propagated from parents to children 'either because the soul is infected by the contagion of the body, as a good ointment by a fusty vessel; or because God, at the very moment of creation and infusion of souls into infants, doth utterly forsake them'.[5]) Thus there is in man 'not only an impotency to good, but such a forcible proneness and disposition to evil, as we can do nothing but sin'.[6] Our best thoughts, desires, affections and endeavours, 'even those that come most near to true holiness, are not only contrary to God, but even enmity itself'.[7] The evil in the heart of man 'is like a huge sea, the banks whereof cannot be seen, nor the bottom searched'.[8]

In detail, discussing the question whether fallen man retains

[1] 'God's free grace and man's free will', *Works*, I, 728.
[2] 'Exposition of the Creed', *Works*, I, 161.
[3] *Ibid.*   [4] *Ibid.* 153.
[5] 'Golden Chain', *Works*, I, 20.   [6] 'God's free grace', *Works*, I, 730.
[7] 'A reformed Catholic', *Works*, I, 559.   [8] 'Exposition of Creed', *Works*, I, 163.

anything of the image of God, Perkins considered in turn the mind, the conscience, the will, the affections, and the body. The affections, briefly, have received 'disorder':[1] the body, 'fitness to begin' and 'execute sin'.[2] The mind has received ignorance, 'a want, or rather a deprivation of knowledge in the things of God, whether they concern his sincere worship or eternal happiness'; impotency, 'whereby the mind of itself is unable to understand spiritual things, though they be taught'; and vanity, 'in that the mind thinketh falsehood truth, and truth falsehood'. In short, 'the remnant of God's image' in the mind 'is certain notions concerning good and evil: as that there is a God, and that the same God punisheth transgressions: that there is an everlasting life: that we must reverence our superiors, and not harm our neighbours. But even these notions, they are both general and corrupt, and have none other use but to bereave man of all excuse before God's judgement seat.'[3] The remnant of the image in the conscience is 'an observing and watchful power, like the eye of a keeper'.[4] The will received of Adam 'an impotency, whereby it cannot will, or so much as lust after that which is indeed good; that is, which may please, and be acceptable to God;...it utterly abhorreth that which is good, desiring and willing alone that which is evil'.[5] It is here that the Calvinist dogmatic of will finds its symmetry: 'There is an excellent harmony, and generally it stands in this, that God's will hath a sovereign Lordship over the will of man.'[6] The important point is: 'man's will wholly depends on the will of God. That vessels be some of honour, some of dishonour, it is not in the power of the clay, but in the will of the potter. The first cause orders the second, and not the second the first. To make God's will depend on man's will is to put God out of his throne of majesty, and to set the creature in his room.'[7]

And the Church of Rome, said Perkins, does precisely that.

[1] 'Golden Chain', *Works*, I, 21. [2] *Ibid.*
[3] *Ibid.* 20. [4] *Ibid.*
[5] *Ibid.* 21. [6] 'God's free grace', *Works*, I, 739.
[7] *Ibid.* 741.

'It is a thing most evident that the present religion of the Church of Rome is an enemy to the grace of God'; and this because 'it exalts the liberty of man's will, and extenuates the grace of God'.[1] For the papists say that 'the power of free will to do that which is good and acceptable to God, is only attenuated and weakened before conversion, not quite taken away, and therefore man can of himself work a preparation to justification';[2] they also say that 'man's will concurreth and worketh with God's graces in the first conversion of a sinner, by itself, and by its own natural power: and is only helped by the Holy Ghost'.[3] Thus, argued Perkins, 'the Church of Rome doth too much extol the power of man, and his natural strength':

it saith that all actions of man unregenerate are not sins, and that original sin needeth no repentance, that a man may have some free will to do spiritual things, that a man by mere naturals, may love God above all things..., that the gentiles may gather out of philosophy knowledge sufficient to salvation, that a man without the help of the Holy Ghost may perform things acceptable to God: that the mind of man understandeth of itself many things which be spiritual and heavenly, that a man regenerate may fulfil the whole law of God: that a man may prepare himself to receive grace, and after preparation merit grace at God's hand: that he may do works of supererogation, etc. By this it appeareth that the Church of Rome ascribeth too much to man, which in himself is only and altogether evil.[4]

In his *A Reformed Catholic*, published in 1598 (and translated into Spanish in the following year), Perkins set forth the differences between the Church of England and that of Rome by a variation on the image of the prisoner. Both Churches, he said, talk of the sinner as a prisoner: but there is a difference. The Church of Rome supposeth the said prisoner to lie bound hand and foot with chains and fetters, and withal, to be sick and weak, yet not wholly dead, but living

---

[1] 'God's Free Grace', *Works*, I, 718.   [2] 'Golden Chain', *Works*, I, 99.
[3] 'A reformed Catholic', *Works*, I, 559.
[4] 'Treatise tending to a declaration whether a man be in the estate of damnation or the state of grace', *Works*, I, 397.

in part: it supposeth also, that being in this case, he stirreth not himself for any help, and yet hath ability and power to stir. Hereupon, if the keeper come and take away his bolts and fetters, and hold him by the hand, and help him up, he can and will of himself stand and walk, and go out of prison.

In other words, 'if the holy Ghost come and do but untie his bands, and reach him his hand of grace, then can he stand of himself, and will his own salvation, or anything else that is good'. To the Church of England, on the other hand,

such a prisoner must he be, as is not only sick and weak, but even stark dead. Which cannot stir though the keeper untie his bolts and chains, nor hear though he sound a trumpet in his ear; and if the said keeper would have him to move and stir he must give him not only his hand to help him, but even soul and life also: and such a one is every man by nature: not only chained and fettered in his sins, but stark dead therein; as one that lieth rotten in the grave, not having any ability or power to move or stir; and therefore he cannot so much as desire or do anything that is truly good of himself.[1]

Such was the Puritan answer (late Elizabethan period) to a Christian humanism.

We are now at Chapter 15, 'Of Election and of Jesus Christ the Foundation thereof'. Election is one part of predestination: 'God's decree, whereby of his own free will he hath ordained certain men to salvation to the praise of the glory of his grace'; the 'foundation' of this decree being 'Christ Jesus, called of his Father from all eternity, to perform the office of Mediator, that in him all those which should be saved, might be chosen'.[2] It is here convenient to insert what Perkins was to say about election in his *Treatise of Predestination*, printed in 1598—a treatise to which Arminius was to write a reply, posthumously published in 1612.

There are two acts in election: 'to be distinguished in the mind (for order's sake, and for the better unfolding of it)'. The first act

---

[1] 'A reformed Catholic', *Works*, I, 559.   [2] 'Golden Chain', *Works*, I, 24.

is 'a purpose, or rather a part and beginning of the divine purpose, whereby God doth take certain men which are to be created, unto his everlasting love and favour, passing by the rest'. This act 'is of the sole will of God, without any respect either of good or evil in the creature'. This is not injustice in God, not to elect all, 'because he is tied to none: and because he hath absolute sovereignty and authority over all creatures'. Thus anyone who argues that election is due to God's 'foreknowledge or foreseeing of future faith, he is manifestly deceived':[1] 'What is this but to set the creature in the throne of Almighty God?'[2] The second act in election is 'the purpose of saving or conferring glory, whereby he doth ordain or set apart the very same men which were to fall in Adam, unto salvation and celestial glory'. Perkins was careful clearly to emphasize that election is 'in Christ': 'to dream of any election out of him is against all sense'.[3] The potential efficacy of the Cross of Christ is the redemption of all men. But the actual efficacy is the redemption only of the elect: and Christ 'prayeth only for the elect and for believers', he 'doth sanctify only the elect and such as believe, therefore he was a sacrifice only for them'.[4] God indeed commands all men to believe. But this command is more universal than his promise: 'the promise is made only to believers; but the commandment is given to believers and unbelievers also'.[5]

The decree of election is 'the cause of and foundation of all saving gifts and works in men. From hence is true faith.'[6] How is faith begotten? By the preaching of the Gospel. How is it confirmed? By the sacraments: whereby 'Christ and his saving graces, are by certain external rites, signified, exhibited and sealed to a Christian man'[7]—when they are apprehended by faith. Perkins attacked the doctrine of the Church of Rome, that 'the very action of the minister dispensing the sacrament as it is the

---

[1] 'Treatise of predestination, *Works*, II, 607–8.
[2] *Ibid.* 627.
[3] *Ibid.* 608.
[4] *Ibid.* 609.
[5] *Ibid.* 608.
[6] *Ibid.* 610.
[7] 'Golden Chain', *Works*, I, 71.

work done, gives grace immediately'. Grace is not conferred 'by the efficacy and very force of the sacramental action itself'.[1] Rather, the sacraments 'confirm grace'.[2] 'Now a sacrament doth confirm our faith, not by any inherent or proper power it hath in itself, as hath a sovereign medicine received by a patient, the which, whether a man sleep or wake, confirmeth his strength: but rather by reasoning, and using the signs'.[3] In this way, claimed Perkins, the Church of England keeps 'the middle way, neither giving too much, nor too little to the sacraments'.[4]

Chapter 33 of *A Golden Chain* dealt with baptism. The important point here, again, concerns the theological view of human nature. Baptism takes away the guilt of sin: it does not take away 'the error and corruption of nature', for what remains in us after baptism (call it 'concupiscence' if you like, in the Tridentine phrase) 'must properly be a sin'. This sin 'is not at the first quite taken away, but successively: and by little and little it is extinguished'.[5] Renovation, in the elect, is certain. In 'the very first instance of the conversion of a sinner, sin receiveth his deadly wound in the root, never afterward to be recovered'. (This was Perkins's answer to the popish allegation that the Protestants teach 'that original sin after baptism is only clipped or pared, like the hair of a man's head, whose roots still remain in the flesh':[6] it was not quite a fair answer, for the connection between baptism and conversion was not made clear in the argument.) To elucidate the truth about baptism, another chart was inserted in the text at this point. In the next chapter there was a further chart, depicting the doctrine of the Lord's Supper, of the bread and wine as 'signs and seals of the body and blood of Christ', the reception of which, by the believer, 'sealeth his application of Christ by faith'.[7]

Perkins now passed on to the problem: How is the decree of

---

[1] 'A reformed Catholic', *Works*, I, 610.   [2] 'Golden Chain', *Works*, I, 99.
[3] *Ibid.* 72.   [4] 'A reformed Catholic', *Works*, I, 611.
[5] 'Golden Chain', *Works*, I, 98.
[6] 'A reformed Catholic', *Works*, I, 562.
[7] 'Golden Chain', *Works*, I, 75.

election manifested? First, he said, by effectual calling: 'whereby a sinner being severed from the world, is entertained into God's family'.[1] This is accomplished by 'the saving hearing of the word of God':[2] which in the elect is

as salt in them, to draw out their inward corruption; it is to them the sword of the spirit, and as a sacrificing knife in the hand of God's minister, by which their flesh is killed and they are offered up in a living sacrifice to God: it is spirit and life to quicken and revive their souls that are dead in sin; and the reason of this is plain: the word of God preached is as a cup of wine: the true Christian is the Lord's guest, but he that hath sauce of his own, he bringeth his sugar with him, namely his true faith, which he tempereth and mingleth with God's word, and so it becometh unto him as a cup of sweet wine, and as water of life.[3]

Faith is 'a certain power, both apprehending and severally applying the promises of God in Christ, whereby a man doth assuredly set down that his sins are forgiven him, and that he is reconciled unto God'.[4] At its most, faith gives us a 'plerophoria', 'a full assurance, which is not only a certain and true, but also a full persuasion of the heart'.[5] This we achieve 'after the sense, observation and long experience of God's favour and love'.[6] Those who have achieved this degree of faith are 'perfect men in Christ'. Those who have not are, as it were, 'yet in the womb, and have their mother the church travailling of them'; or, later, 'new born babes feeding on the milk of the word'.[7] For there are degrees of faith, and 'God doth not despise the least spark of faith', the 'little or weak faith, like a grain of mustard seed'.[8] The title of a treatise Perkins published in 1595 was: *A Graine of Musterd-Seede: or, the least measure of grace that is, or can be, effectuall to salvation.* The aim of this work, as expressed in the preface, was

---

[1] 'A Golden Chain', *Works*, I, 77.   [2] *Ibid.* 78.
[3] 'Treatise tending to a declaration', *Works*, I, 373.
[4] 'Golden Chain', *Works*, I, 100.   [5] *Ibid.* 80.
[6] *Ibid.* 81.
[7] 'Treatise tending to a declaration', *Works*, I, 366.
[8] 'Golden Chain', *Works*, I, 80.

'to teach that a man is even at that instant already entered into the kingdom of heaven, when the Lord, that good husbandman, hath cast but some little portion of faith or repentance into the ground of the heart; yea though it be but as one grain of mustard seed'.[1] Yet this, though it is an 'infolded faith'[2] is not an 'implicit faith', in the popish sense. 'The foresaid beginnings of grace are counterfeit, unless they increase':[3] the spark of grace may go out, unless men 'labour to increase and go on from faith to faith', by the Word, the sacraments and prayer. If it remains but a spark, God will despise it, and it will be false—that is, not a true and lively faith. But that having been said, and with that reservation in mind, it is possible to say that where

men are displeased with themselves for their offences and do withal constantly from the heart desire to believe, and to be reconciled to God, there is faith, and many other graces of God infolded: as in the little and tender bud, is infolded the leaf, the blossom and the fruit. For though a desire to repent and to believe be not faith and repentance in nature, yet in God's acceptance it is.

And so, 'if any shall say, that without a lively faith in Christ none shall be saved: I answer, that God accepts the desire to believe for lively faith in the time of temptation, and in the time of our first conversion'. Perkins quoted Calvin here to prove that the 'weakest having the seeds of grace is the child of God; and faith in his infancy is faith'.[4] Not because such infant faith, like the Thomist 'fides informis', is 'perfect in the perfection which suffices for the nature of faith':[5] but because it is accepted by God as lively faith, conditional upon its going forward and increasing into a true, lively faith.

The second manifestation of the decree of election is justification: 'whereby such as believe, are accounted just before God,

---

[1] *Works*, I, 636.   [2] 'Golden Chain', *Works*, I, 80.
[3] 'Grain of mustard seed', *Works*, I, 642.
[4] 'A reformed Catholic', *Works*, I, 605–6.
[5] II–II, Q. 6, art. 2: in *Nature and Grace* (selections from the *Summa*), tr. A. M. Fairweather, 287–8.

through the obedience of Christ'.[1] Our sins are remitted, and the righteousness of Christ is imputed to us. The 'material cause' of justification is 'the obedience of Christ in suffering and fulfilling the law for us': the 'formal cause' is 'imputation, which is an action of God the Father, accepting the obedience of Christ for us, as it were our own'. This, said Perkins, is deliberately contrary to the popish assertion that 'infused or inherent justice is the formal cause of justification'.[2] Nor, as against the Church of Rome, does the Church of England believe that there is a preparation to justification, wrought partly by the Holy Spirit 'and partly by the power of natural free will'.[3] (If, commented Perkins, 'there were no more points of difference between us, this one alone were sufficient to keep us from uniting our religions'.[4]) Those who are justified 'are accepted of God as his own children'; and 'the elect have in themselves the spirit of Jesus Christ, testifying unto them, and persuading them that they are accepted children of God'. For 'as in a bargain when part of the price is paid in earnest, then assurance is made, that men will pay the whole: so when the child of God hath received thus much from the Holy Ghost, to be persuaded that he is adopted and chosen in Christ, he may be in good hope, and he is already put in good assurance, fully to enjoy eternal life in the kingdom of heaven'.[5]

The third manifestation of the decree of election is sanctification: 'whereby such as believe, being delivered from the tyranny of sin, are by little and little renewed in holiness and righteousness'.[6] In justification the sinner was 'made righteous by the righteousness of Christ imputed to him';[7] now, 'an inherent holiness being begun, is still augmented and enlarged'.[8] The mind, the conscience, the affections, the will and the body are 'freed from the bondage

[1] 'Golden Chain', *Works*, I, 81.
[2] *Ibid*. 102.
[3] 'A reformed Catholic', *Works*, I, 567.   [4] *Ibid*. 568.
[5] 'Treatise tending to a declaration', *Works*, I, 369.
[6] 'Golden Chain', *Works*, I, 83.
[7] 'Treatise tending to a declaration', *Works*, I, 368.
[8] 'Golden Chain', *Works*, I, 83.

and tyranny of sin': the elect Christian is 'by little and little
enabled through the spirit of Christ to desire and approve that
which is good, and to walk in it'.[1] And so the pilgrim passes to the
fourth and final manifestation of the decree of election: that is,
glorification, the 'perfect transforming of the saints into the
image of God'.[2]

Perkins now dealt, in parenthesis, with some differences between
the English and the Roman Churches in their theology of election.
The Church of Rome says that the decree of election is dependent
upon God's foreknowledge of our faith, thus Rome 'hath the
cause of it in man'; and it maintains that the decree does not
'constrain or enforce any necessity upon the will of man', an
assertion of 'the inherent power of free will'. Rome also believes
that God would have all men saved: that he 'hath appointed and
disposed all men so, as they might obtain eternal salvation'. And
it believes that 'he which is justified may be a reprobate, and
perish eternally': therefore that 'predestination is not certain,
seeing it may be lost'.[3] It is true, said Perkins, that in the elect
Christian 'grace may in part, and for a time be lost': 'but that
there is any total, or final falling from grace, we utterly deny'.[4]
Grace may be 'by his own default lessened' in the elect Christian:
'buried in him, and covered for a time so that he may be like
a man in a trance who both by his own sense and the judgement
of the physician is taken for dead'. But the elect man 'after that
he is sanctified he receiveth from God another special grace, which
may be called corroboration. For he hath in him not only the
sanctifying but also the strengthening power of Christ.'[5] And so
there is one manner of sinning in the godly, and another in the ungodly,
though they fall both into one sin. A wicked man when he sinneth in
his heart he giveth full consent to the sin: but the godly though they
fall into the same sins with the wicked, yet they never give full consent:

[1] 'Treatise tending to a declaration', *Works*, I, 370.
[2] 'Golden Chain', *Works*, I, 92.   [3] *Ibid.* 95.
[4] *Ibid.* 103.
[5] 'Treatise tending to a declaration', *Works*, I, 377–8.

for they are in their minds, wills and affections partly regenerate, and partly unregenerate, and therefore their wills do partly will, and partly abhor that which is evil.[1]

Finally, as against the Church of Rome, Perkins asserts that the elect, 'from the nature of faith'[2] (*ex natura fidei*) are 'sure of [*certi*] Election in Christ'.[3] 'True faith is both an infallible assurance [*certa infallibilis*], and a particular assurance of the remission of sins, and of life everlasting. And therefore by this faith, a man may be certainly and particularly assured [*securus*] of, the remission of sins, and life everlasting.'[4] The papists hold that a man is certain of his salvation only by hope: both Churches, said Perkins, teach a certainty (*certitudo*);[5] but 'we by faith, they by hope'. We 'avouch that our certainty by true faith is infallible: they say their certainty is only probable'.[6] Thus a man can be as certain of salvation as he is 'of the articles of the Creed'.[7] Every faithful man must believe that he is elected: for this is not a matter—as the papists assert—of 'especial revelation':[8] it is a general revelation to 'all the elect having the spirit of grace'.[9] There can be no question that 'there be many now, that by long and often experience of God's mercy, and by the inward certificate of the Holy Ghost [*interno testimonio ac certificatione Sancti Spiritus*] have attained to full assurance [*certitudinem*] of their salvation'.[10] Perkins quoted the Tridentine verdict: 'No man, so long as he liveth in this mortal life, ought so much to presume on the secret mystery of God's Predestination, as to determine undoubtedly that he is in the number of them whom God hath ordained to eternal happiness.'[11] And he dismissed it as a denial of the nature of

[1] 'Treatise tending to a declaration', *Works*, I, 372.
[2] 'A reformed Catholic', *Works*, I, 564.
[3] 'Golden Chain', *Works*, I, 113. *Armilla Aurea* (second edition).
[4] 'A reformed Catholic', *Works*, I, 564. Latin in the Geneva edition of Perkins's *Works* (1618–24), I, 377.   [5] Geneva edition, I, 374.
[6] 'A reformed Catholic', *Works*, I, 563.   [7] *Ibid.* 565.
[8] 'Golden Chain', *Works*, I, 104.   [9] 'A reformed Catholic', *Works*, I, 563.
[10] *Ibid.* 566. Latin in Geneva edition, I, 379.
[11] 'Golden Chain', *Works*, I, 96.

faith and election: 'our infallible knowledge and certainty, being contrary to doubting, must needs proceed from true faith'.[1]

That concludes the section of *A Golden Chain* (chapters 15–51) concerned with the decree of election. In chapter 52 Perkins turned to the decree of reprobation.

Reprobation is 'that part of predestination, whereby God, according to the most free and just purpose of his will, hath determined to reject certain men unto eternal destruction, and misery, and that to the praise of his justice'.[2] A decree which 'declareth the liberty and very great perfection of God'. The cause of reprobation 'is the sole will of God, yea even without respect of any sin at all'; that will of God which is 'the cause of causes'. And yet—such are the Calvinist gymnastics—it was still possible for Perkins to assert that 'those which are forsaken of God, do themselves first forsake God'. For reprobation, like election, has two acts: the first is God's decree to forsake some men; the second is his 'ordaining of them to punishment or due destruction'. This second act, said Perkins, is 'not without respect of original and actual sins': for, 'in regard of order', sin 'goeth before' this second act.[3] So we do not, said Perkins, 'set down any absolute decree of damnation, as though we should think that any were condemned by the mere and alone will of God, without any causes inherent in such as are to be condemned'.[4] But at the same time, we can by these scholastic subtleties assert that 'sin is not the cause of the decree of reprobation'.[5]

How is God's decree of reprobation effected? In reprobate infants, 'the execution of God's decree is this: as soon as they are born, for the guilt of original and natural sin, being left in God's secret judgement unto themselves, they dying are rejected of God for ever'.[6] In adults, they might not be called at all; or they might

---

[1] 'A reformed Catholic', *Works*, I, 564. [2] 'Golden Chain', *Works*, I, 105.
[3] 'Treatise of predestination', *Works*, II, 610–11.
[4] 'Golden Chain', *Works*, I, 105.
[5] 'Treatise of predestination', *Works*, II, 611.
[6] 'Golden Chain', *Works*, I, 105.

be called 'by an uneffectual calling'.[1] A sign of this is that the reprobate, though he 'may be persuaded of the mercy and goodness of God towards him for the present time in the which he feels it', has not the persuasion 'of his eternal election before the foundation of the world' which is enjoyed by the elect.

The reprobate, when he repenteth he cannot come unto God, and seek unto him: he hath no power, no not so much as once to desire to give one little sob for the remission of his sins: if he would give all the world he cannot so much as give one rap at God's mercy gate, that he may open to him. He is very like a man upon a rack, who crieth and roareth out for every pain, yet cannot desire his tormentor to ease him of his pain.

He may indeed have the comfort of being able to do 'outwardly all those things which true Christians do': and this has its reward, for 'he may lead such a life here in this world, that although he cannot attain to salvation, yet his pains in hell shall be less'.[2] Perkins used a striking image to bring this point home to his Cambridge hearers and readers:

A master of music hath his house furnished with musical instruments of all sorts; and he teacheth his own scholars artificially to use them, both in tuning of them, as also in playing on them: there come in strangers, who admiring the said instruments, have leave given of them of the master to handle them as the scholars do: but when they come to practise, they neither tune them aright, neither are they able to strike one stroke as they ought, so as they may please the master and have his commendation. This world is as a large and sumptuous palace, into which are received, not only the sons and daughters of God, but also wicked and ungodly men: it is furnished with goodly creatures in use more excellent than all musical instruments: the use of them is common to all: but the godly man taught by God's spirit, and directed by faith, so useth them as that the use thereof is acceptable to God.[3]

[1] 'Golden Chain', *Works*, I, 106.
[2] 'Treatise tending to a declaration', *Works*, I, 357–8.
[3] 'Treatise tending to a declaration', *Works*, I, 416.

The 'use' of this dogmatic of election and reprobation is to persuade the reader to 'diligently try and examine himself, whether he is in the state of damnation, or in the state of grace'.[1] And also to reassure him that in the economy of grace 'a papist cannot go beyond a reprobate'.[2]

At this point, in chapter 54, Perkins considered the errors of 'a new devised doctrine of Predestination taught by some new and late divines': he referred especially to divines 'in Germany', and inserted another chart in the text to demonstrate their absurdities.[3] These divines fear 'lest they should make God both unjust and unmerciful'. And thus they turn the causes of election and reprobation 'upside down' by maintaining that there is 'a certain universal or general election' whereby God 'hath decreed to redeem by Christ and to reconcile unto himself all mankind wholly';[4] that God foreknew but did not foreordain the Fall of Adam, and therefore the Fall was 'without the agent permission of God'; that reprobation is because God 'did foresee the disobedience of some, or, that they would contemn the gospel';[5] and that 'God's calling to the knowledge of the Gospel is universal, yea of all men, and every singular person'.[6] Perkins replied that if all men were elected, 'election' would be a meaningless word: and Christ said (John xvii, 19) 'I pray not for the world but for them which thou has given me'—thus 'Christ is only an advocate for the faithful'.[7] Perkins's exegesis of the prayer followed that of Calvin. Calvin took the prayer as proving

that the whole world belongeth not to the Creator of it, saving that grace delivereth a few from the wrath of God, and from eternal death, which otherwise should have perished: but the world itself is left in his own destruction to which it was appointed. In the mean time although Christ put himself mean between, yet he claimeth to him-

[1] *Ibid.* 361.
[2] *Ibid.* 396–404.
[3] 'Golden Chain', *Works*, I, 106.
[4] *Ibid.* 107.
[5] *Ibid.* 110.
[6] *Ibid.* 111.
[7] *Ibid.* 108.

self the power of choosing in common with the Father. I speak not (saith he) of all: I know whom I have chosen (John xiii. 18). If any man ask from whence he hath chosen them, he answereth in another place, Out of the world, which he excludeth out of his prayers when he commendeth his disciples to his Father (John xv. 19). This is to be holden, that when he affirmeth that he knoweth whom he hath chosen, there is signified some special sort in the general kind of men: then, that the same special sort is made to differ not by the quality of their own virtues, but by the heavenly decree....The sum is, that God maketh them His children by free adoption whom He will have to be His children: and that the inward cause thereof is in Himself: because He is content with His own secret good pleasure.[1]

Perkins admitted that 'many places of scripture' seem to affirm that 'the benefit of Christ's death doth appertain unto all'. But 'all' must be taken to mean 'of all sorts some, not every singular person of all sorts':[2] 'God will not have every one of every kind, but the kinds of every one to be saved, that is to say, of every estate and condition some.'[3] (Discussing the Pauline text 'God will have all men to be saved', Calvin had claimed that 'all men' meant 'all degree of men'.[4]) Moreover, it is 'absurd' to say that 'God appointed all to be saved, with the caveat and condition, *If they believe*': this would make the decree of God dependent upon the will of man; it would be a 'conditional proposition' which 'quite taketh away the certainty of God's decree'. The fact is, said Perkins, that God 'did upon his mere pleasure elect some and reject others eternally, not moved or urged thereunto by anything whatsoever out of himself': he might have decreed 'that even all men should utterly have been rejected, and yet he should have been never whit either cruel nor unjust'. It is equally absurd to assert that 'the foreseeing of the contempt of grace in any, was the first and principal cause of the decree of reprobation'. We are

[1] Calvin, *Institutes*, 3/22/7; tr. T. Norton (1611 ed.), 459.
[2] 'Golden Chain', *Works*, I, 108–9.
[3] 'Treatise of predestination', *Works*, II, 623.
[4] *Institutes*, 3/24/15.

clay in the hands of the potter: and 'the potter when he purposeth to make some vessel, doth not consider the clay, and regard in it some inherent quality to make such a vessel, but he maketh it of such and such a form, to this and that use, even of his own free-will and pleasure'. It would be preposterous to assert that God intended and foreknew all mankind created, fallen and redeemed in Christ, and then afterwards 'ordained them so foreknown to life or to death':

For the end is the first thing in the intention of the agent: neither will a very unskilful workman first prepare means by which he may be helped to do a thing, before he hath set down in his mind all the ends, both such as are most near, and them that are very far off. Now we know this, that man's creation, and his fall in Adam, are but means to execute God's predestination and therefore are subordinate to it: but the end of God's decree, is the manifestation of his glory, in saving some, and condemning others.

It is therefore certain that 'God would not have all men called unto Christ': and that 'the greatest part of the world hath ever been out of the covenant of grace'.[1] It is counterfeit and feigned (Perkins was to write in 1598) to bring in here any distinction of God's will: to say that God by a 'universal, precedent and conditional will' wished all men to be saved. God's will to save some and reject others 'is both absolute and first'.[2] Any theology of universal saving grace—of what Père Rondet has recently called the 'Optimism of Grace'[3]—was rejected by Perkins as 'a plausible device of man's brain': an 'impairing of effectual and Christian grace'.[4]

The final chapter of *A Golden Chain* has the title: 'Of the Application of Predestination'. What is the use of all this for the life of the individual Christian? How can it give men that 'peace

---

[1] 'Golden Chain', *Works*, I, 109–11.
[2] 'Treatise of predestination', *Works*, II, 624.
[3] H. Rondet, *Gratia Christi*, 139.
[4] 'Treatise of predestination', *Works*, II, 628–9.

of conscience' for which the precepts of true religion were directions—and which the precepts of the Church of Rome so conspicuously failed to give?[1] The point of Perkins's dogmatic lay in his assertion of the 'full persuasion' of election: this was the foundation-stone of the confidence of the Calvinist. But the theological emphasis on, and detailed description of, the decree of reprobation was not calculated to instil a Christian calm into the hearts and minds of a congregation.

> Teach us to care and not to care,
> Teach us to sit still.

The only pastoral answer to the problem was to assume that all pious hearers of the word were elected: however Calvinist in the study, the preacher must be Arminian in the pulpit. There are those among you, preached Perkins, that have not yet felt in your hearts the effects of election, such as I have described them. But let not such a man 'presently conclude that he is a reprobate: but let him rather use the word of God, and the sacraments, that he may have an inward sense of the power of Christ, drawing him unto him, and an assurance of his redemption by Christ's death and passion'. All, then, must have an assurance of hope. For those who have passed to the assurance of faith the 'use' of the Calvinist exegesis is obvious:

Such as are persuaded that they are elected, and adopted children of God, they will love God, they will trust in him, and they will call upon him with their whole heart....Now, if so be all the effects of the spirit are very feeble in the godly, they must know this, that God trieth them, yet so as they must not therewith be dismayed, because it is most sure, that if they have faith, but as much as a grain of mustard seed, and be as weak as a young infant is, it is sufficient to engraft them into Christ, and therefore they must not doubt of their election, because they see their faith feeble and the effects of the Holy Ghost faint within them.[2]

[1] 'Treatise tending to a declaration', *Works*, I, 396.
[2] 'Golden Chain', *Works*, I, 113.

Such was—in the words of a number of Masters of Cambridge colleges in the summer of 1595—'the comfortable certainty of true faith'; as against 'the Popish doctrine of doubtfulness of our salvation'.[1]

The argument is finished. But it must not be mistaken for the book. This chapter has been dry bones; and the point about Perkins is that he, more than any other preacher of late Elizabethan Cambridge, made the dry bones live. Of his careful and ordered arrangement of the Calvinist theses, of his practical applications of doctrine (at its best in the chapters on the Ten Commandments in *A Golden Chain*) and of the force and poetry of his imagery, it has been impossible to give more than a hint. Stated baldly, his theology sounds like an English version of 'Master Calvin of blessed memory';[2] and perhaps not much more. But it must be noted that, for instance, in his tightly argued and clear-cut *Treatise of God's Free Grace and Man's Free Will* he quoted Calvin only once, and Luther once also: but St Thomas Aquinas five times, St Augustine twelve times; and the Old Testament, the New Testament, and St Paul over fifty times each. Moreover, although his system has the clarity of the Frenchman's, his style was thoroughly English. At times Perkins seems as far removed from Calvin as Shakespeare from Racine.

If one point alone were to be made about Calvin and Perkins it would be this: they both of them believed that 'all the works of God are done in contrary means'.[3] 'You see that here', Calvin had written, is 'a comparison of contraries, and that here is declared that he which will obtain the righteousness of Christ, must forsake his own righteousness'.[4] It is a cast of mind. 'The middle of humanity', said Apemantus to Timon, 'thou never knewest, but the extremity of both ends.' It is the same with

[1] Heads to Whitgift, 12 June 1595. Trinity College, Cambridge, MS. B/14/9, p. 23.
[2] 'Treatise of predestination', *Works*, II, 616.
[3] 'Grain of mustard seed', *Works*, I, 644.
[4] *Institutes*, 3/11/13; tr. Norton (1611 ed.), 356.

some theologians. In his sermons on 'The Right Way of Dying Well', published in 1595, Perkins wrote:

All the works of God are done in and by their contraries. In the creation, all things were made, not of something but of nothing, clean contrary to the course of nature. In the work of redemption, God gives life, not by life, but by death: and if we consider aright of Christ upon the cross, we shall see our paradise out of paradise in the midst of hell. For out of his own cursed death doth he bring us life and eternal happiness. Likewise in effectual vocation, when it pleaseth God to convert and turn men unto him, he doth it by means of his gospel preached, which in reason should drive all men from God. For it is as contrary to the nature of man, as fire to water, and light to darkness: and yet for all this, though it be thus against the disposition and heart of man, it prevails with him and turns him to God. Furthermore, when God will send his own servants to heaven, he sends them a contrary way, even by the gates of hell.[1]

The way of negation, then, not that of affirmation. Grace does not perfect nature, but destroys it.

All these works of Perkins were preached or written when he was in his thirties: for he died when he was forty-four. And they are still worth study, not least for their insight into the human condition. 'Alas poor souls, we are no better than passengers in this world, our way it is in the middle of the sea, where we can have no sure footing at all, and which way soever we cast our eyes, we see nothing but water, even opening itself to devour us quick.' The Church of Rome passes in the ship with us: and she 'hath long taken upon her to rule the helm'. But she

dealeth too unkindly with us: she unlooseth our anchors: and cutteth in pieces our cables, she telleth us that we may not presume to fasten our anchor on the rock: she will have us freely to rove in the middle of the sea in the greatest fogs and the fearfullest tempests that be: if we shall follow our advice, we must needs look for a shipwreck; for the least flow of wind shall overturn us, and our poor souls shall be plunged in the gulf of hell.[2]

[1] *Works*, I, 492. [2] 'Treatise tending to a declaration', *Works*, I, 398.

Logan Pearsall Smith drew attention to Donne's use of the imagery of the sea:[1] Perkins's use of it is no less striking. The pastoral use of such sea imagery would make an interesting study, on the lines of W. H. Auden's fine *The Enchaf'd Flood* (1951). In turn, 'the love of God is like a sea, into which when a man is cast, he neither feels bottom, nor sees bank'.[2] God 'of his great and endless mercy hath brought us to Christ, as to a sure anchor-hold'.[3]

In the decree of election, the inward testimony of true saving faith, and the assurance of salvation, the elect Christian finds again the lost harmony and order of the universe. Perkins wrote, like Calvin, for 'poor consciences that seek steadfast assurance of eternal life':[4] to answer the ultimate 'Case of Conscience, the greatest that ever was: How a man may know whether he be the Child of God or no'. And to generations of Cambridge consciences, through his preaching, and to future generations in Old and New England, Perkins brought and was to bring that assurance. 'The anchor of hope must be fixed in that truth and stability of the immutable good pleasure of God: so that albeit our faith be so tossed, as that in danger of shipwreck, nevertheless it must never sink to the bottom, but in the midst of danger take hold upon repentance as on a board and so recover itself.'[5]

[1] In his introduction to *Donne's Sermons: selected Passages* (1920), xliv.
[2] 'Right way of dying well', *Works*, I, 492.
[3] 'Treatise tending to a declaration', *Works*, I, 398.
[4] *Institutes*, 1/7/1; tr. Norton (1611 ed.), 20.
[5] 'Golden Chain', *Works*, I, 114.

CHAPTER XIII

THE CALVINIST ASSERTION: 1595

In July 1595 a short statement of 'the truth of religion publicly and generally received'[1] was sent from Cambridge to Lambeth, signed by eight heads of houses: John Duport of Jesus, Roger Goad of King's, Humphrey Tyndall of Queens', Edmund Barwell of Christ's, John Jegon of Corpus, Laurence Chaderton of Emmanuel, Robert Some of Peterhouse, and William Whitaker of St John's. They intended 'to testify our own opinions for the defence and preservation of that truth of doctrine in some substantial points which hath been always in our memories both here and elsewhere, taught, professed and continued, and never openly impugned amongst us but by some persons of late'.[2] These 'persons' were the supporters of William Barrett of Caius, whose recantation, delivered in Great St Mary's in May,[3] also serves as a convenient hand-book to the dogmatic of the academic Cambridge Calvinists in those 'substantial points' around which the controversies of 1595 revolved. William Whitaker, Regius Professor of Divinity, was the most learned and the most respected of this Calvinist group: and in a letter which he wrote to Whitgift in June,[4] and, more extensively, in a sermon preached in Great St Mary's in October about election and reprobation, the loss of grace, and the assurance of salvation, Dr Whitaker set forth with

[1] Trinity College, Cambridge, MS. B/14/9, p. 27. Covering letter to the actual statement, which is at pp. 51–2. This volume is a copy-book belonging to Whitgift, and stamped with his arms, containing transcripts of all the important papers in the Barrett and Baro cases, 1595/6.

[2] *Ibid.* p. 30. Letter of the Heads, 16 July.

[3] Recantation in University Archives, Registry Guard Books, vol. 6 (i), no. 33—wrongly catalogued as a letter of Baro. Copy in Trinity MS. B/14/9, pp. 39–41. Printed at the time as a broadsheet; reprinted by Prynne, *Anti-Arminianism* (1630 ed.), 67–70; and by Strype, *Whitgift*, III, 317–19. Translated into English by Prynne (*op. cit.* 56–62); and also by Fuller, *History of Cambridge* (ed. Prickett and Wright), 283–5.

[4] Trinity MS. B/14/9, pp. 47–9. Printed in Strype, *Whitgift*, III, 337–9.

clarity his own firm interpretation of the detailed matters under debate. (This sermon was his 'Swan Song':[1] for he died in December.) Robert Some also put pen to paper in 1595. Some was a Johnian, one of the first Elizabethan undergraduates, having gone up to the college under James Pilkington in 1559; he had then gone to Queens' as Fellow in 1562, and remained at that college for over twenty-five years, becoming in turn bursar and Vice-President, and being, in 1570, a supporter of Cartwright; he succeeded Andrew Perne as Master of Peterhouse in 1589. John Legate published Dr Some's little English tract—vivid, clear, with an imaginative use of imagery in the best Puritan tradition—in 1596: *Three Questions Godly, Plainly and Briefly Handled. I: They which are endued of God with a justifying faith, cannot utterly lose the same. II: The true believer, by faith, is assured of the forgiveness of his sins. III: Christ died effectually for the elect alone: therefore not for every several man.* From these half-dozen documents the Calvinist verities—as applied and discussed in the lecture rooms and pulpits of the university in the summer of 1595—can be exactly induced.

'Election', Calvin had written, 'is the mother of faith': 'to election faith indeed is fitly joined, so that it keeps the second degree'.[2] That was an unambiguous statement of the special and peculiar perspective in which the Calvinist surveyed Christian territory; or, to change the metaphor, a statement of the characteristic way in which he shook the kaleidoscope. The Cambridge Calvinists of the 1590's were in one point at least the heirs of the men of the White Horse Inn, seventy long years away: 'there is only one true, justifying faith.'[3] Barrett was made to acknowledge the distinction between a temporary, and therefore feigned, faith (*fides temporaria et ficta*) and 'that saving faith whereby sinners apprehending Christ are justified before God for ever'.[4] This was unobjectionable: so long as it was interpreted in the framework

[1] Printed by Legate at Cambridge in 1599; *Cygnea Cantio Guilielmi Whitakeri.*
[2] *Institutes*, 3/22/10; tr. Norton, 1611 ed. 461.
[3] Trinity MS. B/14/9, p. 51.
[4] Recantation (tr. Fuller), *History of Cambridge*, 284.

of the 'grain of mustard seed', of which Perkins so eloquently and extensively wrote in that very year of 1595. But what the early Cambridge reformers could not have foreseen was the interpretation of *sola fide* as dependent upon, almost secondary to, the decree of election. John Overall was to fall foul of Robert Some, Roger Goad and Laurence Chaderton on this very point in the summer of 1599: 'They answered that they held none justified but the elect'; 'but I said, that I meant...all men justified, whether elect or not elect; and whether all men justified were elect, was another question'.[1] This argument of 1599 was especially piquant because Overall was Whitaker's immediate successor as Regius Professor of Divinity: to Dr Some, he seemed to have sold the pass to the Pelagians.

Whitaker, discussing predestination in his Last Sermon, considered himself to be correctly interpreting Article XVII of the Thirty-nine Articles of Religion. He was careful not to make too much of his Master: 'I refrain from speaking about Calvin.'[2] Any reasonable Church of England man, he said, cannot doubt my point. The point is that election does not depend upon God's foreknowledge of our faith or works: 'faith, and perseverance, and all the services of grace, and any good in us' are the effect of election, not the cause.[3] Correspondingly, 'the only will of God is cause of reprobation'.[4] As Calvin had written: 'if we cannot declare a reason why he vouchsafeth to grant mercy to them that be his, but because it so pleaseth him: neither also shall we have any other cause in rejecting of other, than his own will'.[5] It is true that Perkins was subtly to subdivide the decree of reprobation into two acts, the second of which was 'not without respect of original and actual sins':[6] it is true that the heads maintained that 'in the execution of God's decree, there is always respect to sin,

---

[1] University Library, Cambridge, MSS. vol. Gg/1/29, fol. 103a.
[2] *Cygnea Cantio*, 16. The translations from this sermon are mine.   [3] *Ibid.* 6.
[4] Trinity MS. B/14/9, p. 48. Whitaker to Whitgift, June 1595.
[5] *Institutes*, 3/22/11; tr. Norton, 462.
[6] 'Treatise of predestination', *Works*, II, 611.

and the cause of damnation is in the wicked themselves'.[1] But, as Perkins concluded, the cause is 'the sole will of God, yea even without respect of any sin at all'.[2] 'In predestination itself', wrote the heads, 'there is no respect or cause either of holiness in the elect, or of sin in the reprobate, but it dependeth wholly on the mere will and good pleasure of God.'[3]

A crucial text in the Cambridge disputes of 1595 was John xvii. 9—'I pray not for the world, but for them which thou hast given me.' Dr Some, like Perkins, drew from these words a strict inference: 'Christ prayeth not for every several man; therefore he died not effectually for every several man.' Christ, continued Some, laid down his life 'for the sheep' (John x. 15): 'that is, for the elect only: therefore not for every several man. And that we are not to understand every several man by sheep Christ himself proves in these words: "ye believe not, for ye are not of my sheep" (John x. 26)'.[4] What then of St Paul's assertion that God 'will have all men to be saved'? It is, said Some, a 'device of the Pelagians' to interpret this text as meaning that 'God will have all, that is, every several man to be saved, if they themselves be willing: and God is ready to shew mercy, if man be willing'.[5] St Paul meant that 'God would have of all kinds of men some to be saved'.[6]

The elect, and the elect only, have a true and justifying faith. The question now arises: can this faith be forfeit? The answer of the Calvinist heads was, of course, uncompromising: 'That true justifying faith whereby we are ingrafted into Christ, is so fixed and certain to continue, that it can never be utterly lost or extinguished in them which have the said justifying faith.'[7] This point had been put into the mouth of Barrett in May:

I freely protest that the true and justifying faith whereby the faithful are most nearly united into Christ is so firm, as also for the time so certain,

---

[1] Trinity MS. B/14/9, p. 51.
[2] 'Treatise of predestination', *Works*, II, 611.
[3] Trinity MS. B/14/9, p. 51.
[4] Some, *Three Questions*, 20.
[5] *Ibid.* 30.   [6] *Ibid.* 28.
[7] Trinity MS. B/14/9, p. 51.

that it can never be rooted out of the minds of the faithful, by any temptations of the flesh, the world, or the devil himself, so that he who hath this faith once, shall ever have it: for by the benefit of that justifying faith, Christ dwelleth in us, and we in Christ: therefore it cannot be but increased (Christ growing in us daily), as also persevere unto the end because God doth give constancy.[1]

Robert Some considered the question in the context of I John v. 18: 'whosoever is born of God sinneth not'. 'The meaning of the Apostle is that the regenerate man doth not sin either wholly or finally. Not wholly; for there are always some gifts and graces abiding in him; not finally, for the wicked toucheth him not... that is to say, with a deadly wound. The shield of faith may be battered, but it cannot be pierced through.'[2]

Whitaker, in his sermon, considered this point in its general context of the relation of nature and grace. The things of grace, he said, are never so widely accessible as the things of nature: nor are grace and nature commingled, as the Pelagians assert. And to say that grace can belong to each and every man is almost to out-Pelagian the Pelagians.[3] Again, there are gifts of the Spirit which can be lost: but grace in the true sense—expressed in faith working through charity: a firm anchor of the Spirit, giving a firm and secure hope (*spes tuta ac firma*)—such grace cannot, by definition, be forfeit.[4] We may indeed 'depart from grace given' (*recedere*): those are the words of Article XVI. But we cannot utterly fall from it (*excidere*):

We admit that men truly justified and regenerate can indeed sin, and gravely offend God, and deserve and bring upon themselves great punishment, and, as the Articles say, depart from grace. But it would be mere ignorance to interpret the Articles as asserting that we can completely fall from grace. To depart from grace means to obey the lusts of the flesh, and to struggle against the moving of the Spirit: which is far from being a fall from grace, an extinguishing of the

[1] Tr. Fuller, *History of Cambridge*, 284.   [2] *Three Questions*, 3.
[3] *Cygnea Cantio*, 14.   [4] *Ibid.* 17.

Spirit, a retaining of not one spark of grace. Our Confessional Articles speak nowhere in these latter terms: but quite the contrary.[1]

Dr Some made the same claim, in a homely and vivid way which recalls Perkins. Faith can be 'lulled asleep, and eclipsed for a time': but in the elect it will shine out again, like the sun from behind a black cloud; like a palm tree which springs up after being pressed down.[2] 'It is like unto the fire covered over with many ashes, which afterward breaketh forth into a flame. It is like the anchor of the ship, which being cast into the bottom of the sea, seems to be overwhelmed, and carried away with waves and tempests, but yet it abideth. It is like the tree whose root is living, although it bring forth no fruit.'[3]

Calvin 'bid the faithful to fetch out of the word of the gospel' a 'sure stablishment of election' (*certum electionis stabilimentum*). He asked them to feel 'that affiance of heart with which I say that the assuredness [*certitudo*] of our election is stablished'. Paul, continued Calvin, when he warns us of the dangers of 'security', is talking of a carnal and careless security, not of a true and valid Christian *securitas*.[4] Thus Whitaker could regard his aim as Regius Professor to teach *de certitudine et securitate salutis*:[5] and he, with the other Calvinist heads (concerned, like Macbeth, to 'make assurance double sure') could emphasize the 'spiritual security' of the Christian:

he which hath a true justifying faith, remaineth not in a continual wavering and doubtfulness, but is assured of his salvation, and that by the ground and certainty of that justifying faith: because by that faith only, we apprehend and apply Christ to ourselves, whereby we have peace with God etc., and consequently a certainty and spiritual security, which term, for that kind of security, is not only by some late writers and preachers, but by many ancient and Catholic Doctors of the Church, so used.[6]

---

[1] *Ibid.* 20.
[3] *Ibid.* 3–4.
[5] *Cygnea Cantio*, 4.
[2] Some, *Three Questions*, 6.
[4] *Institutes*, 3/24/7; tr. Norton, 476.
[6] Trinity MS. B/14/9, p. 51.

319

The elect and true believer is also assured of the remission of his own particular sins; he is, in the words of Whitaker, 'sure and certain thereof by infallible testimony of the Holy Ghost'.[1] Finally, the Calvinists interpreted the prayer of Christ recorded in Luke xxii. 32—'But I have prayed for thee, that thy faith fail not'—as a petition not only for Peter, nor for the Apostles only, but for 'all those that should believe in Christ'.[2] 'I acknowledge', Barrett was ordered to say in May, 'that Christ did pray for the faith of every particular believer: and that by virtue of that prayer of Christ, every true believer is so stayed up, that his faith cannot fail.'[3] This followed Calvin's exegesis of the Lucan text: 'Whereby we gather, that they are out of danger of falling away, because the Son of God, asking steadfast continuance for their godliness, suffered no denial. What would Christ have us to learn hereby, but that we shall perpetually be safe, because we are once made his?'[4] Thus Whitaker, in his 'Swan Song', summed up one aspect of his half-century of study by asserting that the Fathers and the Scriptures and even the better instructed papists teach that the Christian may have *certitudinem veram, et sanctam securitatem*.[5] As Barrett was made to say in May, they which are justified by faith ought to be 'certain and assured of their own salvation, even by the certainty of faith itself'[6] (*de salute sua, fidei ipsius certitudine, certos esse et securos*). These were the claims of Calvinist assurance. This was the central point at issue in the Cambridge controversies of 1595.

Such was the doctrine; and it lived with a fire and a force to which the Cambridge pulpit gave eloquent witness. When clothed in the pastoral concern of a Perkins or a Some, it became possessed of a power which still speaks to us across the gap of three and a half centuries, and speaks to us in Cambridge terms. Dr Some, like Master Perkins, set an evangelical optimism into

[1] Trinity MS. B/14/9, p. 48. Whitaker to Whitgift.
[2] *Ibid.* p. 51. Heads to Whitgift.
[3] Tr. Fuller, *History of Cambridge*, 283.   [4] *Institutes*, 3/24/6; tr. Norton, 476.
[5] *Cygnea Cantio*, 25.   [6] Fuller, *op. cit.*

the framework of his doctrinal pessimism. Christ came into the world to save sinners: 'therefore let no man despair by reason of his sins, although they be in number more than the stars of heaven, and in weight they surpass the sand of the sea. A man shall not so soon repent, but God will be ready to receive him.'[1] He ended his little book with a practical exhortation to men 'overcharged and oppressed almost with the burden and sense of their sins':[2] adding 'a proposition full of comfort, very godly and plainly expressed: to wit, They which have most grievously offended the majesty of God, ought not to despair of His mercy'.[3] It was, as he said, an exhortation against suicide.

This, then, was 'the truth of religion publicly and generally received'. It is true, said Whitaker, that Barrett may not have preached against the Articles: but he has contradicted 'the religion of our church publicly received, and always held in her Majesty's reign, and maintained in all sermons, disputations, and lectures'.[4] That remark was disarmingly moderate. In fact Barrett was forced to acknowledge in his recantation that he believed 'concerning the doctrine of election, and reprobation, as the Church of England believeth and teacheth in the book of the articles of faith, in the article of predestination'.[5] In other words, the Calvinist heads of 1595 were taking it upon themselves to be the only true and infallible interpreters of the doctrine of the Church of England. That was intolerable; as intolerable—and inaccurate —as the resolutions on religion to be drawn up by the committee of the House of Commons in February 1629, objecting to 'the suppressing and restraint of the orthodox doctrine, contained in the Articles of Religion, confirmed in Parliament, according to the sense which hath been received publicly, and taught as the doctrine of the Church of England in those points, wherein the Arminians differ from us'.[6] It was all very well for Whitaker to

[1] *Three Questions*, 33.　　　　[2] *Ibid.* 31.　　　　[3] *Ibid.* title page.
[4] Trinity MS. B/14/9, p. 48. Letter to Whitgift.
[5] Fuller, *History of Cambridge*, 285.
[6] S. R. Gardiner, *Constitutional Documents of the Puritan Revolution* (1889), 80.

say that his teaching on grace was not contrary to the Articles of Religion; but it was dogmatic of him to go on to assert that his teaching and his teaching alone was contained in, or could be deduced from, those Thirty-nine Articles. It was the claim of the Calvinist heads that the details of their doctrinal system, in the points of nature and grace, of election and reprobation, and of Christian assurance, were unambiguously and exclusively 'set down in the book of Articles, in the Homilies allowed in the book of Articles, in the Apology of the Church of England and Defence of the same, in Catechisms commanded by authority to be used, and in the Book of Common Prayer'.[1] That claim was of course false. In order to examine it the more closely, it will be necessary to devote a chapter to a study of the Prayer Book and the Articles of Religion; to discover what exactly, in these disputed points, were the positive and negative limits of 'the doctrine established by authority'.

[1] Trinity MS. B/14/9, p. 57. Heads to Whitgift, October.

CHAPTER XIV

GRACE AND PREDESTINATION:
THE DOCTRINE ESTABLISHED
BY AUTHORITY

I

FIRST, what is the Universe of Grace explicit in the Book of Common Prayer?

The 'nature and property' of God 'is ever to have mercy and to forgive'; he is the 'giver of all good things', more especially 'giver of all spiritual grace'; and he has 'ordained and constituted the services of angels and men in a wonderful order'. Within this Order, man was 'created after' his 'own image and similitude'.[1]

Yet we are born 'in original sin, and in the wrath of God'. We are compelled to dwell in 'the miseries of this sinful world' and should 'see how frail and uncertain our own condition' is. 'All men are conceived and born in sin (and that which is born of the flesh, is flesh) and they that are in the flesh cannot please God, but live in sin, committing many actual transgressions'; 'through our sins and wickedness, we are sore let and hindered in running the race that is set before us'; to speak particularly, we suffer from 'blindness of heart; from pride, vain-glory, and hypocrisy; from envy, hatred, and malice, and all uncharitableness'. 'We have erred and strayed from thy ways like lost sheep, We have followed too much the devices and desires of our own hearts, We have offended against thy holy laws, We have left undone those things which we ought to have done, And we have done

---

[1] See Prayers and Thanksgivings; Form of the Making of Deacons; Form of the Solemnization of Matrimony; Collect for St Michael and all Angels; Form of Matrimony.

323   21-2

those things which we ought not to have done, And there is no health in us.'[1]

Men by nature cannot achieve Heaven: 'that which by nature they cannot have'. For 'none can enter into the kingdom of God, except he be regenerate and born anew'. Indeed, what can we achieve by nature? We 'have no power of ourselves to help ourselves'; 'through the weakness of our mortal nature we can do no good thing without thee'.[2]

We can do no good thing without grace. 'Thou art not able to do these things of thyself, nor to walk in the commandments of God, and to serve him, without his special grace; which thou must learn at all times to call for by diligent prayer.' The Collects ask for grace: or for 'thy holy inspiration', 'the abundance of thy mercy', 'the grace of thy Holy Spirit', 'the healthful Spirit of thy grace': 'Grant that we being regenerate, and made thy children by adoption and grace, may daily be renewed by the Holy Spirit.' The lines cross, in a great exchange in and to the divine glory: 'The grace of our Lord Jesus Christ, and the love of God, and the fellowship of the Holy Ghost.'[3]

Grace is 'bountiful' and in 'abundance'. It comes to 'strengthen' us; to 'prevent and follow us'; to 'bless and keep' us; to 'direct, sanctify, and govern'. The imagery is varied: 'bright beams of light', a 'true circumcision of the Spirit', 'the right hand of thy Majesty'; it is 'strength and protection', 'comfort', a force to 'Cleanse the thoughts of our hearts', 'to inspire continually... with the spirit of truth', 'to assist us'; it is—most poetically—a 'continual dew'.[4]

[1] See Order of Private Baptism; Order for the Burial of the Dead; Order for the Visitation of the Sick; Order of Baptism for those of Riper Years; Collect for Fourth Sunday in Advent; the Litany; General Confession (Morning and Evening Prayer).

[2] See Order of Baptism for those of Riper Years; Order of Publik Baptism; Collect for Second Sunday in Lent; Collect for First Sunday after Trinity.

[3] See the Catechism; Collect for Fifth Sunday after Easter; Collect for Twelfth Sunday after Trinity; the Litany; Prayer for Clergy and People (Morning and Evening Prayer); Collect for Sunday after Christmas Day; the Blessing (Morning and Evening Prayer).

[4] See Collect for Fourth Sunday in Advent; Collect for Twelfth Sunday after Trinity; Collect for Innocents' Day; Collect for Seventeenth Sunday after Trinity; the Litany;

Grace is given to man 'truly to believe'; 'that the new man may be raised up in him'; 'that all carnal affections may die in him, and that all things belonging to the Spirit may live and grow in him'; that 'we may think those things that be good', 'do always such things as be rightful', and 'have a right judgement in all things': and that 'we may worship him, serve him, and obey him'. Grace is necessary to 'give us true repentance'; and, that given, 'to amend our lives according to thy holy Word', 'the words, which we have heard this day with our outward ears' being 'through thy grace...so grafted inwardly in our hearts, that they may bring forth in us the fruit of good living'. Thus, 'serving him duly in our vocation with thanksgiving', we ask that 'grace may always prevent and follow us, and make us continually to be given to all good works'. That being granted, we have 'such strength and protection, as may support us in all dangers, and carry us through all temptations'. This strength is granted through 'the means of grace': the sacraments being, in the phrase of John Overall, 'an outward and visible sign of an inward and spiritual grace'.[1]

After matins and evensong, in the absolution, comes this petition: 'Let us beseech him to grant us true repentance and his Holy Spirit, that those things may please him which we do at this present, and that the rest of our life hereafter may be pure and holy; so that at the last we may come to his eternal joy.'[2]

Such is the liturgical setting of the relationship of Nature, Man and God. But we do not look to a liturgy for strictly detailed

Order of the Ministration of Holy Communion (Collect after Offertory); Collect for St John the Evangelist's Day; Collect for the Circumcision of Christ; Collect for Third Sunday in Lent; Collect for Fourth Sunday after the Epiphany; Collect for Fourth Sunday in Lent; Order of the Ministration of Holy Communion (First Collect: Prayer for Church: Collect before Gloria); Prayer for Clergy and People (Morning and Evening Prayer).

[1] See Collect for St Bartholomew the Apostle; Order of Publick Baptism; Collect for Fifth Sunday after Easter; Collect for Ninth Sunday after Trinity; Collect for Whitsunday; the Catechism; the Litany; Order of the Ministration of Holy Communion; a Commination; Collect for Seventeenth Sunday after Trinity; Collect for Fourth Sunday after Epiphany; Prayers and Thanksgivings (General Thanksgiving); the Catechism.

[2] See Absolution (Morning and Evening Prayer).

doctrine. In order to determine what was the teaching of the Church of England on the precise points debated in Cambridge in the 1590's—or, perhaps more important, to determine what it was not—it is necessary to consider in detail certain of the Articles of Religion.

In 1551 Cranmer began to prepare doctrinal articles 'for the abolishing of conflicting opinions, and the establishing of agreement in true religion'.[1] These articles, forty-two in number, were drawn up during 1552 and printed in May 1553. The King died within a month, and orders for assent to the articles were abortive. Nine years later, in 1562, Parker worked over the articles: they were further revised by Convocation, reduced to thirty-nine, printed in 1563, and further affirmed by Convocation and confirmed by Parliament in 1571.

II

Article IX, 'Of Original or Birth-sin', defined Original Sin in the following way:

it is the fault and corruption of the nature of every man, that naturally is engendered of the offspring of Adam; whereby man is very far gone from original righteousness,[2] and is of his own nature inclined[3] to evil.... And this infection of nature doth remain, yea in them that are regenerated.[4]... And although there is no condemnation for them that believe and are baptized, yet the Apostle doth confess, that concupiscence and lust hath of itself the nature of sin.

That the phrase 'very far gone from original righteousness' seemed inadequate to the Calvinists was shown in 1647, in the Westminster Confession of Faith, which declared that man had been 'deprived of original righteousness'[5] and was 'wholly

---

[1] J. Lamb, *Historical Account of the Thirty-nine Articles*, 3.
[2] Cranmer had written: 'the former righteousness which he had at his creation'.
[3] Cranmer: 'given'.
[4] Cranmer: 'baptized'.
[5] 'Justitia...originali...exciderunt'; as opposed to 'longissime distet'. P. Schaff, *The Creeds of the Evangelical Protestant Churches*, 615.

defiled',[1] 'utterly indisposed, disabled and made opposite to all good'.[2] Now, the Church of England had naturally insisted that 'all is imperfect that is within us',[3] that the image of God in man has been 'darkened' and the judgement 'corrupted',[4] that 'by reason of the frailty of our nature we cannot always stand upright'.[5] In the words of Article X, 'The condition of man after the fall of Adam is such, that he cannot turn and prepare himself, by his own natural strength and good works, to faith, and calling upon God': that being a phrase added, when the forty-two Articles became thirty-nine, to Cranmer's original words: 'we have no power to do good works pleasant and acceptable to God, without the grace of God by Christ preventing us, that we may have a good will, and working with us [Cranmer's wording had been 'in us'] when we have that good will'. *Gratia co-operans*, then; even when the statement of the early 1550's that God 'enforceth not the will' (in the original Article X of the forty-two) was dropped in the early 1560's. There are good things of nature as well as of grace, though 'whatsoever good thing is in us, of grace, of nature, of fortune, is of God only'.[6] And it was unnecessary for the *Ecclesia Anglicana* uncritically to follow Calvin in the implicit doctrinal assumptions of his portrait of the state of man as (in the Augustinian image) an exile.[7] For Calvin the image of God in man is 'so corrupted that all that remaineth is but ugly deformity', 'so corrupted and almost defaced, that nothing remaineth since that ruin, but disordered, mangled and filthily spotted'.[8] When this imaginative insight into the human condition was translated into text-book dogmatics, the result was

---

[1] 'Penitus contaminati'. *Ibid.*   [2] *Ibid.*

[3] Cranmer's Homily of Salvation, *Book of Homilies* (S.P.C.K. ed.), 29.

[4] 1552 Catechism; in J. Ketley (ed.), *Liturgies etc. in the reign of Edward VI* (Parker Society, 1844), 499. Alexander Nowell took over these phrases for his later Catechism (ed. G. E. Corrie, Parker Society, 1853), 139.

[5] Collect for Fourth Sunday after Epiphany.

[6] Sermon for Rogation, *Homilies*, 507.

[7] *Institutes*, 2/2/12; tr. Norton (1611 ed.), 116.

[8] *Institutes*, 1/15/4; tr. Norton, 77–8.

not the Thirty-nine Articles but the Westminster Confession: and there was almost a century of dispute and definition between them. Man, said the Anglican Article, 'is of his own nature inclined to evil'. 'Inclined' was Parker's phrase: Cranmer had written 'given'. The Westminster Confession had 'wholly inclined'.[1]

'Concupiscence...hath of itself the nature of sin': 'rationem peccati'. This was a reference to the remarks on *concupiscentia* by the Council of Trent in 1546. In Baptism, said the Tridentine Fathers, 'the whole of that which has the true and proper nature of sin' is 'taken away'.[2] There remains 'concupiscence': this is 'an incentive to [*fomes*] sin', it is 'of sin and inclines to sin' (*ex peccato est, et ad peccatum inclinat*); but it is not 'truly and properly [*vere et proprie*] sin in those born again'.

Calvin, commenting on this interpretation, wrote that those theologians who define original sin as concupiscence 'have used a word not very far from the matter, if this were added which is not granted by the most part, that whatsoever is in man, even from the understanding to the will, from the soul to the flesh, is corrupted and stuffed full with this concupiscence: or, to end it, shortlier, that whole man is of himself nothing else but concupiscence'.[3] Bullinger agreed that it was permissible to say that 'concupiscence remaineth in them that are baptized'; so long as it was emphasized that concupiscence 'is sin, and therefore that sin remaineth in them that are baptized'. After baptism, continued Bullinger, the sin is not 'taken away'; but it is 'not imputed' to us.[4] ('So', he concluded, 'did St Augustine resolve this knot.')

The Westminster Confession was to assert what the Council of Trent had denied: that concupiscence is 'truly and properly sin'.[5] Cranmer and Parker had trodden carefully between the

---

[1] 'Ad malum omne proclives penitus'; Schaff, *Creeds of Ev. Prot. Churches*, 615.
[2] Fifth decree on original sin; tr. J. Waterhouse, *Canons and Decrees of the Council of Trent* (1848).   [3] *Institutes*, 2/1/8; tr. Norton, 108.
[4] H. Bullinger, *Decades*, II, 418 (Third Decade).
[5] Schaff, *Creeds of the Ev. Prot. Churches*, 616.

possible extremes, resolving the knot by moderation. Concupiscence in the Anglican Articles, as against Trent, has 'the nature of sin': but it is not said to be 'truly and properly sin'.

The phrase 'have the nature of sin' was also used in Article XIII to describe 'works done before the grace of Christ and the inspiration of his Spirit'. Here again was a balancing on razor edges. Cranmer neatly side-tracked the burning issue of the sinfulness of works before justification (debated by Bucer and John Young in the Cambridge of 1550) by altering the draft phrase 'works before justification' to the final 'works before grace.'[1] The Council of Trent condemned the proposition that works before justification were 'truly sins': but what of works before the inspiration of the Holy Spirit? The precision tools of the Tridentine Fathers cannot bite the English material here. And the precision of the Westminster Confession was also to contrast with the Anglican Article; works done by the unregenerate, it was asserted in 1647, do not merely have the nature of sin; they are sinful—'sunt peccata'.[2] That was clear enough. But it was not the doctrine of Cranmer and Parker.

III

Article XVI of the thirty-nine ('Of Sin after Baptism') must now be considered. The Article runs: 'Not every deadly sin willingly committed after baptism is sin against the Holy Ghost, and unpardonable. Wherefore the grant of repentance is not to be denied to such as fall into sin after baptism. After we have received the Holy Ghost, we may depart from grace given, and fall into sin, and by the grace of God we may arise again, and amend our lives.' There were two Calvinist objections to this Article. First—argued a Puritan petition of 1584—does not the phrase 'deadly sin' 'savour of that popish distinction of sin,

---

[1] E. C. Gibson, *The Thirty-nine Articles*, 418. H. E. Symonds, *The Council of Trent and Anglican Formularies* (1933), 27, made much of this point.

[2] Schaff, *Creeds of the Ev. Prot. Churches*, 636.

deadly and venial'? Secondly, the Puritans of 1584 asked 'whether it be not dangerous to say: a man may fall from grace'.[1] This second objection had been previously voiced in the Second Admonition to Parliament in 1572: 'the Book of the Articles of Christian religion speaketh very dangerously of falling from grace'.[2]

The Council of Trent declared that those who commit deadly sins 'are separated from the grace of Christ'.[3] (Just as the Homily, 'How dangerous a thing it is to fall from God', had made clear that 'as by pride and sin we go from God, so shall God, and all goodness with him, go from us';[4] that 'as we forsake God so shall he ever forsake us'[5]—'he will take away from us all his aid and assistance'.[6]) Recovery, in Tridentine theology, is by means of the sacrament of penance. One of the basic Calvinist assertions, on the other hand, in the words of the Westminster Confession, was: 'They whom God hath accepted in his beloved, effectually called and sanctified by his Spirit, can neither totally nor finally fall away from the state of grace.'[7] This statement seems at variance with the letter of the Anglican Article—though William Whitaker, as we have seen, agreed that the elect may 'depart from grace' (*recedere*), but emphasized that they cannot 'fall from it'[8] (*excidere*). This complicated question of the fall from grace, which was one of the points at issue in the Arminian controversy in Holland at the beginning of the seventeenth century, was raised in Cambridge by William Barrett in 1595. The authorities, not having done their homework on the question, were caught with their briefs unprepared. Whitgift thought that faith may be lost totally, but not finally.[9] Lancelot Andrewes confessed that 'he was in doubt on the subject' of a total (as distinct from a final) fall, whether 'the Holy Spirit may for a time be taken away or

[1] Peel, *Second Part of a Register*, I, 197.   [2] Frere and Douglas, *Puritan Manifestos*, 118.
[3] Chapter xv of the decree of justification.
[4] *Homilies*, 81.   [5] *Ibid.* 84.   [6] *Ibid.* 86.
[7] Schaff, *Creeds of the Ev. Prot. Churches*, 636.   [8] Whitaker, *Cygnea Cantio*, 20.
[9] Trinity College, Cambridge, MS. B/14/9, p. 3. Letter of June 1595.

extinguished'.[1] John Overall, at the Hampton Court Conference, was to argue that the elect, certainly, can never fall away finally or totally; but, through sin, they could become subject to damnation, and their renewal depended on repentance.[2] In emphasizing this point Overall brought the issue back to its true centre. We can 'depart from grace'; whether we can fall completely from it, totally or finally, is debatable; but the fact to be emphasized about Article XVI is the importance it gave to repentance (as Trent gave to penance) as a condition of Christian assurance.

It is now necessary to consider the question of assurance. Christian confidence, of course, is a New Testament virtue. 'I am persuaded', said Paul, that nothing 'shall be able to separate us from the love of God.' The Authorized Version followed the Geneva Bible in using 'I am persuaded'[3] as the translation of πέπεισμαι. The Vulgate translation of the Greek was 'certus sum'; the word 'certus' being also used as a rendering of βέβαιος, which was translated as 'sure' in the Geneva and Authorized versions.[4] So the Christian can at the most be *certus* of his calling: persuaded, assured, sure. Paul gave him a 'full assurance of faith'[5] (*plenitudo fidei*) and a 'full assurance of hope' (*expletio spei*):[6] the Greek word for the Genevan and Authorized 'full assurance' here is πληροφορία; plerophoria. But in spite of this persuasion and assurance the Christian must work out his salvation in fear and trembling. His status can never be one of safety. The word ἀσφάλεια, which the Vulgate translates as *securitas* and the Genevan and Authorized versions as 'safety', is only once used by Paul—and then to warn

---

[1] *Articuli Lambethani* (1651), 29. Opinion of 1596.

[2] Barlow's account of the conference; in E. Cardwell, *History of Conferences*, 186.

[3] Romans viii. 38; cf. Romans xv. 14 and II Timothy i. 12. For II Tim. i. 5 the Geneva Bible had 'assured', the A.V. 'persuaded'.

[4] II Peter i. 10. βέβαιος is usually rendered *firmus*, 'sure'; Rom. iv. 16; II Pet. i. 19; Heb. iii. 14—A.V. 'stedfast'.

[5] Heb. x. 22. The Revised Version altered 'full assurance' to 'fulness'. Mgr. Knox has 'full assurance'.

[6] Heb. vi. 11. Knox has 'fulfilment'.

us of its dangers: 'For when they shall say, Peace and safety; then sudden destruction cometh upon them.'[1] And the adjective *securus* is not once used in the New Testament. As the Tridentine Fathers declared in 1547, with regard to final perseverance: 'let no one herein promise himself anything as certain with an absolute certainty [*certi absoluta certitudine*]; though all ought to place and repose a most firm hope in God's help'.[2] An assurance of hope, then; and, as St Peter made clear, to make 'calling and election sure' (*certus*) we must have 'diligence'.[3] 'The trial of all these things', the Book of Homilies stated, 'is a very godly and Christian life':[4] 'all they that be sorry and truly repentant and will therewithal stick to God's mercy, they may be *sure* they shall obtain mercy'.[5] Christian men, 'if they truly repent them of their sins, and die in perfect faith', may 'put their whole trust and confidence' in the death of Christ:[6] on these conditions they may, in the words of Cranmer, have 'a sure trust and confidence in God's merciful promises to be saved'.[7] The insistence of the Anglican Fathers that, in the life of the individual Christian, the assurance of faith and hope is dependent upon true repentance and amendment of life was nowhere more clearly emphasized than in the debates about predestination among the imprisoned prelates of 1554. One of them declared himself to be 'most sure and certain of my salvation'; and Bishop Ridley gently pointed out that, 'although the hope of his mercy is my sheet anchor of eternal salvation, yet I am persuaded, that whosoever wittingly neglecteth and regardeth not to clear his conscience, he cannot have peace with God, nor a lively faith in his mercy'.[8] Amongst those who sided with the ex-Master of Pembroke here was an ex-Fellow of Pembroke, John Bradford: who had been taught by Bucer and who had taught John Whitgift.

[1] I Thess. v. 3.
[2] Decree of justification, chapter XIII.   [3] II Pet. i. 10.
[4] *Homilies*, 43.   [5] *Ibid.* 90. My italics.
[6] *Ibid.* 357.   [7] *Ibid.* 30.
[8] R. Laurence, *Documents relative to the Predestinarian Controversy under Mary*, xl.

Of course, as every pastor is aware, one of the great Christian temptations is false doubt. He is a lucky pilgrim whose way does not pass through the *selva oscura*. Richard Hooker, preaching in 1585, comforted his troubled hearers by insisting that the faith of them 'which are of God', 'when it is at the strongest, is but weak; yet even then when it is at the weakest, so strong, that utterly it never faileth'.[1]

Better it is sometimes to go down into the pit with him, who, beholding darkness, and bewailing the loss of inward joy and consolation, crieth from the bottom of the lowest hell, 'My God, my God, why hast thou forsaken me?' than continually to walk arm-in-arm with angels, to sit as it were in Abraham's bosom, and to have no thought, no cogitation, but 'I thank my God it is not with me as it is with other men'. No, God will have them that shall walk in light to feel now and then what it is to sit in the shadow of death. A grieved spirit therefore is no argument of a faithless mind.[2]

For we have the word of the promise of God to his people: 'I will not leave thee nor forsake thee.' And 'upon this the simplicity of faith resteth, and it is not afraid of famine'.[3] Christ had 'prayed for thee that thy faith fail not':[4] and thus, 'No man's condition is so *sure* as ours: the prayer of Christ is more than sufficient both to strengthen us, be we never so weak; and to overthrow all adversary power, be it never so strong and potent.'[5] Hooker ended his sermon by quoting St Paul: I am persuaded that nothing can separate us from the love of God; but be ye not slothful—show 'diligence to the full assurance of hope unto the end'.[6] Such 'assurance of my hope I will labour to keep as a jewel unto the end; and by labour, through the gracious mediation of his prayer, I shall keep it'.[7]

---

[1] R. Hooker, *Works*, III, 473–4.   [2] *Ibid.* 474–5.

[3] *Ibid.* 477.

[4] Luke xxii. 32. The question whether this prayer was for Peter alone, or for all the disciples, or for all the elect, was to be much debated in Cambridge in 1595.

[5] Hooker, *Works*, III, 480. My italic.   [6] Heb. vi. 11.

[7] Hooker, *Works*, III, 481.

That was and is the answer to false doubt. But there is another and greater, because less subtle, Christian temptation—false security. No one, wrote Bullinger, is saved 'as it were of necessity, that, do what they will against the word of Christ and commit they never so heinous offences, they cannot possibly choose but be saved'.[1] Hooker also was concerned to stress that 'such is our weak and wavering nature, we have no sooner received grace, but we are ready to fall from it';[2] and therefore 'the strongest in faith that liveth upon the earth, hath always need to labour, and strive, and pray, that his assurance concerning heavenly and spiritual things may grow'.[3] Security, St Thomas said, engenders negligence.[4] That is why, he continued, God does not reveal to us whether we are predestined to life or not; though predestination may be revealed to some by special privilege. The Anglican Article XVII also declared that God's decree of election is by a 'counsel secret to us'. Uncertainty is perhaps the most under-rated of Christian virtues: 'Wherefore let him that thinketh he standeth take heed lest he fall.'[5] At the Hampton Court Conference of 1604 James I pointed out with his usual perceptive and informed good sense (which has earned him the reputation of pedantry at the hands of the imperceptive) that a theology of 'the necessary certainty of standing and persisting in grace' entails a 'desperate presumption'.[6] Bancroft had taken 'occasion to signify unto his Majesty, how very many in these days, neglecting holiness of life, presumed too much of persisting of grace, laying all their religion upon predestination. If I shall be saved, I shall be saved.'[7] Cranmer had been equally aware, in the reign of Henry VIII, of the pastoral problems which might be involved in the tendency to emphasize assurance of election or reprobation.

[1] *Decades* (ed. Parker Society), III, 32 (Fourth Decade).
[2] Hooker, *Works*, III, 476.
[3] *Ibid.* 577 (answer to Travers).
[4] I, Q. 23 (Of predestination), art. I; ed. Fairweather, *Nature and Grace*, 103.
[5] I Corinthians x. 12.
[6] Barlow's account, in Cardwell, *History of Conferences*, 181.
[7] *Ibid.* 180.

Such a tendency would encourage dissoluteness of life : in fact, if we have faith in our election, then the value of that faith is the impetus it gives to good works; and it should both spring from, and lead to, repentance.[1]

It was William Barrett's point in Cambridge in 1595 that the Calvinist exegesis of election, justifying faith, and Christian assurance entailed a 'desperate presumption'; in this criticism he was supported by Peter Baro, Lancelot Andrewes and John Overall; and also by John Whitgift. Whitaker and his followers, as we have seen, spoke in 1595 of the Christian's 'spiritual security'. 'He which hath a true justifying faith... is assured of his salvation, and that by the ground and certainty of that justifying faith.'[2] Not only *certus*, persuaded, sure; but also *securus*: 'fidei ipsius certitudine, certos esse et securos'.[3]

Lancelot Andrewes, chaplain to Whitgift and the Queen, preaching before the court in 1594,[4] had dwelt, as St Paul had dwelt, on the dangers of 'security'. Barrett, within the year, made the same point in Cambridge. *Securitas*, he said, springs from impiety and pride; no one can be *securus* in salvation by the certainty of faith.[5] Saravia, another chaplain to Whitgift, supported Barrett in his distinction between *securitas* and *certitudo*:[6] the latter was a New Testament word; the former was not. And Whitgift agreed with him: 'security', the Archbishop wrote in June 1595, 'is never taken in good part, neither doth the scripture so use it'.[7]

The Christian, then, may have a confidence, a 'certainty', if you wish. But of what order is this certainty? Can we, in the Tridentine phrase, be 'certain with an absolute certainty'? As

---

[1] *Reformatio Legum Ecclesiasticarum* (published 1571); ed. Cardwell, 21–2.
[2] Letter of Whitaker and the heads, 7 July 1595. Trinity MS. B/14/9, p. 51.
[3] Barrett's recantation in Strype, *Whitgift*, III, 317.
[4] Andrewes, *Sermons*, II, 72.
[5] Barrett's recantation, in Strype, *Whitgift*, III, 317.
[6] Saravia's censure of Barrett's recantation is in Trinity MS. B/14/9, pp. 169–83; printed in Strype, *Whitgift*, III, 321–37.
[7] Trinity MS. B/14/9, p. 3.

certain as we are, for instance, of the truths of the Christian revelation in the Creed? Barrett argued that certainty of salvation could not be of that order. Here again Whitgift saw his point of view.[1] And in the Lambeth Articles of November 1595 the point was to be made that a Christian may be *certus* of salvation; not by *certitudo fidei* (the words of Whitaker's original draft[2]); but, in the Pauline phrase, by *plerophoria fidei*.

Whitgift went beyond the Calvinist exegesis to the mind of Paul.

IV

Finally, it is necessary to grasp the nettle of Article XVII: 'Of Predestination and Election'. 'Predestination to Life', wrote Cranmer, 'is the everlasting purpose of God, whereby (before the foundations of the world were laid) he hath constantly decreed by his counsel secret to us, to deliver from curse and damnation those whom he hath chosen in Christ out of mankind.' Those so delivered,

they which be endued with so excellent a benefit of God be called according to God's purpose by his Spirit working in due season: they through Grace obey the calling: they be justified freely: they be made sons of God by adoption: they be made like the image of his only-begotten Son Jesus Christ: they walk religiously in good works, and at length, by God's mercy, they attain to everlasting felicity.

Then, in typical fashion, the pastoral importance of the dogma is described. A 'godly consideration' of 'our election in Christ' is 'full of sweet, pleasant, and unspeakable comfort to godly persons': 'it doth greatly establish and confirm their faith of eternal salvation to be enjoyed through Christ, as because it doth fervently kindle their love towards God'. It draws up our mind to 'high and heavenly things'; and 'in our doings, that Will of

---

[1] Trinity MS. B/14/9, pp. 13–14. 30 September 1595.
[2] Whitaker's draft articles were printed in *Articuli Lambethani* (1651).

God is to be followed, which we have expressly declared unto us
in the Word of God'. Finally, 'we must receive God's promises
in such wise, as they be generally set forth to us in holy Scripture'.

It is convenient first to consider that last phrase. 'Generally'
(*generaliter*) means to all men, universally. In other words, as
Bullinger made clear, 'Christ and the preaching of Christ his
grace declared in the gospel doth belong unto all':[1] 'The holy
gospel of Christ doth generally preach to the whole world the
grace of God, the remission of sins, and life everlasting.'[2] The
word 'generally' was to be played upon by Hooker and Overall,[3]
as well as by Baro. God, argued Hooker in 1599, has a 'general
will', a 'general inclination', that 'all men may enjoy the full
perfection of that happiness which is...their end':[4] the signs of
this general will of God are 'all promises which he maketh in
holy Scripture'. Three years before, Baro had quoted the concluding phrase of Article XVII in support of his point that the
will of God was to save all men, and Christ died for all men.[5]
He also quoted a phrase from Article XXXI: 'The offering of
Christ...for all the sins of the whole world.' Now, the Calvinists
objected to the doctrine of Universal Redemption (to use the
text-book phrase). The Puritans in 1572, for example, had
regretted the fact that 'we pray in the Litany, that all men may
be saved'.[6] Whitgift, at the time, specifically replied to this
objection in these words:

We do so indeed; and what can you allege why we should not do so?
St Paul (I Tim. ii) saith 'I exhort therefore, that, first of all, supplica-
tions, prayers, intercessions, and giving of thanks, be made for all men
&c.' And adding the reason he saith, 'For this is good and acceptable

---

[1] *Decades* (ed. Parker Society), III, 32 (Fourth Decade).
[2] *Ibid.* 33.
[3] Overall, 'Sententia de praedestinatione' (*c.* 1610), University Library, Cambridge,
MSS. Vol. Gg/1/29, fol. 10b; printed in 1651, *Articuli Lambethani*, 42.
[4] 'Answer to a Christian letter', in R. Bayne's edition of *Ecclesiastical Polity, Book V*,
671–2.
[5] Baro to Burleigh, Feb. 1595/6. Lansdowne MSS. vol. LXXX, no. 69.
[6] Frere and Douglas, *Puritan Manifestos*, 144.

22   337   PR

in the sight of God our Saviour, who will that all men shall be saved, and come unto the knowledge of the truth'. The apostle doth here will us in plain words to pray for all men, even that they might be saved.[1]

The Calvinists were not convinced. In the Westminster Confession a phrase such as 'God's promises generally set forth' was conspicuous, so to say, by its absence.

The shifting emphasis of Reformed theology between 1530 and 1560 is demonstrated by the fact that there was no mention of election in the Lutheran Augsburg Confession of 1530, the Genevan Confession of 1536, or the Swiss Confession of 1536; yet articles concerning it were to be central in the French Confession of 1559, the Scotch Confession in 1560, and the Belgic Confession of 1561. Disputes about election began in England in the second part of the reign of Edward VI. John ab Ulmis wrote from Oxford in April 1550 about the disagreement on the subject among English theologians,[2] and in September 1552 the Dean of Chichester, Bartholomew Traheron, chid Bullinger for his leanings towards the moderate views of Melanchthon on the matter: 'the greater number among us, of whom I own myself to be one, embrace the opinion of John Calvin as being perspicuous, and most agreeable to holy scripture'.[3] Not all the dignitaries of the Edwardine Church agreed with the former Cambridge Franciscan. The Italian Bernardino Ochino, prebendary of Canterbury, for example, preached a notable series of anti-Calvinist sermons on the subject, translated in 1550 and reprinted in 1570. The Frenchman Peter Alexander also lectured on predestination in Canterbury; Parker kept the manuscript of his lectures, which is now in the library of Corpus.[4] But the most famous Predestinarian debate of the 1550's was conducted in prison in 1554. The leading spirit was John Bradford of Pembroke.

[1] Whitgift, *Works*, III, 383–4.
[2] *Original Letters relative to the English Reformation* (Parker Society), II, 406.
[3] *Ibid.* I, 325.
[4] Corpus Christi College Library MSS. vol. 115.

This debate[1] was concerned with election, and not in detail with reprobation; and the subject arose in discussion of the problem of free will. Bradford emphasized that 'faith of God's election...is of all things which God requireth of us, not only most principal, but also the whole sum'.[2] There has always been 'with God, even before the world was máde, an election in Christ of all those that shall be saved'.[3] Election in Christ; and Christ died for all men— 'the Lord himself would have all men saved, and damnation cometh of ourselves'.[4] For Bradford, 'it is unseemly for us to seek out' the causes of reprobation.[5] But, if we persist in doing so, then it becomes clear that the cause of reprobation is God's foreknowledge of our sin: 'God, foreseeing their condemnation through their own sin.' Thus the reprobate 'have cause to lament their own wilfulness, sin and contemning of Christ, which is the cause of their reprobation'.[6] John Bradford made quite clear then, in the shadow of martyrdom in 1554, that 'Election is not to be looked on, but in Christ, nor reprobation but in sin'.[7]

Calvin himself had been careful to link election, the ultimate immutable and sovereign decree of God, to the saving death of Christ. 'Christ therefore is the mirror, in which we both must, and without deceit may behold our election',[8] he wrote; Bullinger used the same image.[9] But one of the dangers of 'Calvinism' was that emphasis upon the eternal and arbitrary act of God's will tended to overshadow the saving death of Christ. Parker, by adding the words 'in Christ' to the phrase of the 1552 Articles ('those whom he hath chosen out of mankind'), made clear that any such emphasis was false. This, together with the fact stated in Article IX, that 'there is no condemnation for them that believe

---

[1] Strype, *Cranmer*, I, 503–5 and *Memorials*, VI, 325–34; R. Laurence, *Documents relating to the Predestinarian Controversy*; Bradford's sermons on the subject were printed in 1562.
[2] Bradford, *Sermons*, 307; 'Defence of election'.
[3] *Ibid.* 211: 'Of election and free will.'   [4] Laurence, *Documents*, ix.
[5] *Ibid.* 25.   [6] Bradford, *Sermons*, 219.
[7] *Ibid.* 220.
[8] *Institutes*, 3/24/5; tr. Norton (1611 ed.), 474.
[9] Second Helvetic Confession, 1566; Schaff, *Creeds of the Ev. Prot. Churches*, 253.

and are baptized' (baptism being, in the words of Article XXVII, a visible sign and seal of 'our adoption to be the sons of God'), left open the way for an insistence on faith and repentance as conditions of election. The Homilies had insisted on the primacy of faith; and so did Bullinger. 'The end of predestination', said Bullinger, 'is Christ': 'For God hath ordained and decreed to save all, how many soever have communion and fellowship with Christ...; and to destroy or condemn all, how many soever have no part in the communion or fellowship of Christ.'[1] Bullinger here quoted John iii. 36: 'He that believeth on the Son hath everlasting life: and he that believeth not the Son shall not see life.' This text was also to be quoted in the first Arminian Article of 1610. Bullinger concluded the passage by indicating the pastoral dangers of overmuch disputation on matters of election: 'Touching these points some have diversely disputed; and many verily, curiously and contentiously enough; and in such sort surely, that not only the salvation of souls, but the glory of God also, with the simple sort is endangered.'[2] The debates in Cambridge in 1595 demonstrated that the dangers were not confined to 'the simple sort'.

But the most important fact about Article XVII is that there is no mention of a specific decree of reprobation. Here the article significantly contrasts with the Confession of Westminster: 'The rest of mankind God was pleased, according to the unsearchable counsel of his own will, whereby he extendeth or withholdeth mercy as he pleaseth, for the glory of his sovereign power over his creatures, to pass by, and to ordain them to dishonour and wrath for their sin, to the praise of his glorious justice.'[3] We are faced with Calvin's 'terrible decree':[4] God's condemnation 'even of little children in the mother's womb',[5] 'for no other reason but

---

[1] *Decades* (ed. Parker Society), III, 186 (Fourth Decade).   [2] *Ibid.* 185.
[3] Schaff, *Creeds of the Ev. Prot. Churches*, 610.
[4] *Institutes*, 3/23/7; tr. Norton, 466.
[5] 'Confessio fidei Gallicana', drawn up by Calvin in 1559. Schaff, *Creeds of the Ev. Prot. Churches*, 366.

because he saw that thereby the glory of his name should be worthily set forth'.[1] Calvin's 'Articles Concerning Predestination',[2] which most probably date from the last decade of his life— that is, the years before 1564, the years when the English Articles of Religion were prepared—were the most concise expression of his views. To demonstrate the moderation of the English Article XVII it is only necessary to compare it with a statement such as this: 'While the reprobate are the vessels of the just wrath of God, and the elect vessels of his compassion, the ground of the distinction is to be sought in the pure will of God alone, which is the supreme rule of justice.' Or to examine the objections to the article which were made by the Calvinists. A Puritan protest of 1584 asked:

> Whether the 17th article, speaking of election, be well put down, that maketh no mention of reprobation, seeing Paul, speaking of the one, speaketh of the other? And whether the doctrine of predestination of itself is dangerous, and may cause a dangerous downfall to any, as is put down in the article?[3]

To sum up. The Edwardian tradition, exemplified by John Bradford, said first that it is unseemly for men to seek out the causes of reprobation; and secondly, that in so far as there is a cause known to us, it must be 'sin and contemning of Christ'. In a world in which, as the Homilies argued, God 'made every man's death uncertain',[4] the reprobate are 'all them that in this world be unfaithful unto God and uncharitable unto their neighbours, so dying without repentance and hope of God's mercy'.[5] Barrett and Baro fell foul of the Cambridge Calvinists in 1595 for maintaining these very points. But Whitgift, the pupil of Bradford, supported them in their teaching on reprobation; as he also supported Andrewes, who had said in the

---

[1] *Institutes*, 3/23/8; tr. Norton, 467.
[2] In Calvin, *Theological Treatises*, 178–80.
[3] Peel, *Second Part of a Register*, I, 197.
[4] *Homilies*, 91. [5] *Ibid.* 94.

Cambridge of the 1580's that 'we are not curiously to enquire and search out God's secret will touching reprobation or election'.[1] 'As His mercies be infinite', Whitgift had written in the 1570's, 'so be His judgements unsearchable.'[2] This attitude of Bradford and Whitgift and Andrewes might perhaps appropriately be called the Pembroke contribution to English theology.

V

During the reign of Elizabeth there were those who realized that disputes concerning the mystery of predestination might do more harm than good.[3] But many divines found it difficult to avoid inordinate dogmatism in these high and weighty matters, to tread the mean path between the extremes noted by Calvin (in another connection): 'those things which the Lord hath laid up in secret, we may not search: those things which he hath brought openly abroad, we may not neglect'.[4] Others contrived, with care, to tread it. Lancelot Andrewes, writing in 1596, said that during the whole period of his ministry—that is, since 1580—he had refrained from preaching on the disputed points.[5] How easy to be lost in the 'wand'ring mazes' of the subjects debated by Milton's fallen angels:

> Of providence, foreknowledge, will and fate,
> Fix'd fate, free will, foreknowledge absolute.

In 'matters disputable' silence was the best policy. Better by far than to claim as revelation (and this was Whitgift's grievance against the Cambridge Calvinists of 1595) a mere opinion on 'a matter disputable and wherein learned men do and may dissent

---

[1] Andrewes, *Sermons*, v, 197. [2] *Works*, I, 189.

[3] See for instance the commentary on the 1552 Articles by a group of returned Marian exiles, Corpus Christi College MSS. vol. CXXI, no. 20, printed by R. W. Dixon, *History of the Church of England*, v, 108–15. Or, again, a petition of 1562; Strype, *Annals*, I, 495.

[4] *Institutes*, 3/21/4; tr. Norton, 451.

[5] Trinity College MS. B/14/9, p. 89. Printed in 1651, *Articuli Lambethani*, 21.

without impiety'.[1] The Anglican suspicion of claims to the infallible revelation of absolute truth has been most memorably expressed in the concluding pages of Shorthouse's *John Inglesant* (1881): '"If there be absolute truth revealed, there must be an inspired exponent of it, else from age to age it could not get itself revealed to mankind." "This is the Papist argument," said Mr Inglesant: "there is only one answer to it—Absolute truth is not revealed."'[2] And this suspicion was as operative a virtue against Geneva as against Rome.

Rome and Geneva may have called a spade a spade. The Church of England, like Gwendolen in *The Importance of Being Earnest*, is thankful that it has never seen a spade.

[1] Trinity MS. B/14/9, p. 3. Whitgift to heads, 19 June 1595.
[2] Chapter xxxix. Whether Shorthouse gave his Romance thirty-nine chapters by design or accident has never been discussed.

CHAPTER XV

THE QUESTION OF CHRISTIAN
ASSURANCE: WILLIAM BARRETT

I

ON 29 April 1595,[1] William Barrett, the young chaplain of
Gonville and Caius College,[2] preached to the university in Great
St Mary's. His sermon included the following assertions:[3] that
no one may be so bolstered up 'by certainty of faith' that 'he can
of necessity be assured [*securus*] of his salvation'; that Christ's
prayer 'for thee, that thy faith fail not' (Luke xxii. 32) did not
apply to the elect but only to Peter; that the gift of perseverance
is not certain but dependent upon our individual nature, and so
'certainty concerning the time to come' is both proud and most
wicked; that true justifying faith is not to be rigidly differentiated
from other forms of faith; that no one can with certainty know
that his sins have been forgiven him; and, 'against Calvin, Peter
Martyr and the rest', that the decree of reprobation was due to
God's foreknowledge of sin: 'Sin is the true, exclusive and first
cause of reprobation.' Barrett rounded off his sermon with a full-
blooded attack on Calvin. The congregation was stunned by this
extraordinary and daring performance. Here was a man, protested
the senior Calvinists of the university, not yet turned thirty-five,
who this afternoon

laboured to prove that justifying faith may finally decay and be lost,
and consequently did maintain and teach the popish doctrine of doubt-

---

[1] The date was given in a summary of the case now in the University Archives,
Registry Guard Books, vol. 6 (i), no. 39, fol. 11.

[2] Barrett had matriculated from Trinity in 1580.

[3] This summary of his points is taken from his Retractation (10 May), in University
Archives, Registry Guard Books, vol. 6 (i), no. 33; printed Strype, *Whitgift*, III, 317–19;
tr. Fuller, *History of Cambridge*, 283–5.

fulness of our salvation, against the comfortable certainty of true faith taught and preached in this our Church ever since the first planting of the Gospel amongst us: with most bitter railing upon those worthy men Calvin, Peter Martyr, Beza, Zanchius, and others, to the great offence of the godly.[1]

It was altogether intolerable.

The Vice-Chancellor was John Duport of Jesus, who called Barrett before him for a private interview.[2] This meeting was not a success, and Duport, uncertain of what next to do, wrote for advice to Whitgift. The Archbishop, in reply, reminded the Vice-Chancellor of his prime duty to have new contentions appeased; he asked to be kept informed of developments, and promised that he would carefully think about the matter and write to Cambridge again.[3] While the Archbishop was musing at Lambeth, the routine machinery of the university was set in motion. But unfortunately for the prospects of moderation, Duport was away from Cambridge for the next week; and on 5 May, when Barrett was called before the Consistory Court, the presiding chairman was the deputy Vice-Chancellor—Robert Some.

During the week there were three long meetings of the court:[4] attended by Barwell of Christ's, Jegon of Corpus, Chaderton of Emmanuel, Goad of King's, Clayton of Magdalene, Preston of Trinity Hall, and—most decisively—by Tyndall of Queens' and Whitaker of St John's. Barrett was 'laboured with to be won from his errors, and to have made a quiet end'.[5] At last he was ordered to read a retractation, 'drawn up by them and given to him by Dr Some'.[6] Barrett asked Some whether this might be read not in Great St Mary's but in the Regent House.[7] Some refused.

[1] Trinity College MS. B/14/9, p. 23.
[2] *Ibid.* p. 38.   [3] *Ibid.* p. 1.
[4] The account of the trial in the Consistory, in the hand of Registrary Thomas Smith, is in University Archives, Registry Guard Books, vol. 6 (i), no. 29.
[5] Trinity College MS. B/14/9, p. 38.
[6] *Ibid.* p. 64.   [7] *Ibid.* p. 38.

And so on 10 May, nearly a fortnight after the offending sermon, Barrett officially recanted in the university church. (Later, much to Whitgift's annoyance, the recantation was printed and copies distributed.[1])

A twelve-day wonder, it might have seemed. But there were factors in the situation which, working together for mischief, made inevitable more than a storm in a tea-cup. The matter was taken up by the usual vociferous extremists; and by May 16 a petition had been whipped together complaining not only that the original sermon had been 'very corrupt, savouring of popish doctrine,...so strange and offensive, both to us, and all others of sound religion in our university, as we never heard the like preached in Cambridge, or elsewhere, since the beginning of her Majesty's most gracious reign'; but also that 'for his retractation (being done and read in very unreverent, profane and impudent manner) it rather added new offence, and grief of heart unto us, and many others, than any satisfaction'.[2] This petition was signed by nearly sixty dons (including eighteen from St John's).[3] Nine of the fifty-six had been petitioners for Francis Johnson in 1589— including the Johnians Henry Alvey, John Allenson, Abdias Ashton and Henry Briggs, and Thomas Harrison of Trinity. Other Fellows of St John's whose signatures were attached included Roger Morrell and Robert Hill. Fifteen Fellows of Trinity signed; five of Christ's, including John Smyth; four of Gonville and Caius, among them Stephen Perse; four from Emmanuel, including William Bedell; and three dons from Queen's, three from King's, two from Peterhouse, and even a young Fellow of Magdalene. The petitioners, it must be noted, had found no supporters on the Fellows' tables of the Clare of Thomas Byng, the Corpus of John Jegon, the Jesus of Duport, the St Catharine's of Edmund Hound, or the Pembroke of

---

[1] *Ibid.* p. 14. William Prynne wrote in 1629 that some copies were still extant; *Anti-arminianism* (1630 ed.), 66.
[2] Trinity College MS. B/14/9, p 43.   [3] *Ibid.* p. 42.

Lancelot Andrewes. These petitioners had been effectively captained by Henry Alvey. But some Masters, no less than their Fellows, had been offended by the manner of Barrett's recantation. During the week in which the petition had been going the rounds, in fact, Barrett had been summarily called again before the Consistory and 'threatened to be expelled the university'.[1] So intensive was the opposition that Barrett found himself compelled to write to Whitgift[2] complaining of the activities of the puritan Johnians both in Cambridge and in London—where Daniel Munsay had been instrumental in circulating a libellous broadsheet giving an inaccurate version of the April sermon. Barrett, rather high-handedly, advised the Archbishop to call the authors of this broadsheet before the ecclesiastical commissioners. But Barrett believed that these separate and minor intrigues were bound together into a unity: the master mind behind them, he claimed, was that of the Master of Peterhouse. Robert Some, the letter continued, had organized a deliberate smear campaign, soliciting all his influential friends (including 'a certain little man called Perkins') to agitate in his cause. Barrett had been to see Some and 'complained of this kind of inveighing, and of others also, using the like liberty against me in St Mary's pulpit'. But in obstinacy the two men were well matched: 'he answered me that he had countenanced and would countenance all those that would appear against me to the uttermost of his power'.[3]

Barrett was obviously not a very pleasant young man; and his natural aggressiveness was sharpened and embittered by this sense of standing alone against the world. In another letter to Whitgift later in May he complained more desperately of his 'adversaries':[4] they are prepared to go to any lengths to expel me from the university, so will you not please first write to the heads to call a halt to these proceedings, and then write to the university declaring, once and for all, whether I have 'impugned the doctrine

[1] *Ibid.* p. 79.   [2] *Ibid.* pp. 33–6.
[3] *Ibid.* p. 36.   [4] *Ibid.* p. 37.

347

of the church in this land'? As May passed into June, the tensions in Cambridge became more and more stubborn, and more dangerous too.

By the second week in June the university authorities clearly saw that their 'hard' policy had not only failed to subdue Barrett, but had also failed to satisfy Whitgift. 'Being given to understand', they wrote to the Archbishop on the 12th, 'that your Lordship hath conceived somewhat hardly of our proceedings against one Mr Barrett',[1] they had decided that Some should go down to Lambeth with a copy of the offending sermon and a full account of the discussions in the Consistory; apologizing (rather late in the day) for the fact that, because many of the Masters had been away from Cambridge in the second half of May, the Archbishop 'was not made so soon and so fully acquainted' with the trials 'as was convenient'. Dr Some also took to London a letter for the Chancellor, to whom he talked about the case 'at good length'.[2] This was an important *tête-à-tête*. A day or two before, Whitgift had visited Burleigh to discuss the proceedings of the heads against Barrett; and had said 'that I for my part did think they had done unadvisedly therein'.[3] Burleigh therefore decided to write to the Vice-Chancellor to call the parties before the High Commission. Now, however, after half an hour with the persuasive Some, the Chancellor allowed himself to be convinced that the question of university privilege was involved, and that clause 45 of the statutes of the university, interpreted by the wisdom of the Consistory, was quite adequate to deal with the affair. He therefore dashed off a note to the heads confirming 'that they should further proceed against Barrett as they thought good'.[4] Burleigh was bored and irritated by the affair, and had reminded Some rather testily that he was 'daily occupied in other matters concerning the public state of the realm'.[5] It would have

[1] *Ibid.* p. 17.
[2] Cecil Papers (Salisbury MSS. Hatfield House), vol. 136, no. 30.
[3] Trinity College MS. B/14/9, p. 9.   [4] *Ibid.*
[5] Cecil Papers (Salisbury MSS.), vol. 136, no. 30

been wiser for him to have thought a little more carefully. As it turned out, he had effectively added another contribution to the sorry story of ill-judged and over-hasty proceedings. Whitgift was furious at the Chancellor's change of front. They talk of university statutes, he wrote to Burleigh: it may not have escaped your notice that I drew up those statutes and therefore might be expected to know a little about university privilege: and in this case the university authorities have behaved with a cavalier disregard of my advice and authority: 'My request therefore to your Lordship at this time only is, that you would write unto them to forbear any further dealing in these causes, until your Lordship be thoroughly informed therein, and until the state of the controversy be better made known unto you.'[1] There were, after all, other experts besides the Master of Peterhouse.

Whitgift followed up this note to Burleigh by a long and considered letter to the heads on 19 June. He put forward three constitutional objections to their tactics.

First the hasty and rash proceedings against him, not giving unto him liberty to confer with others nor time to consider of those points wherewith he was charged: a peremptoriness not used by the papists: nor in any well governed church of protestants, and indeed a rash and intolerable and consistorian-like kind of proceeding.

Secondly, in that they knowing my care, to have these new occasions of contention appeased, and to that end writing my advice therein to the Vice-Chancellor to be imparted to the rest of the Heads; knowing also, or at least ought to know, that in matters of religion it hath pleased her Majesty to commit the especial care to me, that university also being within my peculiar charge, in respect of the vacancy of the Bishopric of Ely, yet they would not vouchsafe to make me acquainted therewith as in duty they ought to have done, which I cannot take in good part, neither yet suffer.

Thirdly, for that they have proceeded in matters wherein they have no authority, no not by the statute by them alleged, these points not being within the letter or meaning thereof, although they have suffered and daily do suffer, both in their colleges and in other places in

[1] Trinity College MS. B/14/9, p. 9.

349

the town, men to offend against the very letter of that statute without reproof.[1]

This was bad enough; but worse was to come. The heads had assumed that Whitgift's judgement on the theological points at issue would be firmly against Barrett and in favour of the Calvinist interpretation, as expounded by Some and Whitaker. They were wrong. Whitgift was sufficiently detached to be quite aware (as he wrote to Burleigh) that 'some of the points wherewith they charged him and which they had caused him to recant (without either your Lordship's knowledge or mine) were such as the best learned protestants now living varied in judgement upon them'.[2]

II

When he was Master of Trinity, Whitgift had made clear that although he thought of Calvin as an authority, that authority was not unique or infallible. 'I reverence M. Calvin as a singular man, and worthy instrument in Christ's Church; but I am not so wholly addicted unto him, that I will contemn other men's judgements that in divers points agree not fully with him, especially in the interpretation of some places of the scripture, when as, in my opinion, they come nearer to the true meaning and sense of it in those points than he doth.'[3] Twenty years later his attitude had not changed. He could not approve of Barrett's undisciplined pulpit calumnies against Calvin, though he pointed out that such equally learned theologians as Jerome (shades of Erasmus!) and Augustine had been 'often and many times abused in that university without controlment'.[4] But he pointed out to the heads that if a man should conscientiously criticize Calvin or Beza or Peter Martyr for their

peremptory and false reproofs of this Church of England in divers points and likewise in some other singularities, I know no Article of

[1] *Ibid.* p. 2.
[2] *Ibid.* p. 9.
[3] Whitgift, *Works*, I, 436.
[4] Trinity College MS. B/14/9, p. 3.

Religion against it, much less do I know any cause why men should be so violently dealt withal for it, or termed ungodly, popish, impudent: for the doctrine of the Church of England doth in no respect depend upon them.[1]

That Calvin was a worthy man, one of the best Christian writers, was obvious: to Whitgift, as to Andrewes[2] and Overall.[3] But his judgement should be used in the same way as we 'use the judgement of other learned men'.[4]

One of Barrett's points—that no man can be specifically sure of the remission of his own sins—Whitgift believed to be quite untrue, the result of ignorance. Here 'he should have been better instructed and in a more Christian manner'. The Archbishop disapproved also of Barrett's teaching about the grades of faith; but this error was 'without the compass of their authority, having no Article directly against it: and an error of that nature that may be solved by distinction, worthy of reprehension, not of recantation, for any thing I can yet understand'.[5] Whitgift then went on to discuss the points of the loss of grace, of the assurance of salvation, and of the nature of reprobation. These were the important matters; and on each of them, in this letter of 19 June, Whitgift came down against the heads.

Barrett had argued that justifying faith and grace may be lost in some finally; and in the elect, totally but not finally. Of this assertion—which had caused especial grief to the Master of St John's[6]—Whitgift asked: 'against what Article of Religion established in this church is it? It is a matter disputable, and wherein learned men do and may dissent without impiety'.[7] Barrett had also preached that no one *certitudine fidei*, 'de salute sua debeat esse securus'. And in a letter to Whitgift in May he had elaborated his position by emphasizing the distinction between *certitudo* (which, with reservations, a Christian might have) and *securitas*

[1] *Ibid.* p. 4.
[2] Andrewes, *Sermons*, v, 20.
[3] Overall, *Convocation Book* (1844 ed.), 154.
[4] *Works*, I, 257.
[5] Trinity College MS. B/14/9, p. 3.
[6] *Ibid.* p. 21. Letter of Whitaker.
[7] *Ibid.* p. 3.

(which was presumption): the faithful may be *certi* of salvation, but not *securi*.[1]

In the previous year, 1594, Dr Lancelot Andrewes, Master of Pembroke, prebendary of St Paul's, and chaplain to both the Queen and the Archbishop, had taken the opportunity in a sermon preached at Hampton Court to echo St Paul's warning about the dangers of false assurance:

Now perseverance we shall attain, if we can possess our souls with the due care, and rid them of security. Of Lot's wife's security, as of water, was this salt here made. And, if security, as water, do but touch it, it melts away presently.... And, to avoid security, and to breed in us due care, St Bernard saith, 'Fear will do it'. *Vis in timore securus esse? securitatem time*; 'the only way to be secure in fear, is to fear security'. St Paul had given the same counsel before, that to preserve *si permanseris*, no better advice than *noli altum sapere, sed time*.[2]

In a later sermon on the same theme, against those who 'think that presumption in being secure of their salvation is good divinity', Andrewes was to quote words of St Augustine: 'We may in some cases advise men to have great hope that they shall be saved, but in no case give them warrant of security.'[3] Whitgift asked Andrewes in 1595 for his judgements on the points at issue in the Barrett case. The Master of Pembroke, in this judgement,[4] repeated the argument of his Hampton Court sermon: St Paul said that we should show 'diligence to the full assurance of hope unto the end', that sudden destruction comes upon those who speak of *securitas*; therefore we can never be *securi* of our salvation, but must work out that salvation in fear and trembling, lest *certitudo* degenerate into *securitas*. Another of Whitgift's chaplains was the Dutchman Hadrian Saravia, sometime pastor at Antwerp

[1] Trinity College MS. B/14/9, p. 33.
[2] *Sermons*, II, 72.
[3] *Ibid.* v, 531.
[4] 'Censura Censurae D. Barreti de Certitudine Salutis', *Articuli Lambethani* (1651), 33–40; reprinted in *Pattern of Catechistical Doctrine etc.* 301–5.

and professor at Leiden, who had come to England in 1587. He also was asked for his opinion. And he also emphasized that a man may be *certus* of his salvation but not *securus*: 'There is a great difference', Saravia wrote, 'between *certitudo* of salvation, and *securitas*. Certainty springs from faith, security from presumption and arrogance.'[1]

Thus the views of the Archbishop's chaplains on the subject of Christian assurance coincided precisely with those of William Barrett. And any of the protagonists of 1595 who had been in Cambridge thirty years before, when Whitgift was Lady Margaret Professor, might fruitfully have remembered an oration[2] of the future Archbishop on this very topic; when he had eloquently argued that we are subject to the incomprehensible counsel of God, and that although the Christian be persuaded that nothing can separate him from the love of God, the persuasion is of faith and hope, not of infallible fact. Whitgift had not forgotten his theology. In his letter to the heads in 1595 he dealt with the point thus: 'to affirm *neminem debere esse securum de salute*, to what Article of Religion established in this church it is contrary I see not: seeing security is never taken in good part, neither doth the scripture so use it. And what impiety is it to affirm that a man ought to be *certus de salute* but not *securus*?'[3]

Finally, the point of reprobation. Whitaker had written to Whitgift in that very month of June to insist 'that the only will of God is cause of reprobation...not only St Paul and Augustine have taught, but the best and learnedest schoolmen have largely and invincibly proved'.[4] The ground of the distinction between elect and reprobate must be sought—the Calvinist heads argued —in the pure and sovereign will of God, which is the supreme and unconditional rule of justice. This doctrine, as it was expressed in

[1] Strype, *Whitgift*, III, 321. Strype printed this judgement of Saravia from Trinity College MS. B/14/9, pp. 169–83.
[2] Divinity Act 'de certitudine salutis', University Library, Cambridge, MS. Ff/1/9. Printed in Whitgift, *Works*, III, 622–3.
[3] Trinity College MS. B/14/9, p. 3.   [4] *Ibid.* p. 48.

23   353   PR

Cambridge in 1595, was to Whitgift improper. His letter continued:

In some parts of his retractation they have made him to affirm that which is contrary to the doctrine holden and professed by many sound and learned divines in the Church of England, and in other churches likewise, men of best account; and the which for my own part I think to be false and contrary to the scriptures; for the scriptures are plain that God by his absolute will, doth not hate and reject any man without an eye to his sin. There may be impiety in believing the one, there can be none in believing the other, neither is it contrary to any Article of Religion established by authority in this Church of England, but rather agreeable thereunto.[1]

III

Thus Whitgift urged toleration of Barrett's opinions for two reasons: because there was no Article of Religion against them; and because they were concerned with matters disputable. Both reasons succinctly demonstrate what might be called the 'negative capability' of Anglican theology.

To Whitgift there were matters 'disputable' in doctrine as there were matters 'indifferent' in church government or ritual; matters not of the substance of revealed faith, in which there could be informed private judgement but no infallible revelation. John Overall was to make the distinction very clear in 1609.[2] There is, Overall wrote, 'matter of faith religiously to be observed'; defined as 'that which is agreeable to the doctrine of The Old and New Testament, and collected out of the same doctrine by the ancient fathers and catholic bishops of the church'. There are also 'matters not belonging to the substance of faith and religion'; where we have only the 'private opinions' of 'particular men', who may 'take some liberty of dissenting from the ancient fathers...in divers expositions of some places of scripture,

---

[1] *Ibid.* pp. 2–3.
[2] Preface to the 1609 edition of Jewel's *Apology*; Jewel, *Works*, IV, 1306.

so long as they keep themselves within the compass of the apostle's rule of the proportion of faith and platform of sound doctrine'. Now, the point of the Cambridge Calvinists in 1595 was that the assertions of William Barrett were 'not about inferior points or matters indifferent, but of the substantial ground, and chief comfort and anchor hold of our salvation'.[1] The point of John Whitgift was that the Calvinists were attempting to impose a particular private judgement as the revealed doctrine of Christ's Church in England; and that the attempt was mistaken and pernicious.

Benjamin Whichcote was to regret the activities of those who 'have been busy, and created a great deal of disturbance in the church of God, that have been over industrious to make out the revelation of God, beyond what God hath said, or that will impose upon others their own sense'.[2] Lancelot Andrewes had made a similar point in 1619:

even some that are far enough from Rome, yet with their new perspective they think they perceive all God's secret decrees, the number and order of them clearly; are indeed too bold and too busy with them. Luther said well that every one of us hath by nature a Pope in his belly, and thinks he perceives great matters. Even they that believe it not of Rome, are easily brought to believe it of themselves.[3]

At the time of the Barrett controversies Andrewes declared that Predestination was a great mystery, to be wondered at, not to be analysed.[4] In an address given in Pembroke in the 1580's he had touched on the same point: 'God's "judgements", which are the fountain of reprobation, are *abyssus magna*; and his mercy, extended to all that by faith apprehend the same, is *abyssus et profunditas*, "a great depth". Therefore we are not curiously to enquire and search out God's secret will touching reprobation or election, but to adore it.'[5] We murder to dissect. And though

---

[1] Trinity College MS. B/14/9, p. 52.
[2] *Works* (1751), I, 155.
[3] *Sermons*, III, 328.
[4] *Articuli Lambethani* (1651), p. 21.
[5] *Sermons*, V, 398.

Calvin had described the question of election and reprobation as a labyrinth, there were varying opinions on how far the Christian was capable of penetrating its heart. Whitgift, no less than Andrewes or Overall or Whichcote, regretted the dogmatism of those 'over industrious to make out the revelation of God'.

That is the theological basis of the law of charity and tolerance which was never better stated than in an exhortation in the Communion Office of the Prayer Book of 1549: 'in all things to follow and keep the rule of charity, and every man to be satisfied with his own conscience, not judging other men's minds and consciences; whereas he hath no warrant of God's word to the same'.[1] Whitgift was convinced that the Cambridge Calvinists had broken that rule in their dealings with William Barrett. And so in June 1595 he found them wanting, on moral and doctrinal no less than on constitutional grounds: 'the premises considered, I think they have dealt in matters not pertaining to their jurisdiction: and if it remain doubtful which of these points are contrary to the doctrine professed in this Church of England and which not, I hope they will not take upon them to determine thereof'.[2]

IV

On 2 July the plot thickened. Barrett, taking heart from the disputes, revoked his recantation.[3]

So July and August passed in a flurry of letters and petitions and enquiries and conferences. The inner circle of heads defined their privileges and their theology and decided to make a firm stand. Whitgift revived his quarrel with Burleigh. And Richard Clayton, Master of Magdalene, the Archbishop's most reliable resident Cambridge correspondent, watched the situation within the university degenerate from bad to worse. The troubles, he wrote to Whitgift on 7 July, are 'now daily increasing in our

[1] *Liturgies etc.* (ed. Ketley, Parker Society), 82.
[2] Trinity College MS. B/14/9, p. 4.   [3] Strype, *Whitgift*, II, 246.

university'. Clayton had continually attempted to calm the tempers and moderate the intransigence of Whitaker, Tyndall, Some, and their supporters among the heads; both privately and in the Consistory. But it had been wasted effort. They were still determined to proceed against Barrett in the old way:

taking upon them to justify all their former proceedings in all points, both for the manner thereof, and the whole doctrine in the recantation; and in all these matters they will be their judges, immediately under her Majesty; and in no case acknowledge any authority your Grace hath any way in those causes over them, either to determine what the doctrine is of the Church of England, or otherwise, howsoever; but stand peremptorily upon their privileges, which they take to be a sufficient warrant for all their dealing.[1]

Of course, the responsible and learned and subtle theology of the Master of St John's was one thing. The indiscretion of the Master of Peterhouse was quite another. In early July Some, filling at the last moment a sudden vacancy in the list of university preachers, took it upon himself to launch an attack on Barrett which was unprecedented in its fervour. Whitgift was extremely annoyed. Barrett requested that Some be called before the Consistory, and Duport was compelled to grant the request.[2] Honour seems to have been satisfied in Cambridge on this particular matter; but in spite of that, Some was called to Lambeth and personally reprimanded by the Archbishop. On his return to Cambridge, making play with Whitgift's Christian name, Some preached against the powers of the ecclesiastical commission, taking as his text Acts iv. 6:[3] 'And Annas the high priest, and Caiaphas, and John, and Alexander, and as many as were of the kindred of the high priest, were gathered together at Jerusalem. And when they had set them in the midst, they asked, By what power or by what name, have ye done this?' At the end of 1595

---

[1] Trinity College MS. B/14/9, p. 25.
[2] Ibid. p. 31.   [3] Strype, *Whitgift*, 253-4.

Whitgift was to write to the Master of Trinity and give vent to one of the firmest impressions of the year: 'the foolery of Dr Some hath done no good to the cause' ![1]

V

In September, the more precisely to examine Barrett's theology, Whitgift prepared a questionnaire of eight items, upon which Barrett was examined in Cambridge on the 12th: by Duport, Tyndall, Barwell and Chaderton, with Whitaker as chairman. A report on Barrett's answers, together with the comments of the board, was drawn up for the Archbishop. He did not receive it until the 29th. He replied on the 30th, giving his own full opinion.

The central points were again those of Christian assurance. Was the Lucan prayer of Christ for Peter or for all the elect? was the assurance of Paul due to special and private revelation? can the Christian believe in the personal remission of his sins? can justifying faith make us assured of our salvation? And the fact is that although this precise and official inquiry showed up many weak points in Barrett's theology, Whitgift was still prepared to give him the benefit of many doubts. The Archbishop certainly objected to Barrett's introduction, in discussion, of the distinction between formed and unformed faith: Whitgift and the five heads felt, as Luther had felt, that *fides informis* was 'simply not faith';[2] whereas Barrett, following St Thomas Aquinas,[3] has argued that whereas unformed faith was imperfect, lacking the form it ought to have, yet it still had the nature of faith, and was 'perfect in the perfection which suffices for the nature of faith'. This, indeed,

---

[1] Trinity College MS. B/14/9, p. 119.

[2] Luther's judgement; quoted by Rupp, *The Righteousness of God*, 168. But: 'The barest kind of faith, *fides informis*, mere assent in its unattractive nakedness, still has some impact upon the will, as many of the best Reformation divines recognized'; Owen Chadwick, in *Good Friday at St Margaret's* (ed. Charles Smyth, 1957), 116.

[3] II–II, Q. 6, art. 2: 'Whether Fides Informis is a gift of God', in *Nature and Grace* (ed. Fairweather), 287–8.

was 'popish'.[1] Whitgift also disliked Barrett's statement on the remission of sins, with its talk of penitential acts. But he maintained (in contradiction to Whitaker) that Christ's prayer that faith should not fail 'cannot be drawn to all the elect'. The only difficulty Whitgift saw in exegesis of the text was whether Christ prayed for Peter alone or for all the Apostles; and on this point 'men may without impiety vary in opinion'.[2] This was true also of the question of the revelation to Paul, which was 'of the nature, that men may answer unto it, *pro* and *contra*, without impiety'.[3]

The board of inquiry bluntly tore through the subtleties of Barrett's extended argument on assurance: 'that a man may be assured of his salvation by certainty of faith, he denieth'.[4] What Barrett had actually said was that the faithful Christian can trust in salvation with confidence and certainty; but not with that sort of certainty of faith by which we are assured, for example, that God is One and Three. Whitgift again came down on the side of Barrett here. He had defined assurance without rushing into the dangerous presumption of security.

His answer...is direct, that *Electi* or *Fideles* are *certi de salute*; and I do not take it, that he denieth that *fideles* may be assured of their salvation by the certainty of faith; but he denieth that they are assured, *ea certitudine fidei, qua tenent omnipotentiam, unitatem et sacrosanctam personarum trinitatem* &c. Whereby he expoundeth, what he meaneth *per certitudinem fidei* in that place. Wherein whether I do not yet perceive that his opinion doth differ from any Article of Religion professed by this Church of England, is questionable: and therefore requireth further conference of learned men.[5]

For the rest, Whitgift did not approve of Barrett's brash dismissal of Calvin and Beza; though 'we must take heed, that their bare names and authorities carry not men so far as to believe their errors, or to give unto them that honour and forbearance

---

[1] Trinity College MS. B/14/9, p. 71. Heads to Whitgift.
[2] *Ibid.* p. 13.   [3] *Ibid.* p. 14.
[4] *Ibid.* p. 71.   [5] *Ibid.* pp. 13–14.

of reproof, which is not yielded to any of the ancient Fathers'.[1]
The recantation of 10 May still seemed to the Archbishop to have
been forced on Barrett 'without due consideration', and worthy
to be condemned 'as containing in it some untruths'. And as
Barrett had now, in September, offered to accept the judgement
of those 'who have chiefest authority to decide these controversies', this, thought the Archbishop, 'ought in conscience
and charity to satisfy you, if you seek his reformation and not his
overthrow and destruction. The fierceness and peremptoriness of
some in these causes, doth more harm than good.'[2] His letter of
30 September ended with two positive proposals: that 'no man
in pulpit within that university deal in these causes to or fro,
until further order be taken'; and that during the Michaelmas
term there should come to Lambeth 'some one or two of you'
and 'likewise the parties offending'.

I will bear with no man's contempt or undutiful behaviour towards
superiors; neither may I tolerate any man that impugneth the Articles
of Religion set down by authority. And therefore in punishing such,
you shall not need to doubt of my joining with you. But, I must first
be duly informed, not by report of others, but by hearing the parties
themselves:...you shall perceive that I will deal in these causes as an
honest man ought to do, and one that esteemeth as much of the
privileges of that university as any man living. And therefore
I require this of you, not by any authority I have, but of good will and
friendship towards you and of duty towards the Church and that
university: thinking that to be the best course for the ending of these
controversies, and for the avoiding of further troubles.[3]

VI

The Archbishop's request of 30 September that no one should
preach in the university about the disputed matters was apparently
not felt to apply to the Regius Professor of Divinity. At the
beginning of the new academic year Whitaker found himself 'by

[1] *Ibid.* pp. 14–15.　　　[2] *Ibid.* p. 15.　　　[3] *Ibid.* pp. 15–16.

duty moved to entreat of certain points of religion, which some amongst us have begun of late to call into question, and so have bred some difference of judgements in the minds of many; and greater offence and trouble is to be feared, if good order be not taken and provided to the contrary in time'.[1] And so on 9 October he preached his sermon on election and reprobation, the loss of grace, and Christian assurance; the sermon which was, as it turned out, his swan song. Three weeks later, at the beginning of November, Whitaker and Tyndall went up to Lambeth with William Barrett.

At the ensuing conference Whitgift, face to face for the first time with the trouble-maker, became much less sympathetic towards him. The eight questions were put to Barrett once more; and, awed perhaps by the formalities of Lambeth, his answers were more penitent than they had been in September. He was still able to insist, however, with the encouragement of the Archbishop, that the elect could not be *securi* of salvation, and that the retractation had been unjust. He also maintained that the assurance of St Paul was due to special revelation. But he acknowledged his fault in attacking Calvin so violently; he gave lip service to the distinction between a lively and a dead faith; and he agreed to accept the interpretation of the Lucan prayer of Christ as not only for Peter (as he had preached in April), nor for the Apostles only (as Whitgift himself had formerly been inclined to believe), but for all the elect.[2] During the interview Whitgift—who had called the conference 'to the end I might the better understand the controversies'—came to see that 'Barrett had erred in divers points...some of his opinions being indeed popish'.[3] And he decided that Barrett should read a second retractation in Cambridge; this to be a shorter and less positive document than the first, and to be drawn up to Barrett's own dictation.

[1] Lansdowne MSS. vol. LXXX, no. 10, fol. 26. Whitaker to Burleigh, 19 November.
[2] Trinity College MS. B/14/9, p. 73. [3] *Ibid.* p. 80.

The fair copy of this document was officially shown to Barrett on 10 January by the new Vice-Chancellor, Goad of King's. There had been some delay because of the young man's lack of co-operation, and there was to be more delay yet. At the meeting of 10 January 1596, wrote Goad to Whitgift,

he acknowledged the same to be his own words, and seemed willing to perform the same, if he might first have some respite for further conference to be more fully persuaded that the points he should acknowledge are indeed errors. For which he requiring only a fortnight's time, I did (notwithstanding it was his own fault that all this time he came to none for conference) allow unto him respite for almost three weeks, viz. until the last of this January: appointing unto him, certain persons to confer with to his own good liking, namely Dr Chaderton and Mr Overall, Professor in Divinity.[1]

If the slippery Barrett had wished to delay matters he could not have done better than to count on the possibility that Laurence Chaderton and John Overall would disagree among themselves!

There is in fact no record that Barrett ever delivered his second recantation. However, he remained in Cambridge for at least another year; and made preparations to go abroad in the spring of 1597. On 30 May of that year Whitgift wrote to the Vice-Chancellor to say that Barrett was not to 'depart this realm into foreign parts' without an express royal licence, and without personal permission from the ecclesiastical commissioners.[2] It seems certain that he did in fact go abroad. He also became a Roman Catholic. His Calvinist opponents would have been heartened by the reflection that only in the next century were their successors to be confronted by men who 'found a way to reconcile the opinions of Rome to the preferments of England'.[3] But it was surely flattering to Barrett, when he returned to England, to find that as time went by his name and his opinions,

[1] Trinity College MS. B/14/9, p. 132.
[2] University Library, Cambridge, Baker MSS. vol. xxiv, p. 348.
[3] Falkland's comment on Bishop Goodman of Gloucester; quoted by Charles Smyth, *The Genius of the Church of England* (1947), 33.

far from fading into obscurity, became more and more the subject of discussion and polemic. For Barrett survived to see the theological battles of the 1620's; and he was living in England, a man of nearly seventy, 'a professed papist in the quality of a layman,' when the second edition of William Prynne's *Anti-Arminianism* was published in 1630.[1]

But the importance of the Barrett affair is this: that the extreme Cambridge Calvinists had attempted to impose their interpretation of the mysteries of grace and assurance as the official and sole theology of the Church of England. So far as Cambridge was concerned they had failed. In order to consider their success or failure in the English Church as a whole it is necessary now to examine the most important by-product of the Barrett case; that is, the Lambeth Articles of November 1595.

[1] University Library, Cambridge, Baumgartner MSS. vol. x, no. 60: Thomas Baker to John Strype, April 1712.

CHAPTER XVI

THE LAMBETH ARTICLES

I

W HEN Whitaker and Tyndall went down from Cambridge to Lambeth with William Barrett in November 1595 they took with them a set of dogmatic propositions relating to the points which for six months had caused bitter debate in the university. The interpretation of the limits of Christian assurance, of 'the comfortable certainty of true faith',[1] was dependent upon a whole conception of the nature of election and reprobation; and this wider question had flickered uneasily through the summer quarrels. Whitaker, well conscious of the wider issues of the Barrett affair, had taken as the first and leading point in his university sermon of 9 October the question of predestination. He sent a copy of this sermon to the Chancellor with a covering letter, one of his last, written on 19 November from the London house of his uncle Alexander Nowell, Dean of St Paul's:

I thought it my duty to acquaint you with our troubles, and these controversies raised in your university, whereof I desire and beseech almighty God to see a good and quiet end. And for that purpose am I sent hither from the university to labour with the chief governors of ecclesiastical causes under her Majesty for establishing a peaceable order; wherein what success God doth give unto our labours I will certify your Lordship ere it be long.[2]

The letter concluded with an appeal for more lucrative preferment; especially as the Regius chair, which Whitaker had now occupied for sixteen years, did not allow him sufficient leisure for the cause he really had at heart—apologetic against the Church of Rome.

[1] Trinity College MS. B/14/9, p. 23.
[2] Lansdowne MSS. vol. LXXX, no. 10, fol. 26.

To 'see a good and quiet end' to the disturbances in Cambridge: 'a peaceable order'. That was the aim of the discussions at Lambeth in the middle of November, between Whitgift, Whitaker, Tyndall, and some of the ecclesiastical commissioners. Most probably, the insipid Dr Richard Vaughan was present at the discussions. He was a Johnian, archdeacon of Middlesex, canon of Wells and chaplain to the Queen; on 22 November he was elected Bishop of Bangor, the *congé d'élire* having been issued on the 6th. The other commissioner most concerned was Dr Richard Fletcher, former Fellow of Corpus, who had been for almost a year Bishop of London. At the time, Fletcher was excluded from Court, and from February to July he had been suspended from his episcopal functions, because of his unfortunate second marriage, which had followed hard upon his election to London. Fletcher died in June 1596, of a surfeit of tobacco (so it was said); at the time of the Lambeth Conference his son John, the future playwright, was beginning his fifth year at Corpus.

During the discussions Whitgift 'delivered mine opinion of the propositions brought unto me by Dr Whitaker: wherein some few being added, I agreed fully with them and they with me. And I know them to be sound doctrine, and uniformly professed in this Church of England, and agreeable to the Articles of Religion established by authority.'[1]

Now, the original propositions of Whitaker were printed, from his manuscript, in a book about the Lambeth Articles published in 1651.[2] Translated, they read as follows:

I: God from eternity has predestined some men to life, and reprobated some to death.

II: The efficient cause of Predestination is not the foreseeing of faith,

[1] Trinity College MS. B/14/9, p. 80.

[2] '*Articuli Lambethani*': *Cura et impensis F. G. Ecclesiae Sancti Nicolae apud Trinobantes Ministri. Londini. Typis G. D. An. Dom. 1651.* Number A 3890 in *Short Title Catalogue 1641–1700.* Translated in 1700. This is a book of fifty-six pages, with five sections:

(1) A History of the making of the Articles. There is a manuscript version of this in University Library, Cambridge, MS. Gg/1/29 (a copy-book belonging to a pupil of

or of perseverance, or of good works, or of anything innate in the person of the predestined, but only the absolute and simple will of God.

III: There is a determined and certain number of predestined, which cannot be increased or diminished.

IV: Those not predestined to salvation are inevitably condemned on account of their sins (*necessario propter peccata condemnabuntur*).

V: A true, lively and justifying faith, and the sanctifying spirit of God, is not lost, nor does it pass away (*non excidit, non evanescit*) either totally or finally in those who once have been partakers of it (*in iis qui semel eius participes fuerunt*).

VI: The truly faithful man—that is, one endowed with justifying faith—is sure by certainty of faith (*certus est, certitudine fidei*) of the remission of his sins and his eternal salvation through Christ.

VII: Grace sufficient to salvation (*gratia sufficiens ad salutem*) is not granted, not made common, not ceded (*non tribuitur, non communicatur, non conceditur*) to all men, by which they might be saved, if they wish.

VIII: No one can come to Christ unless it be granted to him, and unless the Father draws him: and all men are not drawn by the Father to come to the Son.

IX: It is not in the will or the power of each and every man to be saved.

Now, so far as the Barrett controversy was concerned, these articles were not completely uncompromising. Even if the *causa efficiens* of election was *sola et absoluta et simplex voluntas Dei*, the reprobate were condemned 'on account of their sins'. Con-

Overall), ff. 112b–114a. This *History* has been thought to be the work of John Cosin; J. S. Brewer's edition of Fuller's *Church History*, v, 221 (footnote).

(2) Whitaker's original draft of the Articles.

(3) Whitaker's draft, side by side with the comments of other theologians at Lambeth. Manuscript version in U.L.C. MS. Gg/1/29, ff. 114b–116a. Reprinted in 1846 in Anglo-Catholic Library ed. of Andrewes's *Pattern of Catechistical Doctrine, etc.* 289–94; and in 1876 in Charles Hardwick, *History of the Thirty-nine Articles*, 364–7.

(4) Two pieces by Lancelot Andrewes: (a) his judgement on the Lambeth Articles; MS. copy (1596) in Trinity College MS. B/14/9; (b) his censure of Barrett's recantation. Both pieces reprinted in 1846, *Pattern of Catechistical Doctrine*, 294–305. They are almost certainly the documents which Andrewes mentioned in 1617 as having been drawn up for Whitgift, and lent to Richard Hooker, who never returned them; Birch (ed.), *Court and Times of James I*, II, 47.

(5) John Overall on predestination. Manuscript copy in U.L.C. MS. Gg/1/29, ff. 10b–13b. Probably dating from *c.* 1610.

demned *necessario*; but, as Andrewes pointed out, if men are condemned *propter peccata* that means 'because they sin', and therefore the necessity is not absolute but provisional.[1] Barrett had been made to agree, in May, that if sin were the *causa reprobationis*, then no one could be saved.[2] Whitgift, objecting to this, had insisted that 'the Scriptures are plain that God by his absolute will, doth not hate and reject any man without any eye to his sin'.[3] The Calvinists cut that knot by some such proposition as: 'In the execution of God's decree, there is always respect to sin, and the cause of damnation is in the wicked themselves. But in predestination itself there is no respect or cause either of holiness in the elect or of sin in the reprobate, but it dependeth wholly on the mere will and good pleasure of God.'[4] But as an interpretation of the article, Andrewes's gymnastics were quite as convincing as those of his Calvinist colleagues, and they preserved Whitgift's point. Andrewes also agreed that all men are not drawn by the Father to come to the Son; though he argued the cause of this to be not the absolute will of God but the depraved will of man.[5] Again, the phrase 'certus est, certitudine fidei' was acceptable to Barrett. It all depended, as Whitgift had seen in September, upon the interpretation of 'certainty of faith': and the Archbishop had then defended Barrett's interpretation against that of Whitaker.

II

'Wherein some few being added.' said Whitgift, 'I agreed with them.' The alterations can be seen by comparing Whitaker's propositions with the final Articles signed on 20 November. The point is that all the changes are in the direction of making the original draft less uncompromising and more scriptural.

Four of the nine propositions remained unchanged: I, III, VIII and IX. But it is worth remembering, before we refer to Whitgift

---

[1] *Articuli Lambethani*, 28.   [2] Strype, *Whitgift*, III, 317–20.
[3] Trinity MS. B/14/9, p. 2.   [4] *Ibid.* p. 51.   [5] *Articuli Lambethani*, 32.

as a 'remorseless predestinarian',[1] that Thomas Aquinas would have been perfectly happy about at least the first and the third. Andrewes, following St Thomas, agreed it to be 'uncontroversial' that God 'in his eternal prescience or foreknowledge saw that some would be elected' and some not.[2] (He then went on, as John Bradford had done, to emphasize that election was 'in Christ' and reprobation 'on account of sins'.[3]) In the *Summa*, again, it was proved that 'the number of the predestined is certain';[4] part of the Thomist proof was a statement of St Augustine, 'The number of the predestined is certain and cannot be increased or diminished'; that statement was also quoted by Andrewes in his approving comment on the third Article;[5] and indeed Whitaker may have based his wording on it. If the Calvinists were 'remorseless', or if they brought something new to the history of the doctrine of predestination, the reason lies not in their interpretation of election but in their emphasis on, and confident analysis of, the decrees of reprobation. And, with regard to reprobation, Whitgift was not prepared to be emphatic or presumptuous.

In number two there were three alterations. First, 'efficient cause' was changed to 'moving and efficient cause'. Foreknowledge of faith is not the moving or efficient cause of predestination. St Thomas had written that foreknowledge was the *final* cause of election,[6] so he might have agreed with the Lambeth theologians here. Calvin, one feels, who had attacked the 'silly subtlety of Thomas' on this very point,[7] might have felt that Whitaker and Whitgift were being equally offensively subtle in their scholastic distinctions. Andrewes, in his comment,[8] passed quickly over this distinction of causes to emphasize the 'order' or

---

[1] F. W. Maitland, in *Cambridge Modern History*, II, 597.
[2] *Articuli Lambethani*, 22.   [3] *Ibid.* 23.
[4] I, Q. 23, art. 7. In *Nature and Grace*, ed. Fairweather, 113–16.
[5] *Articuli Lambethani*, 28.
[6] I, Q. 23, art. 5; Fairweather, *op. cit.* 110.
[7] *Institutes*, 3/22/9; tr. Norton (1611 ed.), 460.
[8] *Articuli Lambethani*, 23–7.

'series' which God observes, attacking the 'chain of the moderns', which destroys the true nature of election by concentrating on the absolute act of God and almost ignoring the work of Christ. (It was probably Perkins's *Golden Chain*, that Cambridge text-book of the 'nineties, which Andrewes had in mind.) Thus, said Andrewes, the phrase 'in Christ' should be added to this article, as Parker had added it to Cranmer's article on predestination. The next change in Article II was that 'predestination' was altered to 'predestination to life'. Thus election alone was an act of 'the sole will of God'; and Whitgift had guarded against the danger that reprobation might also be thought of exclusively in those terms. The alteration prevented the Lambeth Articles from assuming the finality of Calvin's own 'Articles Concerning Predestination', drawn up forty years earlier, which had contained such propositions as 'While the reprobate are the vessels of the just will of God, and the elect vessels of his compassion, the ground of the distinction is to be sought in the pure will of God alone, which is the supreme rule of justice,'[1] and which had contained no suspicion of a suggestion that reprobation might in any way be *propter peccata*. To the Lambeth theologians, election might not take into account 'anything innate in the person of the predestined'; but reprobation might perhaps do so. Thirdly, 'absolute and simple will of God' was modified to 'the will of the good pleasure of God', *voluntas beneplaciti Dei*, a phrase which echoed not Calvin but St Paul: 'Having predestinated us unto the adoption of children by Jesus Christ to himself, according to the good pleasure of his will.'[2] The phrase brings to mind also the distinction made by Andrewes in the 1580's between God's secret will (*voluntas beneplaciti*) and his revealed will (*voluntas signi*).[3] Election, as the seventeenth Anglican article stated, is 'the everlasting purpose of God...by his counsel secret to us'.

In his draft of Article V Whitaker wrote that faith cannot fail

---

[1] Calvin, *Theological Treatises*, 179.   [2] Ephesians, i. 5.
[3] *Sermons*, v, 397.

in 'those who have once been partakers of it': the revised article had that faith cannot fail in 'the elect'. This change was a recognition that others besides the elect may be, for a time, *participes* in *vera fides*; although, as Barrett had said, those who are not of the elect will finally lose that faith.[1]   And the change therefore contradicted the assertion in Barrett's recantation that anyone who once has such true faith has it for ever.[2] Barrett had agreed that the elect can never lose faith *finally*, though (unlike the Fifth Lambeth Article) he believed that they could lose it *totally*. (In June Whitgift had included the question whether the elect can lose faith totally among matters 'disputable and wherein learned men do and may dissent without impiety'[3]: in November he no longer did so.) Andrewes also believed that the faith of the elect does not finally fail:[4] though 'whether the Holy Spirit may for a time be taken away or extinguished is, I think, yet a question. I confess that I am in doubt on the subject.'[5] It was Peter Baro who was most carefully to interpret Article V in terms of the tradition of the Homilies and Articles of Religion, by agreeing that the elect cannot lose faith finally, nor can they lose it totally— in the sense that it can be restored to them by repentance.[6] The elect, as Overall was to argue at the Hampton Court Conference, can through sin become 'subject to God's wrath...until they repented'.[7]

'Grace sufficient to salvation' was not, in Whitaker's draft of Article VII, given to all men. In the finished version 'saving grace' (*gratia salutaris*) is not so given. Efficacious saving grace is not granted to all: but sufficient grace perhaps is.

But perhaps the most significant change was that made in Article VI. The phrase *certus est certitudine fidei* became *certus est plerophoria fidei*; full assurance of faith, the Pauline phrase; or,

---

[1] Trinity College MS. B/14/9, p. 3.   [2] Strype, *Whitgift*, III, 318.
[3] Trinity College MS. B/14/9, p. 3.   [4] *Articuli Lambethani*, 29.
[5] *Ibid.* Tr. William Goode, *Effects of Infant Baptism* (ed. 1850), 126.
[6] Trinity College MS. B/14/9, p. 84; Strype, *Whitgift*, III, 340–2.
[7] Barlow's account, in Cardwell (ed.), *History of Conferences*, 186.

as Perkins translated it, 'a full persuasion of the heart'.[1] Peter
Baro approved of this Lambeth Article: 'He who is endowed with
justifying faith, is assured through faith of the remission of his
sins, and of eternal life; not absolutely, but through Christ, as the
Article says: that is, if he holds to Christ until the end.'[2] But what
was important—as Whitgift had made quite clear in his revision—
was not the Calvinist interpretation of certainty but the Pauline
doctrine of assurance. Whitgift had moved the issues back beyond
the quarrels of Whitaker and Barrett to Augustine and the New
Testament.

The Articles were finally approved by Whitgift and the
ecclesiastical commissioners on 20 November. They now read, in
translation,[3] thus:

I: God from eternity has predestined some men to life, and reprobated some to death.

II: The moving or efficient cause of predestination to life is not the
foreseeing of faith, or of perseverance, or of good works, or of anything
innate in the person of the predestined, but only the will of the good
pleasure of God.

III: There is a determined and certain number of predestined, which
cannot be increased or diminished.

IV: Those not predestined to salvation are inevitably condemned on
account of their sins.

V: A true, lively and justifying faith, and the sanctifying Spirit of
God, is not lost nor does it pass away either totally or finally in the elect.

VI: The truly faithful man—that is, one endowed with justifying
faith—is sure by full assurance of faith of the remission of sins and his
eternal salvation through Christ.

VII: Saving grace is not granted, is not made common, is not ceded
to all men, by which they might be saved, if they wish.

VIII: No one can come to Christ unless it be granted to him, and
unless the Father draws him: and all men are not drawn by the Father
to come to the Son.

IX: It is not in the will or the power of each and every man to be saved.

[1] Perkins, 'A Golden Chain', *Works*, I, 80.
[2] Strype, *Whitgift*, III, 341-2.   [3] Latin text in Strype, *Whitgift*, II, 280.

III

On 24 November Whitgift sent a manuscript copy of the articles (they were never printed) to the Vice-Chancellor, 'praying you to take care, that nothing be publicly taught to the contrary'. These propositions, he continued, 'we are persuaded to be true'; but the Archbishop was to make quite clear that he intended them to be taken 'as our private judgements, thinking them to be true and correspondent to the doctrine professed in the Church of England, and established by the laws of the land; and not as laws and decrees'.[1] 'My earnest and hearty desire', he informed the Vice-Chancellor, 'is to have the peace of the Church generally observed in all places; especially in that university, whereof I am a member.'[2] The Articles of Lambeth had been 'with some care and diligence drawn out and set down' specifically for 'the better observation and nourishing of the said peace'.[3] But, if they were to be discussed in Cambridge, Whitgift commanded that 'discretion and moderation be used, that such as shall be in some points differing in judgement, be not of purpose stung or justly grieved; and especially that no bitterness, contention, or personal reproofs or reproaches be used by any towards any'.[4] And that might have been the last of the matter.

Unfortunately, as an attempt at 'a peaceable order' in the university, the articles misfired badly. They are reminiscent of that earlier blunder in which Whitgift had been involved; when, in November 1565, precisely thirty years earlier, he had signed (as Lady Margaret Professor) the letter from the heads to the Chancellor asking him not to enforce the regulations about the surplice.[5] Whitgift was in those days prepared to sacrifice much for the sake of a charitable peace; and he was prepared to do so now. But the 1595 articles, like the 1565 appeal, in fact incurred

[1] Trinity College MS. B/14/9, p. 17. [2] *Ibid.* p. 77.
[3] *Ibid.* p. 17. [4] *Ibid.* p. 77.
[5] Strype, *Parker*, III, 125–6.

the active displeasure of the Chancellor. If the Lambeth Articles have achieved a certain notoriety in the history of Anglican theology, the credit or the blame rests squarely on the shoulders of Burleigh.

The facts are these. A day or two after the conclusion of the conference at Lambeth, Whitaker visited Tyndall in London and suggested that Burleigh should be told of the proceedings.[1] Tyndall was not keen on the idea, for he had seen Burleigh recently about the state of affairs at Ely (where he was Dean), and had made 'no mention of any university cause'. Whitaker, however, having written to Burleigh on the 19th and sent him a copy of his October sermon, felt it proper that he should 'go to his house and so signify what had been done in these late controversies'. Tyndall eventually agreed to accompany Whitaker; 'so accordingly I went, and we delivered his Lordship a copy of those conclusions'. Burleigh read through them, mentioned that he had also perused Whitaker's sermon and confessed that 'the matters were too high mysteries for his understanding'. More, he

seemed to dislike of the propositions concerning predestination, and did reason somewhat against Dr Whitaker in them, drawing by a similitude a reason from an earthly prince, inferring thereby they charged God of cruelty and might cause men to be desperate in their wickedness. Master Dr Whitaker seeing then his Lordship's weakness, did in wisdom forbear to answer my Lord, but only said that nothing was in that behalf set down, but was delivered in the Articles set out by public authority. So saying that these matters were too deep for him, his Lordship bid us farewell, and gave us thanks that we made him acquainted with those things.

It is probable that Burleigh, in turn, made the Queen acquainted with them. On 5 December Robert Cecil wrote to Whitgift that Elizabeth 'hath commanded me to send unto your Grace that she mislikes much that any allowance hath been given by your Grace and the rest, of any points to be disputed of Predestination, being

[1] Tyndall to Whitgift, 19 Dec.; Trinity College MS. B/14/9, pp. 127–8.

a matter tender and dangerous to weak ignorant minds, and thereupon requireth your Grace to suspend them'.[1] There was a tradition, reported by Thomas Fuller in 1655, that the Queen jestingly told Whitgift that his calling a council without royal consent had made all his goods forfeit to her,[2] and some said that she wished all the Lambeth theologians to be prosecuted for offending against the statute of praemunire.[3] However that may be, Whitgift was certain of one thing, that the propositions had been reported to the Queen 'in evil sense, and as though the same had been by me sent down to the university to be disputed upon, or (I know not how) published'. In fact the Archbishop had always been careful to insist that 'there be no publication thereof, otherwise than in private'. He claimed that the Queen was persuaded of the truth of the propositions, but considered it unfit that such matters should be publicly preached or disputed upon.[4] Moreover, in a letter to the Master of Trinity (Nevile) on 8 December, he angrily complained that things would never have come to such a pass had it not been for the indiscipline of the Cambridge authorities.[5] One of the Cambridge authorities, however, was beyond human criticism. Whitaker, who had returned to St John's on 28 November, died there on 4 December.

The spark had been applied; and during December the debates on the articles grew in intensity, both in the university and at the court. (The puzzled John Young, Bishop of Rochester, wrote to Whitgift on the 24th objecting to a rumour that he had attacked the propositions in London: 'I having never seen or scarce heard of them until this morning.')[6] In Cambridge there was one consolation for the Archbishop. His old friend Whitaker (whose notes and papers on a projected treatise against Stapleton Whitgift

---

[1] Trinity College MS. B/14/9, p. 117.
[2] Fuller, *Church History*, v, 226.
[3] This story, first printed in 1651, in the 'Historia' section of *Articuli Lambethani*, was written up by Peter Heylyn in 1670; *Aerius Redivivus*, 343–4.
[4] Trinity College MS. B/14/9, pp. 118–19.
[5] *Ibid.*   [6] *Ibid.* p. 141.

had collected and filed at Lambeth)[1] was succeeded as Master of St John's by another friend, Richard Clayton. The business of filling the vacant Regius chair was more tricky. Nevile wrote to Whitgift to recommend one of his Fellows, John Overall. Whitgift replied on 8 December that he had been informed that 'Mr Overall is something factious'. Actually, Overall was a friend and disciple of Peter Baro, the Lady Margaret Professor of Divinity, whose other disciples included William Barrett. But with due care, and with Whitgift's admonition in mind that the university elect 'such an one, as shall be in all points conformable',[2] John Overall was during December elected Regius Professor of Divinity.

Whitgift's letter to Nevile on 8 December had contained a note about Peter Baro. It was Baro who now took the stage in Cambridge; and by March 1596 the controversies which he inspired had led to fierce public debate on all the issues of predestination which had been implied in the disputes of 1595.

In fact, it would have been better for 'peaceable order' in the university if the Lambeth Articles had never existed.

[1] *Ibid.* p. 118.   [2] *Ibid.*

CHAPTER XVII

PETER BARO: UNIVERSALITY OF GRACE

I

A COMPLAINT made to Burleigh about Peter Baro in 1596 claimed that the Lady Margaret Professor had

for the space of these fourteen or fifteen years, taught in his lectures, preached in sermons, determined in the Schools and printed in several books divers points of doctrine...contrary to that which hath been taught and received ever since her Majesty's reign, yet agreeable to the errors of popery,...so that we (who for the space of many years past, have yielded him sundry benefits and favours in the university, and forborne him when he hath often himself, busy and curious *in aliena republica*, broached new and strange questions in religion)...cannot ...but continue to use all good means, and seek at your Lordship's hand some effectual remedies, lest by permitting passage to these errors, the whole body of popery should by little and little break in upon us.[1]

Now, Baro had been Lady Margaret Professor for twenty-two years, having been elected in 1574. He was born at Étampes, thirty miles south of Paris, in 1534; by the time he was twenty-three he was bachelor of law of Bourges, and an *avocat* in the Paris *Parlement*; in 1560 he was ordained at Geneva by Calvin.[2] In 1572 Baro came to England as a religious refugee, and in April 1573 he was elected a fellow commoner of Peterhouse, of which college Andrew Perne was Master. Baro was then forty. And for the next quarter of a century he lived in Cambridge with his wife and family, in a house belonging to Peterhouse—where three more sons were born to him.[3] (His eldest son, Peter, was elected Fellow

---

[1] Trinity College MS. B/14/9, pp. 184–5; letter of 8 March 1595/6 to Burleigh, from Goad, Some, Legge, Jegon, Nevile, Preston, Tyndall, Montagu, Barwell and Chaderton.
[2] University Library, Cambridge, Baker MSS. vol. XXIX, p. 185.
[3] T. A. Walker, *A Biographical Register of Peterhouse Men*, I, 297–8.

of the college in 1585). In addition to his Lady Margaret lectures, Baro taught Hebrew at some colleges.

It is significant that Baro was senior to most of the men concerned in the theological disputes of 1595. He was only two years younger than Whitgift: and two years older than Laurence Chaderton, six years older than Robert Some (who had succeeded Perne as Master of Peterhouse in 1589), thirteen years older than Whitaker, and twenty-five years older than Perkins. Again, he was twenty years older than Andrewes, twenty-five years older than Overall, and thirty years older than Barrett. A man, then, to be reckoned with, speaking with authority. He was personally popular in the university, where he won respect both as a saintly man and a scholar.[1] But his theological position was perfectly clear, and well known to the Cambridge divines. In the late 1570's, for example, he had delivered a memorable disputation speech in the Schools on the theme 'God's purpose and decree taketh not away the liberty of man's corrupt will'. His conclusion to the 'Question' was this:

God the creator and governor of all things is not the destroyer of the order by him appointed, but the preserver. For he would that in the nature of things there should be divers and sundry causes, namely some necessary and othersome also free and contingent: which according to their several natures, might work freely and contingently, or not work. Whereupon we conclude, that secondary causes are not enforced by God's purpose and decree, but carried willingly and after their own nature: for because that God is the preserver of the order by him set and appointed, and not the destroyer: who worketh by Satan and the wicked, not as by a stone or brute beast: but according to the quality and disposition of that nature which he hath put in them.[2]

[1] The description is that of a university letter in 1579; University Library, Cambridge, Baker MSS. vol. 'D', p. 208.

[2] From *Two Theames or Questions, handled and disputed openly in the Schooles at Cambridge, in the Latin tung*. Printed in 1579, with Baro's lectures on Jonah, and translated with four sermons preached by Baro in Great St Mary's in his *A speciall Treatise of Gods Providence and of comforts against all kinde of crosses and calamities to be fetched from the same. With an exposition of the 107. Psalme. Heerunto is added an appendix of certaine Sermons & Questions (conteining sweet and comfortable doctrine) as they were uttered and disputed ad clerum in*

His teaching, certainly, had led to occasional complaints. In 1581 (the year after the publication of his book *De fide, eiusque ortu et natura explicatio*) Baro publicly quarrelled with Laurence Chaderton about the nature and form of faith.[1] But his lectures on Jonah, published with some sermons and disputation speeches in 1579 had occasioned no extensive opposition at the time. It is a measure of the essentially rear-guard nature of the Calvinist protest of the 1590's (and the especial intensity of the popish scare in 1595) that it was not until June 1595 that any combined stand was made against him. In that month the Vice-Chancellor and eight heads (including Whitaker, Tyndall, Chaderton and Some) wrote to Whitgift demanding that the opinions of William Barrett be censured 'both in him and in some others, whose disciple he is'.[2] And on 7 July Peter Baro was called before the Consistory Court.

At this meeting, the Lady Margaret Professor was asked to give his opinion on those points of Christian assurance which Barrett had raised in April, beginning with the question whether faith could be totally lost. Baro offered instead to prepare a considered criticism of the published teaching of Robert Some on these matters. But Some did not think this a reasonable request, and insisted that Baro set down his opinions in writing in answer to the specific points. At that juncture the meeting was adjourned;[3] and Baro appears to have been unmolested for the next five months.

Then, in November, to a Cambridge where 'the pulpits ring of these novelties and differences',[4] came the articles decided upon at Lambeth. The Vice-Chancellor, Goad of King's, did

shortly after the receipt use means by the Heads and Presidents that every several college should take knowledge and warning thereof: and

Cambridge. The translator was John Ludham, a Johnian (B.A. 1564), Vicar of Wethersfield (where Richard Rogers was lecturer). The date of the publication of the book is not given: but the *Short Title Catalogue* puts it at 1588(?). The printer was John Wolfe of London. The book was to be reprinted in 1602. The quotation is at pp. 519–20.

[1] W. Dillingham, *Life of Chaderton*, 6.   [2] Trinity College MS. B/14/9, p. 19.
[3] This account of the meeting is based on a letter written on the same evening by Richard Clayton to Whitgift. Trinity College MS. B/14/9, p. 26.   [4] *Ibid.* p. 12.

unto some particular persons, of whom I doubted, as namely Dr Baro the Frenchman, I gave knowledge and caveat by causing him to see and read over the propositions, as also that clause of the said letters that nothing should be publicly taught to the contrary.[1]

But within a few days of that interview—that is, at the beginning of December—Baro had publicly commented upon the articles. Whitgift wrote to the Master of Trinity on 8 December that the Queen herself had heard of this, and was 'greatly offended' with Baro. Whitgift had had a difficult time explaining to Elizabeth the Frenchman's official standing in Cambridge, and he ended his letter with a sharp insular comment on prying foreigners. Meanwhile, Baro must be ordered 'utterly to forbear to deal therein'.[2]

Baro defended himself to the Archbishop in a Latin letter dated 13 December. He was insisting (he said) on only two points, neither of which was condemned by the articles: that God condemns men because of their sins, and that men cannot have security of salvation. However, he was called down to Lambeth and interviewed twice by Whitgift at the end of December. The Archbishop 'showed unto him the Propositions, and demanded his opinion of every one of them severally'. At the second interview Baro did indeed 'make some frivolous and childish objections against one or two of them'; but on the whole Whitgift was satisfied. Baro had agreed that the articles were 'all true'. He had also ominously said that 'they did not impugn any of his assertions'.[3]

There was now, in Cambridge, a fortnight of deceptive calm. The anxious Vice-Chancellor—who was so concerned for peace and quiet that he vetoed the printing of Whitaker's last sermon[4]— was attending the university disputations and sermons with both ears alert for the least whisper of trouble. But, as he wrote to Whitgift during the first week in January, 'I have not heard the

[1] *Ibid.* p. 130.
[2] *Ibid.* pp. 119–20.
[3] *Ibid.* p. 135. Whitgift to Goad, 19 Jan.
[4] *Ibid.* p. 26.

least contradiction: and on the other side so far off from personal provoking, as there hath been seldom or never maintaining or mentioning the truth set down in any of those points, their texts of scripture not occasioning thereunto'.[1] In fact, after nine months of academic groaning and travailing, a great calm seemed to have descended on Cambridge.

Seemed to have: but Baro was at work in his study on the text of his next university sermon, to be preached on 12 January. It proved to be a bigger bombshell even than Barrett's sermon of April 1595. The text was innocuous enough: 'If anyone is to offer service pure and undefiled in the sight of God, who is our Father, he must take care of orphans and widows in their need and keep himself untainted by the world' (James i. 27). The congregation settled down to hear a little wholesome doctrine, tempered by the comforts of practical divinity. These comforts were to be denied. Not only did Baro choose to continue the discussion of the points raised nine months before by his pupil Barrett, but, spurred by the Lambeth Articles, he took the disputes back to the fundamental basis of the theology of election, reprobation and grace: 'the whole course of his said sermon (excepting some entrance he made in the beginning) was concerning the said controversies, and especially the three last propositions about *universalis gratia*, contrary to the doctrine in the same contained, with more earnestness and vehemency, than is remembered that ever he showed before'.[2]

II

In letters to Whitgift on 14 January[3] and to Burleigh on 9 February,[4] Baro summarized the main points of his sermon. God created all men in his image, to eternal life; Christ died 'sufficiently' for all men, his offering being—in the words of the Thirty-nine Articles (Article XXXI)—a 'perfect redemption...

---

[1] *Ibid.* pp. 30–1.   [2] *Ibid.* p. 131. Goad to Whitgift, 13 Jan.
[3] *Ibid.* pp. 87–8.   [4] Lansdowne MSS. vol. lxxx, no. 69, fol. 172.

for all the sins of the whole world'; we must—as Article XVII made clear—'receive God's promises in such wise, as they be generally set forth to us': universally, to all men.

A complaint, giving a summary of the argument of the sermon, was drawn up on the evening of 12 January, while indignation was still hot, by six dons: George Downham of Christ's, and Abdias Ashton, John Allenson and William Nelson of St John's— four men who had petitioned against Barrett in the previous May—and James Crowther and John Hooke, also of St John's.[1] On 21 January, depositions on an official indictment were taken before the Vice-Chancellor, Tyndall, Chaderton and Barwell.[2] The deponents were Thomas Harrison of Trinity, George Estey of Caius, John Blyth of Peterhouse and Thomas Bendes of St John's —all four of whom had also petitioned against Barrett; Ralph Furness of St John's (who had supported Francis Johnson in 1589); Francis Savage, Thomas Monck and Thomas Crouch; and Cuthbert Bainbrigg of Christ's.

A study of the complaint and the indictment enables the following sketch of Baro's assertions to be made. By his primary, or antecedent will, God created each and every man to eternal life; reprobation is an act of the consequent will of God, a result of man's own rejection of the grace offered him. (A king, Baro said, adapts his laws to the capacities of his subjects; a father does not beget a son for the gibbet; a farmer does not plant a tree only to uproot it.) To each and every man God desires to give grace sufficient for salvation, for Christ died for each and every man. Thus if we are not saved the fault is ours. 'Men shut themselves out of heaven, not God.'

Such a distinction between the antecedent or conditional will of God, and his consequent will is found also in Thomas Aquinas:

---

[1] The original of this complaint is in the University Archives, Registry Guard Books, vol. 6 (i), no. 32. Copy in Lansdowne MSS. vol. LXXX, no. 60.

[2] Indictment in University Archives, *ibid.* Copy in Lansdowne MSS. *ibid.* no. 64. Registry Guard Books, vol. 6 (i), no. 31, is an account of the proceedings, in the hand of Registrary Thomas Smith.

'Antecedently, God wills that all men should be saved. But this is to will conditionally, not absolutely. God does not will this consequentially, which would be to will it absolutely.'[1] More important for the history of Elizabethan theology, Richard Hooker had made precisely the same distinction in a sermon preached in 1581: 'in God there were two wills; an antecedent and a consequent will: his first will, that all mankind should be saved; but his second will was, that those only should be saved, that did live answerable to that degree of grace which he had offered, or afforded them'.[2] (Walter Travers had objected to the conception of 'conditional' being applied to the sovereign and immutable will of God.)[3] Also, Samuel Harsnet, aged twenty-three and a new Fellow of Pembroke, had spoken at Paul's Cross in 1584 of the distinction between the 'absolute will' of God and 'his will with condition'.[4] So the distinction was no new thing in England in 1595; and Hooker's emphasis in 1597 on God's 'general inclination' that all men might be saved, and his 'more private occasioned will which determineth the contrary'[5] expressed a position he had begun to work out twenty years before. Overall, as Regius Professor of Divinity at Cambridge—appointed barely a month before Baro preached his sermon—was to be in the same tradition: writing of the 'conditional will of God', a 'general grace', a 'universality of grace'; as opposed to 'a more special grace of God...whereby according to his absolute will and constant purpose, he doth effectually enlighten, call and bring some men to repentance, faith, perseverance, and salvation. Which effectual grace is not universal but proper to the elect.'[6]

Thus the argument passed from the will of God to the grace of

---

[1] I, Q. 23, art. 4; in *Nature and Grace*, 107–8.
[2] From Walton's *Life*, in Hooker, *Works*, I, 22.
[3] Hooker's Answer to Travers; *Works*, III, 592.
[4] Sermon printed as appendix to *Three Sermons* by Richard Stuart (1656), 154.
[5] *Works*, II, 216.
[6] University Library, Cambridge, Baker MSS. vol. XXVI, p. 341. Note of *c.* 1600.

God. The seventh Lambeth Article, Baro agreed, is perfectly true. Saving grace is not 'granted' to all men. But—he went on to say —it is *offered* to all men.[1] Andrewes made the same point in his comments on the articles.[2] And so in January 1596 Baro argued with Goad in the Consistory that there were degrees of true grace, and to some men was offered more, some less; just as fifteen years before he had argued with Chaderton that there were degrees of true faith—a point which his disciple Barrett made in the same court in September 1595. Goad was not to be shaken. Even the Turks, he admitted, have some gifts from God; but to dignify such with the name of grace was intolerable. Grace meant grace effectual to salvation.[3]

It is possible, Baro continued, to resist grace: the Holy Spirit imposes no necessity on man.[4] The reprobate are 'the unbelievers, the rebels, those stubborn in sin'.[5] Here again, a passage of Hooker springs to mind: 'without grace there is no salvation. Now there are that have made themselves incapable of both, thousands there have been, and are, in all ages, to whose charge it may truly be laid, that they have resisted the Holy Ghost, that the grace which is offered, they thrust from them.'[6] Correspondingly, the elect are 'the believers'. Faith or perseverance may not be the efficient or moving cause of election—the Lambeth Articles, agreed Baro, are correct here. But they are the means by which we are made partakers of election: and without faith and perseverance and good works no man can reach heaven.[7]

Baro's theology stands or falls, however, by his most forcefully argued point—that Christ died for all men, for the sins of the whole world. Hooker elegantly made the same assertion:

God being desirous of all men's salvation, according to his own principal or natural inclination, hath in token thereof for their sakes whom he

---

[1] Baro's interpretation of the Lambeth Articles. Trinity College MS. B/14/9, pp. 83–5. Printed in Strype, *Whitgift*, III, 340–2.
[2] *Articuli Lambethani*, 31.
[3] Lansdowne MSS. vol. LXXX, no. 65.
[4] Strype, *Whitgift*, III, 342.
[5] *Ibid.* 340.
[6] *Works*, II, 590.
[7] Strype, *Whitgift*, 340.

loved, bestowed his beloved Son....he tasted death for all men....As therefore the gospel itself, which Christ hath commanded to preach unto all creatures, is an apparent effect of his general care and providence: so Christ, the principal matter therein contained and taught, must needs likewise have been instituted by the selfsame general providence to serve for a most sufficient remedy for the sin of mankind, although to ordain in whom particularly it shall be forceable and effectual be an act of special or personal providence.[1]

III

Besides the Vice-Chancellor, only two heads had been present in Great St Mary's on 12 January to hear Baro's sermon: Clayton and Chaderton. (In fact only about five heads were resident in Cambridge at the time.) Immediately after leaving the church, Goad discussed the matter with his two colleagues, both of whom were 'much grieved, to marvel he durst revive such matters'.[2] So blatant seemed Baro's disregard of 'former order taken' that Goad was uncertain what to do; especially as the question of Barrett's second recantation was under discussion at the same time —Barrett had just been allowed until the end of the month to confer with Chaderton and Overall. So he wrote to Whitgift for advice and help. The Lambeth Articles had been 'by your honourable consent and others in the High Commission approved';[3] so was not Baro's public and contrary teaching a matter for the ecclesiastical commissioners? Whitgift—who feared that Baro had been encouraged by those at court 'that seem to take some account of his judgement in these points', and by hearing of 'some misliking of the said Propositions by some in authority' —was for the moment prepared to leave matters to the Vice-Chancellor.

My advice to you is to call him before you and to require a copy of his sermon or at least to cause him to set down the special points thereof;

---

[1] *Works*, II, 574.
[2] Trinity College MS. B/14/9, p. 132.   [3] *Ibid.* p. 133.

and likewise to demand of him what should move him to continue
that course notwithstanding order taken to the contrary.....But forasmuch as there is something ado here about the same propositions &c
I would not have you to proceed to any determination against him, till
you have advertised me of his answer and the particular points of his
sermon, and received back again from me what I think fittest to be
done by you in this matter.[1]

On 17 January Baro was called for 'a private and quiet conference'[2] before Goad, Barwell, Chaderton, Tyndall, Clayton,
and John Overall.[3] Baro gave an account of this meeting to
Lancelot Andrewes.[4] He was cross-examined by each of the six
men in turn. Clayton was rather on his side; and Overall flatly
agreed with him. Baro complained of the attacks which had
been made upon him by Robert Some; and also of the gratuitous
ill-feeling of Goad and Chaderton—both of whom, he said, 'have
been badly disposed to me for many years now'.[5] He also objected
to a sermon preached the previous Sunday in St Clement's by
William Perkins, in which the new Regius Professor had been
criticized.[6] All in all, the quiet conference was not a conspicuous
success. 'Whereof', reported Goad, 'not ensuing so good issue
as was expected by reason of Dr Baro's uncertain and insufficient
answers.'[7]

Baro came before the heads in Consistory on 22 January, after
the depositions had been taken from nine auditors of the sermon.
The main charge, that he had spoken against the Lambeth
Articles,[8] Baro denied. These meetings too were unfruitful. On
the 29th Goad wrote to the Chancellor, to ask him, in turn, for
advice.[9] But Burleigh, much to the Vice-Chancellor's discomfort,
turned out to be on Baro's side. He strongly disapproved of the
treatment of a Lady Margaret Professor 'as if he were a thief'—

[1] Ibid. pp. 135–6.   [2] Ibid. p. 137.
[3] Account in Lansdowne MSS. vol. LXXX, no. 65.
[4] Trinity College MS. B/14/9, pp. 139–40.   [5] Ibid. p. 157.
[6] Ibid. p. 140. Perkins's sermon against Overall also mentioned ibid. p. 98.
[7] Ibid. p. 137.
[8] Lansdowne MSS. vol. LXXX, no. 59, fol. 149.   [9] Ibid. no. 58, fol. 147.

especially, Burleigh acidly commented, as 'the witnesses do not agree'. 'You may punish him', the letter concluded, 'if you will: but you shall do it for well doing in holding the truth, in my opinion.'[1]

And in fact no further action was taken against Baro. In March Goad went down to Lambeth to see Whitgift about the affair, but he found a very unsympathetic Archbishop. And on the 22nd of that month Baro wrote to Whitgift thanking him for his protection, and for saving him from his old enemy Goad. Whatever had actually happened, Baro saw in the dropping of the case a proof of the benevolent patronage of the Archbishop: 'I have no doubt that your Grace is the cause of it.'[2]

We may perhaps legitimately infer that Whitgift helped Baro, as he had defended Everard Digby, not because of an agreement in opinions, but because of the feeling that there had not been fair play.

IV

Shortly after Baro had written his note to Whitgift, he sent off to Denmark a letter for Niels Hemmingsen, sometime professor at Copenhagen, and former pupil of Melanchthon, in which he complained of the sudden intolerance of the Cambridge authorities: 'In this country we have hitherto been permitted to hold the same sentiments as yours on grace; but we are now scarcely allowed publicly to teach our own opinions on that subject, much less to publish them.'[3] Actually, Baro had completed a short essay on predestination over a year before—he had mentioned it to Fulke Greville in a letter of March 1595.[4] With his letter to Hemmingsen, Baro enclosed the manuscript of this work: his *Summa trium de praedestinatione sententiarum*, not to be published until 1613.[5]

[1] Trinity College MS. B/14/9, p. 129.　　　　[2] *Ibid.* p. 160.
[3] April, 1596. Quoted in J. Nichols (ed.), *The Works of Arminius*, I, 92.
[4] Letter in the MSS. of Sir John Coke, Melbourne Hall, Derbyshire; *Historical Manuscripts Commission, Twelfth Report, Appendix, Part One*, 16.
[5] There is a copy in the University Library, Cambridge. I have used, with a few modifications, the translation by J. Nichols, in his edition of *The Works of Arminius*, I, 92–100. Whitaker's last sermon (*Cygnea Cantio*) was also printed in the 1613 volume.

The essay summarized the three views about predestination held in the Reformed Church. There was first, argued Baro, the opinion of Calvin, Beza and Robert Some, which was also the opinion of the mature Augustine and Luther. This view maintained that God, in making his decrees of election and reprobation, 'had no regard whatever to Christ the Mediator or to faith', or 'to any kind of sin either original or actual'. He decreed absolutely to elect and to reprobate 'without respect to anything out of himself, but solely because thus it pleased him to display his own glory'.[1] If this view is held, said Baro, 'it is scarcely... possible to understand how God may not be accounted the author of that which is evil'.[2]

Secondly, there was the view of Zanchius, of St Augustine in his middle period—and also of Bellarmine. This was more 'liberal', as the decrees of election and reprobation were dated only from the Fall:[3] and the 'material cause' of election was Christ, and of reprobation, sin. But, commented Baro, the distinction between elect and reprobate still sprang 'from the absolute will of God';[4] and although all men might be invited to repentance, the elect were given an 'efficacious' grace which the rest of mankind could not expect;[5] Christ had died only for the elect, and the benefits of his passion had no more reference to the rest than 'to brute beasts or stones'.[6] This second view, like the first, imposed on man 'an inevitable necessity—on the one description of men the necessity of being saved, on the other the necessity of perishing. Numberless absurdities arise from these sentiments'[7].

The third opinion, which Baro took to be true, was that of Hemmingsen, of Melanchthon, of the early Fathers, and of Augustine before the conflict with Pelagius. 'God, who is in his nature good, created man for what is good, that is, for a life of blessedness.'[8] God 'every day truly calls and invites all men,

---

[1] *Summa*, 1. [2] *Summa*, 2. [3] *Summa*, 3. [4] *Summa*, 5.
[5] *Summa*, 4. [6] *Ibid*. [7] *Ibid*. [8] *Summa*, 6.

without any limit, to repentance, faith and salvation'.[1] For Christ is 'the stone of probation, by which the elect may be discerned from the reprobate'.[2] 'God has predestined such as he from all eternity foreknew would believe on Christ (who is the only way of life eternal), that they might be made conformable to him in glory. But he hath likewise from all eternity reprobated all rebels, and such as contumaciously continue in sin, as persons unfit for his kingdom.'[3] At this point Baro introduced the distinction between the 'antecedent' will of God that all and every one may be saved, and his 'consequent' will, by which certain men are damned 'through their own perverseness and depravity'.[4] This third view, Baro concluded, 'though it allows predestination to be immutable in the Divine Mind, yet it denies that such predestination renders the wills of men immutable, and imposes necessity on them, lest by such conclusions it should cause God to appear as the author of sin and of man's destruction'.[5] And the watchwords of this tradition are these: 'It is the will of God that all men be saved and that none perish'; 'Christ has died for all.'[6]

Thus Baro analysed the place of his opinions in the history of Christian theology; in a tract written in Cambridge in 1594. He was, then, one of the 'new Pelagians' roundly trounced by William Perkins in July 1592:[7] those who 'place the causes of God's predestination in man; in that they hold, that God did ordain men either to life or death, according as he did foresee, that they would by their natural free-will, either reject or receive grace offered'. Perkins himself, desiring 'among the rest, to cast my mite into the treasury of the Church of England', had his own 'true view'. This was that 'the cause of the execution of God's predestination is his mercy in Christ, in them which are saved; and in them which perish, the fall and corruption of man: yet so, as that the decree and eternal council of God, concerning them

---

[1] *Ibid.* [2] *Summa,* 6–7. [3] *Summa,* 7.
[4] *Summa,* 8. [5] *Summa,* 9. [6] *Summa,* 8.
[7] Epistle to the reader, 'A Golden Chain', *Works,* I, 10.

both, hath not any cause beside his will and pleasure'. This attack by Perkins on the new-style Pelagians, countered by Baro's angry dismissal of the description as an 'illiberal calumny'[1], helps to set the Cambridge disputes of the mid-1590's in their true context in the history of Christian ideas. They are one chapter of a long story. Baro, by relating the question of Christian assurance to the whole issue of election and reprobation, of the universal saving will of God, and of universal grace, showed what the story was really about. It was a tale of European interest. A reply to William Perkins's writings on predestination was undertaken by Arminius himself; a reply which Perkins never saw, for it was finished only in 1602[2], the year before Arminius went to Leiden, the year in which Perkins died. The Cambridge quarrels, therefore, were one of the tributaries which were to feed the ever-broadening stream which, by circumstances, took its name from the professor at the University of Leiden.

But in 1595 Arminius was only thirty-five—a year younger than Perkins. (He was born in 1560 at Oudewater, between Gouda and Utrecht: a district in which the youthful Erasmus had lived and moved.) His name was not much known outside Amsterdam. To the orthodox Calvinist, at least in England, it was the name of Baro, a quarter of a century the Dutchman's senior, which might have seemed the obvious label for the 'new Pelagianism'.

V

In September 1596 Baro wrote to Burleigh asking for assistance in the re-election to his professorship, in spite of the inadequate stipend.[3] On 26 November Whitgift wrote to the new Vice-Chancellor, Jegon of Corpus, about this matter:

I am loath to commend any man to you for the Lady Margaret's Lecture, partly because I would give no impediment to Dr Baro's

[1] *Summa*, II.
[2] Arminius's 'Modest Examination of Perkins's Pamphlet' is translated in *The Works of Arminius*, III (ed. W. Nichols, 1875), 252–484.
[3] Lansdowne MSS. vol. LXXXII, no. 91, fol. 193.

re-election, if any of his friends be disposed to help thereunto, but especially because I know your wisdoms and discretions to be such, as that you will make choice of the best and fittest for that office. Notwithstanding if there be no intent again to elect Dr Baro, then I would pray you to be favourable to Master Dr Playfere, whom I take to be a very sufficient man.[1]

And in fact, at the beginning of December, Thomas Playfere, Fellow of St John's, was elected Lady Margaret Professor. His tenure of office was to be curious: in 1602 he was reported to be 'crazed for love', and he died insane in 1609. However, on 4 December 1596 Jegon wrote to Whitgift:

I easily perceive by letters from your Grace your good opinion and gracious meaning to that reverend old man Dr Baro, who hath been here long time, a painful teacher of Hebrew and Divinity to myself and others. To whom I am (as I have always been) very willing to show my thankful mind. But he hath lately found some heavy friends among us, to the prejudice of his former credit and his present re-election. But if he returns, and please to take pains, in reading Hebrew lectures in private houses, I doubt not but to his good credit, there may be raised as great a stipend.[2]

But Peter Baro did not return to Cambridge. ' "*Fugio*", saith he, "*ne fugarer*", I fly for fear to be driven away.'[3] He died in London in 1599, at the age of sixty-five, and was carried to his grave by six doctors of divinity.[4]

[1] University Library, Cambridge, Baker MSS. vol. xxiv, p. 349.
[2] *Ibid.* p. 356.
[3] Fuller, *History of Cambridge*, 289.
[4] University Library, Cambridge, Baker MSS. vol. xxix, p. 186.

CHAPTER XVIII

TWO ELIZABETHAN CAMBRIDGE DIVINES: ANDREWES AND OVERALL

'It is a certain rule in divinity that grace does not destroy nature.'

JOHN OVERALL[1]

I

IN 1595 Lancelot Andrewes, for the past six years Master of Pembroke, was forty; four years older than William Perkins. It is usual to think of Andrewes as essentially a Jacobean figure: Bishop of Chichester (1605–9), of Ely (1609–19), and of Winchester (1619–26). But in fact he was as much a part of the history of Elizabethan Cambridge as Some was, or Whitaker, or Chaderton. He had matriculated from Pembroke, at the age of sixteen, in 1571; during the term when the university was split by the intensive campaign against Whitgift's new statutes. He won his fellowship at Pembroke in 1575, and in 1580, the year of his ordination, he was appointed junior treasurer of the college. William Fulke had been elected Master in 1578. Andrewes became senior treasurer in 1581; and he began to set in order the somewhat shaky college finances, dividing up the accounts in his neat hand, calling in 'a number of arrears and irregular debts',[2] insisting on retrenchment and reform. According to Henry Isaacson, whose biography of Andrewes was published in 1650, he found Pembroke in debt and left it with over £1000 in the treasury.[3] During the early 1580's he was also catechist of the college. On Saturday and Sunday afternoons at three he lectured on the Ten Commandments in the college chapel—lectures attended not only by Pembroke men, but by students from other

---

[1] *Convocation Book*, book II, chapter 2; ed. 1844, 87.
[2] A. Attwater, *Pembroke College*, 51.   [3] Ed. S. Isaacson, 40.

colleges and admirers from the town and the surrounding villages.[1] Notes of his addresses were handed down and passed from hand to hand; until a set of such notes was printed in 1642 under the title *The Moral Law Expounded*. The Introductory Epistle, by John Jackson, claimed: 'the work itself is such, as in those days when it was preached, he was scarce reputed a pretender to learning and piety then in Cambridge, who made not himself a disciple of Mr Andrewes by diligent resorting to his lectures; nor he a pretender to the study of Divinity, who did not transcribe his notes.' The style, though Andrewes was still under thirty, was recognizably there: rapid, terse, fresh, orderly, with what Mr Eliot has called a 'precision in the use of words, and relevant intensity'.[2] Andrewes himself, at that time, had noted the importance in preaching of 'a perspicacious order and orderly delivery'.[3] The preacher should have 'authority, gravity, and modesty, as knowing it is not his own, but the everlasting truth of God'.[4] This was not unlike the rule which Perkins was to lay down in *The Art of Prophesying*. But Andrewes's 'eager movement, gradually accelerating',[5] that method which 'takes a word and derives the world from it; squeezing and squeezing the word until it yields a full juice of meaning which we should never have supposed any word to possess'[6]—this was not at all like Perkins. For one thing, there was not much imagery; and what there was was brief and clipped.[7] For another, his 'pedantic ingenuity, his use of assonance and antithesis',[8] did not always correspond with Perkins's speech both 'simple and perspicuous, fit both for the people's understanding and the majesty of the Spirit':[9] though Andrewes no less than Perkins knew that there

---

[1] *Ibid.* 29. [2] T. S. Eliot, *Essays Ancient and Modern*, 16.
[3] *The Moral Law Expounded* (1642), 406.
[4] *Ibid.*
[5] Charles Smyth, *The Art of Preaching*, 127.
[6] Eliot, *Essays Ancient and Modern*, 21.
[7] The best appreciation of Andrewes's style is by J. B. Mozley, in *The British Critic*, XXXI, no. 61 (1842), 169–204.
[8] Smyth, *op. cit.* 123. [9] Perkins, *Works*, II, 670.

'is no speaking of the Spirit without the Spirit, no hearing neither'.[1] These lectures of the 1580's were at times almost contemplative, the alone communing with the alone. They were also immensely scholarly—'having an eye to the Greek word'.[2] (Andrewes had been one of the first holders at Pembroke of the Greek scholarship founded by Thomas Watts, chaplain to Grindal; besides Greek, Latin and Hebrew, he was said eventually to have mastered Chaldee, Syriac, and Arabic, besides many modern languages.) But besides the style, the thought and the temper are there too. 'Grace does not abolish nature but perfects it.'

Man, certainly, is fallen; his nature 'hath received a great wound'.[3] If man 'hath none to direct him but his own natural knowledge, he shall come to more grossness and absurdities, than the very beasts. We are all destitute of the knowledge of God by nature.'[4] It is true that 'the Gentiles do by nature the things of the law'. That is to say, they perform their moral duties, 'for the very light of nature doth guide us to the doing of them'.[5] But 'whatsoever good thing we do by the direction of natural reason, it is without all respect of God, except he enlighten us before'.[6] Man must, then, 'resign all his glory to God, and so the building may begin'.[7] 'To supply the defect that is in nature grace is added, that grace might make that perfect which is imperfect.'[8] The universe of Andrewes was a universe of grace:

It is dangerous to ascribe too little to the grace of God for then we rob him of his glory, but if we ascribe too little to ourselves there is no danger; for whatsoever we take from ourselves, it cannot hinder us from being true Christians; but if we ascribe that to the strength of our own nature which is the proper work of grace, then do we blemish God's glory.[9]

[1] Andrewes, *Sermons*, III (1875), 132.   [2] *The Moral Law Expounded*, 261.
[3] *Ibid.* 124.   [4] *Ibid.* 128.
[5] 'Sermons on prayer', preached in the 1580's, printed in 1611; reprinted in 1642, with *The Moral Law Expounded*, and in 1846, *Sermons*, V (1880 ed.), 315.
[6] *Ibid.*   [7] *The Moral Law Expounded*, 191.
[8] *Sermons*, V, 323.   [9] *Ibid.* 316.

But grace perfects God's creation. It does not destroy it. 'Nature, *qua natura*, is "good", yet imperfect; and the Law in the rigour of it not possible, through the imperfection of it. Nature is not, the Law is not taken away—"good" both; but grace is added to both to perfect both.'[1] Thus God's creation, and his gift of reason—the candle of the Lord—are not hindrances but aids to the vision of God:

As the sun giveth light to the body, so God hath provided light for the soul; and that is, first, the light of nature, which teacheth us that this is a just thing...from this light we have this knowledge, that we are not of ourselves but of another, and of this light the Wise Man saith, 'The soul of man is the candle of the Lord'. They that resist this light of nature are called *rebelles lumini*. With this light 'everyone that cometh into this world is enlightened'. Howbeit this light hath caught a fall, as Mephibosheth did, and thereupon it halteth; notwithstanding, because it is of the blood royal, it is worthy to be made up.[2]

This image of 'the blood royal', with relation to the son of Jonathan who 'fell, and became lame', first used by Andrewes in the early 1580's, was to be a favourite conceit of his: he employed it again, for instance, in a sermon preached on Whitsunday 1621: 'The light of nature, for rebelling against which, all that are without Christ suffer condemnation. Solomon calls it "the candle of the Lord searching even the very bowels", which though it be dim and not perfect, yet good it is; though lame, yet, as Mephibosheth, it is *regia proles*, "of the blood royal".'[3] Forty years in time separate the two passages: the thought is identical.

Thus the young catechist of Pembroke argued about the human condition and the nature of God, not (as Perkins was to do at Christ's) in terms of will, but in terms of reason and nature. We have the 'principles of religion naturally bred in us. The principles of divinity always agree with true reason: truth disagreeth not with truth:...Warrant, that reason agreeth with religion, Acts xvii. 24, etc. The true worship of God proved by natural

[1] *Ibid.* III, 370 (Sermon of 1621).   [2] *Ibid.* V, 327.   [3] *Ibid.* III, 376.

reason. True reason, an help to faith, and faith to it.'[1] With his
reason, fulfilled by faith, Andrewes looked to 'the mutual order
of all things in nature'.[2] In this he followed the Homilies:
'Almighty God has created and appointed all things in heaven,
earth and waters in a most excellent and perfect order...in all
things is to be lauded and praised the goodly order of God...
where there is no right order, reigneth all abuse, carnal liberty,
enormity, sin, and Babylonical confusion.'[3] He followed also
a tradition of European thought which goes back beyond Plato
at least to the perfect ratios of Pythagorean mysticism, which was
expressed in Christian terms by Augustine in his treatise 'On
Order', and which was a foundation—as Dr Tillyard has shown—
of 'the Elizabethan World Picture'. Le Corbusier has confessed
as the inspiration of his architectural theories the conviction that
'toute marche dans une harmonie douce et tranquille';[4] medieval
Christian builders saw in their careful proportions a perfection
which made of a building an image of heaven, just as 'the Biblical
description of the Heavenly City is pervaded and transfigured by
the vision of an ineffable harmony';[5] Piero della Francesca took
to painting because of a passion for geometry and the architectural theories of Alberti; Mozart expressed a belief that wrong
notes would be a denial of the principles of the universe.[6] And
Hooker, no less than Shakespeare, wrote memorably on the theme
of order. Even the most pessimistic of Christians might believe
that the harmony remained, even in a fallen universe, that the
heavenly spheres, if nothing else, still choired in perfection, that
'if His special goodness were not everywhere present every
creature should be out of order and no creature should have his
property wherein he was first created'.[7] Sir Thomas Browne

[1] The Moral Law Expounded, 23.   [2] Ibid. 41.
[3] 'Homily of obedience', Book of Homilies, 109–10.
[4] In a talk on the B.B.C. Third Programme, September 1951.
[5] Otto von Simson, The Gothic Cathedral (the Origins of Gothic Architecture and the
Mediaeval Concept of Order), (1956), 38.
[6] Alfred Einstein, Mozart, 207.   [7] Homilies, 508.

saw even in tavern music 'a sensible fit of that harmony which sounds in the ears of God'.[1] And Andrewes too worked out the implications of the correspondence of musical consonance and the harmony of God's universe: 'Where there are divers natures most discrepant, and these are brought into an harmony and concord, it must necessarily be argued, that there was one that accorded them, that tuned them; as in a lute tuned; so the world being full of varieties of natures, yet they agreeing in a wonderful sympathy, there must needs be a tuner of this so great a harmony.'[2] Grace and nature, then, work together, like reason and revelation, not in discord, but in order.

Such a conception of the Christian world picture was being expounded then—and popularly expounded—in the Cambridge of the early 1580's, as Perkins was working through the master's course in arts. But it must be emphasized that these lectures on the moral law were primarily an outline of practical divinity. Godly pastors such as Richard Greenham (also of Pembroke) might not have approved of Andrewes's firm statement that 'God would have all men saved';[3] they would have been startled by the assertion that 'sitting at prayer time, is not warranted by the word'[4] but kneeling is—'we must glorify him... with our bodies'.[5] (Perkins's sermon in Christ's College against kneeling was, we recall, in 1586.) But they would have whole-heartedly approved of his practical advice about the Christian life, his case-histories, his very frank discussion of sexual morality.[6] For Andrewes there was 'no article of faith or mystery of religion at all, but is as a key to open, and a hand to lead us to some operative virtue'.[7] In this he resembled Greenham. Indeed Thomas Fuller was to link together the two sons of Pembroke: 'I dare boldly say, if Greenham gained any learning by Andrewes, Andrewes lost no religion by Greenham.'[8] Even as a young priest in the 1580's Andrewes was noted

[1] *Religio Medici*, part 2.   [2] *The Moral Law Expounded*, 29.
[3] *Ibid.* 369.   [4] *Ibid.* 275.   [5] *Ibid.* 272.
[6] For example his reflections on adultery; *ibid.* 763.
[7] *Sermons*, v, 196 (1607).   [8] Fuller, *Church History*, v. 191.

as 'a man deeply seen in all cases of conscience, and he was soon sought to in that respect'.[1] This work as spiritual director was continued, at St Paul's when he became a prebendary in 1589, the year in which he was elected Master of Pembroke. And perhaps, in the last resort, when all the puns were forgotten, and the alliterations, and the assonances, and the antitheses, Andrewes deserved to be remembered because—as Fuller was to say of Greenham—'his masterpiece was in comforting wounded consciences'.[2]

II

Andrewes resigned the mastership of Pembroke in 1605, on his election to Chichester. During the sixteen years of his mastership he had also been chaplain to Elizabeth and to Whitgift (1586); prebendary of St Paul's and vicar of St Giles's Cripplegate (1589); prebendary of Westminster (1597); and Dean of Westminster (1601). When he left Cambridge for Chichester, Dr John Overall, his junior by five years, had been for three years Dean of St Paul's; succeeding Alexander Nowell, who had died in 1602 at the age of ninety-five.

Overall had gone up to St John's as a sizar in 1575, when John Still was Master and Henry Alvey a young bachelor of arts. In 1577 Still succeeded Whitgift as Master of Trinity; and Overall went down the street to Trinity too, commencing bachelor from that college in 1578. In 1581 he was elected Fellow of Trinity, and ten years later he became junior dean.[3] In 1591 also, he was instituted as vicar of Trumpington; and he added to this parochial charge in 1592 the livings of Epping (Essex) and Hinton (Berkshire). At the end of 1595, when he was thirty-five, Overall was elected Regius Professor of Divinity, in succession to William Whitaker.

Two years later Edmund Hound, the Master of St Catharine's,

---

[1] H. Isaacson, *Life of Andrewes*, 30.   [2] Fuller, *op. cit.* 147.
[3] W. W. R. Ball and J. A. Venn (ed.), *Admissions to Trinity College*, II, x.

died. The election of his successor took place in March 1598. It was a disputed election: for of the six Fellows the three senior were for Overall and the three junior for Dr Simon Robson of St John's. The seniors declared Overall elected. But the juniors objected to this overbearing decision, and appealed to the Vice-Chancellor, Jegon of Corpus, who—after four days of inquiries and consultations—declared Robson elected instead. Whitgift and the Queen, however, were in favour of Overall; and after poor Dr Robson had been in office for a week, Overall was appointed Master and admitted on 16 April.[1]

It could hardly have been expected, save by the most wishful of Cambridge thinkers, that Overall's tenure of the Regius chair would be uneventful. The trouble came to a head in 1599. In the spring of that year some of his auditors began to take 'great offence' about 'certain points of doctrine by him publicly delivered in the Schools in his divinity lectures and determinations'.[2] A series of tiresome complaints was made to the Vice-Chancellor (Jegon again) both by word of mouth and in writing, and by 20 June things had come to such a pass that Jegon decided to refer the matter to a committee, consisting of two heads—Provost Roger Goad, and Laurence Chaderton.[3] Overall, in his own account of these events, claimed that this decision was due entirely to the chicanery of Robert Some; for at a meeting of the Consistory the Master of Peterhouse 'put up a complaint against me, for teaching some erroneous points of doctrine, as he says, in my readings and determinations in the schools: which he exhibited written in a paper, but somewhat otherwise than I had delivered them'.[4]

Although the committee had been asked to sit at the beginning of July, as soon as possible after the Commencement, Goad and

[1] University Archives, Registry Guard Books, vol. 90, nos. 22 to 32.
[2] Account of the case by Goad and Chaderton. Cecil Papers (Salisbury MSS. Hatfield House), vol. 139, ff. 120–1.
[3] Overall's account of the case; University Library, Cambridge, MS. Gg/1/29, fol. 102a.   [4] Ibid.

Chaderton did not in fact meet until 31 August. On that day they worked out, from the various documents in the case, five points for discussion.[1] Of these, the most important were the first two, concerning the fall from grace and faith: does the elect and justified man who falls into gross sin lose his justifying faith—totally, if not finally—until he repents? This was the heart of the matter.

At the beginning of September Overall and his two examiners met in the Provost's Lodge at King's. The five points were shown to him, as a basis for discussion. The Regius Professor outlined his position with great care. In the matter of the fall from grace he insisted that the verb *carere* (to be destitute of) expressed his meaning better than *amittere* (to lose). He did not wish it to be suggested that the remission of sins once pardoned could be forfeit; only that a 'new guilt' was 'brought upon man by new gross sins committed against conscience, whereby the person became, of justified, unjust before God, and subject to God's wrath and judgement until he repented'.[2] This point made, another day was fixed for the continuing of the discussions, and the three men rose to go. But Overall, taking a last glance at the articles, noticed an ambiguity in one of them. This concerned the phrase 'for a time' in the position: 'can man lose justifying faith for a time?' This might mean, and Overall meant it to mean 'until he repents': it was a conditional remark. But Overall suddenly realized that it might also mean merely 'for some time' —'implying a certainty of return'.[3] And this certainty he would not grant to all men justified—but only to the elect. Goad and Chaderton irritably answered

that they held none justified but the elect, and so calling for the paper again, interlined the word 'Electus', to both the questions; but I said, that I meant both the Questions of all men justified, whether elect, or

[1] Points in Cecil Papers (Salisbury MSS.), vol. 139, fol. 120; and in University Library, Cambridge, MS. Gg/1/29, 102b.
[2] University Library, Cambridge, MS. Gg/1/29, fol. 102a–b.   [3] *Ibid.* fol. 103a.

not elect. And whether all men justified were elect, was another question. But whether they were or not, my meaning was of all men justified, whether elect or not, which should willingly sin, and lie in sin against their conscience.[1]

The Regius Professor, having delivered this body blow to the Calvinist assertion, left King's and returned to his own lodge.

The next day he crossed to King's again, hoping that the discussions might really begin. But there had been a misunderstanding. Goad and Chaderton produced written scripts of their arguments, and asked Overall to show them his. 'I answered, that I made account to confer in speech, until we had beaten out the full meaning and grounds of the opinions on both sides, wherein we differed: otherwise, we might perchance spend time and labour, in proving or confuting that which was not stood upon be avouched.' The Provost and the Master of Emmanuel stared at the Master of St Catharine's in annoyed amazement: and 'said they would have no conference but in writing, and thereupon another day was appointed'.[2]

The day appointed was 11 September. Overall, however, when the time came, found it impossible to keep the appointment, 'being the Fair time, and besides some extraordinary business falling upon me by the death of a near friend'.[3] During September Goad and Chaderton asked on numerous occasions for his 'anwers in writing'.[4] But their demands were always fobbed off, until the two heads extracted a definite promise from their colleague that he would let them have the material by 21 September.[5] On that very day, however (a Friday), Dr Some entered the picture again. Against the specific order of the Vice-Chancellor that both sides should abstain from handling the disputed points in public, Some preached a sermon entirely concerned with them.[6] Overall was rather pleased, thinking this might sabotage the

[1] University Library, Cambridge, MS. Gg/1/29, fol. 103 a.   [2] Ibid.
[3] Ibid.   [4] Cecil Papers (Salisbury MSS.), vol. 139, fol. 120 b.
[5] Ibid.   [6] University Library, Cambridge, MS. Gg/1/29, fol. 103 b.

conference altogether. But Goad and Chaderton were adamant; finally, on 5 October, a month after the first meeting in King's, Overall sent them some notes in writing on his doctrine. Now Overall had cause to complain—because he heard nothing for a fortnight. Then, on 20 October, after dinner, 'I was suddenly called into the Consistory, without any forewarning, to hear a certain confutation, which they had compiled against my arguments.'[1]

Those present, besides Overall, Jegon, Goad and Chaderton, were Barwell, Clayton, Montagu (of Sidney Sussex) and Some. Overall's statement and its confutation were read. Then the meeting broke down into trivial arguments; at one point resolving itself into a bad-tempered exchange about the merits or otherwise of a particular adversary of Bellarmine.[2] Finally, Jegon complicated the whole issue by wondering whether Whitgift should be informed of the proceedings: perhaps he remembered the Archbishop's anger four years previously at the 'rash and intolerable and consistorian-like kind of proceeding' against Barrett. This, said Overall, put everyone in a 'great muse'.[3] One or two of the heads discreetly suggested that such a course was unnecessary: 'It would be a trouble to his Grace; his Grace would not like of it; that his Grace's judgement was utterly against those points; that it would diminish the authority of the university; that it would be smothered, and come to no good; finally, that the matter was not yet ripe.'[4] So Jegon handed back the papers to the three parties, and looked forward to a more detailed discussion at the end of term.

At the end of December Goad and Chaderton sent to the Vice-Chancellor their revised and extended confutation, together with the minutes of the last meeting. (Overall was very annoyed because he never received a copy of either.) There had been, by

[1] *Ibid.*
[2] *Ibid.* fol. 104a; also in Cecil Papers (Salisbury MSS.), vol. 139, fols. 120–121b.
[3] University Library, Cambridge, MS. Gg/1/29, fol. 104a.
[4] *Ibid.* fol. 104a–b.

this time, a further twist of the knife. The new Vice-Chancellor was Robert Some.

Naturally the pulpits had been set ringing once more. There were—for the first time in Elizabethan Cambridge—some disputes about the Real Presence. Overall's opponents asserted that he had taught the real and substantial presence of the body and blood of Christ in the Eucharist. Overall had replied that 'In the sacrament of the Eucharist, the body and blood of Christ, and the whole Christ, is offered to the worthy receiver, not by transubstantiation, nor by consubstantiation, but by the Holy Spirit working through faith'.[1] But the main point at issue was again that of Christian assurance. In a sermon preached in March 1600 Goad attacked as 'a popish opinion, that justifying grace might be lost by mortal sins'; and affirmed that 'perpetuity of justifying grace once given, and certainty of salvation, was our freehold, and therefore in no case to be let go'.[2] Overall, in replying to this sermon,[3] made once again his point that repentance was a necessary condition of assurance: 'I think it a vain fancy and dangerous presumption for a man to have a persuasion, that he hath faith, or that he is justified and elected, so long as he is void of true repentance.' The Christian can be 'fully persuaded' by faith 'of the remission of his sins, and free justification, and thereby conceive also sure hope and trust of his election': but only if he 'in true repentance flieth to the throne of grace, and there apprehendeth Christ, with his merits, in the promises of the Gospel'. There was, then, an element of 'if': and of 'hope'—and hopes can be dupes, just as fears may be liars. An element too of freedom of choice: there has been 'free liberty and mutability left unto the will, even under grace'. Many men may receive 'good affections and motions of grace' and begin 'to believe and live in the Spirit'; but 'afterwards by their negligence, lusts and security' they 'fall away and end in the flesh'. And although the

---

[1] University Library, Cambridge, MS. Gg/1/29, fol. 105a.   [2] *Ibid.* fol. 104b.
[3] University Library, Cambridge, Baker MSS. vol. XXVI, pp. 343-4.

elect 'after that they be effectually called and soundly rooted and grounded in faith and grace' do not fall away from grace either totally or finally, yet they can 'fall into such gross and criminal sins, as that thereby they do grievously wound God's graces in them'; they become 'unjust and guilty of God's wrath and judgement'; and so they remain 'until by God's merciful visitation (which faileth not his elect) they be through a new act of repentance and faith again renewed'.

And so the case dragged on, like all the other cases: weary, stale, flat and unprofitable. Eventually a meeting of the Consistory Court was held in the Regent House on 4 June 1600 'touching the end of the Conference with Dr Overall'.[1] Goad and Chaderton handed over to Some their narrative account of the long drawn-out proceedings, and Some 'earnestly desired Dr Overall to join with him and the rest in the acknowledgement of the truth, whereof all present would be glad'. Overall refused to rise to the occasion: 'he answered that he was not so persuaded in his conscience and therefore could not'. In face of this, all Some could do was to hope that God might better enlighten the mind of the Regius Professor of Divinity, and to require him to forbear impugning in public any of the points of doctrine proved by Goad and Chaderton in their confutation. The heads seemed unusually nervy; with Whitgift in the background and the peace of the university at stake, that was understandable. Nor was the summer to calm their nerves—for within a month of that June meeting the quarrel between Overall and Some flared up again: at the disputations during the Commencement.

For the divinity disputation on Commencement Eve (30 June) two questions had been prepared, and approved by Whitgift: they concerned private confession, and purgatory.[2] Robert Some was moderator of the disputation; and on the 30th he made a speech on the purgatory motion, in which he determined 'against

[1] Cecil Papers (Salisbury MSS.), vol. 139, fol. 123.
[2] *Ibid.* fol. 122.

the popish sort, soundly and perspicuously'.[1] Overall, when he was called upon by the bedell to reply, unfortunately lost his temper, and launched into a violent refutation of the Vice-Chancellor's determination. Dr Some interrupted the flow of rhetoric by commanding Overall to silence; regretting that the Regius Professor had nourished any errors, and condemning his making them public in such a university assembly. And it was probably true, in the circumstances, that the spirit of the meeting was in support of the Vice-Chancellor, Overall's action being 'offensive to the auditory, in regard both of matter and manner'.[2]

For the Master of St Catharine's and the Master of Peterhouse thus to wash their clean linen in public was unfortunate. It was perhaps even more unfortunate that the moderator appointed for the Commencement Day disputation on 1 July was Dr Thomas Playfere, Lady Margaret Professor, who less than a month before had been a possible candidate for the mastership of Clare—one of the other prospective candidates being Overall himself.[3] At the disputation Playfere took it upon himself to dot the i's and cross the t's of Some's speech of the previous day. But the asperity with which he defended the Vice-Chancellor and attacked the Regius Professor was such that even his strongest supporters felt themselves obliged to apologize for it.[4] In fact, the Commencement ceremonies of 1600 had been the most bad-tempered within living memory.

The debate continued: and its echoes were heard nearly four years later at a higher level—at the Hampton Court Conference

[1] *Ibid.* fol. 124a. Some's speech is in Cecil Papers (Salisbury MSS.), vol. 144, fol. 162.

[2] Cecil Papers (Salisbury MSS.), vol. 139, fol. 124a. Overall's own account of the Commencement of 1600, in Latin, is in University Library, Cambridge, MS. Dd/3/85, no. 5, fol. 4a *ad fin.*, said to be in his hand. The copy-book, University Library, Cambridge, MS. Gg/1/29 has a rather fuller version, printed in 1721 by Archibald Campbell, Bishop of Aberdeen, in *The Doctrines of a Middle State between Death and Resurrection*, 203–26.

[3] The election at Clare was held in May, on the death of Thomas Byng. A letter mentioning Overall as a possible successor is in Cecil Papers (Salisbury MSS.), vol. 79, fol. 60. That referring to Playfere is *ibid.* vol. 136, fol. 70. A certain William Smith was elected.

[4] Cecil Papers (Salisbury MSS.), vol. 139, fol. 124.

of January 1604. This conference was the perfect appendix to the past decade of theological controversy in Cambridge. On the second day John Reynolds, Dean of Lincoln and President of Corpus Christi College, Oxford (who, with John Knewstubb and Laurence Chaderton, represented the Puritans), petitioned the King that the wording of Article XVI ('we may depart from grace given') might be amended, as seeming contrary to the doctrine of predestination as expressed in Article XVII. Reynolds suggested that the phrase 'yet neither totally nor finally' be added. He also asked that 'the nine assertions orthodoxal...concluded upon at Lambeth'[1] be officially added to the Articles of Religion. This latter appeal fell rather flat, because James had never heard of the Lambeth Articles. It was explained to him that by reason of some Cambridge controversies Whitgift had 'assembled some divines of especial note, to set down their opinions...for the appeasing of those quarrels'. James replied, with fine lack of pedantry, that 'when such questions arise among scholars, the quietest proceeding were, to determine them in the universities, and not to stuff the book with all conclusions theological'.[2] Richard Bancroft then took up the argument of the fall from grace: informing the King that as against the 'true doctrine of predestination' (whereby 'I trust that God hath elected me') there were those nowadays who 'presumed too much of persisting of grace' and assumed that 'though I sin never so grievously, yet I shall not be damned: for whom he once loveth, he loveth to the end'.[3] Bancroft concluded by pointing out that, as Article XVII made clear, God's promises must be 'generally' understood. The King took up this phrase, which he 'very well approved'. He then treated the assembled company to a royal variation on the Pauline theme that salvation must be worked out in fear and trembling. Perhaps, said James, we might clear the

---

[1] Barlow's account of the Conference; in Cardwell (ed.), *History of Conferences*, 178.
[2] *Ibid.* 185.
[3] *Ibid.* 180–1.

doubts of Dr Reynolds by inserting the word 'often' in the phrase
'we might depart from grace'; but in the mean time he

wished that the doctrine of predestination might be very tenderly
handled, and with great discretion, lest on the one side, God's omnipotency might be called in question, by impeaching the doctrine of
his eternal predestination, or on the other, a desperate presumption
might be arreared, by inferring the necessary certainty of standing
and persisting in grace.[1]

Shortly after this admirable judgement, Overall knelt, and
signified to the King

that this matter somewhat more nearly concerned him, by reason of
a controversy between him and some other in Cambridge, upon a
proposition which he had delivered there; namely that whosoever
(although before justified) did commit any grievous sin...did become,
ipso facto, subject to God's wrath, and guilty of damnation, or were in
state of damnation...until they repented.

It was true, Overall again said, that 'those which were called or
justified according to the purpose of God's election' could 'never
fall, either totally from all the graces of God, to be utterly
destitute of all the parts and seed thereof, nor finally from
justification'; for howsoever they sinned they 'were in time
renewed by God's spirit unto a lively faith and repentance'. But
it was very false to teach that 'all such persons as were once truly
justified', however grievously they sinned, 'remained still just, or
in the state of justification, before they actually repented of those
sins'. For no man 'should be justified and saved without
repentance'.[2]

James, to conclude the debate, could do not better than to
approve and repeat the sentiments of Dr Overall, insisting on 'the
necessary conjoining repentance and holiness of life with true
faith'. For, the King agreed, 'although predestination and
election depend not upon any qualities, actions, or works of man,
which be mutable, but upon God his eternal and immutable

[1] *Ibid.* 181.   [2] *Ibid.* 186.

decree and purpose; yet such is the necessity of repentance, after known sins committed, as that, without it, there could not be either reconciliation with God or remission of those sins'.[1] That judgement of the second Solomon ended the discussion.

After the conference Overall returned to his house—his house as the Dean of St Paul's, where, just over eight years before, Whitaker had lodged with his aged uncle Alexander Nowell during the Lambeth Conference. Whitgift—whose comments at Hampton Court on these matters of grace and predestination have not been recorded—went back to Lambeth by river. On that same river, a fortnight later, he was to catch a severe February chill. For a tired man of more than seventy, this was the beginning of the end: and on 29 February 1604 John Whitgift died at Lambeth after a stroke. The Hampton Court Conference had been, as it were, his last official engagement. There could hardly have been a more appropriate ending to his forty years of service under the Supreme Governor.

III

At the same time as representations were made to the Vice-Chancellor about the teaching of Overall in his Cambridge lectures, complaints were being made to the Bishop of London concerning his preaching as Vicar of Epping. The aggrieved included John Cakebread, a Queens' man, rector of South Hanningfield, twenty miles from Epping, and another Essex rector called Joseph Bird, a Trinity man;[2] but the chief complainer was Robert Hill, Fellow of St John's, friend and editor of William Perkins, and devoted disciple of the late Dr Whitaker. Hill objected to Overall's doctrine that 'the decree of reprobation is for sin'; that 'Christ is offered to every singular man'; and that 'Christ died for all, that is, for every singular man in the world'.[3]

[1] Ibid.
[2] Complaints in University Library, Cambridge, MS. Gg/1/29, fol. 122a.
[3] Hill's complaint, ibid. 119a–121b.

Overall's reply to the inquiry of Richard Bancroft has never been printed.[1] It deserves better:

The occasion of my speech of this matter was this: I was requested to come visit some of my parish that were sick; and coming, found them sicker in mind than in body. The thing that troubled their minds, as they said, was this. They could not be persuaded that Christ died for them. Wherein, having by the comforts of the Gospel, as I thought best, somewhat eased and persuaded them, I took occasion afterward in my sermon, for their sakes, to handle this point, that every one was bound to believe in Christ, that is, that he died for his sins, and namely, to gather them out of the general, Christ died for all (II Corinthians v. 15), where the Apostle (laying down that the love of Christ, which is the great commander of our life and actions, riseth from this persuasion, that Christ died for us), gathered the same from this General, that Christ died for all, almost in manner of syllogism: If one died for all, then all were dead; but one died for all, so all were dead. And so Augustine urgeth his reason against Julian the Pelagian often.

Christ died for all men sufficiently, for the believers only effectually; as the sun that shineth sufficiently to give light to all, though it doth it effectually, only to them that open their eyes; as water that is sufficient to quench all the thirst, but doth it only to them that drink it; as physic that is sufficient to cure all maladies, but doth it effectually only when it is applied. So Christ, the sun of righteousness, the water of life, the heavenly medicine.

Overall was concerned, of course, with the same points as those around which revolved the controversies in Holland and the United Provinces; from which sprang the adjectives 'Arminian' and 'Remonstrant' as descriptions of the 'movement of thought in the direction of a more liberal theology'.[2] But the Cambridge school was an indigenous growth. It would be improper to use the word 'Arminian' of any English theologian before 1610. Indeed, Dr A. W. Harrison had written that it was not until 1613, when Grotius defended the theology of his compatriot before James I, that we can 'begin to discern the first glimmerings of an English Arminian school of thought'.[3] Thomas Goodwin, who

[1] *Ibid.* 122b.   [2] A. W. Harrison, *Arminianism*, 5.   [3] *Ibid.* 64–5.

went up to Christ's in 1614, wrote of his period as an under-graduate: 'As I grew up, the noise of the Arminian Controversy in Holland, at the Synod of Dort, and the several opinions of that controversy, began to be every man's talk and enquiry, and possessed my ears.'[1] The Synod of Dort (on the left bank of the Old Meuse, about fifteen miles south-east of Rotterdam) began in November 1618. The canons were promulgated in the following May: the month in which Bishop Overall died at Norwich. Of the six Englishmen who attended the synod officially, four were Cambridge men: Joseph Hall, Dean of Worcester and sometime Fellow of Emmanuel, who retired after a short time because of ill health; Dr Thomas Goad, sometime Fellow of King's, chaplain to Archbishop Abbot, and son of the Provost Roger Goad who had crossed swords with Baro and Overall: he replaced Joseph Hall; Dr Sam Ward, Master of Sidney Sussex, who had once confided to his undergraduate diary his sorrow at the deaths first of Whitaker, then of Perkins';[2] and Dr John Davenant, President of Queens', who had succeeded Playfere as Lady Margaret Professor in 1609, and whose Cambridge lectures, 'in which he most clearly confuted the blasphemies of Arminius, Bertius, and the rest of that rabble of Jesuited Anabaptists', had been greatly admired in 1618 by the young Symonds D'Ewes of St John's.[3] The four men must have been quite at home in Dordrecht. The issues there discussed were those which had been debated in Cambridge in the late 1590's and which had been causing argument in the Church of England since the early 1580's.

IV

The Five Points of the Arminians, condemned at Dordrecht in 1619, had been published in 1610. The Remonstrant assertions were these: that God elected 'in Christ, for Christ's sake, and

---

[1] T. Goodwin, *Works* (1704), v, x.
[2] M. M. Knappen (ed.), *Two Puritan Diaries*, 125 (Whitaker), 130 (Perkins).
[3] D'Ewes, *Autobiography*, I, 120. Peter Bertius was rector of the University of Leiden.

through Christ' those who 'shall believe on this his son Jesus, and shall persevere in this faith...even to the end'; that Christ died 'for all men and for every man'; that grace was not irresistible in the manner of its working; and that a total and final fall from grace was possible.[1]

At some time between 1610 and his death in 1619 Overall made a summary of these five 'Articles of controversy in the Low Countries'.[2] Respecting these articles 'the Remonstrants or Arminians, and the contra-Remonstrants or Puritans, defend opposite tenets'. But, Overall commented, between the two 'our Church much more correctly (as it appears to me) holds the middle path'.

The position of the Church of England in the disputed points was defined by Overall as follows. With regard to election we assert a 'particular absolute decree', arising not from divine foreknowledge of faith but 'from the purpose of the divine will and grace', respecting the 'salvation of those whom God hath chosen in Christ'. But with this absolute decree we join a 'general and conditional will, or a general evangelical promise'; and we teach 'that the divine promises are so to be embraced by us as they are generally set forth in the Holy Scriptures'. The will of God, as revealed in his word, is clear: 'that God gave his Son for the world or the whole human race; that Christ ordered the Gospel to be preached to all; that God wills and commands all to hear Christ and believe in him, and that he sets forth grace and salvation for all in him.' God, then, in the first place proposed salvation 'in Christ to all, if they believed': for this he gives 'common and sufficient grace'. And in the second place, 'that the salvation of men might be more certain' he adds 'a special grace, more efficacious and abundant' by which men are in fact

---

[1] 1610 Articles in Schaff, *Creeds of the Ev. Prot. Churches*, 545–9.

[2] Copy in University Library, Cambridge, MS. Gg/1/29, fols. 6–14; copies also in British Museum Harleian MSS. vols. 750 and 3142. Printed and translated from the Harleian texts by William Goode, *The Doctrine of the Church of England as to the Effects of Baptism in the Case of Infants* (second edition, 1850), 127–33.

inclined to 'believe, obey and persevere'.[1] Thus the Church of England 'grants the death of Christ for all men': at the same time as it believes in 'the special intention of God', through efficacious grace, to apply the benefits of the passion of Christ 'absolutely, certainly and infallibly, to the elect alone'.[2] We also believe, continued Overall, that men can 'resist the divine call and influence by their free will, and too often do resist'. But we add (he said) that God, 'when he wills and to whom he wills' gives 'grace so abundant, powerful, or suitable (*congruam*), or in some other way efficacious, that although the will is able to resist it, on account of its liberty, yet it does not resist, but certainly and infallibly complies'. God acts in this way 'with those whom he had chosen in Christ, so far as is necessary for their salvation'.[3] Finally, between the Arminian assertion that men can 'by negligence and security fall from (*deficere*) faith and grace', and the Calvinist denial that the believer can do so, Overall set the following doctrine. Believers, 'through the infirmity of the flesh and temptations' may, in the words of Article XVI, 'depart from grace': *recedere*. (Whitaker, it will be remembered, had granted this.)[4] They may even fall from grace and faith: *deficere*. (This Whitaker had denied.) But, on the other hand, 'those believers who are called according to God's purpose and who are firmly grounded in a lively faith' cannot 'either totally or finally fall'. For to them has been granted the special and efficacious grace of perseverance.[5]

These arguments were repeated in Overall's so-called 'Opinions on Predestination', which must have been written in that same decade, and which were to be printed in 1651.[6] It is typical that in this document, even more than in the 'Articles of Controversy',

[1] University Library, Cambridge, MS. Gg/1/29, fol. 6a–b; tr. Goode, *op. cit.* 128–9.
[2] University Library, Cambridge, MS. Gg/1/29, fol. 6b; tr. Goode, *op. cit.* 129.
[3] University Library, Cambridge, MS. Gg/1/29, fol. 7a; tr. Goode, *op. cit.* 129.
[4] *Cygnea Cantio*, 20.
[5] University Library, Cambridge, MS. Gg/1/29, fol. 7a; tr. Goode, *op. cit.* 130.
[6] 'Sententia de Praedestinatione', in University Library, Cambridge, MS. Gg/1/29, fols. 10b–13b; printed in 1651, *Articuli Lambethani*, 42–55.

Overall at every stage based his conclusions on the Thirty-nine Articles, and also on the Book of Common Prayer. In his consideration of the point that Christ died for all men, for instance, he quoted the Consecration Prayer and the Words of Administration in the Holy Communion Office.[1] 'Almighty God, our heavenly Father, who of thy tender mercy didst give thine only Son Jesus Christ to suffer death upon the Cross for our redemption; who made there (by his one oblation of himself once offered) a full, perfect, and sufficient sacrifice, oblation, and satisfaction, for the sins of the whole world.' The liturgy of Cranmer, in its dignity and truth, was a more than adequate support for the theology of Overall.

V

When Overall died in May 1619 he had been Bishop of Norwich for only one year. For the preceding four years he had been Bishop of Lichfield. He had resigned the Regius chair in April 1607.[2]

The two documents on the Arminian controversy date either from Overall's last few years as Dean of St Paul's, or from his period at Lichfield. But neither of them say anything which is new to a student of the Cambridge disputes of 1595, when Overall was a mere Fellow of Trinity. They assert nothing which he had not maintained in his eleven and a half years as Regius Professor of Divinity in the university. And what he maintained

[1] University Library, Cambridge, MS. Gg/1/29, fol. 11 b. *Articuli Lambethani*, 46.
[2] Announcement of the vacancy in University Archives, Registry Guard Books, vol. 39 (ii), no. 1. In 1604 Overall had married, but his wife, a famous beauty, was hardly a model of her kind. John Aubrey was to describe her as 'so tender hearted that she could scarce deny any one', and to print with relish a verse told to him in the 1650's by an elderly matron who had known the accommodating lady:

> The Dean of St Paul's did search for his wife
> And where d'ee think he found her?
> Even upon Sir John Selby's bed
> As flat as any flounder.

(*Brief Lives*, Cresset Press ed.; 161–2; Antony Powell, *John Aubrey and his friends*, 82.)

was significant, in the 1610's as in the 1590's, because it destroyed the case of those Calvinist Puritans who claimed that their interpretation of the mysteries of grace and predestination, and their interpretation alone, was 'the truth of religion publicly and generally received'.[1]

Overall, as everyone has always known, was not alone in his opposition to this claim: Lancelot Andrewes and Peter Baro and William Barrett and their Cambridge supporters have not gone unacknowledged in the story of the 'eclipse of high Calvinism'. But the Calvinist claim was more tenuous, and less overriding, in the Elizabethan Church of England than has sometimes been believed. It has been one of the aims of this study to demonstrate that John Whitgift, too, was aware that 'our Church holds the middle path': *mediam viam tenens.*

[1] Trinity College MS. B/14/9, p. 51. Heads to Whitgift, July 1595.

THE CANDLE OF THE LORD

Religion doth not destroy Nature but is built upon it.

BENJAMIN WHICHCOTE[1]

I

IN February 1626 John Preston (who had been secretly elected Master of Emmanuel in October 1622,[2] on the resignation of Laurence Chaderton at the age of eighty-six) attended a conference in London at York House; to discuss points raised during 1625 by the writings of Dr Richard Montagu (Fellow of King's from 1597 to 1604), concerning 'predestination, falling from grace, liberty of the will'.[3] (Nearly four years before, at the Commencement of 1622, Joseph Mead of Christ's had been much disturbed by the rumours that fourteen Jesuits had been present at the time of the ceremonies, one of them having slipped through the customs at Lynn and come down the river to Cambridge with his trunks, only to be apprehended in the nick of time, as he was hiring a horse for London, and brought before the Vice-Chancellor. He had also been disturbed by the Commencement sermon of William Lucy—sometime fellow-commoner of Caius and now chaplain to the Duke of Buckingham—who had spoken 'totally for Arminianism, wonderfully boldly and peremptorily, styling some passages of the contrary by the name of blasphemy'.[4]) At the 1626 Conference the Master of Emmanuel wished that 'the Synod of Dort might be received and established as the doctrine of the Church of England',[5] as his predecessor,

[1] *Aphorisms*; quoted by E. T. Campagnac (ed.), *The Cambridge Platonists*, 68.
[2] Letter of Joseph Mead, in T. Birch (ed.), *The Court and Times of James I*, II, 339–40.
[3] Letter of Mead, in T. Birch (ed.), *The Court and Times of Charles I*, I, 86.
[4] Letter in Birch (ed.), *Court and Times of James I*, II, 319–20.
[5] T. Ball, *Life of Preston*, 130.

twenty-two years before, had wished the Lambeth Articles to be added to the Thirty-Nine.[1] For Preston there was one basic objection to the theology of Montagu. It seemed to ignore the fact that 'never did strong man glory of his strength more than God doth of his sovereignty and omnipotency'.[2] Yet after the York House Conference Montagu's party talked 'much of the success on their side'[3] (though the Arminians did not quite yet hold all the best bishoprics and deaneries in England). The key figure was the Duke of Buckingham. Until the beginning of 1626 Preston and the Puritans had entertained high hopes of his patronage: but now, wrote Joseph Mead in March, 'the Duke is the great protector of the Montagutians'.[4] And on 13 July, only three months after the conference, when the Duke was at York House solemnly presented to the chancellorship of the university (the Vice-Chancellor and heads having ridden up the day before with their gowns, hoods and caps)[5], it was noticed that at the reception Preston looked much preoccupied and drank but little.[6]

The election of the Duke of Buckingham as Chancellor in 1626 crucially divided opinion in the university. The contest, wrote J. B. Mullinger, 'was essentially one between the two great theological parties of the time'.[7]

The Duke of Suffolk, Chancellor of the University, had died at two in the morning of Sunday 28 March. The news had scarcely arrived in Cambridge when, on the Monday afternoon, the chaplain of the Bishop of London rode in with an episcopal message. (The bishop was George Montaigne, Fellow of Queens'.) The message was this: the King wished Buckingham to be elected as Suffolk's successor. Now, the Duke had been formally

---

[1] Puritan motion, proposed by Reynolds, at the Hampton Court Conference.
[2] Ball, *Preston*, 140.
[3] Mead; in Birch (ed.), *Court and Times of Charles I*, I, 86.
[4] *Ibid.* 105. I. Morgan's biography of Preston, *Prince Charles' Puritan Chaplain*, was published too late (London, 1957) for me to make use of it.   [5] *Ibid.* 127–9.
[6] Ball, *Preston*, 143.   [7] J. B. Mullinger, *The University of Cambridge*, III, 59.

impeached by the House of Commons only three weeks before, and so the situation, to say the least, was very delicate. The heads met together: and the arguments of some who wished to wait the full statutory period of fourteen days before electing, 'to avoid the imputation of folly and temerity'[1], were overborne by the forcefulness of those who were all for Buckingham, and the sooner the better. The most vehement of the Duke's party were William Beale of Pembroke; William Paske of Clare; Leonard Mawe, Master of Peterhouse from 1617 to 1625, and now Master of Trinity; and Matthew Wren, a Pembroke man, sometime chaplain to Bishop Andrewes, who had succeeded Mawe at Peterhouse. So Buckingham was nominated. But the election of a Chancellor was by vote of all the members of the university with the degree of master or above; and to many of these the nomination of Buckingham seemed an arbitrary imposition by an over-powerful clique, resembling nothing so much as an arranged marriage. And on the Monday evening another name was put forward—that of the new Earl of Berkshire[2]; whose supporters unfortunately neglected to inform him of their choice.

The stage was now set. On Tuesday the canvassing and string-pulling began in earnest. All the heads of houses sent for their Fellows and more or less tactfully indicated that they would be expected to vote for Buckingham. But some Fellows were 'so bold as to visit for the contrary in public'. Many others cautiously and tentatively inquired of their colleagues how the land lay. Later on Tuesday Bishop Montaigne himself arrived in Cambridge, with the Duke's secretary; and also John Cosin, sometime secretary to Bishop Overall, and Fellow of Caius, and now chaplain to Bishop Neile of Durham. Cosin brought with him letters from the Bishop of Durham, strongly pressing the claims of the Duke. Throughout Wednesday Montaigne and Cosin and

[1] Letter of Joseph Mead, 3 June 1626; Birch, *Court and Times of Charles I*, I, 108. My account of the election is based on this letter; *ibid.* 107–9.

[2] Thomas Howard (Magdalene), son of Suffolk, had been created Earl of Berkshire on 7 February.

the ducal secretary visited and hectored. And Dr Mawe sent for the Fellows of Trinity one by one—some of them twice over—to argue them into conformity.

The election was on Thursday morning. The Master of Trinity began the day with a persuasive sermon in his college chapel lauding the virtues of unanimity. When the bell of the Schools rang for the election, Mawe caused the Trinity bell to be rung also, as it was always rung for college disputations and acts. He then summoned all the Fellows into the hall, 'to attend him to the Schools for the Duke, so that they might win the honour to have it accounted their College Act'. (Many of them 'got hackneys, and fled to avoid importunity'.) Some dons who had intended to vote for the Earl of Berkshire were persuaded by their 'fearful Masters' to abstain from voting; though they 'kept away with much indignation'. Of all the Cambridge doctors, only one was valiant enough to vote against Buckingham: the admirable Dr Porter. It was a stirring morning. And in spite of all the rumpus, the Duke of Buckingham was elected Chancellor by only three votes. There were those who wished to question the election; but they were soon persuaded of the desperateness of such a remedy. As for Dr Mawe and his supporters among the heads, 'you will not believe', wrote Mead, 'how they triumphed'. The celebrations of the Master of Clare were considered especially inordinate.

II

In 1626 John Milton was in his second year at Christ's. From the Puritan point of view many of the Masters and pastors of contemporary Cambridge were hardly satisfactory. Leonard Mawe died in 1629; but Matthew Wren continued at Peterhouse until 1634, and was successively Bishop of Hereford, Norwich and Ely in the 1630's. Joseph Mead, Fellow of Christ's, had indeed opposed Buckingham in the election campaign, with the Puritans; but his tolerant and rational spirit, which has entitled him to be described as the 'precursor of the Platonic school',[1] was very different from that of William Perkins, who had died the year before Mead went up to Christ's as a sizar in 1603. Before Mead took his M.A. degree in 1610, Samuel Harsnet had been elected Master of Pembroke and Lancelot Andrewes Bishop of Ely; a young man called George Herbert had gone up to Trinity and a younger man named John Cosin to Gonville and Caius. Herbert, who became public orator in 1617, began in the mid-1620's to come under the influence of Nicholas Ferrar, sometime Fellow of Clare, who bought the remote and dilapidated manor-house of Little Gidding in 1625, and who was ordained deacon by Bishop Laud in 1626, when he was thirty-four.

John Cosin left Caius in 1616, when he was twenty-one, to be secretary and librarian to Bishop Overall, first at Lichfield, then at Norwich. Their friendship was brief, for Overall died in 1619; but Cosin always spoke of him as his great teacher, and left in his will £40 for a monument to him in Norwich Cathedral.[2] Cosin returned to Caius as Fellow in 1620, but left Cambridge again in 1624 to go to Durham. He was censured in 1628 by the committee of the House of Commons for religion; and Mead wrote of him in March of that year as 'a most audacious fellow, and I doubt scarce a sound protestant, and takes upon him most impudently to bring superstitious innovations into our Church'. Dr Sam Ward, Master of Sidney Sussex, had shown Mead a letter from Durham, which included the following passage: 'Mr Cosin was so blind at evensong on Candlemas day that he could not read prayers in the Minster with less than 340 candles, whereof 60 he caused to be placed about the high altar. Besides, he caused the picture of our Saviour supported by two angels to be set in the choir upon Bishop Hatfield's tomb'.[3] Others besides Dr Ward must have been apprehensive when Cosin returned to

---

[1] J. Peile, *Biographical Register of Christ's College*, I, 245.
[2] J. Cosin, *Correspondence*, II, 297.
[3] Birch (ed.), *Court and Times of Charles I*, I, 335–6.

Cambridge in 1634 as Master of Peterhouse. Work had begun in 1628, in the second year of the mastership of Matthew Wren, on the new chapel of Peterhouse, to which Cosin was one of the subscribers. The chapel was consecrated in 1632: and the description by Prynne of its interior in the 1630's is well known; of its glorious altar, to which the Fellows and scholars were enjoined to bow; its basins, candlesticks and hanging crucifix; its incense pot and 'special consecrated knife'.[1] The chapel was hardly completed when Richard Crashaw, son of the Puritan William Crashaw of St John's (friend of Perkins and editor of his writings), was elected Fellow and John Hutchinson fellow commoner. Crashaw wrote a poem to extol the consecration. Hutchinson, though a constant worshipper, 'began to take notice of their stretching superstition to idolatry'.[2] Indeed this chapel with 'its negative volutes, its. . . cherub faces, its floral decoration and arabesque lozenges, and its air of fantastic grace'[3] was not sympathetic to the Puritan sensibility. Its internal arrangements under Wren and Cosin were as appropriate to it as they were outrageous to the spiritual successors of George Withers—men such as the infamous William Dowsing, who achieved the masterpiece of his destructive talent when he visited the chapel (Cosin being still Master) in December 1643: 'we pulled down two mighty great angels with wings, and divers other angels, and the four Evangelists, and Peter, with his keys, over the chapel door, and about a hundred cherubims and angels, and divers superstitious letters in gold'.[4] Cosin was the first Master to be ejected by the Earl of Manchester in 1644. He died, as Bishop of Durham, in 1672: at once a link between the Cambridge anti-Calvinists of 1595 and the Caroline high churchmen; and between those high churchmen and the Restoration episcopate.

In the summer of 1604, after the publication of the new

---

[1] W. Prynne, *Canterbury's Doom*; quoted in Willis and Clark, *Architectural History*, I, 46.
[2] J. Hutchinson, *Memoirs*, I, 72.   [3] Basil Willey, *Richard Crashaw*, 6.
[4] Quoted in Willis and Clark, *Architectural History*, I, 46.

Constitutions and Canons Ecclesiastical, Sam Ward, Fellow of Emmanuel, had observed 'two plots laid to bring our college to the wearing of the surplice': for two Masters had unqualifiedly ordered the garment to be worn in the chapels of their colleges— Dr Barnabas Googe of Magdalene and Dr James Montagu of Sidney Sussex. 'Now what remaineth', he demanded of his diary, 'but that we—unless we will be singular—shall take it up. There is no way of escape, for anything I can discern. Our trust is in the name of the Lord.' Next January came the fell day— Wednesday the 18th—when 'the surplice was first urged by the Archbishop to be brought into Emmanuel College'. A further shock to his susceptibilities was in store. In November 1609 there was elected as Master of Ward's old college of Christ's the moderate Valentine Carey: 'Woe is me for Christ's College. Now is one imposed who will be the utter ruin and destruction of that college....O Lord have mercy, mercy, mercy.'[1] Ward, succeeding James Montagu, was to be Master of Sidney Sussex from 1610 until his somewhat surprising ejection in 1644 by his old pupil Edward Montagu, second Earl of Manchester, who had gone up to Sidney in 1618, six months after young Oliver Cromwell left the college without taking a degree. In the report on the state of worship in the university which was drawn up for Archbishop Laud in 1636,[2] probably by Cosin, the chapel of Sidney Sussex was described as 'much like Emmanuel'. Neither of these chapels had been consecrated: but then neither had the Elizabethan chapel of Corpus, where, in spite of royal injunctions, the altar stood in the body of the building (as was also the case in Emmanuel, Sidney, St Catharine's and Trinity) and not at the east end; and where the Fellows and scholars were addicted to singing not hymns but 'long psalms of their own appointing', their behaviour in general being 'with little reverence'. Throughout the university the young men were taught 'to prefer the

[1] Knappen (ed.), *Two Puritan Diaries*, 130.
[2] Cooper, *Annals*, III, 280–3.

private Spirit before the public, and their invented and unapproved prayers before all the liturgy of the Church'. At Trinity, for example, in 'some tutor's chambers (who have three or four score pupils) the private prayers are longer and louder by far at night than they are at Chapel in the evening'. At Cosin's old college of Caius 'if a communion be, all come in with surplices or without, and sit together. The Holy Sacrament, when it is administered, is brought down from the Table to every Fellow and scholar remaining in his own seat, where the priest strides and crowds over some of them with the sacred elements in his hands, not without irreverence and trouble.' The position at St Catharine's was uncertain, for Richard Sibbes, Master since 1626, had died in 1635; under him 'they were as irregular as any, and most like Emmanuel'. But at some four or five colleges 'they endeavour for order and have brought it to some good pass'. Such were Queens', Pembroke and Jesus; and also St John's, under William Beale, who, according to Symonds D'Ewes, 'caused such a general adoration to be practised to and towards the sacraments, that many godly fellows and scholars have left their places in order to avoid the abomination'.[1] William Fulke, in body and spirit, was long dead. But Laurence Chaderton was still alive, though no longer Master of his college: the tradition of the old-style Elizabethan Puritanism lingered on in him. And in the journal of William Dowsing, under the heading 'Emmanuel', there is preserved the cryptic but appropriate comment: 'there is nothing to be done'.[2]

III

The Cambridge of Milton was also that of Jeremy Taylor. The son of a barber in the parish of Holy Trinity, Jeremy went on from the Perse School to Caius in 1626.[3] He attended the lectures

[1] J. B. Marsden (ed.), *College Life in the Reign of James I* (extracts from the unpublished diary of Symonds D'Ewes), 25–6.

[2] Cooper, *Annals*, III, 366.

[3] C. J. Stranks, *Life and Writings of Jeremy Taylor*, 30.

of Dr Sam Ward, now Lady Margaret Professor of Divinity, who took as his especial subject original sin 'and the appendant questions'; these lectures, an echo of the long-dead voice of Perkins, Jeremy found 'useless'.[1] He scored a striking success when, twenty-one and extremely good-looking, he preached before Laud in 1633: three years later he left Cambridge for good. Milton had gone down in 1632. The year before, Henry More had been admitted to Christ's from Eton. At Eton, More had disputed 'against this Fate or Calvinistic Predestination, as it is usually called';[2] and meditating in the recreation grounds of the school he became convinced 'of the existence of God, as also of his unspotted righteousness and perfect goodness, that he is a God infinitely good, as well as infinitely great'.[3] On such schoolboy rambles he developed a taste for 'that which was natural':[4] and perhaps it can be said that the battle for natural theology in Cambridge had been won on the playing fields of Eton. More, refusing all preferment—even the mastership of his college—was to remain at Christ's until his death in 1687. He was not alone in his thirst for a less dogmatic theology. When he was at Christ's in the 1630's John Smith, Ralph Cudworth and Nathaniel Culverwell were at Emmanuel—and so was Benjamin Whichcote.

IV

In September and October 1651, nearly half a century after the death of Perkins, a series of letters[5] passed between Benjamin Whichcote, Provost of King's and Vice-Chancellor, and his former tutor Anthony Tuckney, Master of Emmanuel. The discussion was—in the words of Tuckney—'about the power of reason to judge of matters of faith'.[6] He suspected Whichcote of 'resolving

[1] J. Taylor, *Works* (ed. Heber and Eden), vii, 542.
[2] *Life of Henry More* (ed. M. F. Howard,) 59.
[3] *Ibid.* 61.   [4] *Ibid.* 62.
[5] Eight letters; printed in 1753 in Samuel Salter's edition of Whichcote's *Moral and Religious Aphorisms*.   [6] *Ibid.* 67.

faith into reason'.[1] When you were Fellow of Emmanuel, he said—that is, from 1633 to 1643—you 'were cast into the company of very learned and ingenious men; who, I fear, at least some of them, studied other authors, more than the scriptures; and Plato and his scholars, above others.... And hence in part hath run a vein of doctrine: which divers very able and worthy men, whom from my heart I much honour, are, I fear, too much known by.' The propositions of this 'vein of doctrine' were listed by Tuckney: 'The power of nature, in morals, too much advanced—reason hath too much given to it in the mysteries of faith—a *rectio ratio* much talked of; which I cannot tell, where to find—mind and understanding is all: heart and will little spoken of.' And, more specifically and significantly, 'The decrees of God questioned and quarrelled; because, according to our reason, we cannot comprehend how they may stand with his goodness.' This, together with the emphasis given by Whichcote to 'inherent righteousness', as opposed to 'imputed righteousness', made Whichcote's theology 'a kind of a moral divinity', with 'a little tincture of Christ added'.[2]

Tuckney especially complained about Whichcote's speeches at the Commencement of 1651, which he took to be a deliberate attack on his own Commencement position in 1650.[3] This charge the Provost denied; maintaining that he had been teaching what he said in 1651 since at least 1637, in his commonplaces in the chapel of Emmanuel.[4] He had been asserting it particularly strongly since 1644. In that year, wrote Whichcote, he was preaching in Holy Trinity on Romans, Chapter One, but happened to be struck, as if for the first time, by some verses in Chapter Two: 'when the Gentiles, which have not the law, do by nature the things contained in the law, these, having not the law, are a law unto themselves: Which shew the work of the law written in their hearts.' These words of Paul about natural

---

[1] *Ibid.* 21.
[2] *Ibid.* 38–9.
[3] *Ibid.* 4.
[4] *Ibid.* 12.

law, explained Whichcote, 'have forced upon me all those notions I do entertain, or have publicly delivered, concerning natural light, or the use of reason'.[1] To this, Tuckney retorted that his former pupil was in fact merely imitative; 'Sir, those, whose footsteps I observed, were the Socinians and Arminians: the latter whereof, I conceive, you have been everywhere reading'.[2] Whichcote nicely countered this charge by saying that he did not do much reading, but 'keep myself free to follow reason and scripture':[3] 'while Fellow of Emmanuel college, employment with pupils took my time from me. I have not read many books; but I have studied a few: meditation and invention have been rather my life, than reading: and truly I have more read Calvin, and Perkins, and Beza, than all the books, authors or names you mention.'[4]

More positively, Benjamin Whichcote argued, as John Whitgift had argued, that there was a distinction between the 'substantials' or 'fundamentals' of faith—the 'truths necessary to salvation',[5] and 'revealed by God'[6]—and matters 'in an indifferency',[7] 'matter of opinions',[8] which could not be infallibly determined from Scripture and in which 'good men differ'.[9] (The fundamentals, said Whichcote, revealed in the Scriptures, are 'so clear that there is little danger of good men differing about them'.[10]) He went on to assert that neither the saving truths nor the matters indifferent were 'contrary to the common principles of reason and natural light'.[11] There is nothing '*de fide*, which is contrary to natural knowledge'.[12] This statement Whichcote oddly supported by claiming that it had been acknowledged by 'Mr Perkins, Calvin, and others'. Tuckney agreed that faith might not be contrary to reason: but it is 'in many things much above it'.[13] (That is where the Arminians err, by rejecting those decrees

[1] *Ibid.* 9.
[2] *Ibid.* 27.
[3] *Ibid.* 55.
[4] *Ibid.* 54.
[5] *Ibid.* 56.
[6] *Ibid.* 52.
[7] *Ibid.* 42.
[8] *Ibid.* 55.
[9] *Ibid.* 2.
[10] *Ibid.* 52.
[11] *Ibid.* 99.
[12] *Ibid.* 45.
[13] *Ibid.* 68.

of God which seem contrary to reason.[1]) He strongly objected
to Whichcote's frequent use of Proverbs, xx. 27—'The spirit of
man is the candle of the Lord.'[2] This was the fundamental point.
How, asked Tuckney, can you speak of a right reason in corrupt
nature? For 'there I cannot find right, but more or less distorted
and depraved'.[3] And this made nonsense of Whichcote's position
that 'matters of natural theology' are 'demonstrable by reason'
and that 'matter of faith' is 'satisfactory to reason'.[4]

Perkins had begun by discussing the nature of God in terms of
will. Whichcote, like Andrewes, began by describing it in terms
of reason.

We cannot say worse of God, than that his calls and monitions to his
creatures, are not serious, and in good earnest, and out of love and good
mind. I can make no other explication of that distinction of God's
secret and revealed will, but that they do declare the self same will in
God; but it is his secret will, before he hath declared it: and his revealed
will when he hath made it known....For to speak of a secret and
a revealed will in God, contrary one unto another, is without warrant,
for it is the same will in another state. And this I am well assured and
resolved of, because this would be dishonesty here below in the very
judgement of reason, to pretend and not to intend; to make a shew and
overture, and to resolve in a man's mind the contrary, is a great dishonesty, in the judgement of reason. And we have no other principle
to discern the nature of God by, than the light of reason.[5]

God is bound by his own reason and order. He rules not by
prerogative, but by common law—that is, the Natural Law of
the universe: 'the Laws of God are not impositions of will, or
power, and pleasure: but the resolutions of truth, reason and
justice'.[6] It is thus the duty of reasonable creatures to comply with
these natural laws: 'in all things to be according to the nature,
mind and will of God, the law of justice, the rule of right, the

[1] *Ibid.* 75.
[2] *Ibid.* 49.   [3] *Ibid.* 94.   [4] *Ibid.* 46.
[5] B. Whichcote, *Works* (1751), I, 223–4.
[6] Quoted in Campagnac (ed.), *The Cambridge Platonists*, 70.

reason of things',[1] to do 'that which is comely, that which is regular, decent and directed according to rule, and the standing principle of God's creation'.[2] The reason of things, the nature of things: this was a dominant theme in Whichcote's preaching. 'The laws of nature ought not to be varied from; that is, what is reason, what is right and fit': 'Truth lies in our regularity and conformity with our apprehension of the reason of things.'[3] The voice of a reasonable God, heard by the ear of reason: 'the reason of things is a law and truth which none, either by power or privilege, may transgress'; 'It is that which God will give an account of himself by, to the understandings of his creatures.'[4]

And so, although Whichcote knew as much as most men, and more than some, about the 'very chaos and confusion' of the world, 'the general madness that rules in the commonwealth of men',[5] and about 'the sickly and distempered condition of man',[6] he knew also that the world is a glorious harmony, and that man is noble in reason and infinite in faculty. 'Man, in respect of his mind, is qualified to converse with angels, and to attend upon God':[7]

if we consider man duly, we shall find him to be the glory of God's creation in this lower world, the masterpiece of God's workmanship: that there is more of value and worth in him than in all the creation besides....For the mind of man takes cognisance of God, receives from him and returns to him; and carries a continual sense of God within itself.[8]

The grace of God is necessary for man to 'assist' him to his end.

For though the worst that be said prove true; that man is a bankrupt, and hath suffered shipwreck, is confounded in his principles, marred and spoiled by his apostasy, defection, degeneracy, and consenting to iniquity; admitting that he is perfectly contrary to the true complexion he was in, in the state that God made him, yet all this malady may be cured, and his condition is recoverable...through the assistance of God's grace.[9]

[1] *Works*, I, 71. [2] *Ibid.* 70. [3] *Ibid.* 252–3.
[4] *Ibid.* 66–7. [5] *Ibid.* 119. [6] *Ibid.* 301.
[7] *Ibid.* 195–6. [8] *Ibid.* 299–300. [9] *Ibid.* 286.

Grace assists men, as it were, to be true to themselves, to 'the power and virtue of the principle that God planted in them'.[1] Evil is unnatural, in the Aristotelian sense: a deviation from the norm, from the path to the true end. 'Wickedness in man is as monstrous and unnatural as darkness in the sun': 'To a moral agent, such as man is, he being endowed with reason and understanding, and invested with liberty and freedom, nothing is more unnatural than sin and wickedness. For it is against the reason of our mind, and against the reason of the thing.'[2] Sin is 'contrary to reason';[3] 'a variation from the law and rule of God's creation'.[4] Evil men have 'brought themselves into an unnatural estate'[5] because they 'have contracted evil habits, by ill use, custom and practice'.[6]

God deals with man, as he dealt with Jonah, 'by reason and by argument'.[7] 'This is the rule in all things, that a man act according to reason, which is the candle of the lord set up in him; and by this he should be directed, and see his way before him.'[8] For God does not force: he enables and assists. Religion is a matter of 'grace superadded to nature'.[9] *Gratia non tollit naturam sed perficit.* The 'grace of God doth adjoin itself...to our higher principles. For this end it is given to guide and direct them'.[10] And God 'doth make allowance for our temper, complexion and constitution';[11] making us new creatures 'not by transubstantiating our natures, but by transforming our minds, and mending our tempers':[12] 'it is irrational for us to think, that God having made us intelligent and voluntary agents, that he should force and constrain us: and that he should not expect the use of those powers that he hath given us'.[13] God gave us not a god-like reason to fust in us unused.

---

[1] *Ibid.* 93.
[2] *Ibid.* 212.
[3] *Ibid.* 199.
[4] *Ibid.* 140.
[5] *Ibid.* 44.
[6] *Ibid.* 45.
[7] *Ibid.* 15.
[8] *Ibid.* 193.
[9] *Ibid.* 212.
[10] *Ibid.* 193.
[11] *Ibid.* 234.
[12] *Ibid.* 53.
[13] *Ibid.* 288–9.

God's call, and 'the assurance of assistance'[1] are made to all men. Whichcote's world demonstrated the optimism of grace:

We are now under God's call and invitation. There is no man in the world, that hath the Bible in his hand, or that hath heard anything out of it, who hath any reason to doubt but that he is called of God. What we read in the Bible, we may build upon, and apply to ourselves, with as good assurance, as if God did dispatch an angel from heaven to us. We are in this day of grace, God's invited guests; and we are all of us under the operation of the divine Spirit and may depend upon the assistance of the divine grace.[2]

'No man in the world that hath the Bible in his hand': the ploughman at his plough, the weaver at his loom, the wayfaring man on his journey (or even the don in his study). The Erasmian vision, as it were, had come full circle.

V

The distinguishing temper of a college, no less than that of a family, is capable of change (even of reversal) within a surprisingly short number of generations. Twentieth-century Cambridge provides conspicuous examples of this general truth: and so would any given half-century of university history. In the Cambridge of the 1630's we have John Cosin ruling the college once guided by Robert Some; including among its members Richard Crashaw, to be the most exuberantly baroque of English Catholic poets, and yet the offspring of an Elizabethan Puritan Johnian, the friend of William Perkins. We have high church piety in the chapel of St John's, where Fulke and Alvey had once stirred their colleagues to frenzied hatred of the dregs of popery. In Christ's and Emmanuel, once the homes and now the last ditches of orthodox Cambridge Calvinism, we find groups of

---

[1] *Ibid.* 288.
[2] *Ibid.* 287. Cf. *ibid.* 40: 'where men have never heard, and are without the pale of the church, we leave them to God's mercy, and exclude them not'.

rational and liberal and humanist Protestants. In Whichcote's theology of the 'order of reason', fully preached and discussed in the university of the 1630's, God and man, reason and revelation, grace and nature, worked together for good in that order and harmony from which all things have sprung and in which they will end. The definitions and the details which had so concerned Perkins and Whitaker and Some and Chaderton were sweepingly ignored in the sermons of Whichcote. Tuckney in one way was right when he linked Arminianism to Socinianism and accused Whichcote of treading in the footsteps of both; for, as Dr McLachlan has written, the two movements 'had close affinities and were born of a similar tendency of mind'.[1] The tendency, that is, to emphasize first that 'truth lies in a little compass, and narrow room', that 'vitals in religion are few'[2]: and secondly, that man, though fallen, still positively remains in the image of God—a God who does not do violence to his children, but exercises with charity and patience his sovereign but reasonable power. We are well on the way, then, from 'Puritanism to the Age of Reason'.

'A candle is not lighted', preached Lancelot Andrewes in the Pembroke of the 1580's,[3] 'to be put under a bushel', 'the maxim the Fathers have gathered thence, is this: *Bono debetur manifestatio*; for candles, that have *bonum lucis*, are not to be thrust *sub malo tenebrarum*; so that our candle must be put on a candlestick, to be made known'. The candle of the Lord had been kept alight in the Cambridge of Elizabeth: and by God's grace, in England, it was never to be put out.

---

[1] H. J. McLachlan, *Socinianism in Seventeenth-Century England*, 50.
[2] Whichcote, *Aphorisms*, quoted in Campagnac (ed.), *The Cambridge Platonists*, 72.
[3] *The Moral Law Expounded* (1642), 272.

BIBLIOGRAPHY

I. THE MANUSCRIPT SOURCES

A GOOD deal of the material in the University Archives (housed in the Old Schools) is not yet catalogued or indexed. The series of boxes containing records of the Elizabethan Vice-Chancellor's Court, for example, has no sort of table of contents. Much, obviously, remains to be discovered. The most easily accessible items in the Archives are the Registry Guard Books, a set of bound volumes, with tables of contents by H. R. Luard, a former Registrary. Of these, volume 6 (i), containing documents concerning religious cases in the Consistory Court, from Thomas Aldrich to Peter Baro, has proved most useful. Other interesting volumes are: 4 (Miscellaneous); 6 (ii) (Miscellaneous); 39 (i) (Lady Margaret Professor); 39 (ii) (Regius Professor of Divinity); 52 (Lady Margaret Preacher); 78 (University Miscellany); 88 (Corpus Christi College); 90 (St Catharine's College): 92 (i) (Christ's College); 93 (St John's College); 95 (Magdalene College). There are also manuscripts in boxes, catalogued since the Second World War by Mrs Hall; the most useful for Tudor Cambridge are the five boxes labelled 'Mandates of Elizabeth I'; 'Letters of Elizabeth I'; 'Miscellaneous relating to the Vice Chancellor, 1553–1685'; 'Vice-Chancellor's Court, Documents from the Exhibita, 1559–74'; 'Vice-Chancellor's Court, Parchment Documents from the Exhibita File, 1559–73'. The University Grace Books and Audit Books are also in the Archives.

There is also some unworked material in the colleges. St John's, for instance, bought in 1948 the two previously unknown letters of 1590, by William Whitaker and Eleazor Knox, which I have used in Chapter IX. There are some useful original papers in the bursary of Corpus Christi College, especially in the volume marked 'Miscellaneous Documents, 1430–1700'. In the library of Corpus there is the rich collection of Parker manuscripts, containing much material on sixteenth-century Cambridge; some of this was printed in 1838 by John Lamb, Master of the college, in his *Collection of Original Documents from the Manuscript Library of Corpus . . . illustrative of the History of the University of Cambridge, 1500–72*. Volume 118 of the Corpus MSS. containing papers about the statute disturbances in 1572 is particularly valuable. In the library of Trinity College there is the copy-book once belonging to and used by Whitgift containing transcripts of the letters and papers in the Barrett and Baro cases: MS. B/14/9 (James catalogue no. 295). Strype used this book—or at least the transcript of it sent him by Thomas Baker in 1712; but much of the material in it has never been fully published, including six of Whitgift's own letters.

The University Library, Cambridge, possesses a copy-book belonging to a pupil of John Overall, containing many items relating to Overall: MS. Gg/1/29. (This pupil may have been Overall's nephew John Hayward, who went up to Trinity in 1602 and became a Fellow of Pembroke and rector of Coton.) Whitgift's manuscript of his lectures in 1565 as Lady Margaret Professor, on the Book of Revelation, is University Library, Cambridge, MS. Ff/2/36; and MS. Ff/1/9 contains theses and determinations of Whitgift in the 1560's. Volume 10 of the Baumgartner Papers consists of letters from Thomas Baker to John Strype about Parker and Whitgift—very interesting for the light they throw on the genesis and progress of Strype's works, as well as for the information about sixteenth-century Cambridge given there.

The Cecil Papers (Salisbury MSS.) at Hatfield House contain six volumes with material relating to Cambridge in the 1590's: volumes 36, 79, 85, 136, 139, and 144. Most important is volume 139, with papers about the Overall disturbances in 1599 and 1600.

At the Public Record Office there are the Star Chamber depositions of William Perkins and Henry Alvey in 1591, which, so far as I know, have never been printed or used in a printed work: Star Chamber 5: A: 49/34 (bundle). In volume 238 of the State Papers (Domestic) Elizabeth, there are documents concerning the 1589 synod at St John's. The material about the troubles in St John's in 1565 is in State Papers (Domestic) Elizabeth, volumes 38, 39 and 40. Volumes 3 and 4 of these State Papers have material for the 1559 visitation of the university.

R. F. Scott, Fellow of St John's from 1877 to 1908, and Master from 1908 to 1933, published from 1889 a series of 'Notes from the College Records' in *The Eagle* (the St John's College magazine). The series is very helpful. Volume XXVIII (1907) contains transcripts of most of the Public Record Office material concerning the 1565 disputes.

But the fullest and most important basis for any study of Elizabethan Cambridge is the collection of Burleigh papers in the Lansdowne MSS. at the British Museum. In my book I have used especially volumes 8, 10, 12, 16, 17, 23, 57, 61, 62, 63, 79, 80, 82 and 103. J. Heywood and T. Wright, *Cambridge University Transactions during the Puritan Controversies* (2 volumes, 1854), is an indispensable collection of transcripts of much of this material in the Lansdowne collection.

There remain the Baker manuscripts: forty-two volumes of transcripts of material relating to Cambridge, made by Thomas Baker of St John's (1656–1740). Volumes 1–23 are in the British Museum: Harleian 7028–50. Volumes 24–42 are in the University Library, Cambridge: Mm/1/35–53. The University Library also has four volumes of copies of some of the material in the British Museum: 'Baker A' (Harl. 7031); 'Baker B' (Harl. 7033); 'Baker C' (Harl. 7035–7); and 'Baker D' (Harl. 7037–8). There is an index to the forty-two volumes, published at Cambridge in 1848, by 'four members of the Cambridge Antiquarian Society' (J. J. Smith, C. C. Babington, C. W. Goodwin, and J. Power). Volume 5 of the catalogue of manuscripts in the University Library, Cambridge, contains a catalogue of the contents of the Cambridge Baker MSS. by J. E. B. Mayor (1867).

II. CAMBRIDGE BIBLIOGRAPHY (SELECTED)

(THE PLACE OF PUBLICATION IS CAMBRIDGE IF NOT OTHERWISE MENTIONED)

ATTWATER, A. *Pembroke College* (ed. S. C. Roberts). 1936.

AUSTEN LEIGH, A. *King's College.* London, 1899.

BABINGTON, C. C. *The Infirmary and Chapel of St John's.* 1874.

BAKER, T. *History of St John's College* (ed. J. E. B. Mayor). 2 vols. 1869.

BALL, W. W. R. *Notes on the History of Trinity College.* London, 1899. *Trinity College.* London, 1906. *The King's Scholars and King's Hall.* 1917. *Cambridge Papers.* London, 1918.

BALL, W. W. R. and VENN, J. A. *Admissions to Trinity College.* Vols. I and II. London, 1913–16.

BARTHOLOMEW, A. T. *Catalogue of the Clark Collection of Cambridge Books.* 1912.

BENIANS, E. A. *John Fisher.* 1935.

BOAS, F. S. *University Drama in the Tudor Age.* Oxford, 1914.

BOWES, R. *Catalogue of Books...relating to...Cambridge, 1521–1893.* 1894.

BRITTAIN, F. *A Short History of Jesus College Cambridge.* 1940.

BROWNE, G. F. *St Catharine's College.* London, 1902.

BUSHELL, W. D. *Hobson's Conduit.* 1938. *The Church of St Mary the Great.* 1948.

CAIUS, JOHN. *De Antiquitate Cantabrigiensis Academiae.* London, 1568. *Historiae Cantabrigiensis Academiae.* London, 1574. *The Annals of Gonville and Caius* (ed. J. Venn). 1904. *Works* (ed. E. S. Roberts and J. Venn). 1912.

CLARK, J. W. *Cambridge: Historical and Picturesque Notes.* London, 1890. *The Letters Patent of Elizabeth and James I to the University.* 1892. *Endowments of the University of Cambridge.* 1904.

CLARK, J. W. and GRAY, A. *Old Plans of Cambridge (1574–1798).* 2 vols. 1921.

Collegium Divi Johannis Evangelistae: 1511–1911. 1911.

COOPER, C. H. *The Annals of Cambridge.* Vol. I (to 1546), 1842; vol. II (1546–1602), 1843; vol. III (1603–1688), 1845.

COOPER, C. H. and COOPER, T. *Athenae Cantabrigienses.* 3 vols. 1858–1913.

CORRIE, G. E. *The Interference of the Crown with the Affairs of the English Universities.* 1839.

D'EWES, SIR S. *College Life in the Reign of James I* (extracts from the unpublished diary of Symonds D'Ewes, ed. J. Marsden). 1851.

DIXON, W. M. *Trinity College, Dublin.* London, 1902.

Documents relating to the University and Colleges of Cambridge (published by direction of the commissioners). 3 vols. London, 1852.

DYER, G. *History of the University and Colleges of Cambridge.* 2 vols. London, 1814. *The Privileges of the University of Cambridge.* 2 vols. London, 1824.

EDWARDS, G. M. *Sidney Sussex College.* London, 1899.

EVENNETT, H. O. 'John Fisher and Cambridge', *Clergy Review,* IX (1939).

FORBES, M. D. (ed.). *Clare College: 1326–1926.* 2 vols. 1928–30.

FOSTER, J. E. (ed.). *Churchwardens' Accounts of St Mary the Great: 1504–1635.* (Cambridge Antiquarian Society Publication, 1905.)

FULLER, T. *History of the University of Cambridge* (ed. M. Prickett and T. Wright). London, 1840.

GIBSON, J. 'Cambridge: Nurse of a Nation', *Cambridge Journal,* vol. IV, no. 5 (February 1951).

GOLDSCHMIDT, E. P. *The First Cambridge Press in its European Setting.* 1955.

GOODISON, J. W. *Catalogue of Cambridge Portraits.* Vol. I. 1955.

Grace Books. Grace Book A. (Proctors' Accounts and other University Records, 1454–88.) Ed. S. M. Leathes. 1897. *Grace Book* B, *Part I.* (Proctors' Accounts and other University Records, 1488–1511.) Ed. M. Bateson. 1903. *Grace Book* B, *Part II.* (Proctors' Accounts, 1511–44.) Ed. M. Bateson. 1905. *Grace Book* Γ. (University Records, 1501–42.) Ed. W. G. Searle. 1908. *Grace Book* Δ. (University Records, 1542–89.) Ed. J. Venn. 1910.

GRAY, A. *Jesus College.* London, 1902.

GRAY, J. H. *The Queens' College.* London, 1899.

GUMBLEY, W. *The Cambridge Dominicans.* Oxford, 1938.

HARRISON, K. *The Windows of King's College Chapel.* 1952.

HARRISON, W. J. *Notes on the Masters, Fellows, Scholars and Exhibitioners of Clare.* 1953.

HEYWOOD, J. (ed.). *Collection of Statutes for the University and Colleges of Cambridge.* London, 1840. *Early Cambridge Statutes.* London, 1855.

HEYWOOD, J. and WRIGHT, T. (ed.). *Cambridge University Transactions during the Puritan Controversies.* 2 vols. London, 1854.

INNES, H. M. *Fellows of Trinity College.* 1941.

JACOB, E. F. 'English University Clerks in the later Middle Ages', reprinted in his *Essays in the Conciliar Epoch.* New ed. Manchester, 1953.

JENKINSON, F., ROBERTS, S. C. and BARNES, G. *List of Books printed at the Cambridge University Press: 1521–1800.* 1935.

28   PR

JONES, W. H. S. *A History of St Catharine's College*. 1936. *The Story of St Catharine's College*. 1951.

JOSSELIN, J. (ed. CLARK, J. W.). *Historiola Collegii Corporis Christi*. (Cambridge Antiquarian Society Publication, 1880.)

LAMB, J. (ed.). *Collection of Original Documents from the Manuscript Library of Corpus Christi College, illustrative of the History of the University of Cambridge, 1500–72*. London, 1838.

LANGDON-BROWN, W. *Some Chapters in Cambridge Medical History*. 1946.

LLOYD, A. H. *The Early History of Christ's College*. 1934.

MALDEN, H. E. *Trinity Hall*. London, 1902.

MASTERS, R. *History of the College of Corpus Christi and the Blessed Virgin Mary* (1753). Ed. J. LAMB, London, 1831.

MAXWELL, C. E. *History of Trinity College, Dublin*. Dublin, 1946.

MAYOR, J. E. B. (ed.). *Early Statutes of St John's College*. 1859. *Admissions to St John's College*. 1882.

MOORMAN, J. R. H. *The Grey Friars in Cambridge*. 1952.

MORISON, S. E. *The Founding of Harvard College*. Cambridge, Mass. 1935.

MULLINGER, J. B. *Cambridge Characteristics in the Seventeenth Century*. London, 1867. *The University of Cambridge*. 3 vols. London, 1873–1911. *A History of the University of Cambridge*. London, 1888. *St John's College*. London, 1901.

NEALE, C. M. *The Early Honours List of the University (1498–1747)*. Bury St Edmunds, 1909.

PEACOCK, G. *Observations on the Statutes of the University of Cambridge*. London, 1841.

PEILE, J. *Christ's College*. London, 1900. *Biographical Register of Christ's College*. Vol. I (1448–1665). 1910.

PURNELL, E. K. *Magdalene College*. London, 1904.

RACKHAM, H. *Early Statutes of Christ's College*. 1927. *Christ's College in Former Days*. 1939.

RASHDALL, H. *The Universities of Europe in the Middle Ages* (ed. F. M. Powicke and A. B. Emden). Vol. III: *English Universities*. Oxford, 1936.

ROBERTS, H. *Calendar of Wills proved in the Vice-Chancellor's Court: 1501–1765*. 1907.

ROBERTS, S. C. *A History of the Cambridge University Press: 1521–1921*. 1921.

SALTMARSH, J. 'Tudor Cambridge', *Journal of the Institutional Management Association*, August 1952.

SANDERS, S. *Historical and Architectural Notes on Gt St Mary's*. London, 1869.

SCOTT, R. F. *St John's College*. London, 1907.

SCOTT-GILES, C. W. *Sidney Sussex College*. 1951.

SEARLE, W. G. *History of the Queens' College: 1446–1560*. (Cambridge Antiquarian Society Publication, 1867–71.)

434

SELTMAN, C. T. and BROWNE, A. D. *A Pictorial History of...Queens' College, 1448–1948*. 1951.

SHIPLEY, A. E. *Cambridge Cameos*. London, 1924.

SHUCKBURGH, E. S. *Emmanuel College*. London, 1904.

SORLEY, JANETTA C. *King's Daughters*. 1937.

STAMP, A. E. *Michaelhouse*. 1924.

STOKES, H. P. *Corpus Christi College*. London, 1898. *The Chaplains and Chapel of the University of Cambridge, 1256–1568* (Cambridge Antiquarian Society Publication, 1906). *The Mediaeval Hostels of the University of Cambridge* (Cambridge Antiquarian Society Publication, 1924). *Ceremonies of the University of Cambridge*. 1927.

TANNER, J. R. (ed.). *The Historical Register of the University of Cambridge*. 1917.

TORRY, A. F. *Founders and Benefactors of St John's*. 1888.

TREVELYAN, G. M. *Trinity College*. 1943.

VENABLES, E. *Annals of Great St Mary's*. London, 1869.

VENN, J. *Biographical Register of Gonville and Caius College*. Vol. I. *1349–1713*. 1897. *Caius College*. London, 1901. *Early Collegiate Life*. 1913.

VENN, J. and VENN, J. A. *Book of Matriculations and Degrees 1544–1659*. 1913. *Alumni Cantabrigienses*. Part I (to 1751). 4 vols. 1922–7.

Victoria History of the County of Cambridge and the Isle of Ely. Vols. I and II (ed. L. F. Salzman), London, 1938 and 1948. Vol. IV (ed. R. B. Pugh), London, 1953.

WALKER, T. A. *Peterhouse*. London, 1906. New ed. Cambridge 1935. *A Peterhouse Bibliography*. 1924. *A Biographical Register of Peterhouse Men*. 2 vols. 1927–30.

WARDALE, J. R. *Clare College*. London, 1899. *Clare College Letters and Documents*. 1903.

WILLIS, R. and CLARK, J. W. *The Architectural History of the University of Cambridge and the Colleges of Cambridge and Eton*. 4 vols. 1886.

WINSTANLEY, D. A. *Unreformed Cambridge*. 1935.

III. GENERAL BIBLIOGRAPHY (SELECTED)

(THE PLACE OF PUBLICATION IS LONDON UNLESS OTHERWISE STATED)

A: PRIMARY PRINTED WORKS

AMES, W. *Conscience, with the Power and Cases thereof*. 1639.

ANDREWES, L. *The Morall Law expounded*. 1642. *Sermons* (Anglo-Catholic Library). 5 vols. Oxford, 1841–3. New ed., 1875–82. *A Pattern of catechistical doctrine, and other minor works* (Anglo-Catholic Library). Oxford, 1846.

AQUINAS, T. *Nature and Grace* (selections from the *Summa*, tr. and ed. A. M. Fairweather). 1954.

ARMINIUS, J. *Works* (tr. and ed. J. and W. Nichols). 3 vols. 1825–75.

Articuli Lambethani. 1651. (See page 365, note 2.)

ASCHAM, R. *The Schoolmaster* (ed. J. E. B. Mayor). 1863. *Toxophilus* (ed. E. Arber). 1868.

BANCROFT, R. *Daungerous Positions.* 1593. *A Survay of the Pretended Holy Discipline.* 1593. *Tracts ascribed to Richard Bancroft* (ed. A. Peel). Cambridge, 1953.

BARNES, R. *Vitae Romanorum Pontificum.* Basle, 1535.

BARO, P. *In Jonam prophetam praelectiones.* 1579. *De fide, eiusque ortu & natura explicatio.* 1580. *De praestantia & dignitate divinae legis.* 1587(?). *A speciall Treatise of Gods Providence.* 1588(?). *Summa trium de Praedestinatione Sententiarum.* 1613.

BECON, T. *Early Works* (ed. J. Ayre, Parker Society). Cambridge, 1843. *Catechism, etc.* (ed. Ayre, Parker Society). Cambridge, 1844. *Prayers, etc.* (ed. Ayre, Parker Society). Cambridge, 1844.

BIRCH, T. (ed.). *The Court and Times of James I* (transcripts of 'Historical and Confidential Letters'). 2 vols. 1849. *The Court and Times of Charles I.* 2 vols. 1849.

BRADFORD, J. *Sermons, etc.* (ed. A Townsend, Parker Soc.). Cambridge, 1848.

BROWNE, R. *Writings of Robert Harrison and Robert Browne* (ed. A. Peel and L. C. Carlson). 1953.

BUCER, M. *Scripta Anglicana.* Basle, 1577.

BULLINGER, H. *Decades* (ed. T. Harding, Parker Society). 4 vols. Cambridge, 1849–52.

CALVIN, J. *Institutes.* Tr. by T. Norton (1561). 1611 ed. Tr. by H. Beveridge. 2 vols. 1949 ed. *Theological Treatises* (ed. and tr. J. K. S. Reid). 1954.

CAMPAGNAC, E. T. (ed.). *The Cambridge Platonists.* Oxford, 1901.

CARDWELL, E. (ed.). *A History of Conferences and other Proceedings connected with the Book of Common Prayer, 1558–1690.* Oxford, 1840. *Synodalia (A Collection of Articles of Religion, Canons and Proceedings of Convocation in the Province of Canterbury, 1547–1717).* 2 vols. Oxford, 1842. *Documentary Annals of the Reformed Church of England (a Collection of Injunctions, Declarations, Orders, Articles of Enquiry etc. 1546–1716).* 2 vols. New ed. Oxford, 1844. *Reformatio Legum Ecclesiasticarum: The Reformation of the Ecclesiastical Laws as attempted in the Reigns of Henry VIII, Edward VI and Elizabeth.* Oxford, 1850.

CARTWRIGHT, T. *Cartwrightiana* (ed. A. Peel and L. H. Carlson). 1951.

Constitutions and Canons Ecclesiastical 1604 (ed. H. A. Wilson, Oxford, 1923).

COSIN, J. *Correspondence* (Surtees Society, Vols. 52 and 55). Durham, 1869–72.

CRASHAW, W. *A Sermon preached before the Lord Lawarre, Lord Governour of Virginea (A New-yeeres Gift to Virginea).* 1610.

D'EWES, SIR S. *Autobiography and Correspondence* (ed. J. O. Halliwell). 2 vols. 1845.

ERASMUS, D. *Opus epistolarum Des. Erasmi* (ed. P. S. Allen). 11 vols. Oxford, 1906–47. *The Epistles of Erasmus* (tr. F. M. Nichols). 3 vols. 1901–18. *An Exhortation to the diligent Studye of Scripture* (tr. of the *Paraclesis* by William Roy). 1529. *Colloquies* (tr. N. Bailey). Glasgow, 1877. *The Praise of Folly* (tr. Sir T. Chaloner), 1549; (tr. H. H. Hudson), Princeton, 1941.

FRERE, W. H. and DOUGLAS, C. E. (ed.). *Puritan Manifestos.* Repr. 1954.

FULKE, W. *Works* (Parker Society). 2 vols. Cambridge, 1843–8.

GEE, H. and HARDY, W. H. (ed.). *Documents illustrative of English Church History.* 1921.

GOODWIN, T. *Works.* 5 vols. 1681–1704.

GREENHAM, R. *Works.* (ed. H. Holland). 1599.

GRINDAL, E. *Remains* (ed. W. Nicholson, Parker Society). Cambridge, 1843.

HARRISON, R. *Writings of Robert Harrison and Robert Browne* (ed. A. Peel and L. H. Carlson). 1953.

HARSNETT, S. *Sermon of 1584.* Appended to *Three Sermons* by R. Stuart. 1656.

HOOKER, R. *Works* (ed. J. Keble). 3 vols. Oxford, 1836.

Homilies, Book of. S.P.C.K. edition. 1938.

HUTCHINSON, J. *Memoirs* (ed. C. H. Firth). 2 vols. 1885.

JEWEL, J. *Works* (ed. J. Ayre, Parker Society). 4 vols. Cambridge, 1845–50.

KINGSBURY, S. M. (ed.). *The Records of the Virginia Company of London.* 4 vols. Washington, 1906–35.

KNOX, J. *Works* (ed. D. Laing). 4 vols. Edinburgh, 1846–55.

LATIMER, H. *Sermons* (ed. G. E. Corrie, Parker Society). 2 vols. Cambridge, 1844–5.

LAURENCE, R. (ed.). *Documents relative to the Predestinarian Controversy under Mary.* Oxford, 1819.

LEVER, T. *Sermons* (ed. E. Arber). London, 1871.

Liturgies. *Liturgies etc. in the Reign of Edward VI* (ed. J. Ketley, Parker Society). Cambridge, 1844. *Liturgies and forms of Prayer set forth in the Reign of Queen Elizabeth* (ed. W. K. Clay, Parker Society). Cambridge, 1847.

MUSCULUS, W. *Commonplaces of the Christian Religion* (tr. J. Man). 1563.

NOWELL, A. *Catechism* (ed. G. E. Corrie, Parker Society). Cambridge 1853.

Original Letters relative to the English Reformation (ed. and tr. H. Robinson, Parker Society). 2 vols. Cambridge, 1846–7.

OVERALL, J. *Convocation Book* (Anglo-Catholic Library). Oxford, 1844.

PARKER, M. *Correspondence* (ed. J. Bruce and T. T. Perowne, Parker Society). Cambridge, 1853.

437

PEEL, A. (ed.). *The Second Part of a Register.* 2 vols. Cambridge, 1915. *The Notebook of John Penry* (Camden Society). 1944.

PERKINS, W. *Works.* 3 vols. Cambridge, 1616–18.

PILKINGTON, J. *Works* (ed. J. Scholefield, Parker Society). Cambridge, 1842.

ROBINSON, J. *Works* (ed. R. Ashton). 3 vols. 1851.

ROGERS, R. *Diary:* in *Two Elizabethan Puritan Diaries* (ed. M. M. Knappen). Chicago, 1933.

SMYTH, J. *Works* (ed. W. T. Whitley). 2 vols. Cambridge, 1915.

SOME, R. *Three Questions briefly handled.* Cambridge, 1596.

Trent, Council of. Canones et Decreta. Rome, 1845 ed. *Canons and Decrees* (tr. J. Waterworth). 1848.

WARD, S. *Diary:* in *Two Elizabethan Puritan Diaries* (ed. M. M. Knappen). Chicago, 1933.

WHICHCOTE, B. *Works.* 4 vols. Aberdeen, 1751. *Moral and Religious Aphorisms …to which are added Eight Letters which passed between Dr Whichcote… and Dr Tuckney* (ed. S. Salter). 1753.

WHITAKER, A. *Good Newes from Virginia.* 1613.

WHITAKER, W. *Cygnea Cantio* (in *Praelectiones de Ecclesia*). Cambridge, 1599. *A Disputation on the Holy Scripture against…Bellarmine and Stapleton* (tr. W. Fitzgerald, Parker Society). Cambridge, 1849.

WHITGIFT, J. *Works* (ed. J. Ayre, Parker Society). 3 vols. Cambridge, 1851–3.

WHITTINGHAM, W. *A Brief Discourse of the Troubles begun at Frankfurt.* Reprinted 1846.

Winthrop Papers (Massachusetts Historical Society). Vols. I–V (1498–1649). Boston, 1929–47.

Zürich Letters. First and Second Series (ed. and tr. H. Robinson, Parker Society). Cambridge, 1842–5.

B: PRINTED SECONDARY WORKS

ABERCROMBIE, N. J. *The Origins of Jansenism.* Oxford, 1936.

ALLEN, P. S. *The Age of Erasmus.* Oxford, 1914. *Erasmus: Lectures and wayfaring sketches.* Oxford, 1934.

ANDREWS, C. M. *The Colonial Period of American History.* 4 vols. New Haven, 1934–8.

BAILEY, D. S. *Thomas Becon.* Edinburgh, 1952.

BALL, T. *Life of Preston (1628)* (ed. E. W. Harcourt). Oxford, 1885.

BEARD, C. *The Reformation of the Sixteenth Century.* New ed. London, 1927.

BRADFORD, W. *Of Plymouth Plantation* (ed. S. E. Morison). New York, 1952.

BROMILEY, G. W. *Baptism and the Anglican Reformers.* 1953.

BURGESS, W. H. *John Smyth the Se-baptist.* 1911. *John Robinson.* 1920.

BURRAGE, C. *The True Story of Robert Browne*. Oxford, 1906. *New Facts concerning John Robinson*. Oxford, 1910. *The Early English Dissenters*. 2 vols. Cambridge, 1912. *John Penry*. Oxford, 1913.

CLARKE, S. (ed.). *The Lives of Thirty-two English Divines*. 1677. *The Lives of Sundry Eminent Persons in this later Age*. 1683.

CLAYTON, H. J. *Archbishop Whitgift and his Times*. 1911.

CRAGG, G. R. *From Puritanism to the Age of Reason: a Study of Changes in Religious Thought within the Church of England, 1660–1700*. Cambridge, 1950.

CRAVEN, W. F. *The Southern Colonies in the Seventeenth Century, 1607–89*. Baton Rouge, 1949.

CREMEANS, C. D. 'The Reception of Calvinistic Thought in England', *Illinois Studies in the Social Sciences*, vol. XXXI, no. 1 (Urbana, Illinois, 1949).

DAKIN, A. *Calvinism*. 1940.

DARBY, H. S. *Hugh Latimer*. 1953.

DAVIES, H. *The Worship of the English Puritans*. 1948. *The English Free Churches*. Oxford, 1952.

DAWLEY, P. M. *John Whitgift and the Reformation*. 1955.

DEXTER, H. M. *The Congregationalism of the last Three Hundred Years*. New York, 1880. *The True Story of John Smyth*. Boston, 1881. *The England and Holland of the Pilgrims*. Boston, 1905.

DILLINGHAM, W. *Life of Laurence Chaderton (1700)* (tr. E. S. Shuckburgh). Cambridge, 1884.

DIXON, R. W. *History of the Church of England*. 6 vols. 1878–1902.

Doctrine in the Church of England. (Report of the 1922 Commission.) 1938.

DOD, J. *Memorials* (ed. J. Taylor). Northampton, 1875.

DOWDEN, E. *Puritan and Anglican*. 1900.

FOSTER, H. D. 'Liberal Calvinism', *Harvard Theological Review*, XVI, 1923.

FOXE, J. *Acts and Monuments* (ed. S. R. Cattley). 8 vols. 1837–41.

FRERE, W. H. *The English Church in the Reigns of Elizabeth and James I*. 1911.

FROUDE, J. A. *The Life and Letters of Erasmus*. 1895.

FULLER, T. *The Worthies of England* (ed. P. A. Nuttall). 3 vols. 1840. *The Holy State and the Profane State* (ed. J. Nichols). 1841. *The Church History of Britain* (ed. J. S. Brewer). 6 vols. Oxford, 1845. *Abel Redivivus* (ed. W. Nichols). 1867.

GARRETT, C. H. *The Marian Exiles*. Cambridge, 1938.

GEE, H. *The Elizabethan Clergy and the Settlement of Religion*. Oxford, 1898. *The Elizabethan Prayer Book and Ornaments*. 1902.

GEORGE, E. A. *Seventeenth-Century Men of Latitude*. 1909.

GIBSON, E. C. S. *The Thirty-nine Articles of the Church of England*. 3rd ed. 1902.

GOODE, W. *The Doctrine of the Church of England as to the Effects of Baptism in the Case of Infants*. 2nd ed. 1850.

439

HALLER, W. *The Rise of Puritanism.* New York, 1938.

HARDMAN, O. *The Christian Doctrine of Grace.* 1937.

HARRISON, A. H. W. *The Beginnings of Arminianism to the Synod of Dort.* 1926. *Arminianism.* 1937.

HENSON, H. H. *Puritanism in England.* 1912.

HEYLYN, P. *Historia Quinqu-Articulis* (*the five controverted…points of Arminianism*). 1660. *Aerius Redivivus, or the History of the Presbyterians, 1536–1647.* Oxford, 1670.

HIGHAM, F. *Lancelot Andrewes.* 1952.

HILDEBRANDT, F. *Melanchthon: Alien or Ally?* Cambridge, 1946.

HOLDEN, W. P. *Anti-puritan Satire, 1572–1642.* Yale, 1954.

HOPF, C. L. R. A. *Martin Bucer and the English Reformation.* Oxford, 1946.

HOUGHTON, W. E. *The Formation of Thomas Fuller's Holy and Profane States.* Cambridge, Mass. 1938.

HOWELL, W. S. *Logic and Rhetoric in England: 1500–1700.* Princeton, 1956.

HUGHES, P. *The Reformation in England.* 3 vols. 1950–5.

HUGHES, P. (ed.). *St John Fisher: the Earliest English Life.* 1935.

HUIZINGA, J. *Erasmus of Rotterdam* (Phaidon ed.). 1952.

HUNT, J. *Religious Thought in England.* 1870.

HUNTER, A. M. *The Teaching of Calvin.* 2nd ed. 1950.

HYMA, A. *The Youth of Erasmus.* Ann Arbor, 1930.

ISAACSON, H. *An exact Narration of the Life and Death of…Lancelot Andrewes* (*1650*) (ed. S. Isaacson). 1829.

KENNEDY, W. M. *Archbishop Parker.* 1908. *The 'Interpretations' of the Bishops* (Alcuin Club). 1908. *Parish Life under Queen Elizabeth.* 1914. *Elizabethan Episcopal Administration* (Alcuin Club). 3 vols. 1924.

KNAPPEN, M. M. *Tudor Puritanism.* Chicago, 1939.

KNOWLES, D. *The Religious Orders in England,* vols. I, II. Cambridge, 1950, 1955.

KNOWLES, D. and HADCOCK, R. N. *Medieval Religious Houses: England and Wales.* 1953.

LAMB, J. *Historical Account of the Thirty-nine Articles.* Cambridge, 1829.

LAURENCE, R. *An attempt to illustrate those Articles of the Church of England which the Calvinists improperly consider as Calvinistical.* Oxford, 1805.

LINDSAY, T. M. *A History of the Reformation.* 2 vols. New York, 1916.

MACKINNON, J. *Calvin and the Reformation.* 1936.

MARTIN, C. *Les Protestants anglais réfugiés à Genève, 1555–60.* Geneva, 1915.

MASSON, D. *Life of Milton.* Vol. I. New ed. 1881.

MATHEW, D. *The Social Structure in Caroline England.* Oxford, 1948.

McGINN, D. J. *The Admonition Controversy.* New Brunswick, 1949.

McLACHLAN, H. J. *Socinianism in Seventeenth-Century England.* Oxford, 1951.

MILLER, P. *Orthodoxy in Massachusetts, 1630–50.* Cambridge, Mass. 1933. *The New England Mind: The Seventeenth Century.* 2nd. imp. Cambridge, Mass. 1954. *Errand into the Wilderness.* Cambridge, Mass. 1956. *The American Puritans: their Prose and Poetry.* New York (paperback), 1956.

MILLER, P. and JOHNSON, T. H. (ed.). *The Puritans.* New York, 1938.

MOFFAT, J. *Grace in the New Testament.* 1931.

MORISON, S. E. *Harvard College in the Seventeenth Century.* 2 vols. Cambridge, Mass. 1936. *The Puritan Pronaos: Studies in the intellectual life of New England in the Seventeenth Century.* New York, 1936.

MORRIS, C. *Political Thought in England: Tyndale to Hooker.* Oxford, 1953.

MOZLEY, J. B. *The Augustinian Doctrine of Predestination.* 1855.

MOZLEY, J. F. *William Tyndale.* 1937. *Coverdale and his Bibles.* 1953.

NEAL, D. *History of the Puritans.* 5 vol. ed. 1822.

NUTTALL, G. F. *The Holy Spirit in Puritan Faith and Experience.* Oxford, 1946.

PARKER, T. H. L. *The Oracles of God: introduction to the preaching of Calvin.* 1947.

PARKER, T. M. *The English Reformation to 1558.* Oxford, 1950.

PAULE, G. *Life of Whitgift* (1612). 2nd ed. 1699.

PAULEY, W. C. DE. *The Candle of the Lord.* 1937.

PAWSON, G. P. H. *The Cambridge Platonists.* 1930.

PEARSON, A. F. S. *Thomas Cartwright and Elizabethan Puritanism.* Cambridge, 1925. *Church and State.* Cambridge, 1928.

PHILLIPS, M. M. *Erasmus and the Northern Renaissance.* 1949.

PORTER, H. C. 'Alexander Whitaker: Cambridge Apostle to Virginia', *The William and Mary Quarterly,* Third Series, vol. XIV, no. 3 (Williamsburg, July 1957).

POWICKE, F. J. *Henry Barrow: and the exiled Church of Amsterdam.* 1900. *John Robinson.* 1920. *The Cambridge Platonists.* 1936.

POWICKE, F. M. *The Reformation in England.* Oxford, 1941.

READ, C. *Mr Secretary Cecil and Queen Elizabeth.* 1955.

RONDET, H. *Gratia Christi.* Paris, 1948.

ROWSE, A. L. *The England of Elizabeth.* 1950.

RUPP, E. G. *Studies in the Making of the English Protestant Tradition: mainly in the reign of Henry VIII.* Cambridge, 1947. *The Righteousness of God: Luther Studies.* 1953. *Six Makers of English Religion, 1500–1700.* 1957.

RUSSELL, A. T. *Life and Works of Lancelot Andrewes.* Cambridge, 1860.

SCHAFF, P. *History of the Creeds of Christendom.* 1877. *The Creeds of the Evangelical Protestant Churches.* 1877.

SCHOLES, P. *The Puritans and Music.* 1934.

SCHWARZ, W. *Biblical Translation.* Cambridge, 1955.

SEEBOHM, F. *The Oxford Reformers.* 1867.

SIMPSON, A. *Puritanism in Old and New England.* Chicago, 1956.

SMYTH, C. H. *Cranmer and the Reformation under Edward VI*. Cambridge, 1926. *The Art of Preaching*. 1940. *The Genius of the Church of England*. 1947.

STRANKS, C. J. *Life and Writings of Jeremy Taylor*. 1952.

STRYPE, J. *Memorials of Thomas Cranmer*. 2 vols. Oxford, 1812. *The Life of Sir John Cheke*. Oxford, 1821. *The Life and Acts of Grindal*. Oxford, 1821. *The Life and Acts of Matthew Parker*. 3 vols. Oxford, 1821. *The Life and Acts of John Whitgift*. 3 vols. Oxford, 1822. *Ecclesiastical Memorials*. 6 vols. Oxford, 1822. *Annals of the Reformation under Elizabeth*. 7 vols. Oxford, 1824.

SWEET, W. W. *Religion in Colonial America*. New York, 1942.

SYKES, N. *The Crisis of the Reformation*. 1938. Repr. 1946. *Old Priest and New Presbyter*. Cambridge, 1956.

SYMONDS, H. E. *The Council of Trent and Anglican Formularies*. Oxford, 1933.

THOMPSON, J. V. P. *Supreme Governor*. 1940.

THORNTON, L. S. *Richard Hooker*. 1924.

TILLYARD, E. M. *The Elizabethan World Picture*. 1943.

TORRANCE, T. F. *Calvin's Doctrine of Man*. 1949.

TULLOCH, J. *Rational Theology and Christian Philosophy in England in the Seventeenth Century*. 2 vols. Edinburgh, 1872.

USHER, R. G. *The Presbyterian Movement in the reign of Queen Elizabeth as illustrated by the Minute Book of the Dedham Classis, 1582–1589* (Camden Society, 1905). *The Reconstruction of the English Church*. 2 vols. New York, 1910. *The Rise and Fall of the High Commission*. Oxford, 1913.

WARD, R. *Life of Henry More* (ed. M. F. Howard). 1911.

WERTENBAKER, T. J. *The Puritan Oligarchy*. New York, 1947.

WHITE, F. O. *Lives of the Elizabethan Bishops*. 1898.

WILLIAMS, A. T. P. *The Anglican Tradition*. 1947.

WOOD, T. *English Casuistical Divinity during the Seventeenth Century*. 1952.

WRIGHT, L. B. *The Atlantic Frontier: Colonial American Civilization, 1607–1763*. New York, 1947.

The following books were published in 1957, too late for their use in this work:

ASHLEY, M. *The Greatness of Oliver Cromwell*. London.

BROOK, V. J. K. *Whitgift and the English Church*. London.

COLIE, R. L. *Light and Enlightenment: A Study of the Dutch Arminians and the Cambridge Platonists*. Cambridge.

MORGAN, I. *Prince Charles' Puritan Chaplain* (John Preston). London.

MOSSE, G. L. *The Holy Pretence: A Study of Christianity and Reason of State from Perkins to Winthrop*. Oxford.

And the following in 1958:

MACLURE, M. *The Paul's Cross Sermons 1534–1642*. Toronto.

INDEX

Aarau, 79, 85, 92, 96
Abbot, Archbishop George, 409
Abney, Edward, 202
Abuses, attacks on, 58–9, 61, 136–8, 181
Achurch (Northants.), 246
Act of Supremacy (1559), 101, 103, 147
Acworth, Dr George, 57, 78, 81, 83, 87, 90, 94
Acworth, Thomas, 79, 97
Adam, the first man, 293–4, 307
Admonitions to Parliament, 149, 189, 330
Agawan (Mass.), 231
Agmondesham, Philip, 214
Ainsworth, Henry, 247, 250–1
Albert the Great, St, 23
Alberti, Leo Battista, 395
Alcock, Bp John, 10
Aldrich, Henry, 151, 155
Aldrich, Bp Robert, 31
Aldrich, Thomas, 149–55, 162, 209, 214, 243
Alexander, Peter, 338
Allen, Edmund, 80, 92
Allen, Walter, 237
Allen, William, 105
Allenson, Dr John, 187, 188, 210, 346, 381
Alvey, Edward, 187–8
Alvey, Henry, 187–9, 191, 193–6, 198, 201, 202–3, 205–6, 210, 212, 214, 215, 346, 347, 397, 428
Alvey, Richard, 80, 82, 91, 95, 187, 283
Alvey, Robert, 187
Ames, William, 238, 260, 288
Amondesham, William, 83, 86, 94
Amsterdam, 247–57, 389
Andrewes, Bp Lancelot, 161, 216, 263, 280, 287, 347, 356, 366 n., 377, 385, 413, 416
  and Cambridge biblical studies, 45, 270
  and Cambridge Greek studies, 393
  career of, 391
  catechist of Pembroke, 291, 391–2
  Master of Pembroke, 135, 391
  treasurer of Pembroke, 135, 391
  casuist, 288, 397

on Calvin, 351
on Christian assurance, 330–1, 335, 352, 370
on grace, 383
on grace and nature, 393–6, 429
on predestination, 341–2, 355, 367, 368–9
on the will of God, 369
opposition to D.D. of, 188, 212
style of, 392–3
Anglo-Saxon, study of, 79
Annan, Noel, 230
Antwerp, 105, 352
Apemantus (*Timon of Athens*), 311
Arbella, 256
Aristotle, 4, 31, 36–7, 50–1, 222
Arles, Council of, 284
Arminianism, 424, 429
  in England, 281, 287, 321, 330, 408, 414–15
  in Holland, 330, 340, 409–10
Arminius, Jacobus, 264, 282, 389, 409
Arthur, Thomas, 43
Arts course at Cambridge, 4–5, 50–1
Ascham, Roger, 18, 29, 59, 67–8, 70, 113
Ashby-de-la-Zouch (Leics.), 91, 115, 117, 123, 228
Ashdon (Essex), 219, 222
Ashton, Abdias, 188, 210, 271, 346, 381
Assurance, theology of,
  Andrewes on, 330, 335, 352
  Anglican Articles on, 329, 334, 411
  Arminians on, 411
  Augustine on, 352
  Bancroft on, 334, 405
  Baro on, 335, 379, 389
  Barrett on, 281, 335, 336, 344–5, 351–2, 359
  Bullinger on, 334
  Calvin on, 319, 320
  Cambridge Calvinists on, 311, 317–18, 319, 320, 322, 335
  Cranmer on, 334
  Dr Johnson on, 285
  Goad on, 402
  Homilies on, 332

443

29-2

INDEX

King's College, Cambridge (cont.)
Marian exiles from, 75, 77, 78, 79, 80, 83, 84, 89, 90, 92–3
New England emigrants from, 256, 259
Platonists at, 422
Protestant martyrs from, 42, 65, 72–3
Protestant reformers from, 43, 46, 65
Provost, change of (1558), 101
Provost's Lodge, 399
Puritans from, 126, 210, 213, 214, 219, 263, 409
King's Ditch, Cambridge, 18–19
King's Hall, Cambridge, 8, 15, 68, 80, 83, 93
Kirkland, Christopher, 208
Kitchen, Richard, 106
Knewstubb, John, 190, 191, 192, 203, 208, 213, 227, 270, 405
Knowles, John, 259
Knowles, Mrs, 285
Knox, Eleazor, 85, 145, 195–201
Knox, John, 70, 85–6, 143, 145
Knox, Nathaniel, 85, 188

Lakin, Dr Thomas, 77, 96
Lambarde, William, 79
Lambert, John, 43, 65
Lambeth, 148, 150, 152, 172, 348, 357, 360, 361, 364, 365, 375, 379, 386, 407
Lambeth Articles, 283, 336, 363, 364–75, 378–9, 380, 383, 384, 385, 405, 415
Landbeach (Cambs.), 30
Lansdale, Dr Robert, 214
Latimer, Bp Hugh, 10, 41, 44–5, 48, 49, 55, 58–9, 71, 72, 73, 76, 81, 136, 269
Laud, Archbishop William, 418, 420, 422
Laughton, Thomas, 210
Lawrence, Edmund, 88, 93
Le Corbusier, 395
Legate, John, 190, 264, 289, 315
Legge, Cantrill, 264
Legge, Dr Thomas, 156, 161, 195, 209, 214
Leicester, Earl of, see Dudley, Robert
Leiden, 250, 251–3, 282, 352, 389
Leipzig, 31
Leo X, Pope, 35
Lessius, Leonhard, 284
Lever, John, 77, 85, 96
Lever, Dr Ralph, 75, 77, 85, 90, 96
Lever, Thomas, 7, 67, 75, 76–7, 79, 83, 85, 86, 87, 96, 115, 119, 120, 174
Lewes (Sussex), 10

Lewis, Henry, 151
Ley, Laurence, 214
Libri Sententiarum, 5
Linacre, Thomas, 26
Lincoln, Earl of, see Fiennes, Thomas
Lindsay, T. M., 28
Linsey, John, 121, 127
Lisbon, 4
Lister, Dr Edward, 210
Little Gidding (Hunts.), 215, 418
Little Lever (Lancs.), 96
Little St Mary's Church, Cambridge, 90, 94, 116
Lloyd, Canon Roger, 216
Locke, Thomas, 107
Loftus, Archbishop Adam, 174
Loggan, David, 20
Longworth, Adam, 151
Longworth, Dr Richard, 107, 119–28, 130–35, 184, 185, 215, 244
Longworth, Thomas, 133–4
Lorkin, Dr Thomas, 209, 214
Louvain, 31, 32, 81, 94, 96, 105
Lucian, 28, 33
Lucy, Bp William, 414
Luddington, Richard, 96
Ludham, John, 378 n.
Lupset, Thomas, 31–2
Luther, Martin, 43, 44, 45, 59, 60, 61, 70, 270, 311, 355, 358, 387
Lyford, John, 253
Lyne, Richard, 8, 12
Lynn (Norfolk), 414

Macbeth, 319
McLachlan, H. J., 429
Madingley (Cambs.), 15
Magdalen College, Oxford, 87, 98, 221, 233
Magdalene College, Cambridge, x, 78, 90, 124, 158, 177, 204, 205, 208, 345, 346, 356, 420
founding of, 10
Master, change of (1559), 105
New England emigrants from, 253, 259
Magdalen Islands, 247
Maidstone (Kent), 80, 93, 224
Manchester (Lancs.), 71
Manchester, Earl of, see Montagu, Edward
Marbach, John, 282
Marburg, 95

453

Clare
Hall

Trinity
Hall

Strete

Goueuil
hall

Kinge

44827

S.Benets church

High Str

High Str

ket Hill